The Dictionary of New Media

OTHER BOOKS BY JAMES MONACO

The New Wave
How To Read a Film
Media Culture
Celebrity
Alain Resnais
American Film Now
Who's Who in American Film Now (ed.)
The Connoisseur's Guide to the Movies
The International Encyclopedia of Film (ed.)
The Film Guide (ed.)

The
Dictionary
of
New Media

The New Digital World:
Video, Audio, Print

Film, Television, DVD, Home Theatre, Satellite,
Digital Photography, Wireless, Super CD, Internet

James Monaco

New York   Sag Harbor
Harbor Electronic Publishing
1999

Library of Congress Card Number: 99-091094
ISBN 0–9669744–0-9 (paper)
ISBN 0–9669744–1-7 (cloth)

First Printing August 1999
Printed in the United States of America

CREDITS

Design Director: David Lindroth

Editorial Assistance: Joellyn Ausanka, Curtis Church, William D. Drennan, Kathleen
Fitzpatrick, Joe Medjuck, James Pallot, Rex Pyke, Anne Sanow.

A NOTE ON THE TYPE

This edition of *The Dictionary of New Media* is set in Adobe's release of Meridien.
Designed in 1957 by Swiss typographer Adrian Frutiger for the French foundry
Deberny & Peignot, Meridien's large x-height enhances legibility, while its Latinesque
serifs and flared stems give it a classical Roman elegance. One of the pioneers of "cold
type" design, Frutiger is perhaps best-known for the influential Univers family. The
display types are Bodoni and Trade Gothic.

The book was set by UNET 2 Corporation and printed and bound by Sheridan
Books at their Chelsea plant.

WWW.ReadFilm.com

For my children
and yours
who will have to live in a digital world

In Memoriam

George Monaco
Susanne Monaco

Table of Contents

Introduction   9
  What's it all about?; How this book is organized;
  Finding what you're looking for; A note on the
  illustrations; Further reading; Errors, omissions, and
  the website; Acknowledgements; Dedication

The Digital Quest   15
  The Media matrix; Text; Images; Audio; Video

The Dictionary   29

Notes   283

Introduction

What's it all about?

Words, Numbers, Music, Pictures, Movies:
Media—"in the middle of things."

No area of modern life has seen a greater explosion of language in the last fifteen years than the media. We are bombarded by new words daily. It was complicated enough in the seventies. Even then, literate people needed to know the basic vocabulary of film, television, and books. Now, jargon that was once reserved for professionals becomes a necessity of everyday life as the desktop revolution makes every schoolchild a printer, a filmmaker, a broadcaster, and a Web publisher.

The digital revolution has increased the vocabulary of media by a magnitude, as we strive to find ways to describe scores of new technologies—each with a language of its own—and the relationships between them. And the onslaught of new language shows no sign of letting up. For every three new technical terms, there's a new ethical, political, or esthetic concept that needs to be named and discussed. Behind every acronym, there's a story. Every theory has a history.

Help!

The *Dictionary of New Media* is designed to be your basic handbook for this new world. Because in this quickly converging world of new media you often don't know which area a puzzling term comes from, this should be the first place you look when you run across a new word, or need to understand a confusing technical term more fully.

Because digitization has so radically transformed the media world in the last fifteen years, we start with an introductory chapter on the digital revolution that sets the new digital media in their analog context and suggests the network of concepts and technologies that now connects text, sounds, images, and movies.

The 2,400 entries that follow have been chosen to cover the basic language of the technology, marketing, and business of these media: film, television, radio, audio, print, photography, and video. Special attention is paid to the new worlds of DVD-Video, DVD-ROM, HDTV (high definition television), DSS (satellite television), DVD-Audio, and SACD (the next generation of audio), digital photography, digital cinematography, computer graphics, the Internet, and the World Wide Web.

You'll also find articles on most of the major media companies, as well as critical terms that are useful for discussing media. Some everyday jargon has also been included, but we've tried to avoid slang that is of the moment.

The *Dictionary*'s predecessor, the "Glossary of Film" had a long history. First published by the American Film Institute in 1971, it went through four earlier editions and benefited from twenty-five years of comments and critiques by colleagues. The last incarnation of the "Glossary" was as a basic component of Microsoft's best-selling *Cinemania* CD-ROM in the early 1990s.

Film is the mother of all multimedia, connecting the nineteenth-century multimedium of grand opera with the twenty-first century universe of DVD (and whatever succeeds it). As a result, much of the language of digital media is derived from the world of movies. Even the semiotic critical terms popular in film criticism of the 1970s now find their best use in the analysis of computer interface design.

How this book is organized

We've included an extensive system of cross-references in the *Dictionary of New Media*. In the digital world especially one word is seldom enough to define a concept and these cross-references should help to make things clearer. In addition to the notes at the ends of articles, terms in SMALL CAPITALS are also cross-references. In the articles, words that have been cross-referenced from somewhere else appear in *italics*.

If you are looking for starting points, try these general entries:

➚ For digital basics: BIT, BYTE, and BCD; DIGITAL and DIGITAL RESOLUTION; FILE FORMATS; and MOORE'S LAW.

➚ For digital video: COLOR, COLOR MAPPING, and COLOR MODELS; COMPRESSION; PIXEL, QUANTIZATION, and SAMPLING; and most of the entries beginning with DVD.

➚ For the telecom world: INTERNET and PACKET-SWITCHED NETWORK.

➤ For print: PRINTING TECHNOLOGIES, TYPOGRAPHY, and LOGO.
➤ For the social context: MEDIA, INTELLECTUAL PROPERTY,
KILLER AP, SEMIOLOGY, and PIRACY.
➤ For fun: DEAD TECHNOLOGIES and PLUGS.

Finding what you're looking for

The headwords are listed in a modified ASCII sort. All numbers are
alphabetized as if they were spelled out. Punctuation (hyphens,
slashes, periods) is ignored, but spaces count, so if you are looking for
a phrase like "Real Audio" be sure to look under "RealAudio," as
well.

Anyone who spends more than a few minutes in the digital world
realizes rather quickly that we have developed a new level of language. Acronymania started with the New Deal in the 1930s (WPA,
CCC), increased by a magnitude during World War II (GI, OSS,
WACS, B-17), and took off into the wild black yonder with the space
program in the 1960s (EVA, AOK!). You can't navigate in the digital
world without an appreciation of acronymic oddities. Indeed, sometimes it seems like you're reading ASSEMBLY CODE. For dictionary-mak-
ers this means that the formerly efficient and reliable system of Latin
alphabetic sorting has broken down. It's not only the numerals that
intervene at inopportune times (T-1, X.25, 5.1), it's also the various
flavors of acronyms we've developed over the years. Some are pronounced as words (AFTRA, WYSIWIG) but some are spoken as series
of letters (POV, SMTP). In the latter instance the abbreviations are
sometimes spelled out with spaces, periods, hyphens, slashcs, or
colons (V O, M.O.W., M-A-W, S/N, 4:2:2), but often just strung
together as if they were pronounceable words (AOL, HDTV,
DSS).Sometimes both modes combines (DVD-ROM, DVCAM). Somehow, you the readers have to intuit pronunciation. And we the list-
makers have to figure out how to sort them, guessing where you
might look for them. However, until we all learn ASCII sort order in
grade school (more likely, it will be UNICODE), the traditional Latin
alphabet will have to do.

A note on the illustrations

As you may have noticed, there aren't any—at least not here in the
book version of the *Dictionary of New Media*. No doubt many of the
technical terms described here would benefit greatly from illustration.
However, thc severe economics of book publishing would limit both

the number and the quality of the photos and diagrams that we could include. No such limitations constrain us in the electronic versions of the *Dictionary*: on the web (and on the disc) we can use color, animation, sound, and movies to provide much more effective illustration. You'll find hundreds of David Lindroth's elegant diagrams, photos, audios, and videos at Readfilm.com, the website for the book.

Further reading

The digital world is prodigiously complex. Over the past thirty years the intelligence of tens of thousands of engineers has been applied to solving myriad technical problems so that this structure can work. The *Dictionary of New Media* is meant as an introduction to basic concepts. To peel a few more layers off the onion, you may want to refer to some of these recommended books.

Jim Taylor's *DVD Demystified* (1998) is a superb guide to digital engineering issues. It is both detailed and readable and includes a good glossary. DVD is at the heart of the latest wave of digitization, and Taylor sets it in the context of historic audio and video technology.

Robert Harley has established himself as one of the top gurus for Home Theatre buffs. His *Complete Guide to High-End Audio* (1994, 1998) is the bible for audio buffs, and *Home Theater for Everyone* (1997) bids to become the handbook for video aficionados. Both have good glossaries. Joseph J. Kane Jr of the Imaging Science Foundation is another leader in the field of digital home video. See especially his contributions to the "Imaging Science Theatre 2000" special edition of *Widescreen Review* (1998). This voluminous compendium was published early in 1998, just as the primordial soup of digital video had begun to jell. See also Kane's DVD reference disc, *Video Essentials: Optimizing Your Audio-Video System* (1997).

Mark Long does for Satellite television what Harley does for Home Theatre. His book *The World of Satellite TV* (1983–1998) is now in its ninth edition. He has followed the market and the technology from ten-meter backyard dishes to MPEG-2.

For more technical background on digital audio, see *Digital Audio and Compact Disc Technology, Third Edition* edited by Luc Baert and others (1995).

As of this writing, there have been no definitive books on HDTV—not surprising considering the state of the technology. (Check our website for updates.)

Although it was written before the digital explosion of the 1990s, Steven Lubar's *InfoCulture: the Smithsonian Book of Information Age*

Inventions (1993) is remarkably au courant. (To give you an idea, Lubar was on the Internet before there was a World Wide Web.) This is a superior introduction to the history of information technology in the twentieth century, written with a wise perspective, and heavily illustrated. There is no glossary, but there is an effective index.

Anyone interested in the social context of media technology must read Raymond Williams. His *Television: Technology and Cultural Form* (1975) remains the key introduction to the subject. *Keywords: A Vocabulary of Culture and Society* (1976, 1985) sets the larger context.

For specific areas: Les Brown's pioneering *Encyclopedia of Television* (1977, 1982, 1992), although showing its age, remains a necessary guide to historic television. There are numerous dictionaries of computer terms, and Jerry M. Rosenberg has written many of them. Look for one that is current. *Newton's Telecom Dictionary* (1987–1999), by entrepreneur Harry Newton, is the authoritative wordlist of the telephone and data communications industry, which breeds more acronyms per hour than the rest of the digital world combined. Over the years there have been many dictionaries of film. Recently Ira Konigsberg has cornered the market with *The Complete Film Dictionary* (1987, 1997), now in its second edition.

For professional and desktop publishing check out *The Illustrated Digital Imaging Dictionary* (1998), by Sally Wiener Grotta and Daniel Grotta. For a definitive overview see *The Official Adobe Print Publishing Guide* (1998). Although it is partly an advertisement for Adobe products, this company has defined digital publishing, after all.

Errors, omissions, and the website

More than twenty percent of the terms defined in this book didn't exist five years ago. It looks like the digital revolution has reached a plateau for the moment, so this is a good time to take stock. But you can bet that tomorrow someone will devise a new term or string together yet another acronym that will figure critically in understanding the new media.

You'll find these definitions, not in these pages, printed in mid-1999, but on the website: Readfilm.com. And if they're not there, for some reason, just ask us. We'll do our best to provide them.

Similarly, if you can correct errors, provide further details, or offer illuminating anecdotes, there's a place on the website to communicate with us. The book has already benefited from contributions of early surfers who found a previous edition of the *Dictionary* at Readfilm.com and were kind enough to communicate corrections.

Acknowledgements

My thanks to them. I'm also grateful to editor/producer Curtis Church and producer/Internet entrepreneur Rex Pyke for providing numerous leads and suggestions, as well as to film producer and new media scholar Joe Medjuck for a reality check on Hollywood jargon. Thanks, too, to my wife and children whose dinner-table questions led me to return to the dictionary business.

Dedication

The *Dictionary of New Media* is dedicated to my children (and yours), the first generation of the twenty-first century, who will have to tame this virtual reality that we've bequeathed them.

It is also offered in memory of my parents, George C. Monaco and Susanne Hirschland Monaco, who were born during the Great War, before radio, came of age during the Second World War, spent their maturity in the Cold War, and died as the digital revolution began.

JM
Sag Harbor NY
August 1999

The Digital Quest

The Media matrix

At the turn of the twenty-first century, we find ourselves nearly ready to complete a job begun more than five hundred years ago when Johann Gutenberg invented moveable type. In that moment art and communication entered the world of technology.

For most of the intervening time our communications medium of choice was print. But then in the early nineteenth century our collective attention began to turn to more elusive media. The antecedents of photography date from the late 1830s, and the telegraph, the first means of instant communication over the horizon, from the 1840s.

By 1880 we had the telephone and the phonograph, and printed photographs—and a few years later, motion pictures. By the turn of the last century, the media palette was complete: to printed language, we had added images and sounds. We knew how to record them all, produce numerous copies of each, and transmit them over distance.

We spent the next hundred years working out the kinks.

When the history books are written 300 years from now, the twentieth century will undoubtedly be tagged the Age of Technology. Whatever else we may have accomplished in the fast and furious hundred years just past will fade into insignificance when future historians compare it with our overwhelming obsession with Techno.

Often without thinking why, we've redefined every area of life as a set of technologies—from farming to killing, from transportation to communication—it's all Techno now.

Looking back, it's interesting to note that nearly all the seminal thinking in these areas was done before the twentieth century was truly underway. Those twenty-fourth century historians may make a distinction between our own Age of Technology and the preceding Age of Science—the nineteenth century.

There is perhaps one exception to this century rule—one media invention the twentieth century might claim as its own: digitization. (Yes, Lord Byron's sister Ada was thinking about this even before the first photographs were made, but she never connected the two concepts.)

All of the science involved in recording, reproducing, and transmitting text, images, and sounds had proceeded in an analog universe. Louis Daguerre's plates, Edison's phonograph cylinders, Bell's telephone circuits, and even the moving picture shows of the Lumières, Dickson and Edison, and the Skladanowskys all mimicked the real world. The signals they recorded or transmitted were analogous to the sounds and images they intended to capture. They didn't translate them into an alien coding system; they paralleled them. If you could see a sound wave it would look like the squiggles of a phonograph groove. Photographs are so lifelike that some cultures banned them. No one has to study a new language before taking a telephone call or seeing a movie.

But beginning in the 1950s some technologists saw another interesting way to reproduce media. As computer technology began to mushroom it was evident immediately that it would be useful to code words as well as numbers. By the 1960s images and sounds were also yielding to digital interpretation: the first graphical user interface for a computer was demonstrated in 1968; by 1972 the Lexicon company was selling a digital audiotape recorder. A few years later, digital word processors were popular in offices. By the late 1980s graphics professionals were routinely processing still images on their Macintoshes, digital CDs (introduced in 1982) had taken over the music market from analog vinyl LPs, and filmmakers and sound technicians were beginning to experiment, editing video and audio on workstations.

The next step took a while. DVD, a marketable consumer technology for the digital reproduction of movies, wasn't introduced until 1997. Then the effective digitization of our media palette was complete—only twenty-five years after the Lexicon machine had first gone on sale, and only half a century after the idea had started to germinate!

Instead of mimicking images and sounds, digital systems of recording and reproduction quantify them: a very large set of numbers is calculated to describe the reality in sufficient detail so that when these numbers later drive a reproduction device, an image or sound is created with enough detail to satisfy our unsuspecting ears and eyes.

As you can discern from the brief chronology above, this isn't easy. Theoretically, it is elegant and direct; practically, it has taken a lifetime to achieve. There are two simple problems: (1) you need a hell of a lot of numbers to quantify even simple images and sounds (much less moving pictures with soundtracks); (2) You have to process this gargantuan quantity of information very quickly, especially for time-based media like audio and video. To a large extent, the basic solutions to these problems were understood early on. It was just a question of waiting out a sufficient number of MOORE'S LAW cycles until processing power was equal to the tasks. But along the way we learned quite a bit about how we perceive images and sounds while a legion of geeks burned the midnight pizza developing workarounds for the myriad little glitches.

And now we have finally arrived at the end of the Gutenberg cycle: all the media technologies of the nineteenth century have been translated to the common—and infinitely malleable—language of mathematics. Moveable type broke language into quanta; now, our images, sounds, and movies are equally quantized.

The quantitative task is done; now, what about quality?

Text

Text was relatively easy to digitize. After all, language has been encoded in alphabets for thousands of years. Most of the difficult work had already been done. All the digitizers had to do in the 1940s and 1950s was to find a way to re-encode the "icosahexamal" (base 26) system of the Latin alphabet in binary. Samuel F. B. Morse had shown the way more than a hundred years earlier. The telegraphic coding system that was named after him probably took most of an evening to devise. It's modified dots and dashes (short and long pulses) made up a modified "2-bit, variable bit rate" code.[*] (MPEG-2 is also variable bit rate, just... five or six magnitudes more complex.)

Thirty years after Morse's stroke of brilliance made telecommunication real Émile Baudot refined the system, extending it to a 5-bit unit with a fixed bit rate. Baudot had the insight to add a shift key so that his 32-value code (2^5) could accommodate 64 values—all the capital letters of the Latin alphabet, plus digits and punctuation. Moreover, the fixed bit rate meant that machines could handle the coding more

---

[*] Morse is a 2-bit code because it is composed of four values: dots, dashes, short pauses, and long pauses; it is variable bit rate because each letter or number is represented by as few as one or as many as six dots and/or dashes.

effectively. BAUDOT code served as the basis for the TELEX system for nearly a hundred years.

All the first wave of digitizers had to do was extend the Baudot code to 7 bits (128 values) to handle all the upper- and lower-case letters, digits, and punctuation. Thus was born the 8-bit byte. (One bit was saved, at first, for error-checking.)

Success! Of course this system worked best with English. It didn't handle the accents of Italian, French, German, or Swedish very well. It didn't provide for Cyrillic or Arabic or Greek or Hebrew alphabets. And as for Japanese syllabics or Chinese ideographs, well...! And even with the Latin alphabet, the 8-bit byte of Binary-Coded Decimal only mimicked the already constricted print set of the typewriter: no bold, no italic, not even any underlining (which the typewriter used to make up for its lack of italic and bold). And as for different fonts...!

This is what it is like in the digital world: as soon as you congratulate yourself on solving one coding problem, another layer of the onion of reality makes itself evident.

Even though it took thirty years to institute, the solution to the multiple language-system problem was very simple: a 16-bit, 2-byte unit with 65,536 values can accommodate most of the languages of the world. This is what we now call UNICODE. Font and formatting problems were solved by word-processing and page-layout programs and—surprisingly—still aren't standardized (although the World Wide Web has made some headway with HTML, and eventually we hope that SGML provides the engine for all word processors).

Images

If digitizing the already heavily coded alphabet of language was easy enough for Morse to do in the early nineteenth century, digitizing images was a daunting challenge.

Here there was also a nineteenth-century model: Benjamin Day's halftone system for printing photographs, dating from the 1880s. With considerably more genius than Morse, Day had intuited that the continuous tones of a photograph could be approximated on a black-and-white printing press by varying the density of near-microscopic black dots on a white background. He developed a filter screen that would translate the various levels of gray in a photograph to various concentrations of ink dots on the paper. For the first time, an image had been analyzed into component "picture elements," or "pixels." In a way, Day's halftone screen "binarized" an image without digitizing it. It broke down the continuous range of shades of gray into a set of black and white values. You can see this by looking closely at any newspaper photograph. (You don't need a microscope.)

Much valuable groundwork had also been done in analog television. Day had been limited by the binary black-or-white nature of the printing press. The various inventors of television had a variable signal at their command: the stronger the electron beam in the cathode ray tube, the brighter glowed the phosphor on which it fell.

By the time digital engineers turned their attention to the challenge of reproducing photographs on a cathode ray tube in the 1960s, the NTSC broadcast television standard in the US had given them an inexpensive playing field. The dimensions were 640 pixels wide (more or less) by 480 pixels high.

How did this come about? The NTSC standard called for 525 scanning lines, but since some of these lines were used for other purposes only about 480 actually carried picture information. (This gives us the vertical resolution of the standard VGA computer screen.) The ASPECT RATIO of the television screen, 4:3, was derived from the motion-picture Academy standard. Television engineers didn't have to worry about the number of picture elements in each horizontal line because the cathode-ray-tube beam scanned continuously from left to right, but if you do the math, 480 lines of vertical resolution at a 4:3 Aspect Ratio provides just about 640 lines of horizontal resolution.

By the 1960s television cathode ray tubes were cheap and available. The digital engineers adapted them for computer monitors. At first, there was no thought of reproducing images: the processing power wasn't there. The CRTs were adapted to present a crude layout of 24 lines of 80 characters. Each character cell was composed of a matrix of picture elements, usually 5 x 7 pixels. An electronic module called a character generator drove the screen. The character generator had to know which pixels to light up for any one of 128 characters. (Remember that basic ASCII code was limited to seven bits.) This was a job it could handle.

All this changed with the introduction of the Macintosh in January 1984. (It had been preceded by the Apple Lisa and the Xerox Star, both expensive machines which met with no success in the marketplace.) For the first time, each pixel on the screen was addressable. The first Macintosh came with 128 kilobytes of RAM, twice the memory of any machine available up to that time. It was almost enough to control individually each pixel on a standard black-and-white CRT. (The first Macintosh had a substandard 9-inch screen).

The result was that, not only could you present different fonts on screen, you could also approximate photographs. The resolution of the screen was set at 72 pixels per inch, which was not quite as fine as a rough newspaper photograph. (An 85-line halftone screen is common in newspapers.) There were only two "colors" available—black and white. (This was a function of the lack of necessary RAM and processor speed, not a limitation of the cathode ray tube that served as a monitor.) The Ben Day screen also had only two colors to work with—but in print, the size of the dots could be varied, mimicking grays. On computer screen each pixel is the same size as every other pixel.

So the first challenge was to provide what came to be known as "grayscale." This was relatively easy once RAM and CPU speed increased. The halftone screen had introduced the analysis of the height and width of the image, breaking it down into pixels. Now computer imaging engineers were adding the concept of depth. A 1-bit color depth provides two colors—the bit is on or the bit is off. A 2-bit depth offers four colors—two shades of gray as well as black and white. An 8-bit depth provides 256 shades of gray (2^8). For most purposes this is considered sufficient.

The television engineers had figured out how to do color on a CRT in the early 1950s: three subpixels—one each for red, green, and blue—would combine psychologically to represent all the colors of the spectrum. This trick worked, however, only when the intensity of each subpixel could be varied. This was no problem in analog television where the strength of the electron beam varied continuously. But it was a significant challenge for digital imaging: three times as much information had to be stored and processed as for a black-and-white picture.

With a 3-bit color depth you have eight permutations: black (all the subpixels are off), white (all the subpixels are on), and six colors (the other combinations). With a 6-bit color depth, you get sixteen colors, and this was the standard for early Windows machines. It was enough to provide a little variety in the layout of the screen, but it was not sufficient to reproduce photos. 16.7 million colors is the current digital photographic standard. This is a 24-bit color depth, 8 bits per subpixel, and therefore a logical extension of the 256 grayscale standard (256 x 256 x 256: three "grayscales," one for each of three primary colors). To fully describe a picture 640 pixels wide, 480 pixels high, and 24 bits deep requires 7,372,800 bits—or almost a megabyte of data. To process a signal like this you need a machine 24 times as powerful as the 1984 Macintosh. Luckily, Moore's Law continued to operate flawlessly throughout the late 1980s and 1990s. In addition a better understanding of how we perceive color images led to useful compression technologies, which we'll discuss later.

Before we consider the daunting task of digitizing *moving* pictures, let's take a look at digital sound.

Audio

Recording analog audio is so straightforward it is surprising that Leonardo DaVinci didn't think of it. All that is necessary is an understanding of clock mechanics and the physics of musical instruments. But digitizing audio required a leap of imagination. The technique that gradually developed required the application of two technical concepts: sampling and quantization. To represent an analog audio waveform digitally you measure—or "sample"—the wave numerous times per second and then assign a numerical value to that sample— you "quantize" it.

There are some rough parallels here with the world of digital imaging: the sampling rate (samples per second) is like the resolution (pixels per inch). The quantization is like the color (or grayscale) depth. Standard CD audio is sampled 44,100 times per second and the quantization depth is 16 bits. That is, each sample can be assigned one of 2^{16} (or 65,536) different values. This is enough digital detail to fool most of the people all of the time. For the average listener, a modern digital CD sounds at least as "good" as an old-fashioned analog LP. Because a CD is less subject to physical damage than an LP, and because CDs—and CD players—require less care and attention, the medium now dominates the music business. Audiophiles may disagree, but they occupy a small sliver of the marketplace.

The audio CD standard developed by Philips and Sony was established in 1980 and compact discs went on the market beginning in 1982. The CD standard has lasted through more than ten Moore's Law cycles—an extraordinary achievement. There is no other digital technology standard from 1980 that hasn't been superseded numerous times. This first exploitation of digital technology in the consumer marketplace has also been the most successful.

With the establishment of the DVD standard in 1995 digital audio took a quantum leap. The target sampling rate was increased to 96,000 times per second and the target quantization depth to 24 bits. This is the AC-3, or DOLBY DIGITAL, specification. Some progress had been made in the intervening fifteen years in digital theatrical sound systems, where most of the innovations in digital audio were carried out in the 1980s and early 1990s. DOLBY led the way here, supported by George Lucas's THX, and challenged by DTS and Sony's SDDS.

One result of this development track has been a renewed interest in multichannel sound. Stereophonic recordings, reproducing two channels of sound, came to market in 1958 and quickly became the standard. That FM radio could reproduce stereo was a major factor in its growth in the late 1960s. (AM could not at that time.) In the early 1970s the recording industry attempted to market Quadraphonic equipment and records on the theory that if two channels were good, four were better. That technology died quickly—partly because the analog system at the time was not well equipped to handle that many signals, but mainly because consumers didn't see a great enough advantage to invest in entirely new sound systems.

Movie theaters, however, have been profiting from the aptly named SURROUND SOUND since the 1950s. There's little doubt that hearing sounds coming from behind you increases your involvement in the drama. So the DVD-Video specification calls for 5.1 Surround Sound to heighten the dramatic experience in the Home Theatre as well. (It's called 5.1 because there are five basic channels—left, center, right, left surround, and right surround—plus one low-frequency effects channel.) For musical reproduction Surround Sound may not seem to make much sense—who wants to sit in the middle of the band? But the extra channels can help to increase the realism of what audiophiles call the soundstage—the sense of presence in the recording.

Of course the more channels you add, the more data you have to store and process. The original digital audio CD specification was uncompressed: that is, every bit that was recorded was stored and played. Here's the math: 44,100 samples x 16 bits/sample x 2 channels of stereo require that 1,411,200 bits per second be stored and processed. As digital sound (and digital imaging) progressed, it quickly became evident that some way had to be found to reduce the gargantuan quantities of data spewing forth.

The answer was data compression—a series of increasingly sophisticated mathematical techniques to code more information with fewer bits of data.[*] As COMPRESSION technologies developed in the late 1980s and early 1990s Dolby and other companies employed them

---

[*] To give you an idea how compression works, let's take a look at one of the basic algorithms: Run-Length Encoding. In any set of samples a series of numbers may be identical. If a note is held for two seconds, for example, 88,200 samples will be identical. RLE replaces those 88,200 numbers with two: one for the value, another for the length of the run. This is a significant saving.

for theatrical sound systems like Dolby Digital, SDDS (Sony Dynamic Digital Sound), and DTS (from Digital Theater Systems).

There remains one more important acronym to add to your audio collection: DSD. Direct Stream Digital is the encoding system Sony and Philips have adopted for their successor to the veteran audio CD—which they have named SACD (Super Audio Compact Disc). Other manufacturers are betting on DVD-Audio, which developed out of the DVD-Video specification. But Sony and Philips have done some brilliant lateral thinking.

The DVD-Audio standard comprises a set of sampling/quantization systems all of which are related to the 96 kiloHertz/24-bit resolution of DVD-Video. Direct Stream Digital represents an entirely new way of thinking: the sampling frequency is increased to 2.8224 million times per second while the depth of the quantization is reduced to one bit! The signal information is carried in the frequency of the pulses not their amplitude.* DSD is an elegantly simple approach to digitization using the brute force of the latest microchips. With such a high sampling frequency it is not surprising that a graph of a DSD signal looks very much like an analog signal. To many of the early listeners DSD recordings also sound as good as analog. It may be that in twenty years we look back on the quantization model as a wrong turn—even though it was that technology that helped make the audio CD such a successful consumer product.

Video

If the number of numbers required to digitize an audio signal is mind-boggling, the amount of data necessary for a digital moving picture is...well, 178 times mind-boggling, since that is more or less the ratio between CD audio and contemporary television data flows. When you remember that a DVD-Video disc holds only seven times as much data as an audio CD, you see how important compression techniques have become. The transfer rate of uncompressed digitized studio-quality television is more than 200 megabits/sec. Without compression, a 4.7 gigabyte DVD-Video disc could hold about three minutes of video (although few computers could process that amount of data quickly enough to keep the picture moving).

Indeed, ironically, compression is the bedrock on which the new digital world has been built. This wasn't at all clear in the early days:

---

* Using the historical radio model, you could think of DSD as digital FM as opposed to the AM of audio CD/DVD-Audio coding.

as we've noted, the audio CD didn't need it, nor did the first wave of computer graphics. But the analysis of the sounds and images that was necessary in order to portray them as a series of numbers a CPU could understand put us on a mathematical intellectual track towards compression and we're still riding those rails.

As we've seen, certain basic compression techniques, like Run-Length Encoding, are just mathematical tricks. They are "lossless": no data is lost in compression or decompression. The more sophisticated techniques, however, are "lossy": some data is discarded in the process. We can take this risk mainly because we have learned more about how human beings perceive sounds and images—and that knowledge reveals certain weaknesses that can be mathematically exploited. (Cinema itself was founded more than a hundred years ago on the weakness known as PERSISTENCE OF VISION, so this approach is nothing new.)

In the audio world this lossy approach has come to be known as PERCEPTUAL CODING. This set of techniques depends on our tendency not to hear noise when it is close in frequency to louder sounds—a phenomenon known as AUDITORY MASKING.

In the more complex world of video, there are several key technologies. In the first place we have to distinguish between still images and moving pictures, so there are two general approaches to video compression: spatial and temporal. Spatial compression is applied to each individual frame. Temporal compression is applied over a range of frames. Perceptual weaknesses are exploited in both areas.

Let's look at spatial compression first. The main intellectual breakthrough here was understanding that we perceive the brightness of an image differently from its colors, and that brightness information (luminance) could be separated from color information (chrominance). It was also useful to describe the color information differently—to invent a new color system. (The two existing color models—CMYK from the world of printing and RGB from cathode ray tubes—didn't lend themselves well to compression.) Because our eyes are less sensitive to color information than to brightness, color can be compressed more without noticeably degrading the image. Because we are less sensitive to red and much less sensitive to blue, these colors can be compressed more than green. In addition, our sensitivity to color differences as well as brightness varies over different ranges. In areas where we are less sensitive, we can use more compression.

The YC_BC_R color model lets us apply this multilevel approach to compression. In this model all the luminance information is included in Y, while C_b is the blue chrominance and C_r is the red chrominance. (The green chrominance can be computed from the other two.) If this model seems difficult to comprehend, think of a black-and-white photograph: all the chrominance has been subtracted from it, but you can still understand it. A picture with all the color information but no luminance information, however, would be unintelligible—sort of like iridescent mud. It's the contrast—the luminance—that defines shapes for us.

Although there are numerous graphics file formats that use compression techniques, the standard has become JPEG, named after the Joint Photographic Experts Group, who developed it. JPEG follows this color model, compressing luminance less than blue and red chrominance. It then goes a step further to exploit another perceptual weakness—our lack of sensitivity to visual complexity. The JPEG algorithm divides the image into blocks—groups of sixteen pixels—then performs an operation called a DISCRETE COSINE TRANSFORM on each block. This is the kind of math that separates the geeks from the rest of us, so we won't go into detail here. Suffice it to say that both the chrominance and luminance information in each block emerges from the Discrete Cosine Transform sorted in order of complexity so that we can choose to throw out the more complex values that—the theory goes—we can't perceive anyway.

When it has swept away all this "useless" detail, JPEG can achieve compressions of 80 to 90 percent, producing pictures that most people can't differentiate from the originals. Now we're getting somewhere. (By the way, if you bring HDTV into the equation, multiply the amount of data by five to account for 1,080 scan lines instead of 480.)

But there's more. Temporal compression deals with the differences between frames. Even greater savings occur here. In most films very little changes from one frame to the next. If only the changes are recorded, much less additional data is needed for each succeeding frame.

All temporal compression schemes use a combination of key frames and delta frames. The key frames are always digitized whole (with the necessary spatial compression being applied). The delta frames, as the name implies, record only changes from the key frames. One result of this system is that it is very hard to run compressed video backwards: the delta frames depend on the preceding key frames; they have little relationship to the succeeding ones. Another result is that the picture can be degraded in various ways since the compression architecture is so delicate. Video compression is still an art, and some compressionists practice it better than others.

As in the still-image world, there are numerous compressors (or CODECS) available for movies, but the standard has become MPEG, named for the Motion Picture Experts Group who devised it. The key technique here is not unlike the Discrete Cosine Transform of JPEG. MPEG divides each frame into areas called macroblocks, looks at the next frame to see if and how a particular macroblock has moved, then stores the vector for the macroblock, rather than the macroblock itself. MPEG is capable of calculating and storing three kinds of frames: I-frames are the key frames, full images compressed with JPEG; P-frames are "predicted" using the macroblock difference technique. Some, but not all, MPEG encoders can also produce B-frames. These "bidirectional" delta frames relate to previous as well as succeeding I- and P-frames.

The uneasy marriage of film and television more than fifty years ago had already presented a set of temporal problems that are still with us. One advantage of digital video is that it can obviate some of these problems. Feature films are shot at a standard rate of 24 frames per second. American (and Japanese) television operate at about 30 frames per second. (The precise rate is 29.97 frames/sec, but that's another story.) European television (PAL and SECAM) operates at 25 frames per second. These television frame rates are tied to the frequencies of alternating current in their respective countries.[*]

In order to show feature film on American television, a device called a FILM CHAIN must be used to divvy up 24 film frames into 60 video fields (with two fields per video frame). A lot of approximation (and cheating) is involved. The situation is worse in Europe. When feature films are shown on European television they are actually speeded up four percent (from 24 frames/sec to 25 frames/sec). Whatever problems we may have with digital video pale in comparison to the workarounds that have been employed to adapt theatrical film to television. Moreover, because the DVD standard accommodates all the existing frames rates, when you run DVD on a computer

---

[*] Perhaps this is a good place to note that a lot of sampling, quantization, and even compression have been applied to movies long before they reach the digital stage. If you shoot a film at 24 frames per second, you are sampling reality 24 times a second. If you limit your palette to red, green, and blue (either in the layers of the color filmstock or the subpixels of the video screen) you are quantizing color. What painter would be content to limit himself to three tubes of pigment? If you've shrunk your soundtrack to fit in the narrow space between the frame and the sprockets, you've compressed it.

(or, a digital television set) you can choose the frame rate that matches the original source material.

If there is one law that governs both the analog and digital worlds it is that the technology is only as good as it has to be. 24 frames per second is just fast enough (if you show each frame twice) to avoid flicker. 72 pixels per inch is just barely enough to rival the detail we are used to in printed photographs. 16.7 million colors are just enough to look like a good color photo. The CD sampling rate and quantization depth are just enough to offer a favorable comparison with the analog LP that was the CD's predecessor. The MPEG-2 compression scheme used for DVD-Video (and DSS, digital satellite television) is just good enough to stand up to Laserdisc video.

Anyone who has seen a SHOWSCAN film production running at 60 frames per second knows how inadequate our 24 frames/sec movie standard is. Audiophiles equipped with a modern turntable and well pressed vinyl have no time for digital CDs. Film buffs who have collected Laserdiscs for fifteen years will only buy a DVD if no Laserdisc edition exists. In short, we are just at the beginning of the digital transformation.

The future is—theoretically—limitless. We can envision an electronic book screen with a resolution of 4,000 dots per inch instead of 100 pixels per inch so that it matches or exceeds the resolution of good photographs and print. (Let's assume that a color depth of 16.7 million is sufficient.) If Direct Stream Digital's 2.8 million samples per second rate proves to be not really enough to cut it, then maybe "DSD-2's" 5.6 million samples per second rate will make the grade. Digital audio will then match or exceed the best analog quality. If the MPEG-2 video compression scheme is awkward and gawky, then perhaps "MPEG-8" will solve the problems.

In the digital world in which we now find ourselves, it's only a small question of processing power. If Moore's Law will hold fast for another decade or so, we should be home free.

Then the only remaining question will be philosophical: is it moral, ethical, esthetic, or useful to spend so much time, energy, and intelligence parsing reality—breaking it down into numbers—so that we can image it, record it, modify it, and transmit it?

A

A and B Rolls ⇒ Two or more rolls of film are arranged for printing such that images on one roll are concurrent with black leader on the other roll (and vice versa). The technique is useful for special effects and superimposed titles. The end product usually is a composite master. Since the rolls must run through the optical printer concurrently, the topologies are opposite.

A & E ⇒ Arts and Entertainment. CABLE NETWORK devoted to programming skewed to an educated audience, founded by ABC in 1981, now co-owned with NBC and Hearst. The company now also operates the Biography and History channels.

A Picture ⇒ During the Golden Age of Hollywood, a "major motion picture." Compare B PICTURE, PROGRAMMER.

AA ⇒ Average Audience. A NIELSEN measurement that averages the audiences for each minute of a program.

AAC ⇒ Advanced Audio Compression. A competitor to MP3 from Liquid Audio and other companies that—unlike MP3—supports encryption, watermarking, and copy protection. A potential foundation for MP4.

AAD ⇒ See CD CODES.

A/B ⇒ (1) (n) A switch. (2) (v) To compare two versions of a film or tape by switching back and forth between them or viewing them side by side.

Abby Singer ⇒ The penultimate shot, named after the veteran production manager. Supposedly, Singer was famous for promising that there was "just one more shot to do after this one." Compare MARTINI, WINDOW.

ABC ⇒ (1) American Broadcasting Company, a division of DISNEY, operator of the third American television NETWORK. ABC grew out of two 1940s antitrust cases: the 1943 decision to break up NBC's two-network radio system (the "Blue" network became ABC), and the 1948 consent decree that separated Paramount Pictures from its theater chain. In 1952 ABC merged with United Paramount theaters to form a new television network, competing with DUMONT for third place behind NBC and CBS. ABC was a perennial also-ran until the 1976–77 season, when a string of hits programmed by Fred Silverman gained it a number of new affiliates and the number one ranking. In 1986 ABC merged with Capital Cities Broadcasting, an operator of a number of local stations. In 1995 Capital Cities/ABC was acquired by DISNEY for $19 billion, the largest media merger to that date. The company's ownership of cable networks—especially ESPN—largely accounted for the inflated price. See CBS, NBC. (2) Australian Broadcasting Corporation, the national radio and television network of Australia.

Above-the-Line Costs ⇒ See COSTS.

Absolute Film ⇒ An abstract film that is nonrepresentational, using form and design to produce its effect and often most easily described as visual music. See COMPUTER FILM.

Academy Aperture ⇒ The standard frame mask established by the Academy of Motion Picture Arts and Sciences in 1932. A ratio of width to height of 4:3, or 1.33:1. See also WIDESCREEN, TV MASK, ASPECT RATIO.

Academy Curve ⇒ The audio frequency spectrum set as a standard for film sound in 1938. Because of the inherent noisiness of optical tracks at the time and the minimal quality of theatrical sound systems, the Academy Curve was severely limited, offering audio that was not much better than AM radio. The curve limited soundtrack reproduction well into the 1970s. See ACADEMY APERTURE, DOLBY STEREO.

Academy of Motion Picture Arts and Sciences ⇒ Founded in 1927, the ambitiously named Academy is best known for the annual Oscars ceremony, one of the most-watched television shows around the world. It also has established some basic standards (see ACADEMY APERTURE, ACADEMY CURVE.) It also runs an important library in Los Angeles. But its most important function, perhaps, is to serve as the arbiter of Hollywood nobility.

Accelerated Montage ⇒ A sequence edited into progressively shorter shots to create a mood of tension and excitement. See PARALLEL ACTION.

Access ⇒ The right to make use of a medium. Access to radio and television is limited, while access to the print media is relatively open. REAL-TIME ACCESS permits use of the medium instantaneously without intervening processing (such as publication).

Access Time ⇒ In television programming, the period just before PRIME TIME reserved by the FCC since 1970 for non-network programming. The aim of the access rule was to open up prime time to non-network productions. AFFILIATES usually run syndicated programming—often game shows—during the time period. The original Access Time period was 7:30 pm to 8 pm. Additional Access Time during the period from 6 pm to 8 pm became known as Double Access. See DAYPART.

ACE Awards ⇒ Awards presented annually by the National Association of Cable Television for outstanding original cable programming.

Acetate Print ⇒ See NITRATE PRINT.

Acrobat ⟫ Adobe's universal file format for text and graphics is an ambitious effort to bring a general standard to documents (both text and graphics) presented on a screen, just as the company's PostScript did for printed documents. It is not yet an open standard, which limits its adoption. See Adobe, Image File Formats, Text File Formats.

AC-3 ⟫ The encoding scheme developed by Dolby Laboratories and adopted as the digital audio standard for DVD and HDTV. AC-3 encodes six channels of audio (5.1). It is also the basis for Dolby Digital theatrical sound systems. Employing a variety of compression techniques AC-3 achieves a low bit rate: 328–384 kilobits/sec as compared to the 1,411 kilobits/sec of basic PCM stereo. Compare DTS, MPEG-2.

Active Matrix LCD ⟫ An LCD display screen where each Pixel emits light. Compare Passive Matrix LCD.

Actual Sound ⟫ Sound whose source is an object or person in the scene. See Commentative Sound.

Acutance ⟫ A measure of the ability of a lens to reproduce edges sharply. See Resolution.

Ad Hoc Network ⟫ Temporary grouping of normally nonaligned stations (sometimes mixing independents and network Affiliates) set up by a syndicator to air a special event or program. See Operation Primetime.

A D ⟫ Short for Assistant Director.

A/D ⟫ Analog to Digital conversion.

ADC ⟫ Analog/Digital Converter. DACs are common consumer items, but ADCs are generally reserved for professionals whose job it is to translate and package audio or video that has been captured in an analog format for digital delivery on a CD or DVD.

ADD ⟫ See CD Codes.

Additive Primary Colors ⟫ See Color Models.

Addressable ⟫ A Cable Television tuner that the system operator can control from the Head End is said to be "addressable." Addressable tuners are necessary for Pay-per-View. See Encryption.

ADI ⟫ Area of Dominant Influence. Geographical area in which a television station has significant viewership, as designated by Arbitron. Used in Ratings research and marketing and advertising studies. Compare DMA.

Adjacency ⟫ In television, a commercial time period just prior to or following a program rather than within it.

Adobe ⟫ Founded in 1982 by John Warnock to market his PostScript language, Adobe has been a key organization in the digital revolution, as creative as Apple and as dominant in its own domain as

MICROSOFT. Despite the Apple–Microsoft joint effort of the late 1980s to displace PostScript with TrueType, Adobe's page description language remains the key technology that allows software to control printers of all kinds. Adobe's PhotoShop and Illustrator products dominate the world of graphics professionals, and Premiere is the tool of choice for low-end film and video editing. Acrobat, an ambitious attempt to provide a lingua franca for the screen (much as PostScript had done for printers), is becoming an essential tool of the WORLD WIDE WEB. Adobe may not be a household word like Microsoft or Apple, but the company has invented or developed many of the key technologies supporting today's microcomputer industry.

ADR ➻ Astra Digital Radio. An invention of the SES.

ADR Editor ➻ A sound editor who specializes in "Additional Dialogue Recording." See LOOPING. (The term ADR became popular in the 1980s and is sometimes said to stand for "Automatic Dialogue Replacement," although the process is far from automatic and the dialogue is not always a replacement.)

ADSL ➻ Asynchronous Digital Subscriber Line. A technique for distributing high volumes of information through the standard telephone network. Data moves at 6.312 megabits/sec (T-2 speed) in one direction and 64 kilobits/sec in the other. Compare SDSL, HDSL2.

Advantix ➻ Eastman Kodak film system introduced in 1996 to try to match some of the advantages of digital photography in a traditional photographic system. The Advantix system employs a sealed cassette loaded with filmstock that has been coated magnetically so that the camera can record information about light source, contrast, and picture dimensions which can later be read by the processor so adjustments can be made during developing and printing. (Some of this information is also recorded optically.) Kodak calls this data track *PQIX* (Picture Quality Information eXchange.) Although the filmstock is smaller than 35 mm, three aspect ratios are offered. The cassette form factor makes the film easier to use. See PHOTO CD.

Aerial Shot ➻ A shot taken from a crane, plane, or helicopter. Not necessarily a moving shot. See CRANE SHOT.

AES/EBU Interface ➻ A specification of the Audio Engineering Society and the European Broadcasting Union for the interconnection of digital audio equipment using a BALANCED line and XLR connections.

AF ➻ A feature of RDS that allows an automatic shift to a stronger frequency (for the same station).

Affective Fallacy ➳ A term used in twentieth-century literary criticism to suggest that it is an error to judge a work of art on the basis of its results, especially its emotional effect. Introduced by W. K. Wimsatt (*The Verbal Icon*). See INTENTIONAL FALLACY.

Affiliate ➳ By law U.S. television networks were allowed to own outright a limited number of VHF and UHF BROADCASTING stations. (These restrictions were lifted by the Communications Act of 1996.) The remainder of the network is composed of privately owned stations, which distribute the network's programming and operate under contract. They have some leeway to disapprove shows. The term is also used to describe a station CLEARED by a distributor to carry a SYNDICATED program.

AFI ➳ See AMERICAN FILM INSTITUTE.

AFMA ➳ American Film Marketing Association. Set up in 1980 as the professional association of smaller producers and distributors. The major studios are members of the MPPA. Produces the highly successful American Film Market each winter in Los Angeles.

AFTRA ➳ American Federation of Television and Radio Artists. With SAG, one of the major film and television actors' unions.

AGC ➳ Automatic Gain Control, a feature of many recording devices that adjusts the recording input automatically.

Agent ➳ Agents have always been important members of the film industry community, the grease that allows talent and business interests to mesh. Jules Stein, who founded the Music Corporation of America in 1924, is regarded as the most important of the early agents. MCA quickly moved from agenting to business and, in 1962, acquired the UNIVERSAL studio. As the studio system began to break down in the 1960s, agents acquired unusual power. With the demise of contract players and talent, it was the agent who could put together the PACKAGE that made a film happen. At first, the William Morris Agency held sway. It was joined in the power circle in the 1970s by *ICM* (International Creative Management) and in the 1980s by Michael Ovitz's *CAA* (Creative Artists Agency). Although hot new agencies are always springing up, these three continue to dominate Hollywood today.

Alan Smithee ➳ The unknown soldier of the film industry. If script or direction is credited to Alan Smithee, that means the real writer or director refuses to take credit for his work.

Album ➳ A vinyl phonograph record production consisting of one or more LP records and at least thirty minutes in length. The term derives from the pre-1952 world of 78-rpm wax records when a production with a dozen songs would require six 12-inch disks that would be packaged in a bound set of sleeves that looked very much like a photo album. See SINGLE, LINER.

Algorithm ⇒ A general routine in computer programming that performs a specific task. A precisely defined set of steps that solve a problem.

Aliasing ⇒ An ARTIFACT, or inconsistency, in digital imaging. The misrepresentation of lines caused by inadequate SAMPLING. See NYQUIST LIMIT, JAGGIES. ANTI-ALIASING ALGORITHMS are used to counteract aliasing.

Alienation Effect ⇒ See ESTRANGEMENT EFFECT.

Alpha Channel ⇒ In computer graphics programs an additional channel to provide noncolor information such as masks, transparency levels, textures, and the like. A 24-bit color depth leaves 8 bits for the Alpha Channel.

Alpha Test ⇒ See BETA.

AltaVista ⇒ See SEARCH ENGINES.

Alternate Movies ⇒ A feature introduced with QUICKTIME 3 that permits storage of several versions of a movie at different DATA RATES so that web browsers operating at different speeds can automatically choose the most appropriate one.

Alto ⇒ See XEROX PARC.

AM ⇒ Amplitude Modulation, a system of broadcasting in which the PROGRAM SIGNAL is imposed on the carrier wave by modifying the strength or amplitude of the carrier. See also FM, WAVE MECHANICS.

Ambient Light ⇒ The natural light surrounding the subject, usually understood to be soft: reflected or bounced. See AVAILABLE-LIGHT PHOTOGRAPHY.

Ambient Sound ⇒ The natural sound of a scene, usually outdoors. See PRESENCE, TRACK, ROOM TONE.

AMC ⇒ American Movie Classics. CABLE NETWORK devoted to classic films.

America OnLine ⇒ See AOL.

American Film Institute ⇒ Perhaps because the American film industry already had an august ACADEMY it came late to the Institute game. The American Film Institute was founded in Washington DC—not Los Angeles—in 1969. (The next year, its first publication was pamphlet that was the seed for the book you hold in your hands.) The AFI found its public voice in 1973 when it began its television program for Life Achievement Awards. (The Academy had aggrandized all the others for the Oscars.) The AFI has also been active in compiling a complete filmography of American film.

AMPAS ⇒ See ACADEMY OF MOTION PICTURE ARTS AND SCIENCES.

Amplitude ⇒ See WAVE MECHANICS.

AMPS ➻ Advanced Mobile Phone System. The standard for analog CELLULAR TELEPHONY in the U.S. See TACS, CDMA.

AMS ➻ Automatic Music Search, senses the blank areas between tracks on a tape or disc.

Anaglyph ➻ See 3-D.

Analog ➻ See DIGITAL.

Analytical Editing ➻ See CONTINUITY EDITING.

Anamorphic Lens ➻ A camera lens that squeezes a WIDESCREEN image to conform to the dimensions of the standard frame width. The anamorphic lens on the projector then unsqueezes the image.

Anamorphic Video ➻ First introduced in Europe and Japan, the application of the ANAMORPHIC technique to video became standardized with the introduction of DVD-VIDEO, which supports it as a useful alternative to LETTERBOXING. Whatever its original Aspect Ratio, the image is captured at 1.78:1 (16:9) which is then squeezed to 1.33:1 (the Aspect Ratio of a standard television monitor). Of course, a widescreen monitor is necessary to realize the full effect, but Anamorphic Video can also be LETTERBOXED on a standard monitor. The advantage of anamorphic video over letterboxing is 33 percent better vertical resolution, since the top and bottom of the screen can be used. This is comparable to LINE-DOUBLING.

Angle of View ➻ The angle subtended by the lens. WIDE-ANGLE LENSES have broad angles of view, TELEPHOTO LENSES have very narrow angles of view. Not to be confused with CAMERA ANGLE.

Angle/Reverse Angle ➻ Editing SHOTS of two people in conversation to conform to the 180-DEGREE RULE. See REVERSE SHOT.

Animatic ➻ Simple animation used as a STORYBOARD.

Animation ➻ Methods by which inanimate objects are made to move on the screen, giving the appearance of life. These methods include drawing on the film itself; photographing CELLS (drawings) one at a time; photographing concrete objects one frame at a time while adjusting their positions in between frames (STOP-MOTION PHOTOGRAPHY, PIXILATION); and various computer techniques that are both modeled on these older techniques and unique to computer graphics, such as MORPHS. See ROTOSCOPE, ANIME.

Animatronics ➻ Theme-park figures whose movements are controlled by computer programs. The technology is sometimes used in animated films.

Anime ➻ The Japanese word for animation has been adopted in English to mean Japanese animation, mainly for television. It became popular in the 1980s and remains a collectible. See MANGA.

ANSI ➻ American National Standards Institute, sets standards for many technical fields, including audio and video equipment. Formerly the American Standards Association, whose ASA numbers are one of the familiar gauges of film speed. See ISO.

Answer Print ⯈⁺ The first print of the conformed negative received back from the laboratory. Color values have been corrected. See TIMING, MARRIED PRINT.

Antenne 2 ⯈⁺ The original name of the second French television network formed in the 1970s after the breakup of the state-owned system (and a pun on "entendu"). Now known as France 2.

Anti-Aliasing ⯈⁺ The limited resolution of most computer screens results in JAGGIES on certain typefaces and in many images. Anti-aliasing techniques use ALGORITHMS that calculate intermediate levels of gray (or average colors) for pixels on the edges of letters or images. These computed values fool the eye into perceiving a smooth line. See ALIASING; compare BEN DAY SCREEN.

Antiope ⯈⁺ The original name for the French TELETEL PROTOCOL for encoding VIDEOTEXT graphics, now in disuse.

Anti-Skating Mechanism ⯈⁺ See TURNTABLE.

AOL ⯈⁺ In the early 1980s, the online industry was composed of COMPUSERVE and numerous small BBS systems. A young man from Hawaii by the name of Steve Case thought he saw an opportunity. Most of the traffic on Compuserve (or the BBSes for that matter) had to do with computer-related questions. If you dedicated an online service to a particular platform, you should get most of the traffic for that platform. He found some venture capitalists willing to invest in this classic niche marketing concept and, in 1985, Quantum Link was born. The first platform targeted was the Commodore 64, a cult machine with dedicated followers. After awhile, a service was opened for APPLE users. It was quickly followed by PC Link, for users of the IBM PC and its clones. Usage on these services was OK, but the money wasn't flowing in as expected. (In the 1980s we referred to online as "the industry in search of a business.") The venture capitalists got antsy. Would they ever get their money out of this thing?

The company changed direction (for the first time), deciding to be a general service, like Compuserve, but focusing on more mundane interests. Quantum Link changed its name to America Online. By this time consumers had some mild interest in online services, thanks in part to the entry of IBM into the market with PRODIGY. AOL, as it soon became known, started to grow. The initial public offering took place successfully.

In the early 1990s the company engaged in one of the most massive direct mail campaigns ever seen. There was hardly a computer owner in the country who didn't receive at least one AOL disk in the mail each month. Membership continued to grow. AOL passed Compuserve. Prodigy was failing. Microsoft's MSN hit the ground stumbling in 1995. Then the WORLD WIDE WEB exploded. It was direct competition to a general, proprietary online service like AOL. By rights, the company should have faded quickly, as did Prodigy. Instead, Steve Case, still the CEO, reinvented AOL yet again. The new AOL embraced the Web, and offered access to it through a browser extension hurriedly purchased. The transition was successful (and those disks kept arriving in the mail with predictable regularity). In 1997 AOL acquired arch-rival Compuserve. In 1998 it purchased NETSCAPE, the company most responsible for the Web's success. By this time, AOL had a market value of $20 billion.

AP, APP ➤ Short for APPlication, a computer program, as in "That App takes up too much RAM."

Apple ➤ Founded January 3, 1977 by Steven Jobs, Stephen Wozniak, and A. C. "Mike" Markkula, Apple Computer Inc. has consistently led the microcomputer revolution. The Apple II, introduced in April 1977, established the model for the Personal Computer, providing a platform for VisiCalc, the first popular spreadsheet program, and under the technical leadership of Stephen Wozniak establishing the open architecture that still dominates most of the PC world. The Macintosh, introduced in 1984 under the technical leadership of Steven Jobs, followed the opposite path: a closed architecture on the "appliance" model.

The Macintosh's GRAPHICAL USER INTERFACE (mouse, icons, windows) which Apple borrowed from the work done at Xerox's Palo Alto Research Center in the 1970s proved to be a quantum advance in personal computer science, expanding the purview of the machine from text and numbers to graphics, sound, and images, as well as vastly simplifying users' control. This positioned what began as an office typewriter/calculator tool to become the MULTIMEDIA device of choice in the 1980s, serving as a common ground for the film, television, music, and publishing industries. Although still officially an Apple Fellow, Wozniak left the company in February 1985 to return to school and pursue other interests. Jobs was forced out by CEO John Sculley in September 1985, later founding the NeXT company.

In 1991 Apple formed an alliance with IBM to position itself to expand market share in operating systems and software just as the rest of the personal computer industry was catching up—and therefore finally able to compete—with Apple's pioneering Graphical User Interface. In 1993, the company introduced the Newton, a PENBASED PDA device that foreshadowed a major shift in interface design. Sculley, who had championed the device, was ousted the same year. His second-in-command, Michael Spindler, was installed as CEO, but was himself let go early in 1996 as the company's stock plummeted. In 1994 the company successfully managed the transition to a new CPU architecture based on the PowerPC RISC chip developed in conjunction with Motorola and IBM, although it took several years for the technology to realize its full potential.

In 1997, facing mounting losses, the Apple Board ousted Spindler's replacement and reinstalled Steve Jobs as "interim" CEO. Within a year he had turned the company around, refocusing it on exciting technology and, by the way, reviving his original Macintosh "all-in-one" appliance philosophy with the hot-selling iMac, introduced in 1998.

APS ≫→ Advanced Photo System. Kodak technology for the ADVANTIX system.

Arbitron ≫→ One of the two major U.S. radio and television RATINGS services. Compare NIELSEN.

Arc Light ≫→ Used both on the set and in projectors to provide high energy illumination. An electric current arcs across the gap between two pieces of carbon creating a very white, strong light with a COLOR TEMPERATURE close to 6,000° Kelvin. Formerly the norm, arc lights are seldom used today since cheaper, less dangerous technologies have become available. See XENON LAMP, AVAILABLE-LIGHT PHOTOGRAPHY.

Architext ≫→ See SEARCH ENGINES.

ARD ≫→ Arbeitsgemeinschaft der Rundfunkanstalten Deutschlands. The ARD is the central broadcasting authority of Germany, founded in 1950. The first channel began in 1954. A second channel was added in 1961.

Area of Dominant Influence ≫→ See ADI.

ARPANET ≫→ The network established by the U.S. Department of Defense to connect academic and military participants in the DOD's Advanced Research Project Agency. It was the ARPANET that grew into the INTERNET.

Arri ≫→ Nickname for ARRIFLEX.

Arriflex ≫→ A lightweight, portable camera that became popular in the late 1950s, it was essential to the HAND-HELD technique of the NEW WAVE and the contemporary style of cinematography that followed in the sixties. The Arriflex was soon joined by many imitators, but steadily improved. The Arnold and Richter company in Munich has won Academy Awards twice for the technology of the camera. Compare MITCHELL.

Art ➤ Originally the word was used to refer to any kind of skill, but gradually took on more specific meanings having to do with esthetic activity. It now refers generally to those endeavors that are not strictly utilitarian. Includes the practical arts of design, environmental arts such as architecture, pictorial arts (painting, sculpture, drawing), dramatic arts, poetic and narrative arts, and musical arts. The various earlier senses of the word are still represented in a number of derivations: an "artisan" is a craftsperson; an "artiste" is a performing artist.

Art Director ➤ The designer, generally in charge of sets (and sometimes costumes). Sometimes a major contributor to a film, play, or media presentation.

Art Film ➤ In the midfifties, a distinction grew up between the art film—often of foreign origin—with distinct esthetic pretensions, and the commercial film of the Hollywood tradition. Art films were shown in ART HOUSES, usually small theaters catering to a discriminating clientele; commercial movies were shown in larger theaters. Although the range of film activity is at least as great today, the dichotomy between art and commercial film has largely died out. See FILM D'ART.

Art House ➤ A type of film theater popular in the late 1950s and 1960s that showed ART FILMS—usually foreign—rather than "movies." (Many art houses served espresso instead of soft drinks in the lounge.) The art houses opened the new world of cinema to an entire generation of Americans long before film was considered a serious art and studied in universities.

Articulation ➤ The linguist André Martinet suggested that languages have the power of double articulation—that is, the user of a language must be able to distinguish sounds as well as meanings. The smallest distinguishable units of sound are called PHONEMES; the smallest distinguishable units of meaning are called MONEMES. Christian Metz suggested that cinema does not have the power of double articulation, since signifier and signified are too closely connected. Umberto Eco, however, suggested that cinema is a "language" marked by triple articulation in which "figures" combine to form "signs," which then combine to form "semes."

Artifact ➤ In DIGITAL graphics, a specific GLITCH in the image. ALIASING, CONTOURING, and PIXELLATION are all digital artifacts. Although the term came into general use in the late 1980s with the development of desktop video, the phenomenon is not limited to digital imaging. Analog images also have problems, among them SNOW, RF INTERFERENCE, SMEARING, FRINGING, and STREAKING.

Artificial Intelligence ➻ The area of computer science that studies the qualities of intelligence in an attempt to make machines act more like humans. The dubious premise here is that this would be a good thing. "Open the pod-bay doors, HAL." See ELIZA, TURING TEST.

ASA ➻ See EMULSION SPEED.

ASCII ➻ American Standard Code for Information Interchange. The international standard 8-bit code (ISO 646) that assigns specific numerical values to all Roman alphabetic characters, digits, punctuation symbols, and other characters. (In the 1970s there was a competing standard: IBM's EBCDIC. The micro revolution killed it.) See UNICODE.

ASIC ➻ Application-Specific Integrated Circuit. Most CHIPS are designed to do a variety of computing chores; ASICs are designed with one task in mind which allows them to concentrate their power on the job at hand.

Aspect Ratio ➻ The ratio of the width to the height of the film or television image. The formerly standard ACADEMY APERTURE is 4:3, or 1.33:1. WIDESCREEN ratios vary. In Europe 1.66:1 is most common, in the U.S., 1.85:1. The widescreen aspect ratio chosen for HDTV is 16:9 (1.78:1), somewhere between the U.S. and European standards. ANAMORPHIC processes such as CINEMASCOPE and PANAVISION are even wider, ranging from 2.00:1 to 2.55:1. See also VISTAVISION, TV MASK.

Assembly Language ➻ See MACHINE LANGUAGE.

Astra ➻ The brand name for the satellite operations of SES, the largest satellite broadcaster in Europe.

Asymmetrical Compression ➻ See COMPRESSION.

Asynchronous Sound ➻ Sound that does not operate in unison with the image. See COMMENTATIVE SOUND, CONTRAPUNTAL SOUND; compare SYNCHRONOUS SOUND.

Atari ➻ The company founded by Nolan Bushnell in 1973 to sell his PONG arcade VIDEO GAME. Atari was a huge success in the 1970s. Bushnell sold out to Warner Communications and moved on to his next venture, Chuck E. Cheese pizza theaters. Under Warner's wing, Atari moved into the PC market in the 1980s with machines based on Motorola chips that was inventive but didn't sell well enough to prevent the company from crashing. (Chuck E. Cheese didn't survive either.)

ATAS ➻ See NATAS.

ATM ➻ Asynchronous Transfer Mode. A type of PACKET-SWITCHED network that transmits fixed-length units of data, but asynchronously, and runs at up to 155 Mb per second.

ATRAC ➤ Adaptive Transform Acoustic Coding. Sony's proprietary compression technology used in the MINIDISC and the SDDS theatrical sound system. Like AC-3, ATRAC uses PERCEPTUAL CODING techniques to produce a low bit rate, but its main value for movie sound tracks (where space is limited) is that it merges several channels of sound into one data stream.

ATSC ➤ Advanced Television Systems Committee. Set up in 1987 to develop a consensus on standards for U.S. digital television. See GRAND ALLIANCE.

Attenuation ➤ When an electromagnetic signal is transmitted over a distance it loses power. This is called attenuation.

Attraction ➤ Eisenstein's theory of film analyzes the image as a series or collection of attractions, each in a dialectical relationship with the others. Attractions were thus basic elements of film form, and the theory of attractions was a precursor to modern semiotic theory. See MONTAGE OF ATTRACTIONS.

ATV ➤ Advanced TeleVision, the rather colorless umbrella term adopted by the GRAND ALLIANCE for all flavors of television technically superior to NTSC including: HDTV, EDTV, IDTV and almost anything digital.

Audimeter ➤ The original gadget the NIELSEN company attached to television sets across the country to measure ratings. From "audience meter." Replaced in 1987 by the PEOPLE METER for measuring national ratings. The Set-Tuning Meter, a more recent version of the audimeter, is still used in major markets to measure local ratings.

Audio ➤ (1) The sound portion of a transmission or broadcast. (2) Sound and recording arts in general. See VIDEO, VISUALS.

Audio Interleave ➤ When a movie is digitized the audio and video signals have to be woven into one stream. The size of the audio chunk is known as the Audio Interleave, typically one second or one-half second. The data is stored in a buffer to be played back as necessary.

Audio Offset ➤ Because audio and video tracks on a DVD are not linearly linked as they are on tape or film, synchronization is often a problem. The COMPRESSIONIST has to adjust for Audio Offset.

Audiocassette ➤ Technology introduced by PHILIPS in 1963 that reduced the size of tapes and—just as important—eliminated the handling associated with reel-to-reel tapes. By packaging the technology to make it "consumer-friendly" Philips developed a formidable competitor to the durable LP record. By 1982 sales of cassettes exceeded sales of records.

Audion ⇒ The original name of Lee De Forest's VACUUM TUBE. The simplest type consisted of two electrodes separated by a grid that can modify the current flowing between them, thus permitting amplification and modification of a signal.

Audiophile ⇒ A person with some expertise in and appreciation of the AUDIO arts. A fan. See HIGH-END AUDIO. Compare CINEPHILE, VIDEOPHILE.

Audiotext ⇒ A computerized information system utilizing the telephone as a terminal, with input from the telephone touchtone keypad, and output via recording. In the U.S., simply, 900 numbers and their local equivalents. The term is now dated; see IVR.

Auditory Masking ⇒ The tendency of the human ear not to hear noise when it is close in frequency to louder sounds. A principle of Dolby noise reduction in all its forms. See PERCEPTUAL CODING.

Aural Cable ⇒ The origination and transmission over CABLE TELEVISION systems of FM radio programming.

Auralization ⇒ The process of predicting how a room will sound by applying mathematical formulas to data about its design.

Auteur ⇒ In the French AUTEUR POLICY (1) the prime author of a film; (2) a director with a recognizable style. Compare METTEUR EN SCÈNE.

Auteur Policy, Auteur Theory ⇒ The auteur policy postulates that one person, usually the director, has the artistic responsibility for a film and reveals a personal worldview through the tensions among style, theme, and the conditions of production. The net result is that films can be studied like novels or paintings—as clearly individual productions. The "politique des auteurs" (auteur policy) was first stated by François Truffaut in his article "Une certaine tendance du cinéma français," which appeared in the January 1954 issue of *Cahiers du Cinéma*. It became the policy for that journal and was elaborated on by other writers, mainly André Bazin. Andrew Sarris was the main exponent of the auteur policy in the U.S. See PANTHÉON.

Authoring ⇒ The process of constructing a CD-ROM or DVD. Authoring involves programming, testing, and preparing files to be written to disc. It does not include writing. A strange verb derived from a noun that already had a perfectly good verb behind it. (Authors write, they don't "author"—except in *Time* magazine's lingo.) It may derive from the programmer's understandable desire to share in the artistic credit.

Autowide ⇒ This feature automatically switches a widescreen digital television from 4:3 to 16:9 or LETTERBOX aspect ratios.

AV ⇒ Audio-Video.

Available-Light Photography ⇒ Recent advances in the chemistry of FILMSTOCKS have produced materials with more sensitivity to light, making available-light photography more common. No artificial light is used; the cinematographer confines himself to PRACTICAL LIGHT-ING such as the sun and normal household lamps. See also AMBIENT LIGHT.

Avant Garde ⇒ If ART is seen as progressing and developing chrono-logically, then it will by its nature reveal a cutting edge of artists—the avant garde—more intellectually and esthetically advanced than their contemporaries. In the POSTMODERN period, the concept of the avant garde has lessened in importance. Avant-garde films were often nonnarrative in structure and sometimes deal with contro-versial subject matter. They were almost always self-conscious, emphasizing technique over subject matter. See ABSOLUTE FILM, POETIC FILM.

Average Audience ⇒ See AA.

Avid ⇒ Although other companies manufacture video editing soft-ware, the Avid Technology Inc. system is most popular. The Mac-based Avid Media Composer was first used for a feature film on Martha Coolidge's *Lost in Yonkers* (1992). Since then the software has been ported to other platforms. The great advantage to DIGITAL EDITING systems is that they are nonlinear: any piece of footage can be accessed at any time. Compare MOVIOLA, STEENBECK.

AVLS ⇒ Automatic Volume Limiting System, a feature of some per-sonal audio systems (WALKMANS) that is supposed to prevent poten-tially damaging GAIN levels. See SHISS.

Awareness Factor ⇒ In film and media marketing, a measure of the recognition of a product, usually before it is released. Compare INTENT-TO-RENT, WANT-TO-SEE.

Azimuth ⇒ For magnetic audiotape, the angle of the head to the line of the tape: usually 90°.

B Frame ⇒ See MPEG-2.

B Movie, B Picture ⇒ When double features were the rule, quick, cheap pictures were made to fill the bottom of the double bill. The equivalent today is the MADE FOR TV MOVIE or DIRECT-TO-VIDEO. See PRO-GRAMMER.

B Roll ⇒ See A AND B ROLLS, COVERAGE.

Babelsberg ⇒ The popular name for the historic German film stu-dios outside of Berlin in Neubabelsberg. The first film company set up shop there in 1912. UFA was located there in the 1930s. After the war, the studios were given over to the East German film authority, DEFA. In 1992, Compagnie Générale des Eaux took control. Compare CINECITTÀ.

Baby Bell ⇒ The nickname for the seven regional phone companies carved out of AT&T in 1984: Nynex, Bell Atlantic, Bell South, Ameritech, Southwestern Bell, U S West. and Pacific Telesis. Within 15 years, mergers had reduced the number to four, none of them corporate babies: Bell Atlantic (which absorbed Nynex), Bell South, SBC Communications (Southwestern Bell, Pacific Telesis, and Ameritech), and U S West, which agreed to merge with upstart Qwest.

Back Projection ⇒ See REAR PROJECTION.

Backlighting ⇒ The main source of light is behind the subject, silhouetting it, and directed toward the camera. See also KEY LIGHT, FILLER LIGHT.

Backstory ⇒ Actors often invent detailed pasts for their characters. These are the backstories. The practice is especially common with bit players, perhaps because their characters have so little presence.

BAFTA ⇒ British Academy of Film and Television Arts, founded in 1946.

Balanced Connection ⇒ Professional audio equipment is often interconnected with three-wire Balanced cables. The first wire carries the signal, the second carries it with inverted polarity, and the third provides the ground. There is less sensitivity to RF interference.

Balun ⇒ A type of logical connector that joins COAXIAL cable to TWISTED PAIR cable.

Banana Plug ⇒ See PLUGS.

Band ⇒ (1) A defined group of radio frequencies. (2) A CUT on a record.

Band Printer ⇒ The workhorse of industrial computer printing from the beginning of the industry, the Band Printer relied on a travelling metal tape on which the letters, numbers, and symbols were embossed. When the proper letter was in place, a hammer fired, pressing the embossing into the typewriter ribbon which deposited the ink on the paper. Band Printers were never used with personal computers and were eventually replaced in industrial applications by the LASER PRINTER. See also DOT MATRIX, DAISY WHEEL.

Bandwidth ⇒ (1) The capacity of the frequency range of the RADIO SPECTRUM allotted to an electromagnetic signal such as a television or radio broadcast, or the capacity required for a certain application. Broadband technology is supported by a wide range of frequencies. Narrowband technology depends on a limited range. Bandwidth has become a key buzzword of the 1990s as the rivers of the INTERNET and DIGITAL media flow together to produce a floodtide of information. Bill Gates uses the word to describe people as well as technologies. If Gates tells you, "You're a really high-bandwidth guy," smile and say thank you. (2) A similar frequency range in audio. For example, the human ear has a bandwidth of 20 Hz to 20 kHz.

Bankable ⟫⁺ A star or director is said to be bankable when his or her commitment to a project convinces investors it is worthy of financing.

Barn Doors ⟫⁺ "Blinders" placed on set lights to direct the flow of the light beam in a certain direction.

Barter ⟫⁺ In a barter deal, a television station or cable operator trades advertising time rather than money for programming. The syndicator then sells the ad time to a national advertiser. The station may sell any remaining commercial time.

Baseband ⟫⁺ A primary video or audio signal transmitted at its original frequency, not imposed on a carrier frequency. With satellites, the incoming signal before downshifting. Compare BROADBAND, NARROWBAND.

Baud ⟫⁺ A measure of transmission speed for data communications: the number of separate signals transmitted each second. For slow-speed modems, the Baud rate usually equals the number of bits per second (thus, a 1200-Baud modem transmits 1,200 bits/sec), but at higher speeds more complex coding systems are used. In effect, each Baud carries more than one bit, so the effective speed is considerably higher than the Baud rate. These coding systems, such as Phase Shift Keying, are a main reason modem technology advanced from 300 bits/sec in the early 1980s to 28,800 bits/sec in the late 1990s. The phone lines hadn't changed. Named after Émile BAUDOT.

Baudot ⟫⁺ The coding system used for TELEX, named for telegrapher Jean-Maurice Émile Baudot, who invented it in 1874. This ingenious system was one of the first applications of BINARY-CODED DECIMAL transmission. Baudot used a five-bit unit, which meant it was capable of 32 different characters—not enough for even the Latin alphabet and numerals. So Baudot assigned two of the 32 positions to control characters named LTRS and FIGS. When you hit the LTRS key, everything that followed was alphabetic (capital letters only, of course); when you hit the FIGS key, everything that followed was numeric or punctuation. This supershift idea was later adopted for the escape-sequence commands of UNIX; then the Control, Command, and Alt keys of contemporary computers.

BBC ⟫⁺ British Broadcasting Corporation. The quasi-public authority responsible for the noncommercial television and radio networks of the U.K. founded in 1927. The budget is funded by a special tax on television sets so that the BBC is theoretically free of government interference in programming (unlike public television authorities, which receive allocations from a government). The BBC currently operates two television networks: BBC-1 and BBC-2. Compare ARD, ITV.

BBS ➻ Bulletin Board System. Before the advent of the WORLD WIDE WEB, thousands of small BBSes provided our first taste of network interconnectivity. You could post items in their forums, read the published articles, and usually also chat. But you had to dial in directly to their telephone number and you were limited to an ASCII command-line interface. COMPUSERVE grew to be the largest BBS. See also SYSOP, AOL.

BCD ➻ Binary-Coded Decimal. While digital computers operate with a binary number system, it is often useful to represent decimal numbers (and letters). Eight bits provide 256 decimal values, enough to code the letters of the roman alphabet, numbers, punctuation, and control codes. See BAUDOT, BIT, ASCII, UNICODE.

BDB ➻ British Digital Broadcasting. A consortium of Granada and Carlton Television in the U.K.: a commercial enterprise, not a standard.

Beeb ➻ The longtime colloquial nickname for the BBC.

Below-the-Line Costs ➻ See COSTS.

Ben Day Screen ➻ The array of dots or lines that, when used as a filter, permits the decomposition of the continuous tones of a photograph into the pure blacks and whites used in printing. Invented by Benjamin Day. Also HALFTONE.

Bertelsmann AG ➻ The world's third largest media company at the turn of the century (behind TIME WARNER and DISNEY), Bertelsmann is different in several significant ways: (1) nearly all of its stock is owned by charitable foundations (since 1993); (2) It was founded in 1835, nearly a century before its rivals; (3) its German origins give it status as an international company, unlike its American-based rivals. Reinhard Mohn, a descendent of founder Carl Bertelsmann, rebuilt the company after World War II. He started the first German book club, Lesering, in 1950.

By the mid-1960s the company was ready to expand beyond book publishing. In 1964 Bertelsmann bought what remained of UFA, an important brand name in German film and television. A while later the company purchased an interest in magazine publisher Gruner + Jahr. In the 1970s Bertelsmann began to expand abroad, purchasing a majority interest in Bantam books in 1977 (the purchase was completed in 1981), and U.S. Arista records in 1979.

In the 1980s, under CEO Mark Woessner, the company continued to expand in the U.S. In 1986 it bought RCA Records and control of Doubleday Publishing. (In 1993 Mohn transferred substantial voting shares in the company to the Bertelsmann Foundation.) In 1995 the company teamed up with AOL to produce a comparable online service for Europe. The next year Bertelsmann partnered with CANAL + and Havas to introduce DSS to Europe. In 1996 the company combined its UFA operation with Luxembourg's CLT (Compagnie Luxembourgeoise Télédiffusion). The result was one of the largest broadcasting companies in Europe. In 1998 the company solidified its unique position as an international publisher by completing the purchase of Random House. It also bought a fifty percent interest in Barnesandnoble.com, one of the leading Internet booksellers. The same year Woessner retired; American-trained Thomas Middlehoff became Chairman and declared that the official language of the company would henceforth be English.

Best Boy ➻ The first assistant to the GAFFER, or chief electrician on the set.

Beta ➻ (1) Software is never finished. Early on, the industry devised a way to indicate stages of development. The *Alpha* version of a program is undergoing internal testing. The Beta version has been released to trusted individuals outside the company for testing. Betas usually go through numerous versions. Nowadays, Betas are followed by Release Candidates. They still aren't finished, but they're better than Beta. See BUG. (2) The VIDEOCASSETTE consumer format first introduced by SONY in 1976 as Betamax. By the mideighties, the Beta format had yielded to the technically less sophisticated VHS format in the home market, but was retained for professional use in the BETACAM system.

Betacam, Betacam SP, Betacam SX ➻ The SONY professional half-inch VIDEOCASSETTE technology, introduced in 1981. Betacam SP (Superior Performance) does not record a COMPONENT video signal but approaches that level of quality by recording LUMINANCE and two-color components thereof together with stereo audio. The SP technology has also been applied to the successor to the U-MATIC, *3/4-Inch SP. Digital Betacam*, introduced in 1994, provides a COMPONENT digital format. Betacam SX (1996) offers an improved 4:2:2 Component digital format designed for television news-gathering. (The numbers refer to the OVERSAMPLING ratios.)

Beta-Film ⇨ Leo Kirch's Munich-based film distribution company that served as the foundation of the Kirch media empire, licensing films to television in the 1970s and 1980s.

Betamax ⇨ See BETA and BETACAM.

BFI ⇨ British Film Institute. Growing out of the film club movement, The BFI was founded in 1933. The Institute runs the prestigious National Film Theatre and the National Film and Television Archive, publishes monographs and the venerable *Sight and Sound* magazine, and even dabbles in film production.

BG ⇨ Background, and by implication, the EXTRAS.

Bicycling ⇨ Shipment of prints and tapes by other than electronic means. Years ago, film distributors would save on print costs by literally bicycling individual reels of a print from one theater to another so that the same print could serve more than one theater: as soon as reel one was finished at theater A it would be biked over to theater B, while reel 2 unspooled at theater A.

Bildschirmtext ⇨ The German VIDEOTEXT PROTOCOL of the 1980s. Compare TELETEL, NAPLPS.

Binary-Coded Decimal ⇨ See BCD.

Binary Magnitudes ⇨ Microcomputers are based on a binary number system; most of the rest of the world runs on a decimal system. In the early days of the business some unknown engineer decided to appropriate some of the language we have developed for decimals to use with binaries. The "kilobyte" was born. It was an understandable fudge: after all, 2^{10} is 1,024, which isn't very far from 10^3, or 1,000. And anyway, anyone who dealt with kilobytes or megabits knew their true binary values.

However, as the business became a cultural revolution two things happened: normal people, who knew that a kilometer was 1,000 meters, had to use these words; and vastly increased storage and speed multiplied the discrepancies. The difference between a binary kilo (1,024) and a decimal kilo (1,000) is only 2.4 percent; but the difference between a binary giga (1,073,741,824) and a decimal giga (1,000,000,000) is more than three times as great.

Moreover, computer engineers are not always consistent: sometimes a mega *is* a decimal million, not a binary 2^{20} (1,048,576): this is the case with the familiar "4.7-gigabyte" DVD disc, which really holds only 4.38 traditional binary gigabytes. And even worse, sometimes the two are mixed: the familiar "1.44 megabyte" 3.5-inch diskette is measured in "megabytes" of 1,024,000 bytes (1,000 x 2^{10})!

To bring some order to this muddle the IEEE has recommended to the ISO a new system of prefixes for the binary magnitudes so that there will be no confusion with the decimal values: *kibi, mebi, gibi,* and *tebi* (the second syllable is pronounced "bee") would replace the misused decimal prefixes.

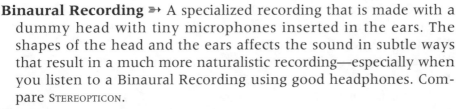

Prefix	Magnitude	Symbol	Origin	Derivation
kibi	2^{10}	Ki	$(2^{10})^1$ kilobinary	$(10^3)^1$ kilo
mebi	2^{20}	Mi	$(2^{10})^2$ megabinary	$(10^3)^2$ mega
gibi	2^{30}	Gi	$(2^{10})^3$ gigabinary	$(10^3)^3$ giga
tebi	2^{40}	Ti	$(2^{10})^4$ terabinary	$(10^3)^4$ tera

Binaural Recording ➻ A specialized recording that is made with a dummy head with tiny microphones inserted in the ears. The shapes of the head and the ears affects the sound in subtle ways that result in a much more naturalistic recording—especially when you listen to a Binaural Recording using good headphones. Compare STEREOPTICON.

Binding Post ➻ See PLUGS.

Biograph ➻ American Mutoscope and Biograph, the company for which D. W. Griffith worked between 1908 and 1913.

Biopic ➻ A filmed biography, especially of the sort produced by WARNER in the 1930s and 1940s.

Bioskop ➻ The camera/projector Max and Emil Skladanowsky developed in Germany between 1896 and 1898.

Bird ➻ A SATELLITE.

Bit ➻ Binary digIT. The smallest unit of DIGITAL computer information. A bit can have only two possible values: 0 or 1, on or off, yes or no. In order to encode Roman letters and numbers, at least 5 bits are required in each group to provide 32 possible combinations. Modern computers have standardized on an 8-bit BYTE that provides 256 combinations: enough for upper- and lower-case letters, digits, and punctuation. See ASCII, BAUDOT, K, MEG, UNICODE.

Bit Budget ➻ Even though DVDs store 4.7 gigabytes or more, a DVD product often needs all that REAL ESTATE. The preliminary storage requirement estimate for all the various elements of a DVD-ROM or DVD-VIDEO is the Bit Budget.

Bitmapped Graphics ➻ Computer graphic images that are generated and described PIXEL by pixel. In contrast, Vector graphics generate and describe the image with mathematical formulas for the lines, points, and curves of which it is composed. As a result, Vector graphics are independent of screen or printer RESOLUTION, while Bitmapped Graphics are affected by screen or printer resolution. See RASTERIZE.

Bits per Pixel ⇒ See COLOR DEPTH.

Black Body ⇒ One of several systems for quantifying color values in print and electronic media. See COLOR MODELS.

Black Box ⇒ (1) Any electronic device or processor whose workings are either mysterious or vaguely illegal. (2) A descrambler used to pirate video signals from either satellites or CABLE television.

Black Comedy ⇒ A type of comedy popular during the late fifties and early sixties that dealt in macabre subjects such as atomic war, murder, mutilation, and overeating. See SLAPSTICK, SCREWBALL.

Black Maria ⇒ The nickname for Edison's early film studio around 1900. Open at the top, the Black Maria revolved to catch the sun, the only source of light strong enough to shoot film at the time.

Blacklist ⇒ See HOLLYWOOD TEN.

Blanking Interval ⇒ See VERTICAL BLANKING INTERVAL.

Blaxploitation ⇒ VARIETY'S 1970s term for EXPLOITATION FILMS aimed at the Black market. See SEXPLOITATION.

Blimp ⇒ A semipermanent soundproofing cover for the camera. Most cameras are now self-blimped—that is, constructed so that they operate relatively noiselessly.

Blind Bidding ⇒ The practice of requiring exhibitors to bid for a film without having seen it. Now outlawed in an increasing number of states. See BLOCK BOOKING.

BLOB ⇒ Binary Large OBject. A very large computer file that operates more like a disc than a file. Example: VOB.

Block ⇒ An 8 x 8 matrix of pixels in MPEG coding, the unit that undergoes the DISCRETE COSINE TRANSFORM calculation to produce luminance and chrominance values. In MPEG-2, a *Macroblock* is made up of 6 blocks, 4 for luminance, 2 for chrominance, from a 16 x 16 matrix. The Blocks are at the heart of the SPATIAL COMPRESSION of the image; the Macroblocks serve a similar function for the TEMPORAL COMPRESSION of the movie.

Block Booking ⇒ The practice of requiring exhibitors to book a package of several films at once, usually including one or two they want, and many they don't. See BLIND BIDDING.

Block Programming ⇒ Segments of DAYPARTS reserved for specific genres of programming, such as children's blocks or news blocks.

Blockbuster ⇒ Jargon term for a film that either is highly successful commercially or has cost so much to make that it must be extraordinarily popular in order to return a profit.

Blocking ⇒ (1) The telltale sign that video has been compressed. When you see blocky images, the compression is too high and the 8 x 8 matrix of the Block is revealed. (2) In theater or film, working out the placement and movement of the actors before the performance.

Blooming ➻ Defocusing of the television image caused by excessive brightness.

Bloop ➻ A small patch placed over a splice in a soundtrack or tape in order to cover the noise made by the splice moving across the sound Head.

Blooper ➻ An error made on the set, usually an actor's error. See Outtake.

Blue Book ➻ See CD Standards.

Blue Box ➻ See Hacker.

Blue Movie ➻ 1950s term for an erotic or pornographic film.

Blue Screen ➻ A process of combining separate images using a Travelling Matte. Nowadays the Blue Screen is often green. See also Chroma Key.

Bluetooth ➻ Standard agreed to by computer and communications industries to use a frequency band at 2.4 gHz for very low power, short-range intraoffice communications. If implemented it would compete with Infrared communications protocols like IRDA.

BMP ➻ See Image File Formats.

BNC Connector ➻ See Plugs.

BO ➻ Varietese for Box Office.

Bonus Spot ➻ Commercial time allotted to an advertiser to make up for a previous Undelivered Audience, or a Spot that did not run because of technical or programming problems. Also called a *Make-Good*.

Booking ➻ The rental of a film to a theater. See Distribution, Exhibition, Blind Bidding, Block Booking.

Bookman ➻ See Data Discman.

Boom ➻ A travelling arm for suspending a microphone above the actors and outside the frame.

Boom Channel ➻ Nickname for the Low Frequency Effects channel—the .1 in 5.1.

Bot ➻ From roBOT, a computer program that performs tasks automatically, usually on the World Wide Web, usually searching for data. See Spider, Chatterbot.

Box Office ➻ (1) Literally, the small booth at the entrance to a theater where tickets are sold. (2) Figuratively, the money collected from ticket sales. The box-office Gross is divided by formula between the exhibitor and distributor.

BPP ➻ Bits Per Pixel. A measure of the Color Depth of an image.

BPS ➻ Bits Per Second. A measure of digital transmission speed. See Modem.

Bravo ➤ CABLE NETWORK devoted to the arts, founded in 1980 by a consortium of cable systems.

Breakaway ➤ Any PROP constructed so that it can be broken without injuring an actor.

Breakdown ➤ The analysis of a script in order to schedule a shoot, including the number and type of actors to be hired.

Breen Office ➤ See PRODUCTION CODE.

Bridging ➤ The television programming technique of countering the popularity of a competing program by scheduling your program to start earlier and—it is hoped—hold its audience once the competition begins. See LEAD-IN, HAMMOCKING.

Bridging Shot ➤ A shot used to cover a jump in time or place or other discontinuity. Examples are falling calendar pages, railroad wheels, newspaper headlines, seasonal changes.

Broadband ➤ Used to refer to services that include voice, data, audio and video. See BANDWIDTH. Compare NARROWBAND, BASEBAND.

Broadcast ➤ Transmission over a wide area. See NARROWCAST, UNICAST, CABLE TELEVISION.

Broadway ➤ The LEGITIMATE THEATER industry in New York, especially those particular theaters in and around Times Square (Broadway and 45th Street) which are defined as the top rank in union contracts. Off-Broadway houses developed in the 1950s as a second rank, often but not always located in Greenwich Village. Off-Off Broadway developed in the 1960s as a third rank in union contracts. A theater does not need a Broadway address to be a "Broadway" theater; conversely, some theaters with Broadway addresses are "Off-Broadway" or even "Off-Off Broadway" theaters.

Brown Noise ➤ See NOISE.

Browser ➤ A Web Browser is software that understands both HTTP and HTML. The term is also used more generically for any application that allows you to view an organized list of files.

B-Sky-B ➤ The British DSB SATELLITE television system formed by the merger in 1990 of Rupert Murdoch's pioneering SKY TV and the competing British Satellite Broadcasting. Compare ASTRA, DIRECTV.

BTX ➤ See BILDSCHIRMTEXT.

Bubble Memory ➤ A magnetic memory storage technology that enjoyed a very brief vogue in the early 1980s. It was never widely disseminated and never competed successfully against traditional disk-based memory.

Buff ➤ A person with an unusual enthusiasm for a subject, especially regarding its details. (From the nickname of early New York volunteer firemen—hence enthusiasts—who wore buff-colored uniforms.)

Bug ➺ An error in a computer program, from the early days when, if something went wrong, it could very likely be traced to a dead insect somewhere in the innards of the computer.

Business ➺ Secondary action in a SCENE. The sort of movement extraneous to the central action that intends to breathe more life into the action. Captain Queeg's steel balls in *The Caine Mutiny* are one example of a famous "bit of business."

Byte ➺ A group of BITS, usually eight. In the binary-coded decimal system used by most microcomputers, a byte equals one character. A *Nibble* is—you guessed it—half a Byte (4 bits). See K, MEG.

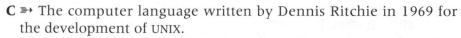

C ➺ The computer language written by Dennis Ritchie in 1969 for the development of UNIX.

CA ➺ Conditional Access. One of a variety of technologies to limit access to SATELLITE channels to those who have paid for the privilege.

CAA ➺ Creative Artists Agency. See AGENT.

Cable Channel, Cable Network ➺ As broadcasting developed, hundreds of local stations were united via coaxial cable to form networks supplied with programming from headquarters in New York and Los Angeles. As cable television developed, the existence of several thousand local system operators presented the same opportunity. When HBO went live on the SATELLITE in 1975, the CABLE NETWORK was born. But whereas the defined number of local television stations in each market limited the growth in the number of broadcast networks, the ever-growing number of cable channels has resulted in a continually expanding number of cable networks, most of which, unlike the broadcast networks, specialize in a particular kind of product. The main cable networks include: HBO, CINEMAX, SHOWTIME, TNT, AMC (all devoted to movies), CNN, HNN, MSNBC (news), ESPN (sports), CNBC (business), MTV, VH-1 (music videos), A&E, BRAVO (the arts), NICKELODEON (children), THE DISNEY CHANNEL, USA (general entertainment), C-SPAN (public affairs), and THE WEATHER CHANNEL (temperatures and precipitation). See also DSS, SUPERSTATION.

Cable Modem ➺ Strictly speaking, not a MODEM at all, but a SET-TOP BOX that performs the same function as a modem, allowing you to transmit and receive digital data over your television cable.

Cable Television ➺ Television transmission via wire rather than broadcast radio waves. Originally developed to permit reception in areas where normal broadcasting was impeded by geographical conditions, cable has developed into a competitor to the broadcast networks providing a great many more channels as well as special services. See PUBLIC ACCESS TELEVISION, CATV, COAXIAL CABLE.

Cablecast ⟫ To transmit solely via CABLE TELEVISION.

Cable-Ready ⟫ Television sets that include tuners equipped to receive the many additional channel frequencies used by cable television systems are said to be "cable-ready." A cable-ready set does not include DESCRAMBLING capability. See BLACK BOX.

CAD/CAM ⟫ Computer-Assisted Design and Computer-Assisted Manufacturing.

Caddy ⟫ The plastic cassette into which CD-ROMs may be loaded before they are inserted into some CD-ROM disk drives, necessary to provide enough stability for the drive to read the disk properly.

Cahiers du Cinéma ⟫ The seminal film journal founded by André Bazin, Jacques Doniol-Valcroze, and Lo Duca in 1951. Godard, Truffaut, Chabrol, Rohmer, Rivette, and others wrote for it. See NEW WAVE, AUTEUR POLICY.

Call Letters ⟫ The three-, four-, or five-letter codes assigned to radio and television stations. The first letter generally indicates the region of the world: the U.S. is divided into W for the East and K for the West (although one of the first radio broadcasters, Pittsburgh's KDKA, breaks the rules). During the last twenty years, traditional call letters have fallen into disuse, replaced by marketing slogans like "Hot 97 FM" that come and go with increasing regularity. For radio amateurs, however, Call letters have an historical resonance and mystique that they are not likely to lose anytime soon. See HAM RADIO.

Camcorder ⟫ Originally SONY'S trade name for its 8 mm VIDEOCASSETTE camera/recorder, the word has now become generic to refer to any video camera/recorder unit.

Cameo ⟫ A small yet significant part in a film, usually played by a well-known actor.

Camera Angle ⟫ The angle at which the camera is pointed at the subject: low, high, or eye-level. Not to be confused with ANGLE OF VIEW. Compare CANTED FRAMING.

Camera Lucida ⟫ A device that permits the projection of a natural scene on a piece of drawing paper where it can be traced. See also CAMERA OBSCURA.

Camera Obscura ⟫ One of the earliest antecedents of the photographic camera. Literally, a "dark room" or box with a pinhole in one side that acts as a lens to focus light rays on the opposite side. See also CAMERA LUCIDA.

Camera-Ready Copy ⟫ Pages laid-out and prepared for commercial printing with illustrations in place. In traditional printing, they are then photographed and the resulting negatives are used to make the printing plates. Compare DIRECT-TO-PLATE.

Caméra-Stylo ⇒ "Camera-pen." The phrase used by Alexandre Astruc to suggest that the art of film is equal in flexibility and range to older arts, such as the novel and the essay.

Canal + ⇒ (Pronounced "Canal-ploos.") Canal + got started in the 1980s as a purveyor of pay-per-view in France. In the early 1990s, the company moved into film production with mixed results. By the mid-1990s Canal + had become a major European broadcaster and one of the first to get involved in digital television. Canal + has their own proprietary conditional access system (SECA) and their own ENCRYPTION system (MEDIAGUARD). The company is now active in Spain, Italy, Belgium, and Poland, as well as France. SECA has been chosen as the CA system for BDB.

Canned Laughter ⇒ See LAUGHTRACK.

Cannon ⇒ See PLUGS.

Canted Framing ⇒ Slanting the orientation of the camera relative to the horizontal plane so that the scene itself appears slanted. Compare CAMERA ANGLE.

Cantilever ⇒ See TURNTABLE.

CAPTAIN ⇒ Character And Pattern Telephone Access Information Network. The Japanese VIDEOTEXT PROTOCOL of the 1980s. Compare TELETEL, NAPLPS.

Carrier Wave ⇒ See WAVE MECHANICS.

Cartridge ⇒ (1) A Phono Cartridge, part of a RECORD PLAYER. (2) A tape system in which the tape transport mechanism is enclosed and operates with a single reel. The tape feeds off the interior of the reel and is wound continuously back onto the exterior. Eight-track cartridges were popular in the 1970s. They have since been entirely replaced by the CASSETTE. (3) A package for ROM such as those used in some VIDEO GAME systems. The word "cartridge" is sometimes used interchangeably with "cassette."

Cash Barter ⇒ A variation of a BARTER deal in which the local station pays a fee for a show or shares production costs in addition to carrying the distributor's SPOTS.

Cassette ⇒ An enclosed prepackaged audiotape or videotape system using two reels. Compare CARTRIDGE.

Cassette Memory ⇒ A feature of DV tape formats. A chip that holds 4–16 kilobits is built into the cassette to record menu and navigation information. This makes the tape easier to access. Compare ADVANTIX.

Cassingle ⇒ A short audiocassette, usually with one song on each side. See SINGLE, ALBUM.

Cat 3, Cat 5 ⇒ Electronic cables are now ranked by CATegory. The higher the number the greater the protection against radiofrequency interference.

Cathode Ray Tube ⇒ A television picture tube, computer screen, or similar device. The face is coated with phosphors that are excited by an electron beam focused by an electromagnetic lens at the opposite end of the tube.

CATV ⇒ "Community Antenna Television." CABLE TELEVISION designed to improve reception in problem areas. Subscribers are connected by cable to a master antenna located high enough to receive a good signal from the broadcasters. Compare SMATV.

CAV ⇒ Constant Angular Velocity. One of the two basic systems used for LASERDISCS. A CAV disk rotates at a constant speed (1,800 RPM for NTSC, 1,500 rpm for PAL). A CLV disc rotates at varying speeds to maintain a "Constant Linear Velocity" for the laser pickup on the track. All CDs and CD-ROMs are CAV discs. CLV videodiscs allow twice as much playing time, but they sacrifice much of the user power that CAV discs provide. The rotational speed of a CLV videodisc varies from 1800 rpm on the inner edge to 600 rpm on the outer edge. (Unlike LPs, CDs play from the inside out.) It is one of the curiosities of the disc system of recording that when the disc revolves at a constant rate the tracks on the outer edge, which are much longer than the tracks on the inner edge, are severely limited to the data density capacity of the inner-edge tracks. CLV systems attempt to correct for this anomaly. No phonograph records operate at CLV, of course, but some computer MAGNETIC DISK systems do. The WOZ MACHINE, the disk drive Steven Wozniak invented for the Apple II, was perhaps the first disk device to avail itself of the greater economy of CLV.

CB ⇒ "Citizens Band" radio. The FCC sets aside certain frequencies in the radio band for use by persons with little or no formal training in broadcasting. CB transceivers permit both reception and transmission of signals in a limited area, usually one mile to ten miles. CB radio was all the rage in the late 1970s; the car phone, then the cell phone, seriously impacted the CB market in the eighties. Compare CELLULAR TELEPHONY.

C-Band ⇒ See SATELLITE BANDS.

CBC ⇒ Canadian Broadcasting Corporation. The state-supported primary television network in Canada.

C_bC_r ⇒ See COLOR-DIFFERENCE SAMPLING.

CBR ⇒ Constant Bit Rate. See VARIABLE BIT RATE.

CBS ⇒ Founded by broadcasting visionary William S. Paley in 1927 to compete with NBC, CBS was an also-ran throughout the 1930s until it discovered the appeal of newscasts at the beginning of World War II with Edward R. Murrow's broadcasts from London. As television broadcasting began in earnest after the war, CBS took an early ratings lead, mainly by appropriating NBC's radio comedy stars Jack Benny, Red Skelton, and Edgar Bergen. Known as the "Tiffany" of NETWORKS for many years, conservative CBS held first place in the ratings race continuously from the early fifties until ABC's ascendancy in 1976.

In the 1950s and 1960s, CBS also attempted to play in the hardware arena, enjoying one major success in competition with RCA: the 12-inch, 33 rpm LP record, which won pride of place over RCA's own 7-inch 45 rpm technology. CBS lost the battle for color television when its sequential system lost out to RCA's all-electronic technology in the 1950s. CBS's last excursion into consumer electronics was the ill-fated EVR system, well ahead of its time, and discontinued in 1972.

In the mid-1980s, after several takeover attempts had failed, Paley brought in Lawrence Tisch of Loew's Corporation as "White Knight." Tisch quickly wrested control from Paley (who died in 1990). After selling its magazine and publishing operations and its powerful music division in the late 1980s, CBS was reduced to running only the broadcast television network in a rapidly declining market. The network regained its leading ratings position in 1992 for a brief period, then declined again.

By 1993 CBS was on the block again. In 1995 Tisch finally unloaded the asset-stripped property to Westinghouse for $5.4 billion. (Ted Turner, who had lost out to Tisch a decade earlier, was prevented by the cable television interests on his board of directors from bidding against Westinghouse.) The deal garncred little enthusiasm among industry analysts, overshadowed as it was by the sale of ABC to DISNEY just weeks earlier for more than three times the price.

CC ➻ The abbreviation in television program listings for those programs which are broadcast with CLOSED CAPTIONS.

CCD ➻ The Charge-Coupled Device converts light into an electrical signal in a video camera. It has replaced the image orthicon tube for that purpose because of its greater sensitivity, lower cost, and better quality. See CMOS.

CCIR ➻ Comité Consultative Internationale de Radiocommunications. The International body devoted to developing radio standards. Subsumed under its parent, the ITU.

CCIR 601 ⇛ The main standard for digital video. Since the CCIR has changed its name to the ITU-R, the more proper designation might be ITU-R BT601. CCIR 601 calls for 8-bit sampling at 13.5 mHz.

CCITT ⇛ Consultative Committee for International Telegraphy and Telephony, sets standards for international communication. A subdivision of the ITU.

CD ⇛ The "compact disc" that uses a LASER device to read a DIGITAL signal that encodes sound information. During the 1980s the CD replaced the thirty-year-old vinyl LP record as the main medium of the music business. CDs are recorded on 120 mm polycarbonate plastic disks coated with a thin layer of evaporated aluminum which reflects the laser. Like their LP predecessors and unlike their AUDIOCASSETTE competitors, CDs can be mass produced quickly and cheaply. The digital technology results in a disc that can contain as much as 74.7 minutes of high-fidelity stereophonic sound, virtually noise-free, with a wide frequency response and a wide dynamic range, although AUDIOPHILES still argue the relative merits of the ANALOG vinyl record versus the digital CD, many claiming that the digitally reproduced sound is cold and lifeless because of the SAMPLING technique which is used to translate naturally analog sounds. SONY and PHILIPS collaborated on the CD technology, the latter firm providing much of the research. The CD was introduced to the market in late 1982 in Japan and in mid-1983 in the U.S. See LASERDISC, CD-ROM, DVD.

CD Codes ⇛ Audio CDs are tagged with a three-letter code which indicates how they are recorded and manufactured: DDD means digitally recorded, mixed and mastered, and manufactured. ADD means recorded in analog, digitally mixed and mastered, and manufactured. AAD means recorded, mixed and mastered in analog, digitally manufactured.

CD DA ⇛ The basic CD standard for digital Audio licensed by SONY and PHILIPS. (The Red Book.) See CD STANDARDS.

CD-I ⇛ Compact Disc-Interactive. PHILIPS's technology for MULTIMEDIA CD-ROMs (supported by SONY and MATSUSHITA) introduced commercially in late 1991. Approaching the technology from the point of view of the consumer electronics rather than the computer industry, CD-I was an attachment to the standard television set, operated by a remote control joystick and lacking a keyboard. It was obsolete almost before it was introduced, but Philips stuck stubbornly with the format for years. Compare CDTV, DVI.

CD+ ⇛ See ENHANCED CD.

CD+G ⇛ The CD audiodisc standard originally set by PHILIPS contained provisions for a number of low data-rate subcode channels in addition to the audio channels. Two of these channels are used for error correction, but the others are free. The vast majority of CDs on the market ignore them, as do the vast majority of players. However, after 1986, a handful of discs and one or two players (mostly KARAOKE) used these channels to provide decorative graphics (the "G" in CD+G). When such a player was connected to a television monitor, a CD+G disc provided song lyrics, or very low-resolution pictures. The concept fizzled quickly. Both CD+G and CDV were replaced by ENHANCED CD.

CD R ⇒ A recordable CD. The common term for CD WO.

CD RW ⇒ A recordable CD that can also be erased so that it can be ReWritten.

CD Single ⇒ A small audio CD.

CD Standards ⇒ The *Red Book* describes the standard for CD DA, the digital audio disc developed by SONY and PHILIPS and now the universal standard for music distribution. (It also included specifications for CD+G.) The *Yellow Book* describes the standard for CD-ROM, the adaptation of the technology which allows the storage of computer data. The *Green Book* lists the parameters for CD-I, the first interactive multimedia application of the technology. The *Orange Book* extends the standard to for writable discs. The *Blue Book* is an apocryphal definition of LASERDISC and CD VIDEO standards. The HIGH SIERRA (or ISO 9660) standard, named for the resort at which it was first discussed, describes a lowest-common-denominator directory structure that can be interpreted by virtually every computer system (a major achievement in the computer world, and still unmatched as a true standard). The CD-ROM XA (eXtended Architecture) standard borrows from the Green Book to add audio compression techniques to the CD-ROM format providing a more flexible platform for multimedia. The *White Book* describes the standard for Video CD. More recently, the Scarlet Book is the Sony/Philips specification for SACD based on DSD. See also CDTV (proprietary), DVI (proprietary), JPEG, MPEG, ENHANCED CD.

CD WO ⇒ A "write once" CD, defined in the Orange Book. Using a suitable CD-ROM drive, you can add data to the disc but cannot erase or replace data already written. The specification was incompatible with standard CD-ROM players. As a result, CD WO has largely been replaced by CD-R, which is compatible. See MO, PHOTO CD.

CDMA ⇒ Code Division Multiple Access. An important MULTIPLEXING technology for CELLULAR TELEPHONY and PCS, CDMA increases capacity by imposing signals on noiselike carrier waves using SPREAD SPECTRUM technology. By using the entire available spectrum it greatly increases the number of calls that can be handled. It is more efficient than Frequency Division Multiplexing (*FDM*) or Time Division Multiplexing (*TDM*), which multiply the signals carried by crowding the frequencies or compressing the time. CDMA is a Direct Sequence (*DS*) application of Spread Spectrum rather than a Frequency Hopping (*FH*) application. Rather than shifting frequencies according to an agreed pattern CDMA assigns a coding—known as Pseudonoise (*PN*) to each signal. If multiplexing generally is hard to visualize, CDMA is impossible. Think of a cocktail party with many conversations going on at once. Then assign a digital signature to each. Now you have a way to pick out the conversation you want to hear. CDMA succeeds because it applies the brute processing power of microchips to old-fashioned waveform communications.

CDPD ⇥ Cellular Digital Packet Data, a WIRELESS technology for the transmission of data, under development since 1994.

CD-ROM ⇥ Championed by MICROSOFT as early as 1986, the CD-ROM borrowed from audio CD technology to create a medium for data storage. ("ROM" is an acronym for "Read Only Memory," a storage medium that a computer reads but does not write to.) The standard 120 mm CD-ROM holds more than 650 megabytes of data, which is about 400 times the capacity of the standard 3 1/2-inch magnetic DISKETTE. As the microcomputer industry rapidly developed techniques for the digitization of still images and then moving pictures in the late 1980s and early 1990s, the huge data capacity of the CD-ROM suggested that it was an ideal medium for the storage of images and sounds—as well as data. The result: MULTIMEDIA. But good digital video proved to be beyond the capabilities of the CD-ROM specification. That had to wait until DVD. Compare LASERDISC, DVD-ROM.

CD-ROM XA ⇥ CD-ROM eXtended Architecture. Introduced in 1989 to allow the mixture of data, graphics, and audio, CD-ROM XA did CD-I better. Although nearly all CD-ROM players supported the architecture within a few years, the interleaving features are seldom used.

CDS ⇥ Cinema Digital Sound. Movie sound reproduction system developed by Kodak and Optical Radiation Corp. and introduced in 1990. (*Dick Tracy* was the first feature released in CDS.) The system was slow to take off, since theater chains resisted installing the necessary hardware due to the recession of the early 1990s. CDS uses a six-track system (like the analog six-track systems common since the 1960s). As in the world of consumer electronics, digitization reduces background noise levels. Compare DOLBY, THX SOUND SYSTEM.

CDTV ➼ Commodore's technology for Multimedia CD-ROMs (before they went out of business). Compare CD-I.

CDV ➼ CD Video. A 120 mm Laserdisc including up to twenty minutes of CD audio as well as five or six minutes of analog video, it was used to distribute Music Videos; introduced concurrently with Philips's combination CD/Laserdisc player in 1989. CDV is not at all the same thing as VCD! Compare CD+G, Enhanced CD.

CED ➼ Capacitance Electronic Disc. The Videodisc technology developed by RCA for its Selectavision product, discontinued in 1984. On a CED disc, a physical stylus rode in a physical groove, much like on a phonograph record, but read electronic capacitance information encoded on the disc rather than the physical waveforms of the groove. Compare VHD, Laserdisc.

CEEFAX ➼ The BBC's Teletext system. See also Oracle.

Celebrity ➼ In Daniel Boorstin's famous phrase, a celebrity is "known for being well known." The rise of the phenomenon is intimately connected with the rise of film and the other Mass Media. See Star.

Cell ➼ (1) Each of the thousands of individual drawings used in Animation. To cut the work involved, combinations of cells may be used: one for the background, which doesn't change from frame to frame; one for the middle ground, which changes only a little; and one or more for the foreground, where most of the action takes place. Also "cel." The concept of Cell animation is now familiar outside the industry as it has transmuted into the layers of graphics program like Photoshop and Illustrator. (2) One of numerous limited broadcast areas that, taken together, make Cellular Telephony possible.

Cellular Telephony ➼ Broadcast radiotelephony existed for a long time before the advent of the cellular technique made it a commercially viable medium in the early eighties. When the telephone broadcast needed to cover an entire city, the Bandwidth was, of course, severely limited: if there were one hundred available channels in the city, only one hundred customers could make a call at any one time. Dividing the city into numerous small "cells" (which is what cellular telephony does) multiplies the number of frequencies by the number of cells. The technique depends on computer software to hand off conversations from one cell to another as the user moves about. See PCS, CDMA.

Censorship ➼ Film and electronic media are normally exposed to a greater degree of censorship than is print. "Prior censorship," which forbids even the release of the film, is more damaging than the kind of censorship that challenges the exhibitor's right to continue showing the film after it has had a formal release. See RATINGS.

Central Office ➻ See LOCAL LOOP.

Centronics ➻ See PLUGS.

CG ➻ (1) Contemporary Hollywood slang for Computer Graphics. See POST HOUSE. (2) See CHARACTER GENERATOR.

CGI ➻ Computer Generated Imaging. See CG.

CGMS ➻ Copy Generation Management System. A technology to either prevent any copies of a DVD-VIDEO from being made, or to prevent copies being made from copies (hence "Generation"). The choices are "Copy Once" or "Copy Never." See CSS, MACROVISION.

Champagne Shot ➻ The last shot of the day. Compare ABBY SINGER.

Changeover Cue ➻ Small dot or other mark in the top right-hand corner of the film frame, in series, that signals the projectionist to switch from one projector to another. Now that most films are mounted on platters that can hold the whole show, Changeover Cues are archaic. If you are watching a tape or disc their presence or absence can be a clue as to whether the production is LETTERBOXED or PAN AND SCAN.

Channel ➻ A fixed band of frequencies set aside for television or radio transmission.

Channel 3 ➻ The name adopted for the British ITV service in 1991 when ITV franchises were redistributed.

Channel 4 ➻ The fourth British television network (after BBC-1, BBC-2, and ITV), founded November 2, 1982, and dedicated to alternative programming. Channel 4 has been an important force in British filmmaking since its founding, providing the financing for numerous films that are released in theaters before airing on the network.

Channel 5 ➻ The fifth British broadcast television network, introduced in 1997.

Channel-Surfing ➻ Slang term that became popular in the 1980s to describe the practice of rapidly switching through dozens of CABLE channels using the REMOTE. It is the main exercise of COUCH POTATOES.

Chapters ➻ DVD-VIDEOS and LASERDISCS can be divided into Chapters, sections that can be addressed via remote control buttons or menus. See PGC.

Character Actor ➻ Any actor who doesn't play lead roles. An actor whose work is generally well regarded but who doesn't have STAR quality. Generally synonymous with supporting actor, but also carries the connotation of craftsmanship: a "character" actor is capable of playing different characters, while a star often just plays another variant of his basic PERSONA.

Character Generator ⇒ A kind of word processor used in video and television to produce credits and subtitles. The CHYRON is a popular brand name. See PAINT BOX.

Characteristic Curve ⇒ The contrast relationship between the input for an image and the output over a range of light values. See GAMMA.

Charge-Coupled Device ⇒ See CCD.

Chatterbot ⇒ A BOT designed to chat automatically, usually with a human. See ELIZA.

Cheat ⇒ To rearrange people or objects in a scene to improve composition. See CONTINUITY.

Checkerboarding ⇒ Television program schedule in which five different programs, usually related by genre, are scheduled during the same weekday time slot. See STRIP.

Cherry-Picking ⇒ Selecting television programming or data from a SATELLITE.

Chiaroscuro ⇒ (Pronounced "kyahro-skooro.") The technique of using light and shade in pictorial representation, or the arrangement of light and dark elements. The two Italian words for "clear" and "dark."

Chip ⇒ Slang for MICROPROCESSOR.

Chopsocky ⇒ *Variety*'s term for martial arts or kung fu EXPLOITATION FILMS.

Chroma, Chrominance ⇒ In order to produce a signal that is compatible for both black-and-white and color television reception, the information of the color signal must be separated in such a way that the color information (hue, saturation) is included in the chrominance part of the signal, while the black-and-white information (intensity) is included in the luminance part of the signal. See COLOR, COLOR MODELS.

Chroma Key ⇒ An electronic television technique like BLUE SCREEN TRAVELLING MATTE that allows the melding of separate images.

Chronophotographic Gun ⇒ The rifle-like camera developed by Étienne-Jules Marey in 1882 that took twelve photographs per second which were printed on a rotating glass plate. The following year, Marey switched to roll paper film. An important advance over Muybridge's system for studying movement on film, which employed multiple cameras to take the necessary series of photographs. See CINÉMATOGRAPHE.

Churn ⇒ In CABLE television and similar businesses, the rate of turnover of subscribers.

Chyron ⇒ A proprietary electronic system for generating CRAWLS and other television graphics. See PAINT BOX.

Cinéaste ⇒ (1) A filmmaker. (2) More generally, anyone associated in a professional capacity with film.

Cinecittà ⇒ (Pronounced "Cheenay-cheetah.") Rome's answer to the Hollywood studio that reached its zenith in the sixties as the home for Fellini and others. Cinecittà was closed in 1993. Compare BABELSBERG.

Cinéma du Papa ⇒ François Truffaut's phrase for the type of established cinema against which the NEW WAVE reacted in the 1950s.

Cinema Nôvo ⇒ The Brazilian movement for a new cinema in the 1960s whose major figures included Glauber Rocha, Nelson Pereira dos Santos, Carlos Dieguès, and Tonino Guerra. Compare NEW WAVE, NEUE KINO.

Cinema Studies ⇒ An academic discipline—devoted to film and video history, theory, and criticism—created in the late 1960s and early 1970s. As the study of film became popular on American campuses, teachers of film—often attached to English, language, or art departments—realized an opportunity to form new academic baronies, replete with all the bureaucratic appurtenances of American university departments. Throughout the seventies, cinema studies departments were one of the prime growth areas in the academic business, along with ethnic studies. What had for a few years been an exciting, interdisciplinary, renegade academic pursuit became by 1980 regularized, codified, and infected with the same academic malaise that still pervades most of American higher education. (But by then, the movies were codified, too.) See EVERSON/MICHELSON DICHOTOMY.

Cinéma Vérité ⇒ A word now often used loosely to refer to any kind of documentary technique, it originally signified a type of 1960s cinema that utilized lightweight equipment, two-person crews (camera and sound), and interview techniques. Jean Rouch was an important figure. See DIRECT CINEMA, DOCUMENTARY.

CinemaScope ⇒ Twentieth Century Fox's trade name for its ANAMORPHIC process; by extension, used to refer to anamorphic processes in general. The ASPECT RATIO was 2.35:1. Compare PANAVISION, VISTAVISION.

Cinemate ⇒ A neologism based on the model of "literate." Compare NUMERACY.

Cinematheque ⇒ A film museum and library. The world-class institutions include the CINÉMATHÈQUE FRANÇAISE in Paris, the Museum of Modern Art Film Library in New York, the BFI in London, and the Library of Congress in Washington.

Cinémathèque Française ⇒ The world's largest film library and museum. Located in Paris, founded privately by Henri Langlois and Georges Franju in 1936, it has a collection of more than 60,000 films. The availability of many of its old films is credited with having an important effect on the development of French film in the 1950s and 1960s. After the "Events of May 1968" the Cinémathèque was funded by the CNC.

Cinématographe ➤ The Lumière Brothers' early camera/projector. See also KINETOGRAPH, BIOSKOP.

Cinematographer ➤ Also known as "director of photography," "DP," or, in the U.K., "lighting director" or "lighting cameraman." Responsible for the camera and lighting and, therefore, the quality of the image.

Cinematography ➤ Motion picture PHOTOGRAPHY.

Cinematology ➤ The study of film itself, as opposed to FILMOLOGY, which is the study of the economic, political, social, and technological causes and effects of film.

Cinemax ➤ HBO's companion CABLE NETWORK, offering a different set of movies.

Cineon ➤ Trade name for Kodak's high-end film digitization process, dating from 1992. A collection of hardware and software products that attempts to set the absolute standard for digital video, scanning up to 4,000 lines per 35 mm frame using 10-bit logarithmic color encoding. The Cineon Lightning laser film recorder can then image an equally high resolution image on filmstock. (In case you were wondering: yes, 4,000 lines is enough to capture all the detail of standard 35 mm color filmstock.)

Cinepak Codec ➤ A high-compression video CODEC that was important during the early 1990s for CD-ROM production.

Cinephile ➤ A lover of cinema.

Cinerama ➤ A WIDESCREEN process invented by Fred Waller that used three cameras synchronized electrically. The first Cinerama film was *This Is Cinerama* (1952). In 1962, after *How the West Was Won*, the three-camera/projector curved-screen system was abandoned in favor of a wide film ANAMORPHIC process marketed under the same name.

Cine-Structuralism ➤ The application of SEMIOTICS to cinema in an essentially sociological or ethnographic way. The British journal *Screen* was the most important journal during the 1970s.

CISC ➤ Complex Instruction Set Chip. See RISC, CPU.

Clap Slate, Clapper Board ➤ A chalkboard photographed at the beginning of a shot, upon which are written the pertinent data for the shot. A clapstick on top of the board is snapped shut and the resultant sound and image are used later to synchronize picture and sound. Nowadays an electronic slate is preferred.

Claque ➤ A group of people hired to applaud and cheer an actor or singer, common in nineteenth-century opera. From the French "claquer," to clap. See Fanning.

Classic ➤ Perhaps the most overused adjective in film criticism. In the 1980s, Art Films, foreign films, and releases for which distributors saw limited prospects became known as "Classics."

Clear, Cleared, Clearance ➤ When a distributor signs a contract to air a program on a local station, the show is said to be "cleared" in that market. Affiliates' acceptance of network or syndicated programming, as in "Our show has been cleared in 67 markets."

CLI ➤ Command Line Interface; CUI, or character-based user interface. Compare GUI.

Clik! ➤ See Digital Film.

Clipping ➤ When an audio system is driven beyond its capacity, the tops and bottoms of the waves are truncated, producing distortion.

Closed Circuit ➤ A television or radio system in which the program is not broadcast but rather distributed by cable to a limited number of receivers.

Closed-Caption ➤ A section of the television Vertical Blanking Interval (line 21) is used to transmit caption translations of dialogue for use by hearing-impaired viewers. A closed-caption decoder is required to receive and display the captions. These decoders are required on all U.S. television sets over a certain size. See also Teletext.

Closed-End Series ➤ A Series of program episodes of limited number, usually involving a more complex plot and more character development than does an Open-End Series.

Closeup ➤ (1) Precisely, a shot of the subject's face only. (2) Generally, any close shot.

CLT-UFA ➤ See Bertelsmann.

CLUT ➤ Color LookUp Table; the palette. See Color Mapping.

CLV ➤ Constant Linear Velocity. See CAV.

CMOS ➤ (Pronounced "sea-moss.") Complementary Metal Oxide Semiconductor. Long used in laptop computers because of their low power requirements, CMOS chips found a profitable new application in cheap digital video devices after engineers figured out how to amplify the light source. CMOS chips began replacing CCDs in inexpensive cameras in 1998.

CMX ➤ An industry standard for interfacing editing systems to VCRs before online editing became common. The EDL controlled the operation of the tape drives.

CMYK ➤ One of several systems for quantifying color values in print and electronic media. The letters stand for Cyan, Magenta, Yellow (the subtractive primaries), and blacK. See COLOR PRINTING, COLOR MODELS.

CNBC ➛ NBC's business news CABLE NETWORK, founded April 17, 1989, as a competitor to FNN, later absorbed that network in 1991 when FNN fell on hard financial times.

CNC ➛ Centre Nationale de la Cinématographie. The French national film archive.

CNN ➛ Cable News Network. Founded in 1980 by Ted Turner, CNN, featuring 24-hour nonstop news, quickly became a standard offering of cable network operators and together with HBO molded the cable world of the 1980s and 1990s. In 1982, when the broadcast networks threatened to compete, Turner added HNN, the "Headline News Network" clone. In the late 1980s Turner took CNN international, offering the service on hotel networks in Europe and elsewhere. CNN thus became the first international television network. By the time of the Gulf War in 1991, CNN could claim superiority to broadcast network news operations.

Coax ➛ Short for COAXIAL CABLE.

Coaxial Cable ➛ The line, composed of a thin copper or aluminum wire, surrounded by insulation, and encased in an outer conducting shell, by which television signals are carried between NETWORK centers and affiliated stations, between HEAD-ENDS and subscribers in CABLE TELEVISION systems, and within the home. The advantage of a coaxial cable is that this arrangement of the conductors is relatively impervious to outside electromagnetic interference. A *Twinax* cable has three lincs—two wires inside and the shell. When buying Coax, you want RG-6 (higher quality), not RG-59. See FIBER OPTIC, BALUN, TWISTED PAIR.

Coaxial Digital Output ➛ Found on some LASERDISC players, this is different from the COAXIAL CABLE used for television signals. It's a digital audio output with an RCA jack.

COBOL ➛ See COMPUTER LANGUAGES.

Codec ➛ From COder–DECoder (or COmpressor–DECompressor), on the model of MODEM. A software algorithm that compresses digital audio or video data for recording, then decompresses it for playback. The invention of efficient Codecs such as MPEG-2 was necessary for the development of DV (digital video). See also COMPRESSION, DVD.

Codes, Subcodes ➛ In SEMIOTICS, the rules and sets of identifiable elements, an understanding of which allows us to interpret a film. Codes are analytic tools constructed after the fact.

Cold Type ➛ Jargon for type set by photographic means. See PHOTOTYPOGRAPHY, HOT TYPE.

Color ➻ Visible light is comprised of one section of the ELECTROMAG-
NETIC SPECTRUM. Perceived color is a function of the wavelength or frequency of the light. Beginning with the longest wavelengths and
progressing toward the shortest, the visible spectrum includes the
colors red, orange, yellow, green, blue, indigo, and violet. These are
the basic hues, known to all students of physics and art by the
mnemonic moniker Roy G. Biv. Two other measurable factors in
the perception of color are intensity and saturation. The intensity of
a color is a measure of its brightness (if it is a light source) or lightness (if it is a reflecting object). The saturation of a color is a measure of the vividness of its hue, or the degree of difference between
the color and a gray of the same lightness or brightness.

　　Color photography, cinematography, printing, and video are
made possible by the fact that combinations of colors can produce
other colors. The "primary" colors of a light source are red, green,
and blue. The "primaries" for a reflecting object, such as pigment,
are red, yellow, and blue. There is a further complication because
color technology utilizes two complementary methods of mixing:
additive and subtractive. For light sources, the additive primaries
are red, green, and blue, while the subtractive primaries are
magenta (a combination of red and blue), cyan (a combination of
green and blue), and yellow. See also COLOR MODELS, TECHNICOLOR, EAST-
MANCOLOR, SOLARIZATION.

Color Depth ➻ The digital precision of a color or GRAYSCALE image. A
data file that represents a black-and-white, or monochrome, image
requires only one bit per pixel: the pixel is either on or it is off; the
color is either black or it is white. Color (and grayscale) images
require more than one bit per pixel to represent the other color values the pixel may have. Four-bit color allows a palette of 16 colors
(2^4), which is not sufficient for photographic images. Eight-bit color
yields a palette of 256 colors (2^8), generally regarded as the bare
minimum for photographic images. Twenty-four-bit color accommodates 16,777,216 different color values, a number most experts
regard as beyond the ability of the human eye to differentiate.

Color-Difference Sampling ➻ In digital color-difference terminology, Y is the luminance and C_b and C_r stand for the two CHROMI-
NANCE signals where the luminance has been subtracted from the
blue and red signals, respectively (B–Y, R–Y). For psychological reasons, the chrominance signals are less important that the luminance component. Imagine watching a video image that had only
color, no difference in intensity: it would look abstract and be difficult to understand. However, an image with only intensity (luminance) is easy to understand: that's just a black-and-white image.

As a result, most coding systems collect less data on the chrominance information than on luminance. The shorthand for these ratios goes like this: 4:4:4 samples all three signals equally. It is used only in the highest quality studio work. 4:2:2 is more common for professional work. DVD-VIDEO outputs 4:2:0. See COLOR, COLOR MODELS.

Color Layering ⟫ See PHOTORET.

Color Mapping ⟫ Representing a sufficient range of color values in a DIGITIZED image to reproduce a sufficiently realistic image requires very large data files. Much of the intellectual effort in the development of digitization has therefore involved schemes to compress the data so that it can be stored, transmitted, and displayed with reasonably priced hardware. One of the more ingenious methods of COMPRESSION is Color Mapping. A palette of 32,000 colors is generally regarded as the minimum necessary for realistic digital color representation. However, for any individual image far fewer colors may be necessary. For many images, as few as 256 colors will suffice. The Color Mapping technique identifies that limited set of colors necessary for a particular image, extracts the set from the complete palette, and stores it in a Color Lookup Table (or CLUT), to which the software can refer when reproducing the image. Of course, if you change from one style of image to another, you have to change the CLUT, which takes time and can cause noticeable GLITCHES. As 24-bit color monitors become the norm and DVD begins to provide the necessary storage capacity, color mapping is less necessary—although it still is common on the WORLD WIDE WEB.

Color Models, Color Systems ⟫ In print and electronic media, several models have been developed to quantify color values so that a reasonable spectrum can be produced on the page or on the screen. The RGB model analyzes an image according to the three additive primary colors, Red, Green, and Blue. It is used in computer monitors. CMYK is the model printers use: values are established for the subtractive primaries—Cyan, Magenta, Yellow—and blacK. Computer software generally analyzes a color according to its Hue, Saturation, and Brightness (or Luminance)—the HSB or HSL system. In television, luminance and chrominance are the parameters, with the chrominance expressed as differences between and among the primaries. This system is known as YUV, where Y stands for luminance or brightness, and U and V for chrominance. (Variants: YIQ or YC_BC_R.) A fourth model, sometimes called Black Body, simply measures the COLOR TEMPERATURE in degrees Kelvin.

Color Printing ⟫ An extension of HALFTONE technology in which three or four colors are printed by three or four separate printing plates. The dot patterns of the colors create the illusion of other colors. This is usually referred to as *Process Color*. The colors used in traditional four-color printing are Cyan, Magenta, Yellow, and Black (CMYK). See COLOR MODELS, SPOT COLOR.

Color Rendering Index ➻ See CRI.

Color Temperature ➻ A measure of the dominant spectrum of light produced by a light source. Lower color temperature light sources tend to the red end of the spectrum, while high color temperatures tend to the blue/violet end. Sunlight (ideal white light) has a color temperature of 6,000° Kelvin, for example, while incandescent house lamps have a more orange color temperature of about 3,200° Kelvin. The human nervous system makes many automatic adjustments for variances in the spectrum of the light the eye perceives: FILMSTOCKS do not, so the cinematographer must make adjustments to correct for this limited response. You can better understand the concept of color temperature when you consider the change in color of a piece of iron (or a star) as it is heated; the color changes from black to red to orange to yellow to white. See BLACK BODY.

Colorist ➻ The technician in charge of TIMING a print, either optically or digitally. See TELECINE.

Colorize ➻ To add artificial color to a black-and-white film. An analog colorization system was introduced by Color System Technologies in 1985. The process was commercialized by American Film Technologies, which became a division of Turner Entertainment, who introduced their digital system in 1987. The color was added, not chemically to a film print of the movie, but electronically to a videotape for distribution via broadcast or VIDEOCASSETTE. Shortly after the technology was commercialized, a number of CINEASTES led by Martin Scorsese banded together to protest colorization as contrary to the artistic intent of the original filmmakers.

Eventually this movement led to the Nation Film Preservation Act. No doubt, most colorization destroys the original intent of the filmmakers; on the other hand, few if any contemporary filmgoers know what original black-and-white prints looked like, since television prints have always been adjusted for GAMMA, or contrast, which just as seriously distorts original artistic intent. Moreover, colorization is the only hope, however slim, for restoring something approaching original color values to old EASTMANCOLOR films which—unlike the TECHNICOLOR prints of the 1940s and 1950s—deteriorate rapidly in a relatively short time.

ColorSync ➻ Apple's proprietary software for calibrating color output on computer monitors and output devices such as printers. This is one of the more difficult problems confronting graphics professionals; ColorSync has become a standard. Microsoft adopted it for Windows 2000.

Columbia ➺ Incorporated in 1924 as the successor to a sales company formed by Harry and Jack Cohn and Joe Brandt in 1920, Columbia reached prominence in the 1930s under the leadership of Harry Cohn, and with the help of Frank Capra. Since Columbia owned no theaters, it was helped rather than hurt by the Paramount decision of 1949 that required other studios to divest their theater holdings. In the early 1950s the studio took the lead in meeting the challenge of television. Screen Gems, Columbia's television production subsidiary, quickly became a leading supplier to the new medium, and the company continued to rise in prominence. Alan Hirshfield and David Begelman managed the studio successfully in the mid-1970s before Begelman was forced to resign in 1978, accused of embezzlement. Frank Price took over as head of production, and was responsible for a number of successes in the early 1980s before he was replaced by David Puttnam, who himself was quickly replaced by Dawn Steel.

Coca-Cola bought the studio in 1982 for $750 million and sold it seven years later to Sony for $3.4 billion. Sony purchased the management team of Peter Guber and Jon Peters from Warner at a high price to run their new acquisition, and took over the prestigious MGM lot to serve as headquarters for the new Sony Pictures Entertainment division. By 1995 the studio was in serious financial trouble, Guber and Peters were gone, and sister studio TriStar had been merged into Columbia in a much-belated effort to control costs. Sony stuck with it (while rival Matsushita did not) and the studio managed to survive.

COM ➺ (1) Computer Output Microform; microfilm and microfiche output directly from computer files. (2) Abbreviation for "communications."

Comb Filter ➺ Like the *Notch Filter* that preceded it, the Comb Filter is the decoder in a television set that converts the incoming signal into RGB signals to drive the Cathode Ray Tube. The Comb Filter provides much higher Video Resolution and better color and is found in high-end systems.

Commentative Sound ➺ Sound whose source is outside the reality of the scene being shot. The opposite of Actual Sound. Compare Asynchronous Sound, Contrapuntal Sound.

Common Carrier ➺ Certain media are defined by law as common carriers: the telephone system and some satellite systems, for example. Common carriers must offer their facilities on an equal basis to all customers who wish to avail themselves of them.

Compact Videodisc ⇒ See CVD.

CompactFlash ⇒ See DIGITAL FILM.

Companding ⇒ A technique of DIGITIZATION. In companding, an analog signal that has been SAMPLED and QUANTIZED is represented by a series of noninteger numbers, rather than integers. The aim is to reduce the noise level.

Compilation Film ⇒ A film composed of SHOTS, SCENES, or SEQUENCES from other films, generally to illustrate features of the genre, stars, filmmakers, or period from which the FOOTAGE comes. See FOUND FOOTAGE.

Compiler ⇒ See COMPUTER LANGUAGES.

Completion Guarantor ⇒ An insurer unique to the film industry who guarantees the completion of a film project. If the director and producer run much over budget, the Completion Guarantor may take over control of the project. Hiring a Completion Guarantor is now as important to securing financing as getting a BANKABLE star. (Imagine if you could hire Completion Guarantors in your line of work!)

Component System ⇒ An audio or video system for the home composed of separate electronic devices—amplifier, CD deck, speakers, for example—usually individually selected by the user.

Component Video ⇒ A video system that separates Red, Green, and Blue (RGB) component signals from each other as well as separating CHROMINANCE from luminance in order to produce a sharper and more accurate image. *Composite Video* combines all color and brightness information into one signal. The American/Japanese NTSC television standard uses a composite signal; nearly all computer monitors use a component signal, which is one of two main reasons that computer monitors produce much higher quality images than their television counterparts even though the physical CRTs may be the same. (The other is PROGRESSIVE SCANNING.) See also NONINTERLACED MONITOR. Compare COLOR PRINTING.

Composite Video ⇒ See COMPONENT VIDEO.

Compositing ⇒ In digital video production work, the job of stitching together the various layers created in the editing process. Now image editors have some of the same MIXING capabilities as sound editors.

Compression ⇒ With the growing interest in DIGITAL technology in the early 1990s, techniques for compressing audio, video, and data signals became increasingly important. The huge quantities of data that digital systems require make the economies offered by various mathematical compression schemes vital to commercial success. The developing standard for still photographs is known as JPEG

(Joint Photographic Experts Group), while the developing standard for motion pictures is known as MPEG (Motion Picture Experts Group), although many other systems are in contention. CD-ROMs use a variant of PCM. *Nonlossy* (or *Lossless*) compression ALGORITHMS ensure that the numbers remaining after decompression are precisely the same as the ones compressed. *Lossy* algorithms trade some precision for greater compression.

The decision about which numbers to lose is a matter of psychology as well as mathematics. If we can only perceive differences among 16.8 million colors, why care about the values in between? But who's to say 16.8 million is enough? The question then becomes philosophical. No one likes to "lose" information, but it must be remembered that analog systems are also inherently "lossy." All photographs have grain; reality has none. No audio system is perfect; real sound is perfect, by definition. Lossy compression is just another step along the media path from reality to abstraction upon which we embarked in the 1830s.

Symmetrical compression requires equal effort for both compression and decompression, while asymmetrical compression calls for more processing power (and time) during compression, less during decompression. Movies are compressed in two dimensions: SPATIAL COMPRESSION reduces the size of each frame, just like still-image compression. TEMPORAL COMPRESSION reduces the size of the entire file by registering only the changes between frames. See also COLOR MAPPING, BITS PER PIXEL.

Compressionist ➻ On the model of Impressionist and Expressionist, the Compressionist is the technician who decides which COMPRESSION algorithms and bit rates are best for each sequence or shot of a film when it is digitized (usually for distribution on DVD-VIDEO). A talented Compressionist can make a big difference in the perceived quality of the final digital product.

Compuserve ➻ In the 1970s Compuserve was a classic TIME-SHARING vendor. Companies bought time on Compuserve's machines, dialing in via modem to the company's massive network. Once connected, they used Compuserve's machines as if they were their own. Of course, most of this activity took place during business hours; the machines were lightly used at night. In 1979 someone at Compuserve had the bright idea to sell some of this wasted capacity to the burgeoning new microcomputer market. Compuserve Information Services was born. CIS quickly became a favorite hangout for hackers and power users. It had one great advantage over the many BBSes that were then springing up: it's size. Because Compuserve sold time all over the world, the new service also had reach. If you had a Compuserve address (they were just DEC user account numbers like 71726,211) other Compuserve members could send you email. There were no inter-network mail protocols at the time so the largest network tended to dominate. Soon there were competitors. (The SOURCE was founded in 1981 with the intention of being a more consumer-oriented, less technical service.) But Compuserve transcended them all because of its size. Through canny marketing AOL eventually beat Compuserve at its own game, but it took years to do so. In 1997 the company was broken up, with the physical network going to MCI and the online service to AOL.

Computer Film ➤ Beginning in the 1950s, a film in which a computer controlled the visual information, usually via a CATHODE RAY TUBE display, and sometimes the sound. In modern filmmaking, computer techniques are so well integrated that the term no longer has much meaning. The algorithms of many 1960s computer films survive in today's screensavers. See ABSOLUTE FILM.

Computer Freak ➤ A person who makes a hobby of manipulating and studying the complexities of computer systems.

Computer Languages ➤ In the beginning, there were only switches. You turned them on or you turned them off to program a computer. You had to speak its language of 1s and 0s. The development of higher-level languages like COBOL and FORTRAN in the 1950s opened up the world of computer programming, providing Englishlike commands that were easier to remember and manipulate. Basis, Pascal, Logo, C, C++, and many other languages simply refined this idea and offered variations fit for one job or another and based on a variety of syntax systems. In order for the machine to understand these higher-level languages the programs must be translated into MACHINE LANGUAGE. There are two ways to do this. An *Interpreter* intercepts the higher-level command at the time of execution and translates it in REAL TIME. A *Compiler* translates the code beforehand. Compiled programs should, therefore, execute faster.

COMSTAR ➤ AT&T's proprietary name for its communications SATELLITES.

Conceptual Art ➤ An artistic movement of the 1970s that suggested that it was no longer necessary actually to do art, merely to describe what might be done. The artistic weight of meaning was shifted from the object to the concept. See POSTMODERNISM.

Concrete Music ➤ Music composed directly on tape from a variety of naturally occurring sounds that may be modulated electronically before they are finally mixed. Introduced by Pierre Schaeffer of the Studio d'Essai of ORTF in 1948.

Conference Call ➤ See TELECONFERENCE.

Confetti ➤ Visual NOISE, usually on a VIDEODISC.

Conforming ➤ The final editing of a video using offline takes and the EDL as a guide to produce an edited master.

Connections ➤ See PLUGS.

Connotation ➤ The suggestive or associative sense of an expression (word, IMAGE, SIGN) that extends beyond its strict literal definition. See DENOTATION.

Constant Bit Rate ➤ CBR. Compare VBR.

Content Curve ➤ A term used to denote the amount of time necessary for the average viewer to assimilate most of the meaning of a SHOT.

Continuity ➤ The script supervisor is in charge of the continuity of a film production, making sure that details in one shot will match details in another, even though the shots may be filmed weeks or months apart. The script supervisor also keeps detailed records of TAKES.

Continuity Editing ➤ *Analytical Editing*. The system of editing, largely developed in the U.S. in the 1910s, that still dominates film language. Striving for seamless spatial and temporal continuity, this approach uses a set of rules whose aim is to hide rather than emphasize the CUT. See EYELINE MATCH, 180-DEGREE RULE, 30-DEGREE RULE, SHOT/REVERSE SHOT, MATCH ON ACTION.

Contouring ➤ An ARTIFACT, or inconsistency, in digital imaging. When too few BITS PER PIXEL are used to define shades of gray or colors, the contours of the image are crude and obvious, appearing as a set of blotches.

Contrapuntal Sound ➤ Sound used in counterpoint to the image. See PARALLEL SOUND, COMMENTATIVE SOUND.

Contrast ➤ Used to refer to both the quality of the lighting of a scene and a characteristic of the FILMSTOCK. High-contrast lighting shows a stark difference between blacks and whites; low-contrast (or soft-contrast) lighting mainly emphasizes the midrange of grays. See GAMMA.

Control L ➤ See LANC.

Convergence ➤ (1) Focusing of the three separate color signals in television reception so that they match. (This is especially critical in projection TV.) (2) Merging of communications technologies as they become DIGITAL. For example: CTI (the integration of computers and telephony); CABLE television companies that sell Internet access; or telephone companies that distribute television programming.

Converter ➻ (1) A CABLE TELEVISION tuner and DESCRAMBLER. (2) Circuitry that converts digital signals to analog signals, or vice-versa—a DAC.

Convolver, Convolving ➻ In computer graphics, algorithms that apply special effects to images (or sounds) are known as Convolvers: they "twist" the original, adding layers—or "folds"—of new information. A simpler synonym is "Filter."

Cool and Hot Media ➻ Marshall McLuhan's terms to indicate the relative degree of audience involvement in varying media. See his *Understanding Media*.

Cool Colors ➻ The colors to the right on the visible spectrum: blue, indigo, violet. Compare WARM COLORS.

Coprocessor ➻ An auxiliary CPU, usually built into the chip, that handles certain tasks for the CPU—math, for example.

Copy Protection ➻ Since digital copies are indistinguishable from their originals, schemes to prevent or limit copying have grown in importance. See GENERATION, MACROVISION, CSS, CGMS, DIGITAL CPS, DONGLE, AAC, and ENCRYPTION.

Copyright ➻ The legal doctrine that grants ownership of a piece of INTELLECTUAL PROPERTY such as a film, book, song, or software program to its author. The U.S. Copyright law of 1976 grants a copyright for the life of the author plus fifty years. If the "author" is a company rather than an individual, the grant is for seventy-five years from the year of first publication or one hundred years from the year of creation of the work. Once the copyright has expired, the work enters the PUBLIC DOMAIN.

Corporation for Public Broadcasting ➻ See PBS.

Costs ➻ Modern film and television budgets are complicated documents. Three terms are important: "Above-the-line costs" include those expenses relating to the period before shooting begins, such as script costs, supervision, salaries of the cast, music, royalties and commissions, some taxes, and fixed costs. "Below-the-line costs" include expenses incurred during shooting and postproduction work on the film: set construction, salaries of technical personnel, equipment rental, transportation, location costs, makeup, wardrobe, special effects and basic lab work, filmstock, editing, and so forth. "NEGATIVE COST" is the sum of above-the-line and below-the-line costs: in other words, the total amount necessary to produce the final edited and prepared negative of the film. Not included in the "negative cost" are expenses that the distributor of the film often shares with the producer: P & A—prints, advertising, and promotion. Since Hollywood discovered the effectiveness of television advertising in the 1970s, these "non-negative" costs have bal-

looned; on some Hollywood features they can approach the negative cost itself.

Couch Potato ⇒ Vivid slang that became popular in the 1980s to
describe television addicts newly liberated from even the pretense
of exercise by the advent of the REMOTE CONTROL and the proliferation
of cable channels. (Now if only somebody could figure out how to
change the videotape without human intervention....)

Counterprogramming ⇒ In a three-network television system any
one network could often garner larger RATINGS than its competitors
by programming against them. If, for example, both NBC and CBS
had scheduled cop series for a particular time slot, ABC might have
"won" that period by programming a variety program against
them. Since the first two networks split the audience for that type
of show, the third had the remainder of the audience to itself, at
least in theory. The technique became less effective when FOX was
added to the equation. See LEAD-IN, HAMMOCKING.

Cover ⇒ In the 1950s and 1960s, when it looked like an original
Black Rhythm & Blues or Rock 'n' Roll song was about to take off,
it was common practice in the music industry to issue a "cover" by
a white musician as quickly as possible. These versions were an
understandable source of contention: promoted more heavily by
larger record companies, the covers always ate heavily into the
profits of the original Black recording. It's interesting how the use
of the word has changed. In the 1990s, a cover is simply a new rendition of an old song; the avaricious connotation has been lost
(although the venal practice still exists). Partly this is the result of
the identity forged in the Rock world between performer and composition—unique among musical genres. A rock song belongs to its
composer in a way no other music does, so any new rendition is a
"cover." Compare SAMPLING.

Cover Shot ⇒ See MASTER SHOT.

Coverage ⇒ (1) The READER'S report, including synopsis of the action
of a book or script and a snap judgment as to its suitability for film.
(2) Footage shot as backup material, often by a SECOND UNIT. Also
called *B-Roll*.

CPB ⇒ See PBS.

CPM ⇒ Cost per thousand, the advertising industry's index of the
cost effectiveness of a print ad or broadcast commercial.

CP/M ⇒ The microcomputer operating system written in 1975 by
Gary Kildall and distributed through his company, Digital Research,
Inc., that dominated the early days of the microcomputer industry,
and served as the model for Microsoft's MS-DOS.

CPU ➼ Central Processing Unit, the main Microprocessor in a personal computer. In recent years, RISC (Reduced Instruction Set) architecture has begun to rival CISC (Complex Instruction Set) architecture. Intel has dominated the industry, first with its 80x86 series, then with the enormously successful Pentium series, but Motorola kept pace with its 680x0 series, then with its PowerPC series, introduced in 1994 and codeveloped with Apple and IBM. Some of the earliest microcomputers used chips from a third company, Zilog. The Z-80 was popular for CP/M machines before IBM introduced their Intel-based PC in 1981. Zilog still exists, manufacturing chips for special uses.

Crane Shot ➼ A shot taken from a crane, a device resembling the "cherrypickers" used by the telephone company to repair lines.

Crawl ➼ The rolling credits common to television, usually at the end of the program.

Credits ➼ The list of technical personnel, cast, and crew of a film or program. In the Golden Age of Hollywood, credits were simple: one or two cards listed the key personnel and most of the technicians on the film—regular employees of the studios—went without recognition. Now, credit crawls can go on for minutes: even interns get to see their names on the screen.

CRI ➼ (1) Color Rendering Index. Measures the consistency of the brightness of a light source in a projector over the visible spectrum. (You'll also find this index on light bulb packages.) (2) Color Reversal Intermediate. A Reversal filmstock used to produce release prints.

Critical Distance ➼ The distance from a sound source at which the direct energy radiated by the source equals the reverberant energy reflected from the walls, floor, and ceiling.

Cross-Cutting ➼ Intermingling the shots of two or more scenes to suggest Parallel Action.

Cross Luminance ➼ *Dot Crawl*. A defect of NTSC composite video that appears as a dot pattern on the edges of colors. Chrominance has leaked into the Luminance signal.

Crosslighting ➼ Lighting from the side. See Backlighting.

Crossover ➼ A circuit that splits a signal into different frequency spectra, common with loudspeakers. See Woofer, Tweeter.

Cross-Ownership ➼ Ownership by a single company of outlets in different news media within the same city—for example, a newspaper and a television station.

Crosstalk ➼ Interference in one electromagnetic signal by another.

CRT ➼ See Cathode Ray Tube.

C-SPAN ➨ Cable Satellite Public Affairs Network. Noncommercial CABLE NETWORK founded in 1979 to provide live coverage of congressional sessions and other government business and which became almost as well-known in the nineties for its talk shows and interview programs.

CSS ➨ The Content Scrambling System built into DVD-VIDEO and mandated by the studios to prevent copying. See CGMS, MACROVISION.

CT ➨ A feature of RDS that provides automatic Clock Time setting.

CTI ➨ Acronym for Computer–Telephone Integration. A technological dream of the microcomputer industry since the mid-1980s, CTI picked up steam in the mid-1990s when the Internet offered a new alternative to the telephone for networking. See CONVERGENCE.

CTV ➨ The Canadian commercial television network, owned by independent stations.

CTW ➨ Children's Television Workshop, the not-for-profit organization founded in 1967 by Joan Ganz Cooney to produce an educational public television program for preschoolers. *Sesame Street* became the cultural touchstone for a generation and was soon joined by *3-2-1 Contact*, *Square One*, and *Ghost Writer*. Only Jim Henson, who was a major contributor to *Sesame Street*, had a greater influence on children's popular culture and myth.

Cubism ➨ The movement in painting in the early years of the twentieth century (Picasso, Braque) that abstracted natural shapes into geometrical compositions in order to extend the boundaries of the art to such subjects as movement and psychology. Compare FRACTAL.

Cue Cards ➨ Large cardboard signs with dialogue printed on them held out of camera range so that actors don't have to memorize their lines. See TELEPROMPTER.

CUI ➨ Character-based User Interface; the acronym for older interfaces such as DOS and CP/M that required the user to issue all commands by typing them. Also CLI. Compare GUI.

Culture Industry ➨ Term for the MASS MEDIA and POPULAR CULTURE used by members of the influential Frankfurt School of theorists in the 1930s and 1940s—especially Theodor Adorno and Max Horkheimer to suggest that ART had become industrialized as a mass-produced commodity, promulgating an ideology, and designed to promote passivity and uniformity among consumers. See MEDIA IMAGE, VALIDATION.

Cut ➨ (1) In film and television, a switch from one image to another. (2) In disc recording, a band of grooves separated from other bands to provide an access reference point.

Cutaway ➳ A shot, usually brief, inserted in a scene to show action at another location; most often used to cover breaks in the main TAKE, as in television and documentary interviews. See REACTION SHOT.

Cutter ➳ See EDITOR.

Cutting-Room Floor ➳ Scenes and sequences that don't make it into the FINAL CUT of a film are said to be "left on the cutting-room floor."

CVBS ➳ Composite Video BASEBAND Signal. This is a satellite signal that includes synchronization information as well as the program signal.

CVD ➳ Compact VideoDisc, an unofficial transposition of the official VCD (Video CD).

CX-Encoding ➳ A system of noise-reduction developed by CBS Labs, used for analog sound on LASERDISCS. It reduces the interference from the video signal on the audio channel.

Cyberpunk, Cyberspace, Cyberworld ➳ The concept of an alternate reality based on online networks and digital representations of reality popularized by William Gibson in his 1984 novel *Neuromancer*. Denizens of Cyberspace are Cyberpunks. Compare HACKER.

Cyclorama ➳ A large curved backdrop at the rear of a stage.

D/A ➳ DIGITAL to ANALOG conversion.

DAB ➳ Digital Audio Broadcasting. A theoretical system of broadcasting requiring a wide BANDWIDTH. Experimental in U.K. in late 1990s, especially for car reception.

DAC ➳ Digital/Analog Converter. Since most television sets and stereo amplifiers are still analog, a DAC is necessary to output a signal from a CD or DVD. See JITTER.

DAD ➳ Acronym for Digital Audio Disc, an adaptation of the basic DVD-VIDEO format to present 24/96 audio. Classic Records issued discs in this transitional format in 1998. Compare DTS, HDCD, DSD.

Dada ➳ European literary and artistic movement, flourishing from 1916 to the mid-1920s, that attempted to rediscover authentic artistic reality by a head-on, comic, derisive assault on established theories, forms, and styles. Dada set the tone for the twentieth-century aesthetic revolution; illogic, parody, and random artistic choice were its tools. The important Dadaist painters and poets included Marcel Duchamp, Max Ernst, Jean Arp, Tristan Tzara, and Kurt Schwitters. Films made under the influence of Dada were notable for their freewheeling technique and deflation of authority, and include works by Hans Richter (*Ghosts Before Breakfast*), René Clair

(*Entr'Acte*, probably the most famous Dadaist film), and Marcel Duchamp himself (who acted in Clair's film and who made *Anemic Cinema*). See THEATER OF THE ABSURD, SURREALISM.

Dailies ➤ See RUSHES.

Daisy Wheel ➤ An adaptation of typewriter technology, first used with dedicated WORD PROCESSORS in the 1970s, then with personal computers in the early eighties. The characters were molded at the ends of fingers (or petals) arranged in a wheel shape. As the proper letter revolved to the top, a hammer fired pressing the molding into the typewriter ribbon which transferred the ink to the paper. Although expensive mechanical devices, Daisy Wheels were popular in the early years of the PC industry because the alternative, the DOT MATRIX printer, produced such poor quality type. The rise of the LASER PRINTER, and then INK JET technology, killed the Daisy Wheel quickly. See also BAND PRINTER.

DAM CD ➤ A CD that includes MP3 files as well as standard audio tracks. Possible acronym from "Digital Automatic Music."

DAT ➤ Digital AudioTape. The application of DIGITAL technology to tape products, introduced by SONY and other consumer audio equipment manufacturers in the late 1980s to compete with the CD. DAT cassettes are not compatible with ANALOG cassettes, and have found a market only in professional applications. The CODEC is based on PCM. The same DAT cassettes are also used in computer backup systems, as are variants of this FORM FACTOR. Compare DIGITAL COMPACT CASSETTE.

Data Discman ➤ SONY's 80 mm CD-ROM technology, introduced in 1990. The discs were read by a hand-held reader and were limited to data only. The data was displayed on a small LCD screen. Also known as *Electronic Book*, the Data Discman came in several versions. The *Bookman* used a 120 mm CD-ROM XA disc. One of the earliest attempts at a hand-held computer, the Discman was not successful in the market and was soon replaced by the PDA.

Data Rate ➤ The effective operation of a DVD-VIDEO (or a CD, for that matter) depends on a constant flow of data from the disc to the CPU. The speed at which the disc can deliver the data to the CPU is the Data Rate. A single-speed CD-ROM had a data rate of about 150 kilobytes/sec. The first DVD players had a transfer rate of 1.3 megabytes/sec. In comparison, the data rate of uncompressed NTSC video is more than 27 megabytes/sec.

Data Types ➤ All computer data is binary, but each data set, or file, is destined to produce a different effect in the real world. These formats are known as data types. With respect to media the important data types are text, image, audio, and video. See TEXT FILE FORMATS, IMAGE FILE FORMATS, MOVIE FILE FORMATS.

Database ⟫ A collection of information organized in records and fields within records. For example, in a mailing list each person comprises a record, and the fields within the record might be name, street address, city, state, and zip code.

Day for Night ⟫ The practice of using filters to shoot night scenes during the day. The French term for this is "La Nuit Américaine" ("the American night"), evoking the economy typical of Hollywood technique.

Day-and-Dating ⟫ BOOKING a film for a first or second run at several theaters at the same time. See EXHIBITION, SHOWCASE.

Daypart ⟫ One of several segments of the day defined for television programming: Morning, Daytime, EARLY FRINGE, ACCESS, DOUBLE ACCESS, PRIMETIME, Late News, LATE FRINGE, and Latenight.

dB ⟫ See DECIBEL.

DBS ⟫ See DSB.

DBS Band ⟫ See SATELLITE BANDS.

DB-25, DB-15, DB-9 ⟫ See PLUGS.

DC ⟫ Digital Camera. See DIGITAL FILM.

DCC ⟫ PHILIPS'S DIGITAL COMPACT CASSETTE.

DCR ⟫ Digital Cable Radio.

DCT ⟫ See DISCRETE COSINE TRANSFORM.

DDD ⟫ See CD CODES.

DD-1 ⟫ SONY'S abbreviation for the first version of the DATA DISCMAN.

Dead Technologies ⟫ Competition is one of the elements that makes the history of technology fascinating. Once a particular technology has won the battle, it becomes a part of our lives; we can't imagine life without it. Early on there was the battle between Direct Current and Alternating Current. Nobody uses DC today (except that it is a part of every electronic device we own).

Lee DeForest's PHONOFILM didn't get anywhere. The first famous sound film used the competing VITAPHONE process. But Vitaphone was dead within a year and systems like Phonofilm still rule film sound today. (The Vitaphone sound-on-disk system was revived successful for DTS more than 60 years later.)

David Sarnoff successfully repressed FM radio in the 1930s. But it was revived in the 1960s, and now competes on a more than equal basis with AM. In the early 1950s CBS's 33 1/3 rpm LP beat RCA's 45 rpm, but the RCA disk found a niche for itself. (What would Rock 'n' Roll have become without the 45?) CBS also championed mechanical color television; RCA's electronic color system won hands down.

In the mid-1970s everyone knew that videodiscs were just around the corner, but the corner kept receding into the future. All of a sudden, videotape cassettes entered the market, and cornered it for 25 years. Discs, when they did arrive a few years later, had to settle for a minor niche. Everyone knows that VHS killed BETA, but, in fact, Beta technology has survived as a professional format.

Nevertheless, numerous graves have been dug in the cemetery of technology over the last 30 years—and occupied.

QUADRAPHONIC sound was the first modern victim of the technology wars. When it failed in the 1970s, only months after its introduction, we were shocked. Until that time anything demonstrably better in media technology had succeeded.

When Philips/MCA's LASERDISC was introduced, it was one of three competing formats for videodisc. The other two, Telefunken/ Decca's TED and RCA's SELECTAVISION, died a quick death.

The VIDEOCASSETTE is one of the great success stories of modern media, but two predecessors, based on film, were non-starters: CBS's EVR and Polaroid's POLAVISION.

Throughout the 1980s, numerous technologies competed in what was then known as VIDEOTEXT for a piece of the online market. Britain's PRESTEL, the pioneer, Japan's CAPTAIN, Canada's TELIDON, Germany's BILDSCHIRMTEXT, and the U.S.'s NAPLPS are all historical curiosities now, instantly outshone by the INTERNET nova of the early 1990s. Only France's MINITEL system survives—for a while longer.

The history of CD-ROM MULTIMEDIA forms a curious parallel with Videotext. Like its online counterpart it never quite fulfilled its promise. CD-I, MMCD, VIS, CDTV, and ULTIMEDIA have been consigned to the historical dustbin. But direct descendent DVD will succeed where CD-ROM failed.

The prize for underachieving zombie technology of the twentieth century goes to HOLOGRAPHY. Like the laser a child of the 1960s, holography promised a 3-D world in every garage. So far, 35 years later, it has succeeded only for security badges on credit cards. (Runner-up is the SMART CARD, a great idea that survives only because it found a niche in the DSS world.)

Then there are the technologies that served their time as productive members of the techno society before gracefully expiring. All of the film industry opticals fall into this category (TRAVELLING MATTES, ROTOSCOPE, FRONT PROJECTION, REAR PROJECTION) done in by their digital software equivalents.

The honorable TELEGRAPH, and its successors TELETYPE, TELEX, and TWX rest in peace after long careers, replaced very quickly in the 1990s by electronic mail. (TELETEX died in infancy.)

Everyone thought that the LP was dead, but VINYL disks surprisingly survive thanks to audiophiles still unsatisfied with digital reproduction.

The featured technology joust on the horizon as we write is SACD vs DVD-AUDIO, but times have changed. Now that everything is digital, it is just a matter of software. Both these technologies are likely to survive because the consumer won't have to make a choice. Software will handle both transparently. From now on, the new digital technologies won't die—but many will simply fade away, almost without our knowing it.

Decibel ➻ A tenth of a Bel. This basic unit of sound power is also used to measure electrical signals. Abbreviated *dB*. The scale is logarithmic, so each unit represents a significant difference.

Deconstruction ➻ Critique of the tradition of Western philosophy developed by Jacques Derrida beginning in the late 1960s and often associated in the U.S. with the work of the "Yale School." A central tenet of POSTSTRUCTURALISM (with which it is often confused), deconstruction questions traditions of thinking obsessed with origins (the "logos") and final destinies (the "telos"). It proposes that a "trace" exists between SIGNIFIER and SIGNIFIED that prevents an exact correspondence. Deconstruction works to unsettle hierarchies and demonstrate that what appears to be freely and naturally articulated (the consummate example is speech) is actually a situated, complex inscription (in other words, a "writing"). Invading the academy in the 1970s, deconstruction really caught on in the 1980s in many areas, including film criticism. Typically, a deconstructive analysis of a text (novel, song, film, ad) will fix on a seemingly insignificant feature and will work it through that text until the coherence of the text is undermined ("deconstructed") so that it loses its integrity and power. In the 1980s, deconstruction was seen as a potent tool for gender, ethnic, and sexuality studies. Digital technology is a fitting companion to Deconstructive thought.

Découpage ➻ The design of the film, the arrangement of its shots. "Découpage classique" is the French term for the old Hollywood style of seamless narration. See CONTINUITY EDITING.

Deep Focus ➻ A technique favored by REALISTS in which objects very near the camera as well as those far away are in focus at the same time. See also SHALLOW FOCUS.

Deep Linking ➻ The technique, inherent to the philosophy of the WORLD WIDE WEB, of linking to pages several levels down on other websites. This democratic reference system lies at the heart of the hypertext concept. However, by using frames, the linker can make the linked pages from someone else's site appear to be part of the linker's site, which is not proper netiquette. As the Web became a commercial powerhouse, "deep linking" was called into question. In 1998, Barry Diller's Ticketmaster sued Microsoft for deep linking to its ticket sales site. The suit was settled out of court early in 1999, so no case law was established on this interesting question.

Deep Space ➻ A MISE EN SCÈNE that establishes a considerable distance between the foreground and background planes of a SHOT. Not the same as DEEP FOCUS.

Definition ➻ As used in regard to FILMSTOCK, the word indicates the power of the film to define the elements of an image—a measure of the GRAIN. See RESOLUTION.

Delphi ➻ Founded by Dan Bruns in 1984, this online system was focused on basic information rather than chat or software advice. (Its predecessor was Wes Kussmaul's digital encyclopedia.) Like all online services that weren't based on marginal costs (as were COMPUSERVE and GENIE) Delphi struggled throughout the 1980s, a leader in the "industry in search of a business." In 1992, Delphi had the unique foresight to focus on Internet access—but the foresight proved premature. Nobody knew what the Internet was, then. Least of all Rupert Murdoch, who bought Delphi in 1993 to serve as a technical support infrastructure for his TV Guide Online (then in development by UNET). A couple of years (and $150 million) later, Delphi was deemed disposable by Murdoch and he sold it back to Bruns. It now concentrates on building and servicing INTERNET communities.

Delta Frame ➻ See KEY FRAME.

Demographics, Demos ➻ The study of the characteristics of a population. Advertisers use demographics to pinpoint specific, potentially profitable audiences in order to increase the efficiency of the advertising media. Often abbreviated "demos." See UPSCALE. Compare PSYCHOGRAPHICS.

Denotation ➻ The strict literal definition of an expression (word, IMAGE, SIGN) as opposed to its CONNOTATION.

Denouement ➻ French for the "unknotting." The closing action of a drama, in which the loose ends are tied up (in English) or the knots are untied (in French). See DEUS EX MACHINA.

Density ➻ (1) The degree of darkness or EXPOSURE of a film image. (2) In theory, a measure of the amount of information an IMAGE or medium communicates.

Depth of Field ➻ The range of distances from the camera at which the subject is acceptably sharp. See FOCUS PLANE.

DES ➻ Data Encryption Standard, from the National Bureau of Standards.

Descrambler ⇒ An electronic device for decoding encrypted—or scrambled—transmission signals. See ENCRYPTION, BLACK BOX.

Designated Market Area ⇒ See DMA.

Desktop Publishing ⇒ The combination of more sophisticated word processing software that can deal with issues of design, layout, and typography together with LASER PRINTER technology that provides high-quality, direct output; collapses the formerly arduous and expensive publishing process so that all the equipment necessary literally fits on a desktop.

Desktop Video ⇒ On the model of DESKTOP PUBLISHING, a system of video and audio editing and mixing that runs on a microcomputer. Just as Desktop Publishing brought the art and science of printing to millions, so Desktop Video brings the tools of filmmaking to everyone.

Detail Shot ⇒ Usually more magnified than a CLOSEUP. A shot of a hand, eye, mouth, or subject of similar detail. EXTREME CLOSEUP.

Deus Ex Machina ⇒ Latin for "God from the machine." A plot device that resolves the action and that is as arbitrary as a god descending magically from the flies (the area above the stage where backdrops are kept). See DENOUEMENT.

Development ⇒ (1) The arduous, seemingly endless process of seeking financing for and preparing for production of a film. Sometimes exaggerated as in, "He's been in development hell most of the year." (2) See PROCESSING.

D-Girl, D-Boy ⇒ A young assistant to a studio executive or producer, always ambitious, often involved in DEVELOPMENT, from which the phrase is derived.

Diachronic ⇒ In linguistic theory, a phenomenon is diachronic when it consists of or depends upon a change in its state, usually across time. Compare SYNCHRONIC.

Dialectics ⇒ The system of thought after Hegel that focuses on contradictions between opposing concepts: historical change occurs through the opposition of conflicting forces and ideas. Some filmmakers (notably Sergei Eisenstein) use the Marxist version of the idea to create meaning out of the juxtaposition of SHOTS.

Diamondvision ⇒ Originally a proprietary term for large video screens used in baseball stadiums (hence "diamond"), the term is now used to refer to any theater-sized video screen. Compare VIDEO PROJECTION.

Diaphragm ⇒ The device that controls the amount of light passing through a LENS.

Dictaphone ⇒ An archaic term for a tape recorder designed for dictation. Before AUDIOCASSETTE recorders were adapted to the task, Dictaphones recorded on a wide, continuous band of magnetic material.

Diegesis ⇒ The DENOTATIVE material of film narrative, it includes, according to Metz, not only the narration itself, but also the fictional space and time dimensions implied by the narrative.

Diffuser ⇒ A gelatin plate that is placed in front of a light to change its quality. See SCRIM, GOBO, FLAG.

Digerati ⇒ On the model of "literati," the digitally well educated class.

Digital ⇒ *Analog* systems of recording or transmitting information—data, sounds, or images—use a structure that attempts to mirror closely the continuous waveforms of the original signal. From Edison's earliest RECORDS to the first VIDEODISCS, analog systems served the media well. With the microcomputer revolution of the 1980s, digital methods of recording and transmitting information began to develop. In a digital system, the original waveform—data, audio, or video—is sampled many thousands of times per second; the samples are translated into numerical values; and those values are stored as data.

Because the information is stored as numbers, digital systems are relatively impervious to degradation and background NOISE: a collection of digits stored on a CD doesn't wear out like the groove of a vinyl record, and the noise inherent in an analog recording simply doesn't exist: there are no spurious numbers. Importantly, the information is now much more susceptible to computer manipulation. On the other hand, analog fans continue to maintain that, no matter how many times you "sample" the music, you aren't recording all of it; they believe digital recordings are therefore lifeless. In the U.S. a digital transmission system was first used in 1978 by PBS to transmit its sound signal from the network to affiliated stations where it was translated to analog for retransmission to the home. Experimental digital recordings were also introduced in that year. See DSD, DSS, DVD, HDTV.

Digital Audiotape ⇒ See DAT.

Digital Betacam ⇒ See BETACAM.

Digital Compact Cassette ⇒ PHILIPS'S DIGITAL audiocassette technology that used COMPRESSION techniques to achieve a standard audiocassette size, compatible with ANALOG audiocassettes. The product was introduced in the early 1990s in an attempt to bring DAT technology to the consumer market, and in competition with Sony's MINIDISC. Philips abandoned the format in 1996.

Digital CPS ➥ Proposed Digital Copy Protection System based on FIREWIRE technology. The DVD-VIDEO deck would do the encryption on the fly, so no changes would be necessary to the disc itself.

Digital Editing ➥ The digitalization of film and tape editing has gone through several stages. Early computer editing systems, such as the *Eddiflex* in the mid-1980s, controlled banks of VCRs on which various takes had been loaded. The process was cumbersome. The AVID Media Composer, introduced in 1989, brought all the takes (or a version of them) onto hard disks where they could be more quickly accessed. The singular aim ever since CBS debuted their million-dollar computerized editing machine in the mid-1970s has been to make the process "Nonlinear." In traditional film (or tape) editing hundreds of individual takes of individual shots are stored on reels or in *Trim Bins*. Finding the one you want (or think you remember) is a very time-consuming business.

Computerizing the operation turns your collection of takes into a DATABASE, with all the facility that provides. You can call up an individual take much more quickly and compare two or more takes more easily. You can also move back and forth from beginning to end quickly (because you are accessing a disc, not a tape). This is why the process is called nonlinear. Of course, working with files rather than a workprint is much safer. You aren't likely to have to spend time splicing back footage if you make the wrong cut: just don't save the file. And you can compare two alternate edits on the screen at the same time if you choose.

To edit film you first have to convert it to tape, then digitize it and compress it. After the *Online Editing* is complete your Edit Decision List (EDL) serves as a blueprint for the actual cutting of the original negative into the master in a process called VIDEO MATCHBACK. (This is the *Offline Editing*.) The process is simpler for analog videotape. You only need to digitize and compress. The EDL serves as the guide for CONFORMING the original tape. With digital tape the process is simplest: the digital signal on the tape is fed directly to disc via a high-speed FIREWIRE connection. The finished edit can be read from disc to tape the same way.

Digital Effects ➥ Most SPECIAL EFFECTS can be accomplished digitally, but the term has special resonance when it refers to processes liking MORPHING that are unique to the digital world. See POST HOUSE.

Digital 8 ➥ SONY's HI-8 digital videotape format, introduced in 1999. The cameras are backward-compatible with analog HI-8.

Digital Film ➥ Sony's MAVICA, the first digital camera, remains the only digital camera on the market to use a standard storage medium, the old-fashioned 1.44 Mbyte diskette. All the other cameras use a confusing variety of media, nearly all of them exceeding the diskette in capacity; all of them increasing the difficulty of getting the image into your computer where it can be edited. Some of these media (as of early 1999) include: *CompactFlash*, Type II *PC Card*, *SmartMedia*, *Miniature Card*, and *Clik!*

Digital Light Processor ➺ See DLP.

Digital Micromirror Device ➺ See DMD.

Digital Pulse Wireless ➺ See ULTRAWIDEBAND RADIO.

Digital Resolution ➺ In the new world of digital imagery, at least five different parameters are called "resolution," which can make things confusing even for sophisticates.

   (1) *Bit Resolution* or bit depth (also called COLOR DEPTH) is a measurement of the number of Bits used to define each Pixel of a color or GRAYSCALE image.

   (2) *Device Resolution* is a measurement of the number of dots or pixels per inch (dpi or ppi) that a piece of hardware presents.

   (3) *Screen Resolution* (or Screen Frequency) is a specification of the number of dots per inch in a HALFTONE screen used to print an image. (It has nothing to do with the computer screen.)

   (4) *Image Resolution* is a measurement of the amount of information that is stored for an image (generally measured in pixels per inch). Note that Image Resolution is independent of both Device and Output Resolution. See RESAMPLING.

   (5) *Output Resolution* is a measurement of the capability (in dots per inch) of a printer or other output device. (Thanks to Adobe Systems Incorporated for this succinct analysis.) See also VIDEO RESOLUTION.

Digital-S ➺ JVC's late 1998 contribution to the plethora of digital tape formats. A 1/2-inch, 4:2:2 format. Compare DVCAM, DVCPRO, MiniDV.

Digital Video Effects ➺ See DVE.

Digitization ➺ The process of converting an analog signal into a DIGITAL signal. See A/D, SAMPLING, QUANTIZATION, and COMPANDING.

DIN ➺ See PLUGS.

Dingbat ➺ Printer's lingo for any decorative type object, such as a bullet, arrow, checkmark, box.

Direct Cinema ➺ The dominant style of DOCUMENTARY in the U.S. since the early 1960s. Like CINÉMA VÉRITÉ, it depends on lightweight, mobile equipment. Unlike cinéma vérité, it does not permit the filmmaker to become involved in the action and, in fact, is noted for its avoidance of narration.

Direct Satellite Broadcasting ➺ See DSB.

Direct Sound ➵ The technique of recording sound simultaneously with image, direct sound has become much more feasible since the development of portable tape recorders and self-BLIMPED cameras. See CINÉMA VÉRITÉ, DIRECT CINEMA.

Director ➵ Generally considered to be the most influential member of the filmmaking team and usually, but not always, its leader. At the very least, the director is in charge of the actors and technicians on the set, but often has considerable input during PREPRODUCTION and POSTPRODUCTION. See AUTEUR POLICY.

Director of Photography ➵ See CINEMATOGRAPHER.

Director's Cut ➵ The director's preferred version of a film. Directors' Cuts blossomed in the 1980s as a marketable feature of SIGNATURE EDITIONS of Laserdiscs. Perhaps the ultimate Director's Cut, however, was Francis Coppola's reworking of *Godfather* I and II together with outtakes in chronological order for a network television broadcast.

DirectShow ➵ Microsoft's successor to VIDEO FOR WINDOWS, software to play back audio and video. Introduced with Windows 98. See MOVIE FILE FORMATS.

Direct-Stream Digital ➵ See DSD.

Direct-to-Plate ➵ In the old days of PHOTOTYPESETTING the process went something like this: An author's manuscript was handed to a typesetter who re-keyed it on a minicomputer designed especially for typesetting. The output of the typesetter was photographic REPRO. A layout artist cut and pasted this Repro on pages. These pages were then photographed to make a negative from which the printing plate could be burned. Although a lot of printing is still done this way, the software tools now available produce digital page layout, which may as well burn the plate as print CAMERA-READY COPY.

Direct-to-Video ➵ Like the MADE-FOR-TV MOVIE, a descendant of the B PICTURE and PROGRAMMER born out of the videocassette revolution of the 1980s. Direct-to-Video movies are sometimes released perfunctorily in theaters but their economics are based entirely on the video market. By 1990 more than a hundred Direct-to-Videos were produced in Hollywood each year.

DirecTV ➵ See DSS.

Disc, Disk ➵ The good news is the bad news about discs: they're round. This geometry offers the advantages of cheap reproduction (discs can be stamped; they don't need to be recorded, like tapes) and near instant access to any point in the recording (because the tracks are laid closely next to each other). Its disadvantages are that it may be highly susceptible to physical damage and that, because it is not linear, it cannot be edited. See DISK, TAPE, LIVE, MAGNETIC DISC, LASERDISC, CD.

Discography ➻ An organized list of records—even if they're CDs—often by a particular performer.

Discovision ➻ Not a dance craze, but SONY/PHILIPS's proprietary term for its laser-based VIDEODISC format introduced in the early 1980s. The technology was later sold to Pioneer. The term is now in disuse. Compare SELECTAVISION.

Discrete Cosine Transform ➻ A mathematical technique used in COMPRESSION that performs an analysis of the digital data that describe an image such that it can be sorted so that the most valuable information comes first (and the least valuable last). Once the data is sorted in this way, more or less of it can be employed to reproduce the image with varying degrees of precision.

Dish ➻ Colloquial term for any ground antenna, especially the parabolic antennas used to capture satellite transmissions. The first dishes were ten meters wide and very expensive. The first dish offered to consumers appeared in the 1979 Neiman-Marcus Christmas catalogue. The price: $36,500, installed. With the advent of three-meter dishes in the 1980s a small but avid consumer market developed for the dishes as aficionados learned to pirate signals from the satellites. More recently, DSS systems aimed at the consumer market use much smaller dishes. See SQUARIAL.

Dish Night ➻ A giveaway promotion common in American movie theaters in the 1930s. Free dishes were handed out to audience members, usually on Tuesdays. To get a service for eight, you'd have to come back week after week. Remarkably, the crockery displayed no corporate logos!

Disk ➻ See DISC. Both spellings are acceptable in English, but "disc" is preferred for LASERDISCS, CDs, and DVDs; "disk" for vinyl and magnetic.

Diskette ➻ See FLOPPY DISK.

Disney ➻ Founded by Walt Disney and his brother Roy in 1923 to produce their animated films, this unusual studio did not enter the live-action field until the 1950s. From the 1950s through the early 1980s Disney concentrated on carefully orchestrated family entertainment and had that field virtually to itself. The company opened its first theme park, Disneyland, in 1955, and this division quickly became a central focus of the organization. Walt Disney died in 1966, and the company began a period of slow decline as family entertainment appeared to lose its attractiveness at the box office. Even animation, Disney's strong suit, was under attack. In 1979 a number of Disney's leading animators, led by Don Bluth, left the organization, disappointed with the low level of standards. Walt Disney's son-in-law Ron Miller took over as CEO in 1983 and began a remarkable turnaround, establishing the Touchstone Pictures division to compete with the other studios on their own turf—adult entertainment—and even returning the company to prominence in television with its own cable network, the DISNEY CHANNEL. Miller lost control to Walt's nephew Roy E. Disney in 1984.

The growth continued, however, under the leadership of chairman Michael Eisner, head of production Jeffrey Katzenberg (both former associates of Barry Diller at PARAMOUNT), and Frank Wells (formerly of WARNER). A second general-interest film division, Hollywood Pictures, was formed in 1990 to exploit lower-budget films. The company even returned to prominence in animation, with a string of hits in the late 1980s and 1990s. Frank Wells died in an accident in 1994. Shortly after, when it became evident that Eisner would not promote him, Katzenberg left to form his own studio—DREAMWORKS SKG—with Steven Spielberg and David Geffen. Although a merger with CBS had long been rumored, Eisner stunned the entertainment world in the summer of 1995 with his announcement that Disney would purchase Capital Cities/ABC for $19 billion. After two decades during which Hollywood studios had been bought and sold like schmattes, the last remaining independent studio had turned the tables—dramatically. Walt's little cartoon studio is now one of the world's largest media conglomerates, second only to TIME WARNER.

Disney Channel ➤ CABLE NETWORK that serves as a channel for Disney film and television product, founded in April 1983.

Dissolve ➤ The superimposition of a FADE-OUT over a FADE-IN. Sometimes called a lap dissolve.

Distance Learning ➤ A slightly awkward term for INTERNET-based educational programs.

Distant Signal ➤ A television broadcast signal not defined by the FCC as local to the community in which the cable system that carries it is located. See SUPERSTATION.

Distribution ➤ The dissemination of media products; the intermediate stage between production and EXHIBITION (or reception).

Distribution Flow ➤ The structure of distribution can be either discrete (composed of separate independent units, such as books, records, or films) or continuous (in which case the units are linked together, as in television and radio). A third variation is the mosaic, which offers a number of immediate choices, as in newspaper and magazine layout or the separate channels of television or the Internet. Distribution flow is also defined as either unidirectional or interactive, the latter allowing intercommunication between sender and receiver. Further, distribution is either BROADCAST or NARROWCAST.

Distributor ➤ The company that markets a film and arranges deals with exhibitors. Often—but not always—a branch of the production company or studio.

Dithering ➤ In computer graphics, a technique that creates the illusion of a color (or GRAYSCALE) where none exists by drawing patterns of two or more other colors (or brightness values). It is an extension of color printing technology and complementary to the technique of ANTI-ALIASING.

DivX ➤ Proprietary DVD player designed to build a one-way rental/purchase market for DVD-VIDEO. Viewers bought the disc for the equivalent of a rental fee and were then licensed to view the movie for a certain limited time. They could then: (1) throw it out; (2) rent another license; (3) buy unlimited viewings. The DivX player included a modem to make all this possible. Discontinued in early 1999.

DLP ➤ Digital Light Processor. A video projection technology developed by Texas Instruments and based on their DMD—Digital Micromirror Device.

DLT ➤ Digital Linear Tape. The tape format in general use for production of DVD-VIDEO and DVD-ROM. Final productions are written to DLT for transfer to disc.

DMA ➤ (1) Designated Market Area. NIELSEN's geographic designation of non-overlapping counties in which a television station has significant viewership. Used in RATINGS research and marketing and advertising studies. Compare ADI. (2) In computer technology, Direct Memory Access, a technique for communicating data between main memory and disk or other peripherals without the intervention of the CPU.

DMAC, D2MAC ➤ See MAC.

DMD ➤ Digital Micromirror Device. A technology developed by Texas Instruments and used in their DLP video projectors. Each chip holds as many as 500,000 or more micromirrors, each controlled by its own circuit. Because the light source is independent of the micromirror controller and the reflection is more efficient than transmission, the technology supposedly offers brightness and accuracy superior to earlier generations of video projectors based on LCD and LCLV technologies.

DME ➤ Dialogue, Music, Effects: these three basic contributing sound tracks are kept separate before the final mix, and are preserved to make POSTDUBBING easier.

DNS ➻ Domain Name Server. A program (or the machine on which it runs) that translates URLs to numeric IP ADDRESSES for the Internet. Hundreds of thousands of DNSes run on the Internet, each updating the others as DOMAIN names are changed or added. Sometimes the updates take several days to trickle down to remote DNSes.

Docudrama ➻ Semifictional versions of actual events, docudramas became popular staples of American television in the early seventies.

Documentary ➻ A term with a wide latitude of meaning, basically used to refer to any film or program not wholly fictional in nature. The term was first popularized by John Grierson. See CINÉMA VÉRITÉ, DIRECT CINEMA, DOCUDRAMA.

Dolby A, Dolby B ➻ A system of recording sound that greatly mutes the background noise inherent in film and tape reproduction. A is the professional system; B is the consumer system. Dolby Laboratories, Inc. began work on the system in the late 1960s. It licenses its technologies to manufacturers The technology evolved into an impressive range of analog and digital processes.

Dolby Digital ➻ Dolby's AC-3 algorithm applied to theatrical cinema. Introduced with *Batman Returns* in 1992. Dolby Digital prints store the digital soundtrack between the sprocket holes, and also include analog soundtracks for backward compatibility. Compare DTS, SDDS.

Dolby Prologic ➻ An advanced form of DOLBY SURROUND decoding that provides better channel separation and adds a center track.

Dolby SR ➻ A successor to the "Dolby A" technique that increases the maximum recording level attainable without distortion, permitting the reproduction of a wider frequency range with less distortion. The most powerful analog Dolby system. The initials stand for Spectral Recording.

Dolby SR•D ➻ A 35 mm release print that includes both Dolby analog (SR) and Dolby Digital (D) soundtracks.

Dolby Stereo ➻ The industry standard soundtrack through the 1980s, Dolby Stereo first gained prominence with the release of *Star Wars* (1977). The system encoded four channels (left, center, right, and surround) into two optical tracks on the print. See SVA.

Dolby Surround ➻ The consumer version of DOLBY STEREO for HOME THEATRE systems: left, right, and surround.

Dolly ➻ A set of wheels and a platform upon which the camera can be mounted to give it mobility. Also called "Crab Dolly."

Dolly Shot ➻ A shot taken from a moving DOLLY. Almost synonymous with, but more fluid than, a TRACKING SHOT. See FOLLOW SHOT.

Domain ➻ An area on the Internet identified by an IP address or an equivalent domain name. Root-level domains identify collections of sites either by type (.com for commercial, .edu for educational, .org for organization) or by location (.fr for France, .de for Germany, .ny.us for New York State in the U.S.). Type and location can also be combined (.co.uk for commercial, U.K.) See DNS.

Domestic Comedy ➤ That form of television (and sometimes film) centering on family relationships.

Dominant ➤ The controlling CODE or ATTRACTION in an image or montage. See SUBSIDIARY, INTRINSIC INTEREST.

D1, D2 ➤ Professional-level digital VIDEOCASSETTE recording formats. D1 is a COMPONENT format using gamma-ferric-oxide tape. D2 is a COMPOSITE format using iron particle tape. D-1 dates from 1987 and D-2 from 1988. Compare DVCAM.

Dongle ➤ (1) A gizmo that serves as a key for protected software. The dongle is plugged into the serial port of the computer. The software looks for it at the serial port and won't work without finding it. (2) By extension, any short cable adapter that "dangles."

Dot Crawl ➤ See CROSS LUMINANCE.

Dot Gain ➤ In most printing technologies, wet ink is deposited on absorbent paper. As the ink penetrates the paper the dots of HALF-TONE images enlarge. This Dot Gain darkens the image and decreases the contrast, problems which must be compensated for in the preparation of the halftone.

Dot Matrix ➤ A computer printing technology of the 1970s that dominated the low-end market in the 1980s before it was largely replaced by INK JET printers. An advance over the ancient BAND PRINTER, the Dot Matrix system relied on an array of pin-like hammers (usually 5 x 9) which fired in a pattern hitting a typewriter ribbon which deposited the ink on the paper. Because of the low resolution, the printed output was relatively crude. See also DAISY WHEEL.

Double Access ➤ See ACCESS TIME.

Double Pumping ➤ The television programming practice of broadcasting the same show twice within days, usually to generate interest for a new series. See STUNTING.

Double-System Sound ➤ The film-production technique in which sound is recorded separately by a lightweight magnetic recorder that is physically separate from the camera although often linked to it for purposes of SYNCHRONIZATION. See SINGLE-SYSTEM SOUND.

Downlink, Uplink ➤ The Uplink is the transmission from the GROUND STATION to the Satellite; the Downlink is the transmission from the Satellite to the Ground Station or home antenna. See HOP, DOWNLINK.

Download, Upload ⇒ You Download a computer file from a host machine to your local machine; you Upload a file from your local machine to the host.

Downmix, Upmix ⇒ Downmixing is the technique of reducing a multi-channel SURROUND-SOUND mix (usually 5.1) to two stereo outputs. A standard feature of DVD-VIDEO, which can do the downmixing in real time during playback. See DVD-AUDIO. In an Upmix the 5.1 channels are synthesized from an original stereo signal.

Downsample ⇒ See RESAMPLING.

DP ⇒ Slang for Director of Photography, or CINEMATOGRAPHER.

DPI ⇒ Dots Per Inch. See DIGITAL RESOLUTION.

Dramatization ⇒ A fictional representation of an actual event.

Dreamworks SKG ⇒ Founded in late 1994 by producer-director Steven Spielberg, former studio chief Jeffrey Katzenberg, and music-industry magnate David Geffen, Dreamworks SKG is the latest attempt at creating a new Hollywood studio, and thus aptly named. After toying with the idea of locating the studio on Long Island, Dreamworks bought the property in Playa del Rey CA where Howard Hughes had built his Spruce Goose. The old aircraft hangars would have served well as sound stages, but Dreamworks abandoned the planned construction in 1999 after years of battling with environmental interests intent on preserving local wetlands. Compare UNITED ARTISTS, ORION, TRISTAR.

Drive-In ⇒ Popular in the 1950s and early sixties, Drive-in movies combined America's twin passions at the time—cars and movies—at the same time that they offered a generation of repressed adolescents a little date-night privacy. By the 1970s Drive-ins were in rapid decline as cars got smaller and the acres of real estate required to accommodate a profitable audience proved more valuable as shopping malls—the social institution that replaced the Drive-in as the meeting place for suburban teenagers.

Drop-In ⇒ A short SYNDICATED television program sold by distributors to be dropped in to news, sports, interview, or other magazine shows. An *Insert Program*.

Drop-Out ⇒ Degradation of the electronic signal on a videotape, usually caused by dirt on the tape or an uneven coating, which reveals itself as lines or spots on the screen. The electronic equivalent of dirt or scratches on a film.

DS ⇒ Direct Stream. See CDMA.

DSB ⇒ Direct Satellite Broadcasting. For many years satellites were used to transmit television signals between major GROUND STATIONS. A DSB system broadcasts intentionally direct to consumers. The first DSB system was launched by Japan in 1984. An attempt to duplicate this product for the U.S. failed shortly after. Rupert Murdoch's British SKY TV (now B-SKY-B) was introduced successfully in 1988. In the mid-1990s, DSB broadcasters like B-SKY-B, ASTRA in Europe, and STAR in Southeast Asia became major factors in international broadcasting. Because of the high penetration of CABLE television in the U.S., DSB has been less influential in North America, although activity picked up in the mid-1990s with the advent of DSS. Sometimes called DBS.

DSD ⇒ *Direct Stream Digital*. Sony/Philips technology for a high-quality digital audio disc CODEC to replace the PCM codec in use on CDs since 1982. Whereas traditional audio CD technology samples the signal 44,100 times per second and encodes each of these values as a 16-bit number, DSD vastly increases the SAMPLING rate to 2.8224 million times per second but stores the values as one-bit numbers. How can one-bit numbers convey any useful information? (A one-bit number has only two possible values.) The amplitude is conveyed in the density of the pulses—not their individual values! (As a result DSD is known as a PWM—Pulse Width Modulation—system.) Where did the sampling rate of 2.8224 megabits/second come from? It is exactly four times the information contained in the old system: 44.1 kilobits/second x 16 x 4. More important, it matches the data capacity of the DVD standard: 96 kilobits/second x 24. Interestingly (and not surprisingly) such extremely rapid sampling produces a signal that looks very much like an analog wave form—and is also easy to convert to analog. DSD is used for the SACD product.

DSI ⇒ Data Search Information. Indexing and other information useful for searches on a DVD-VIDEO. See PCI.

DSL ⇒ Digital Subscriber Line. The phone companies' answer to CABLE MODEMS. See ADSL, SDSL, HDSL2.

DSP ⇒ (1) Digital Signal Processor. A MICROPROCESSOR dedicated to processing digital signals, usually audio and video. (2) Digital Sound Processing. Uncommunicative label for circuitry or software that adds artificial ROOM SOUND to the SOUNDSTAGE.

DSR ⇒ Digital Satellite Radio.

DSS ⇒ (1) Digital Satellite System. The digital DSB product, introduced in 1994 in the U.S. by DirecTV, a unit of Hughes Aerospace, which manufactured the satellite. DirecTV soon found competition from *USSB* (US Satellite Broadcasting) who later merged with *PrimeStar*. As the first exploitation of digital video (DV) technology in consumer markets, DSS met with quick success: two million dishes were sold in the first two years. Broadcasting began using MPEG-1; MPEG-2 became the standard in 1996. (2) In the U.K.,

Domestic Satellite Service, introduced by the Broadcasting Act of 1990.

DTH ➻ In the U.K., Direct-To-Home satellite television.

DTMF ➻ Dual Tone MultiFrequency. The *Touchtone* system of telephone signaling that began to replace the Pulse system beginning in the 1960s. Invented by an engineer named Schenker in the early sixties at Bell Labs, this system, as its name indicates, combines two tones chosen from seven frequencies to code numbers. The three vertical columns and four horizontal rows of the typical telephone keypad visualized the DTMF system: each column and each row has its own frequency; two tones are necessary to specify a key. Is it a coincidence Schenker hit on this idea just at the time grade schools were introducing the "New Math," with its emphasis on set theory? Was this the tiny seed from which the spreadsheet grew? In any event, besides being an enormous productivity tool (DTMF saves me about twenty-five hours per year over pulse dialing), Schenker's scheme remains one of the most elegantly simple inventions of the century. It should be noted that the enormous time savings from DTMF dialing were effective only in the 1970s and 1980s. By the early nineties, the time wasted from computerized response systems (IVR) and voicemail quickly obliterated the hundreds of megahours of annual savings from DTMF: What technology giveth, technology taketh away.

DTP ➻ See DESKTOP PUBLISHING.

DTS ➻ A theatrical digital sound system developed by Digital Theater Systems. The 5.1 or 7.1 channels are encoded with a high-bit-rate algorithm and stored on a CD-ROM which is synced with a TIMECODE printed on the film between the analog track and the picture. Introduced in *Jurassic Park* (1993). Like SDDS and DOLBY DIGITAL DTS uses compression techniques but accepts a higher bit rate. In 1998 the DTS system was adopted for some HIGH-END 5.1 audio CDs for the consumer market. It is also an option for DVD-VIDEO. The DTS discs require special DTS decoder hardware. DTS fans like the system for its higher bit rate. Compare HDCD, DAD, DVD-AUDIO, MLP.

DTS Digital Surround ➻ The consumer version of DTS.

DTV ➻ (1) Generally, DIGITAL TeleVision in all its forms. (2) Specifically, the wide array of U.S. digital broadcast formats devised by the GRAND ALLIANCE and mandated by the FCC. These formats involve combinations of standard aspect ratio (4:3) and widescreen (16:9); a variety of vertical resolutions from 480 (similar to analog NTSC) to 1080; the choice between progressive and interlaced SCANNING; and the choice of three frame rates: 60, 30, and 24 frames/sec. When you do all the permutations of these four variables you get eighteen possible standards! Shorthand for these various formats links the vertical resolution with the scanning method: 1080I, for example, is 1,080 lines of vertical resolution with interlaced scanning. See DV, EDTV, IDTV, ATV, HDTV. (2) See DESKTOP VIDEO.

Dub ⇒ (1) (v) To rerecord dialogue in a language other than the original. (2) (v) To record dialogue or sound effects in a specially equipped studio after the film has been shot. See LOOPING. (3) (n) A copy of a tape or disc: a "dupe," or duplicate. (4) (v) To copy. See WINDOW DUB.

Dumont ⇒ Founded by television inventor Allen B. Dumont in 1946, the Dumont NETWORK never succeeded in garnering a sufficient number of affiliates to survive. It ceased operations in 1955 as ABC rose to the number three position. See FOX.

Dupe ⇒ (1) To print a duplicate negative from a positive print. Also, to print a duplicate REVERSAL print. (2) A print made in this manner. See GENERATION.

DV ⇒ (1) Digital Video in all its forms, including, but not limited to, DSS, DVD, ATV, HDTV, and DVC. Because the digitization of video is several magnitudes more complicated than the digitization of audio, the introduction of DV trailed the debut of digital audio on the CD by fifteen years—ten MOORE'S LAW cycles. (2) The format for consumer-oriented digital videotape introduced in 1995.

DVB ⇒ The set of standards for European Digital Video Broadcasting established by the European Broadcasting Union (EBU) beginning in 1995. DVB-S is the subset of standards for satellite broadcasting; DVB-C is the subset for cable transmission; and DVB-T for terrestrial transmission. Compare ATV.

DVC ⇒ Digital Video Camera, the set of technologies developing as both still photography and motion picture cinematography become DIGITAL. See DVCAM, DVCPRO.

DVCAM ⇒ SONY's professional digital videocassette format, introduced in 1996. See D-1, D-2; compare DVCPRO.

DVCPRO ⇒ MATSUSHITA's digital videocassette format. Compare DVCAM.

DVD ⇒ The name for the new generation of CD-ROM technology. (After arguing whether the letters were an acronym for "Digital Video Disc" or "Digital Versatile Disc," the industry decided in 1998 to let "DVD" stand simply for itself.) The impetus for the development of the format had been the desire to do for (or to) video recording what had been done for (or to) audio recording with the conversion to digital CD in the early 1980s. Recording video digitally requires not only vastly increased storage, but also advanced compression algorithms. Competing technologies introduced by

SONY/PHILIPS and TIME WARNER/Toshiba in early 1995 were combined in the fall of that year to assure a standard which was backward compatible at the same time that it allowed maximum capacity (18.8 gigabytes).

The increased storage capacity of the DVD format results principally from using a shorter wavelength laser that can write and read many more pits (and bits) per square inch. A single-sided, single-layer basic DVD holds approximately 4.7 gigabytes (more than seven times the capacity of the CD that preceded it). But the standard allows for two layers and double-sided discs, as well, so the theoretical maximum capacity is 18.8 gigabytes. DVD-VIDEO players built to be connected to television sets were introduced to the market in early 1997; DVD-ROM drives for computers started shipping in quantity in late 1998. In addition to DVD-Video and DVD-ROM, there are three other "books" in the DVD specification: DVD-R, DVD-RAM, and DVD-RW—with DVD-AUDIO on the way as of mid-1999. By late 1998 three forms of DVD discs were being manufactured: single-layer, single-sided (DVD-5, 4.7 GB); single-layer, double-sided (DVD-10, 9.4 GB); and single-sided, double-layer (DVD-9, 8.5 GB).

DVD-Audio ➺ The proposed application of DVD technology to replace the ubiquitous audio CD. As of mid-1999, no standard had been agreed upon. Sony and Philips were pushing for a backward compatible, single-inventory format: one layer of the disc would include the old CD format while a second layer would offer the higher quality DVD-Audio format. They called this SACD for "Super Audio Compact Disc." Other companies (JVC, Matsushita, Pioneer, Toshiba, Warner) were resisting this eminently sensible approach. The DVD-Audio standard they proposed was entirely scalable: the sampling frequency, word length, and number of channels for any disc would be decided by the producer. Six sampling frequencies were proposed: 44.1 kHz, 48 kHz, 88.2 kHz, 96 kHz, 176.4 kHz, and 192 kHz. Thus, one of these discs might include a two-channel stereo mix at 96/24 together with a 5.1-channel mix with the front channels at 96/24 and the surround channels at 4/16. Or the whole disc could be recorded 192/24 stereo, or 96/24 5.1. (5.1 surround would not be available at the 192-kHz sampling rate because the amount of data necessary would exceed the transfer rates possible.)

If the 96/24 surround configuration were chosen, the player could also downmix to stereo—with or without something called SMART technology. In order to achieve a playing time of 86 minutes of 6-channel 96/24 audio, the proposed standard uses Meridian Audio's Meridian Lossless Packing (MLP) compression. Having aggrandized the video real estate on the DVD disc, DVD-Audio is not content to give up visuals entirely. The standard includes potential onscreen menus, still images, lyrics, and even low-quality video—assuming you play the disc on a DVD-Video player attached to a monitor. First- and second-generation DVD-Video players would not be able to play these discs.

What drives these desperate standards wars? As expert Robert Harley has pointed out, Sony and Philips still derive significant revenue from CD patents, while the Toshiba-Warner group owns potentially lucrative DVD patents. By the time you read this one group or the other may have won, or—more likely—consumers will declare a plague on both their houses and glom on to low-quality MP3, free on the Web. Since the basic DVD standard includes AC-3 audio, which is the state of the art at the turn of the century, one wonders whether a separate audio format is even necessary: just listen, don't watch! In mid–1998 Classic Records adopted this approach for their DAD discs. See HDCD, SACD, DSD.

DVD Books ➻ As for CD-ROM, the standards for DVD are contained in a set of "books," but the DVD books are colorless. Book A: DVD-ROM. Book B: DVD-VIDEO. Book C: DVD-AUDIO. Book D: DVD-R (write-once). Book E: DVD-RAM (rewritable). Compare CD STANDARDS, SCARLET BOOK.

DVD-R ➻ Recordable DVD format. Not to be confused with DVD-RAM.

DVD-RAM ➻ An application of DVD technology that provides a simple backup system. Capacity is on the order of 5 gigabytes. DVD-RAM drives read from and write to special DVD discs housed in cartridges. They are incompatible with DVD-ROM, DVD-VIDEO, DVD-R, and DVD-RW discs.

DVD-ROM ➻ The application of DVD technology to the medium formerly known as CD-ROM. The greater storage capacity of DVD discs allows far better video and audio content using MPEG-2 and AC-3 and other advanced CODECS. DVD-ROM players are attached to computers.

DVD-RW ➻ Recordable and rewritable DVD Format. Not to be confused with DVD-RAM.

DVD Second Generation ➻ Second Generation players were introduced less than eighteen months after the technology debuted. The main difference is speed: 2.642 megabytes/sec transfer rates (precisely 22.16 megabits/sec) rather than the 1.321 megabytes/sec transfer rate (11.08 megabits/sec) of first generation players. In addition the second-generation players can play DVD-R discs.

DVD-Video ➻ The application of DVD technology meant to replace VHS videotape recorders as a playback medium. DVD-Video machines are attached to television sets and offer some limited interactivity: you can change camera angles, film formats, soundtracks, and the like. The standard allows for up to nine camera angles, eight language soundtracks, 32 subtitle tracks, 4:3 or 16:9 aspect ratios, multiple story sequences (and, hence, multiple rating versions), parental locking, REGION CODES, and multiple audio protocols. The standard for video on DVD-Video is MPEG-2. The audio standard is AC-3, although MPEG-2 and PCM audio are also allowed. DVD-Video can accommodate 8 channels of linear PCM audio, 5.1 channels of AC-3, or 7.1 channels of MPEG-2 audio. Compare DIVX.

DVD-Video Disc Formats ➻ There are codes for the various formats of DVD discs: DS-DL, DS-SL, DS-RSDL, SS-DL, SS-SL, SS-RSDL. SS is Single-Sided; DS is Double-Sided; SL is Single-Layered; DL is Dual-Layered; RS is Reverse Spiral. When a disc is formatted with Reverse Spiral the second layer starts where the first layer ends so that the head can pick it up almost immediately without having to pause to move back to the beginning of the disc.

DVD-Video Frame Rates ➻ The DVD-VIDEO specification supports three frame rates: 24 frames/sec progressive from film, 25 frames/sec interlaced from PAL or SECAM video, and 29.97 frames/sec interlaced from NTSC video. How does the television monitor deal with the 24 frames/sec progressive frame rate? The MPEG-2 coding flags the video stream to tell the decoder in the DVD-Video player to perform a translation on the fly. For NTSC, this is the traditional 3:2 PULLDOWN that converts 24 frames/sec progressive to 30 frames/sec interlaced. For PAL/SECAM systems, it is a 2:2 PULLDOWN, which means there is a four percent increase in speed. (Believe it or not, this is the norm for European television.) This system has an interesting side effect: when a DVD-Video is played on a computer rather than a television set there is no need to perform either the 3:2 pulldown for NTSC or the four percent speedup for PAL/SECAM so movies are more clearly and more accurately displayed on a computer. (The computer can also do line-doubling to improve the picture.) I am indebted to Jim Taylor for this insight. See TELEVISION STANDARDS.

DVE ➻ Digital Video Effects. Realtime effects created in a buffer, such as zooms, repositions, freezes, and warps.

D-VHS ➻ Digital VHS for consumer use.

DVI ➻ Digital Video Interactive. A technology developed by RCA in the late 1980s for storing video on CD-ROMs. DVI comprised four specifications: a custom chip set, a runtime software interface, audio and video data file formats, and compression algorithms.

DX ⇒ HAM shorthand for long-distance radio signals and hence the hobby of searching for them.

Dye Sublimation, Dye Sub ⇒ A high quality color printing process in which CMYK dyes are transferred from a plastic film to coated paper and then vaporized. Compare THERMAL WAX, SOLID INK.

Dye Transfer ⇒ A system of printing film used in the TECHNICOLOR process in which inklike dyes are applied to the FILMSTOCK in a manner similar to PLANOGRAPHIC printing.

Dynabook ⇒ Researcher Alan Kay's early 1970s vision of a portable ELECTRONIC BOOK. Compare MEMEX.

E

Early Fringe ⇒ See FRINGE.

Eastmancolor ⇒ The color FILMSTOCK now used almost universally, it employs a chemical process, not a DYE-TRANSFER process like its predecessor, TECHNICOLOR. There are many companies that process Eastman stock in their own ways, but the differences are minimal. The product was introduced in 1950 and was quickly adopted by the industry, ushering in the age of the color standard in movies. But the chemistry of early Eastmancolor was inferior to Technicolor and many of the early negatives have faded badly. The EXR series, with a finer grain, was introduced in 1989. It included KEYKODE barcoding to facilitate increasingly important film-to-tape transfers. In 1996 Eastman Kodak switched branding for their professional filmstocks with the introduction of the "Kodak Vision" series, with even finer grain.

EBU ⇒ The European Broadcasting Union, the organization charged with establishing television and radio standards for the European Union. See DVB, GRAND ALLIANCE.

Écriture ⇒ The French SEMIOTIC term (literally "writing") for that quality of a work of art that is a combination of the artist's personal style and more general social, political, and historical concerns. An articulation of meaning in a particular mode or style by means of the text (novel, film, or poem, for example).

ECU ⇒ EXTREME CLOSEUP in a script. Compare ELS.

ED Beta ⇒ SONY's Extended Definition BETA format, which introduced stereo audio on FM carriers on videotape.

Eddiflex ⇒ See DIGITAL EDITING.

Edge Blanking, Edge Noise ⇒ A video signal usually includes a few pixels of black around the edge. While this Edge Blanking doesn't show up on a television monitor, it will be apparent in a digital capture. Also called Edge Noise, Overscan.

Edit Decision List ⇒ The list of TIMECODE ins and outs generated by a nonlinear, digital editing system (such as AVID) to be used later to produce the FINAL CUT on either tape or film.

Editing ⇒ See EDITOR, DIGITAL EDITING. Also: MONTAGE, DÉCOUPAGE, CONTINUITY EDITING, COMPOSITING, CONFORMING.

Editor ⇒ The cutter. The person who helps determine the narrative structure of a film, in charge of the work of splicing the shots of a film together into final form. See MONTAGE, FINE CUT, ROUGH CUT.

EDL ⇒ EDIT DECISION LIST. In tape or DIGITAL EDITING, a list of starting and ending points for all audio and video segments to be used in the final edit.

EDTV ⇒ Enhanced Definition TeleVision uses more modern encoding and transmission systems to enhance the quality of the television image while maintaining backward compatibility with NTSC. A transitional technology. See HDTV.

Educational Television ⇒ The movement to use television for educational purposes began in April 1954 with the founding of WQED-TV in Pittsburgh, the first community-sponsored educational station, which began telecasting classes to elementary schools in 1955. A loose confederation of educational stations became the formal PBS network in 1969.

EEPROM ⇒ Electronically Erasable, Programmable Read-Only Memory. A ROM that can be erased electronically and reprogrammed. Compare PROM, EPROM.

Effects Track ⇒ The soundtrack on which the sound effects are recorded prior to MIXING.

EFM ⇒ See EIGHT-TO-FOURTEEN MODULATION.

EFM Plus ⇒ See EIGHT-TO-SIXTEEN MODULATION.

EHF ⇒ Extremely High Frequency band. See ELECTROMAGNETIC SPECTRUM.

Eidophor ⇒ Video projection system for large screens, as in movie theaters.

Eight-to-Fourteen Modulation ⇒ In order to increase the amount of information that an audio CD can hold, the coding system requires that transitions from pits to lands (and vice versa) carry the binary information rather than the actual pits and lands themselves. In other words, instead of ones being represented by pits and zeros being represented by lands, a one is represented not by a pit, but by the transition from pit to land or land to pit. Even though there appear to be two different transitional states, they both look the same to the laser reader, so only one value can be represented. Since only one value can be represented, the ones must be separated by zeroes. Of course, the original digital binary signal has a great many pairs of ones. The simple but ingenious system of Eight-to-Fourteen Modulation divides the 16-bit sample in half, then inserts zeroes in each 8-bit half so that no two ones are adjacent. The result is a 14-bit value. As it happens, nine different pit transition lengths result.

Eight-to-Sixteen Modulation ≫ The variant of Eight-to-Fourteen Modulation used for DVD. Also called *EFM Plus*.

Electromagnetic Spectrum ≫ The entire range of radiation extending in frequency from 0 Hertz (cycles per second) to 10^{23} Hertz and including cosmic rays, gamma rays, X rays, ultraviolet rays, visible light, infrared rays, microwaves, radio waves, heat, and electric currents. The usable radio spectrum has been defined as ranging from about 10 kiloHertz (10,000 cycles per second) to 300,000 megaHertz (300,000 million cycles per second) and includes the following areas: very low frequency (*VLF*): 10 to 30 kHz; low frequency (*LF*): 30 to 300 kHz; medium frequency (*MF*): 300 to 3,000 kHz; high frequency (*HF*): 3,000 to 30,000 kHz; very high frequency (*VHF*): 30 to 300 MHz; ultra high frequency (*UHF*): 300 to 3,000 MHz; super high frequency (*SHF*): 3,000 to 30,000 MHz; and extremely high frequency (*EHF*): 30,000 to 300,000 MHz. AM radio transmitters operate in the medium frequency band; FM radio, and television channels 2 through 13, in the very high frequency band; and television channels 14 through 83 in the ultra high frequency band. See Radio Bands, Satellite Bands.

Electron Gun ≫ The device in a Cathode Ray Tube that supplies the electron beam.

Electronic Book ≫ (1) Sony's brand name for the discs that play in the Data Discman. (2) By extension, any computer disc meant to be used as a book. The idea that a book experience could be delivered electronically has been around at least since the mid-1940s when physicist Vannevar Bush proposed the Memex. In the early 1970s, Alan Kay at Xerox PARC dubbed this ideal device the Dynabook. In the early 1990s, Sony tried to market several variations (the Data Discman, the Bookman) which used mini-CD technology, but the screens were too small and lacked sufficient resolution.

At the same time, Bob Stein at Voyager produced a series of books converted into Hypercard stacks and delivered on diskettes. Late nineties laptops and PDAs fulfill some of the functions Kay envisioned for the Dynabook. In 1998 John Warnock's Octavo company began an ambitious program of transferring rare books to CD-ROM with high resolution. The real fulfillment of the Dynabook dream, however, will have to wait for vast improvements in screen technology. The resolution of the average book page remains more than 30 times greater than the resolution of computer screens. And printed books smell and feel better, too.

Electronic Mail ⇢ A broad term to define the transmission of computer files—usually text, but also graphics and applications—via telephone lines and MODEMS or LANs, usually through a centralized HOST, or a network like the INTERNET. Throughout the 1980s and early 1990s, the lack of a universally recognized electronic mail PROTOCOL and a standardized system of host or local storage, limited the use of electronic mail to intra-company communications. The growth of the Internet in 1994 and 1995 changed all that almost overnight, finally providing the necessary common protocol. By late 1996 email was nearly ubiquitous in offices and making inroads at home as well, where parents learned to keep in touch with their wired college students via the Internet. By 1998 the newly popular medium was an important element in trials such as U.S. v Microsoft. See MIME, FAX, TELEX, SMTP.

Eliza ⇢ A computer program designed to simulate conversation, written in 1966 at MIT by Joseph Weizenbaum. Eliza was designed as a psychotherapist, the kind who asks questions more often than she makes statements: "How long have you felt this way?" Versions of Eliza (named after Eliza Dolittle from *Pygmalion*) still live on the Web. Some people think it helps to talk things out with her. See CHATTERBOT, ARTIFICIAL INTELLIGENCE.

ELS ⇢ EXTREME LONG SHOT in a script. Compare ECU.

EMail ⇢ (1) Short for ELECTRONIC MAIL. (2) (n, v) An electronic mail message, as in, "Send me an email on that."

Emmys ⇢ On the model of OSCARS, the awards presented by both the Academy of Television Arts and Sciences and the National Academy of Television Arts and Sciences (The two groups split in 1978.) Many hundreds of Emmys are awarded each year. The name supposedly comes from slang for the IMAGE ORTHICON tube.

Emoticon ⇢ See SMILEY.

Emotion Engine ⇢ SONY/Toshiba graphics chip that serves as the heart of the PLAYSTATION II. Rated at more than 6 gigaflops, the chip is several times more powerful than CPU competitors like the Pentium III.

Emulsion ⇢ The thin coating of chemicals mounted on the base of the FILMSTOCK that reacts to light.

Emulsion Speed ⇢ A measure of the sensitivity of FILMSTOCK to light. Often measured against a scale devised by the American Standards Association (ASA, now ANSI) or the DIN. The faster the speed of the emulsion, the higher the ASA number, and the greater the sensitivity to light. High-speed films generally have a rougher GRAIN than slow-speed films. See SPEED, DEFINITION, AVAILABLE-LIGHT PHOTOGRAPHY.

Encryption ⇒ Scrambling (encryption) technology was the key to the development of DSB and DSS. Cable companies could always cut the wire if you didn't pay, but how was a satellite broadcaster to charge for the service? Your individual antenna wasn't addressable. Smart card DESCRAMBLERS provided an inexpensive and versatile answer. See EUROCRYPT, VIDEOCRYPT, NAGRAVISION, SIMULCRYPT.

Endoscopy ⇒ Surgery using FIBER OPTICS and miniaturized instruments that allow much smaller incisions and therefore far less trauma to the body. See TELEPRESENCE.

ENG ⇒ Acronym for "Electronic News Gathering," an awkward phrase that simply means using videotape rather than film to record news events for television broadcast. See MINICAM.

Enhanced CD ⇒ Although earlier attempts at adding graphics to the standard audio CD had failed (see CD+G, CDV), by 1995 the rapidly expanding multimedia CD-ROM industry gave birth to a new, more successful variant. The Enhanced CD stamped multisession technology, developed by PHILIPS and SONY, allows standard audio CD players to read the audio tracks on the mixed mode Enhanced CD disc while multimedia players can access video information or software as well. The problem had been that audio players were too dumb to know the difference between their own data type and others. If they played another data type as audio, the result could be noise so alien it could damage speakers. The multisession format prevented this. Also known as CD+.

Enhancement ⇒ An electronic method of refining an audio or video recording or image using computer techniques. The computer extrapolates from basic information.

Entr'acte ⇒ The intermission in a long feature film, or the break between sides or discs in a LASERDISC presentation.

EON ⇒ Enhanced Other Network. An additional RDS feature, that allows switching to an Alternative Frequency during a Traffic Announcement.

Epic Theater ⇒ In Brecht's theory, theater that appeals more to the spectator's reason than to his feeling. See ESTRANGEMENT EFFECT, THEATER OF CRUELTY.

EPROM ⇒ Erasable, Programmable Read-Only Memory. A ROM that can be erased—usually by exposure to ultraviolet light—and reprogrammed. Compare PROM, EEPROM.

EQ, Equalization ⇒ The technique of boosting or lowering frequency bands in an audio signal to enhance the quality of the sound. EQ is a standard procedure in audio editing and mixing.

Erlang ➤ A dimensionless unit of telephone traffic intensity. It is numerically equal to the calling rate times the average holding time. It is named for the Norwegian telephone engineer who first popularized the concept.

ESPN ➤ Entertainment and Sports Programming Network. A cable network founded in 1979, that has enjoyed major success attracting advertisers with a wide and never-ending menu of sports events, from the ridiculous (Australian Rules Football?) to the sublime. By 1989 ESPN was strong enough to compete with the broadcast NETWORKS for NFL rights. By 1993 it was the leading cable network, accessible in 61.7 million American homes.

Establishing Shot ➤ Generally a LONG SHOT that shows the audience the general location of the scene that follows, often providing essential information, and orienting the viewer.

Estrangement Effect ➤ Verfremdungseffekt. Essential to Brecht's theory of theater, it keeps both audience and actors intellectually separate from the action of the drama. It provides intellectual distance. See EPIC THEATER.

Ethernet ➤ This protocol for Local Area Networks was devised by Bob Metcalfe in 1973. By the late 1980s it had become the dominant standard for networking office PCs. At first Ethernet required fairly expensive COAXIAL CABLE installations, but by the mid-1980s it was running on cheaper TWISTED PAIR and could thus be integrated with the office telephone network. Two flavors of Ethernet are now common: *10Base-T* runs at 10 megabits/sec. *100Base-T* runs at 100 megabits/sec. What the INTERNET did for the world, Ethernet did for the office. See LAN.

ETSI ➤ European Telecommunications Standards Institute, an international standards body comparable to ANSI.

ETV ➤ See EDUCATIONAL TELEVISION.

Eurocrypt ➤ SMART-CARD-based ENCRYPTION system for DSB used with many MAC transmissions. See VIDEOCRYPT, NAGRAVISION.

EutelSat ➤ Organisation Européenne de Télécommunication par Satellite. A rival to ASTRA.

Everson/Michelson Dichotomy ➤ In American CINEMA STUDIES, the debate between those who put the Cinema first (the Eversonian tradition) and those who put the Studies first (the Michelsonian approach). Perhaps best considered as an academic reduction of the central question posed not so rhetorically by François Truffaut in Day for Night ("Are films more important than life?"), the Everson/Michelson Dichotomy has driven the development of the Cinema Studies business since the 1960s. At its best, the Eversonian tradition celebrates the fact of movies; at its worst, it ignores the art of spectatorship. At its best, the Michelsonian approach empowers the spectator; at its worst, it smothers films in a thick coat of critical cant. Named after two longtime professors at NYU's Cinema Studies Department, William K. Everson, the revered archivist and historian, and Annette Michelson, one of the first film academicians.

EVR ⇒ Electronic Video Recording. A system combining electronic and film techniques for home playback, invented by Peter Goldmark at CBS in the 1960s; a curious predecessor to videocassettes. Discontinued in 1972. See POLAVISION.

Excite! ⇒ See SEARCH ENGINES.

Exciter Lamp ⇒ The light source for the optical sound head that reads a film SOUNDTRACK.

Executive Producer ⇒ See PRODUCER.

Exhibition ⇒ The final link in the theatrical film entertainment chain. See FIRST RUN, GENERAL RELEASE, SHOWCASE, FOUR-WALLING, DAY AND DATING, BLIND BIDDING, BLOCK BOOKING, GO WIDE, PLATFORMING.

Exploitation Film ⇒ A film designed to profit by serving a particular need or desire of the audience. Examples: SEXPLOITATION, BLAXPLOITATION. The term usually has a negative connotation.

Explorer ⇒ Microsoft's Internet Explorer BROWSER. See NETSCAPE.

Export-Union ⇒ Export-Union des Deutschen Films, the German equivalent of UNIFRANCE and UNITALIA.

Exposure ⇒ A measure of the amount of light striking the surface of the film. Film can be intentionally overexposed to give a very light, washed-out, dreamy quality to the print image, or it can be underexposed to make the image darker, muddy, and foreboding. See DEVELOPMENT.

Exposure Latitude ⇒ A measure of a FILMSTOCK's flexibility in regard to EXPOSURE.

Expressionism ⇒ Generally, the kind of film style, borrowing from movements in painting and literature early in the twentieth century, that allows liberal use of technical devices and artistic distortion in order to evoke the emotional state of the characters and in which the art of the medium is always obvious and carries the meaning of the film. See GERMAN EXPRESSIONISM, REALISM, NEOREALISM, FORMALISM.

EXR ⇒ See EASTMANCOLOR.

EXT ⇒ EXTerior, or outdoors, in a script. Compare INT.

Extra ⇒ A minor actor without dialogue. Compare CHARACTER ACTOR.

Extravision ⇒ The CBS TELETEXT system of the early 1980s, now defunct.

Extreme Closeup ⇒ See DETAIL SHOT.

Extreme Long Shot ➻ A panoramic view of an exterior location photographed from a considerable distance, often as far as a quarter mile away. See also ESTABLISHING SHOT.

Eyeline Match ➻ An editing rule: the alternation of two shots, the first showing a character looking off-screen, the second showing what he's looking at. A rough sense of scale and distance is kept, but not necessarily perspective—that is, every POINT-OF-VIEW SHOT is an eyeline match, but every eyeline match is not necessarily a POV shot.

E-Zine ➻ See ZINE.

Facsimile ➻ To everyone else in the world, it's a FAX, but to lawyers it's a facsimile. This is interesting. Lawyers always strive for linguistic precision. It's true that the root of the word "fax" is "facsimile." But why use the ambiguous root when the precise derivation is available—and widely understood? Because lawyers traditionally charge for normal office procedures that every other profession absorbs as a regular expense of doing business. You can't put a "fax" on an invoice: it's not formal enough.

Fade-In, Fade-Out ➻ A punctuation device. In a Fade-In, the screen is black at the beginning; gradually the image appears, brightening to full strength. The opposite happens in a Fade-Out. You can fade to a color other than black, too. See DISSOLVE, IRIS-IN, FOCUS-IN.

Fairness Filler ➻ NBC executive Reuven Frank's phrase in the 1970s for the supposedly "objective" material—statements of opposing opinions, for example—introduced into network television documentaries ostensibly to satisfy the FCC's fairness doctrine. The result is a false sense of objectivity.

Fanning ➻ Actors and others in the entertainment business sometimes hire others to act like fans—screaming and carrying on to draw attention. The demonstration is known as Fanning. The practice goes back more than a hundred years to the CLAQUES that opera stars used to hire to follow them around.

FantaSound ➻ Perhaps the earliest instance of SURROUND SOUND, this system was devised by RCA for Disney's *Fantasia* in 1940. Three optical soundtracks were used for left, center, and right speakers and signals were synthesized from these three tracks for other speakers in the theater. The aim was to reproduce the orchestral experience. Compare PERSPECTASOUND.

Fast Fourier Transform ➻ Baron Joseph von Fourier posited that any complex sine wave could be described by a series of trigonometric functions. (This is a Fourier Series.) The necessary calculations can be done in REAL TIME by a computer, producing a Fast Fourier Transform (an FFT), a graph that is useful to analyze the frequency response of audio equipment.

Fast Motion ➻ Also called accelerated motion. The film is shot at a speed of less than 24 frames/sec so that when it is projected at the normal speed, actions appear to move much faster. The camera is UNDERCRANKED. Often useful for comic effect.

Fax ➻ From "facsimile." A key technology in the history of the digital revolution, the fax machine, which digitizes an image of a printed page, then transmits it via modem from one SCANNER/printer to another. The resolution of current Group IV fax machines is as much as 200 dots per inch. Although in existence since the 1950s, fax did not become the preferred means of textual telecommunications until 1988. Compare TELEX, ELECTRONIC MAIL.

FBC ➻ Fox Broadcasting Corporation; see FOX.

FCC ➻ Federal Communications Commission. The independent government oversight agency established by the U.S. Congress in 1934 to regulate both broadcast and wired communications.

F-Connector ➻ See PLUGS.

FDDI ➻ Fiber Distributed Data Interface, a high-speed network data distribution system based on fiber-optic cable.

FDM ➻ Frequency Division Multiplexing. See CDMA.

Feature ➻ (1) The main film of a multifilm program. (2) Any film considered to be full-length, defined by the MPAA for theatrical distribution as 82 minutes or more. Compare PROGRAMMER, SHORT, FEATURETTE.

Featurette ➻ A twenty- or thirty-minute film meant to accompany a FEATURE. Until the 1960s, a show at your local movie house might include a newsreel, a Featurette, a Short Subject, a Cartoon, as well as the main Feature and, of course, TRAILERS for "coming attractions." All that remains now, are the Feature and the trailers—now repositioned as "PREVIEWS."

Feed ➻ The transmission of a television or radio program from network headquarters to individual stations, from which it is then BROADCAST.

Feedback ➻ (1) A basic phenomenon of electronic technology: in any system that has both input and output, the return of some of the output to the input. Sometimes useful for amplification and other applications. More often a problem in audio when the output is in a loop with the input and a loud high-pitched whine is the result. (2) Response to communication, as in, "Did we get any feedback on that article?" See DISTRIBUTION FLOW.

Feminist Film Theory ⇒ Since the early 1970s, feminist critics and academics have produced a sizable body of writing examining the representation of women on the screen, celebrating women filmmakers, and theorizing about female spectatorship. The feminist movement in film theory was important within the POSTSTRUCTURALIST and POSTMODERN critical debates.

Femto ⇒ Standard prefix for a quadrillionth (U.S.), as in "femtosecond": 0.000000000000001 (10^{-15}) of a second. See also MICRO, NANO, PICO.

FFT ⇒ See FAST FOURIER TRANSFORM.

FG ⇒ Foreground.

FH ⇒ Frequency Hopping. See CDMA.

FIAF ⇒ Féderation Internationale des Archives du Film. The international organization of FILM ARCHIVES, founded in 1938 with more than one hundred member institutions in sixty countries.

Fiber Optics ⇒ A distribution technology for a radio, television, telephone, or data signal that imposes that signal on a visible light CARRIER WAVE. The light beam is generated by a LASER and carried by a thin glass filament, much narrower than a human hair. Because light wavelengths are very much shorter than radio wavelengths, they can carry much greater amounts of information. In addition, the very small width of the glass fiber means that thousands can be bundled together in the space taken up by traditional electronic TWISTED PAIR or COAXIAL CABLE. See CABLE TELEVISION, WAVE MECHANICS, PHOTONICS.

Field ⇒ (1) In television, one of two equal parts into which a frame is divided in interlaced scanning. See RASTER. (2) In DATABASE design, each record is divided into fields.

File Formats ⇒ See TEXT FILE FORMATS, IMAGE FILE FORMATS, MOVIE FILE FORMATS.

Fill Light, Filler Light ⇒ An auxiliary light, usually from the side of the subject, that can soften shadows and illuminate areas not covered by the KEY LIGHT.

Fill Rate ⇒ This is the same as DATA RATE, but measured in PIXELS per second rather than bits per second. The term is used in the video game industry.

Film Archives ⇒ As national libraries are to books, film archives are to film. In the U.S., the Library of Congress serves as the ultimate film archive. In France, it is the CINÉMATHÈQUE FRANÇAISE. See FIAF.

Film Chain ⇒ A device that converts 24-frames/sec film into 30-frames/sec video. Digital video has proved very useful in rationalizing this process. See TELECINE, 3:2 PULL-DOWN.

Film Clip ⇒ A short section of film taken out of context. A "quote."

Film d'Art ⇒ The early movement in French film to produce records of more respectable stage productions. See ART FILM.

Film Gauge ⇒ Filmstock is made in various widths, measured in millimeters: 35 mm stock is the standard for commercial feature films; 65 mm and 70 mm stocks have been used for major epic WIDE-SCREEN productions; 16 mm stock is the standard for most of the rest of the industry; 8 mm stock has been limited to amateur use. Super 8 mm and Super 16 mm greatly increase the available picture area in their respective gauges by making sprocket holes smaller or by eliminating one of the two rows of sprockets.

Film Noir ⇒ Originally a French term (literally "black film"), now in common use, to indicate a film with a gritty, urban setting that deals mainly with dark or violent passions in a downbeat way. Especially common in American cinema during the late forties and early fifties, its themes of existential alienation and paranoia have often been read as signs of postwar malaise and Cold War anxiety.

Film Recorder ⇒ A machine for transferring a digital image to film using either a CRT or LASER as the light source. See CINEON, FILM SCANNER, TELECINE.

Film Scanner ⇒ A machine for capturing a digital image from film generally using a CCD array to capture the image. See CINEON, FILM RECORDER, TELECINE.

Film Strip ⇒ An education technology of the mid-twentieth century that provided an efficient and effective way to present a SLIDE SHOW. The "slides" were just frames on a piece of 35 mm film that was advanced by a ratchet. The slides were never out of order, reversed, or upside-down!

Film Theory ⇒ Consideration of such questions as "What is cinema?" "How do we know cinema?" and "What are the effects of cinema?" Issues in academic film theory include: the nature and ideology of style, representation, and spectatorship. Some of the more important theories of film have been put forth by philosophers, cultural historians, and art critics as well as by filmmakers themselves.

Filmic Space ⇒ The power of the film medium that makes possible the combination of shots of widely separated origins into a single framework of fictional space.

Filmography ⇒ A listing of films, on the model of "bibliography."

Filmology ➻ The study and analysis of film as a social, political, and historical phenomenon. Compare CINEMATOLOGY.

Filmstock ➻ The raw material of film. See FILM GAUGE.

Filter ➻ (1) A plate of gelatin, glass, or plastic placed in front of the lens to alter the quality of the light. (2) An electronic device that alters the quality of sound or image, or modifies the signal in some other way.

Final Cut, Fine Cut ➻ The film as it will be released, as opposed to ROUGH CUT. The guarantee of final cut assures a filmmaker that the producer will not be able to revise the film after the filmmaker has finished it.

Finale, Series or Season ➻ In 1977, the final episode of *The Mary Tyler Moore Show* became a media event that set a pattern for American television series. While the impetus for a grand Finale may have been financial—media events draw huge ratings—television artists appreciated the opportunity to provide denouements to the never-ending story-lines. By the late eighties, many series were scheduling Season Finales to boost ratings during the important May SWEEPS period. In 1998, the *Seinfeld* Series Finale set ad revenue records. Perhaps the most ingenious Series Finale, however, was the final episode of Bob Newhart's second series, in 1990. At the end of the show, Bob wakes up in bed with Suzanne Pleshette, his wife from his *first* series. It turns out the long-running second series has just been a bad dream.

Fin-Syn Rules ➻ See SYNDICATION.

Firewire ➻ The IEEE 1394 standard developed by Apple for very high-speed serial-port communications that is necessary for digital video (DV) production. The standard supports three DATA RATES (100, 200, and 400 megabits/second) and isochronous as well as asynchronous data transfer. An isochronous system maintains a constant data rate, which is very useful for audio and video data types. Up to 64 devices can be chained together. Compare USB.

First Run ➻ One of several stages of film distribution, the first run is the opening engagement, often at a limited number of theaters. A second run is often organized at a larger number of theaters. See GENERAL RELEASE, SHOWCASE, FOUR-WALLING, DAY AND DATING.

First-Run Syndication ➻ See SYNDICATION.

Fish-Eye Lens ➻ An extremely WIDE-ANGLE LENS that has an ANGLE OF VIEW approaching 180 degrees. It greatly distorts the image.

5.1 ➻ (Pronounced "five dot one.") In a 5.1 recording system six channels provide left, center, and right front channels together with left and right rear surround channels and a special effects SUBWOOFER channel (the ".1"). The surround channels should be used only to provide ROOM SOUND to increase the ambiance and enhance the SOUNDSTAGE of the music. See SURROUND SOUND.

Fixed Wireless ➻ See WIRELESS.

Flack ➻ Derogatory slang for a PRESS AGENT or PR person.

Flag ➻ A device placed in front of a light to cast a shadow. See GOBO, SCRIM.

Flare ➻ When the light source is pointed directly at the camera, the optics of the LENS often produce in the image a haze, glow, or aura known as flare.

Flash Cutting ➻ Editing into shots of very brief duration that succeed each other rapidly.

Flash Frame ➻ A shot of only a few frames' duration—sometimes a single frame—that can just barely be perceived by the audience.

Flashback ➻ A SCENE or SEQUENCE (sometimes an entire film) that is inserted into a scene in "present" time and that deals with the past. The flashback is the past tense of film narrative.

Flash-Forward ➻ On the model of FLASHBACK, scenes or shots of future time; the future tense of film narrative.

Flashing ➻ See POSTFLASHING.

Flat Field Noise ➻ Slight variation in uniform areas in a video image. Although this noise is not apparent to the eye, it does cause problems during COMPRESSION.

Flat Lighting ➻ Low CONTRAST lighting. See GAMMA, POSTFLASHING.

Flicker ➻ In film projection, a cyclical fluctuation in the intensity of the light falling on the screen, caused by the passage of the SHUTTER across the light beam. The psychological effect is caused by a projection rate of fewer frames per second than PERSISTENCE OF VISION is able to forge into a continuous image.

Flip ➻ A type of WIPE in which the images appear to be cards flipped one after another.

Flipper ➻ A DVD-VIDEO that you have to flip over to see the whole film. See REVERSE SPIRAL.

Floppy Disk ➻ Inexpensive and widespread system of computer information storage that uses magnetic recording on a thin DISK rather than on tape. The disk format offers the advantage of greatly increased accessibility. IBM introduced the 8-inch Floppy in the early 1970s. The 5 1/4-inch disk became the norm with the introduction of the microcomputer around 1980. In the mid-1980s SONY'S 3 1/2-inch diskette (introduced in 1980), now encased in rigid plastic, won out over a competing 4-inch FORM FACTOR when it was adopted for the Macintosh. It eventually became a universal standard. (Even these rigid disks are known as "floppies.")

FLOPS ⇒ FLoating-point OPerations/Second. A common gauge of CPU speed, usually measured in megaflops or gigaflops. Compare MIPS.

Flutter ⇒ See WOW.

Fly ⇒ The area above a set or stage where scenery is stored. Also a verb: to hoist scenery or props into the fly.

Flyover ⇒ Entertainment industry term for the area of the U.S. situated between the Hudson River (the western boundary of New York City) and the San Gabriel Mountains (just east of Los Angeles).

FM ⇒ Frequency Modulation, a system of broadcasting in which the PROGRAM SIGNAL is imposed on the carrier wave by modifying the frequency (or wavelength) of the carrier. See AM, WAVE MECHANICS.

FNN ⇒ Financial News Network. Pioneering business news CABLE NETWORK founded in 1981, it rode the crest of the 1980s boom before falling on hard times. It was absorbed by its competitor CNBC in February 1991.

F-Number, F-Stop ⇒ The size of the opening of the DIAPHRAGM on a camera lens. The higher the F-number, the smaller the opening, and less light entering the camera. There also exists a system of measurement in T-numbers, which is a more accurate index of the amount of light actually striking the emulsion.

Focal Length ⇒ The length of the lens, a measurement (usually in millimeters) of the distance from the center of the outside surface of the lens to the film plane. Long lenses are TELEPHOTO lenses, short lenses are WIDE-ANGLE lenses.

Focus ⇒ The overall sharpness of the image. A range of distances from the camera will be acceptably sharp. See DEPTH OF FIELD, DEEP FOCUS, SHALLOW FOCUS.

Focus-In, Focus-Out ⇒ A punctuation device. The image gradually comes into focus or goes out of focus. Compare IRIS-IN, FADE-IN.

Focus Plane ⇒ The plane in the scene being photographed upon which the lens is focused, measured as a distance from the film plane. See DEPTH OF FIELD.

Focus Pull ⇒ To refocus during a TAKE: to change the FOCUS PLANE. See RACK FOCUS, FOLLOW FOCUS.

Foley Editor ⇒ A technician who concentrates on sound effects, usually having to do with movement. (The term "Foley" became popular in the 1980s.)

Follow Focus ⇒ To PULL FOCUS during a shot in order to keep a subject in focus as it moves away from or toward the camera. See RACK FOCUS, FOLLOW SHOT.

Follow Shot ⧫→ A Tracking Shot or Zoom that follows the subject as it moves.

Font ⧫→ A style set of alphanumeric characters and symbols in a particular typeface design (for example, Times Roman Italic, Helvetica Medium, Palatino Bold). A group of style sets (for example, Roman, Italic, Bold, and Condensed) in a particular design is more properly known as a font family.

Footage ⧫→ (1) A measurement of the amount of film actually shot or to be shot. (2) "Some" film, as in "Did you see that footage of the fire on the news last night?"

Footprint ⧫→ (1) the area that a piece of electronic equipment occupies on the desktop. (2) The coverage area of a Satellite signal.

Forced Display ⧫→ Subpicture material on a DVD-Video over which the user has no control as, for example, subtitles that appeared in the original movie.

Forcing ⧫→ See Processing.

Forelengthening ⧫→ The linear distortion caused by a Wide-Angle lens: the perception of depth is exaggerated.

Foreshortening ⧫→ The distortion caused by a Telephoto lens: the illusion of depth is compressed.

Form Factor ⧫→ The general form or shape of an electronic device or product. Desktop computers and laptop computers are said to have different Form Factors, as do VHS and Beta videotapes, for example. This slightly stilted construction is necessary to draw attention to the grammar of the design: If you manufacture a VHS cassette, you had better do it according to specifications, or it won't work. If you decide to include the motherboard of the computer inside the monitor case (as the iMac does), you have invented a new Form Factor. (In this case, you've actually reinvented the original Macintosh Form Factor.) But a CD, a CD-ROM, and a DVD-Video all have the same Form Factor.

Formalism ⧫→ (1) Concern with form over content. (2) The theory that meaning exists primarily in the form or language of a discourse rather than in the explicit content or subject. (3) The Russian movement of the twenties that developed these ideas. See Expressionism.

Format ⧫→ (1) The basic structure of a radio or television program. (2) The basic orientation of a radio station: Rock, Classical, All-News, Country, Talk, Educational, and the like. (3) A system of information storage, such as Disc, Tape. See Form Factor.

Formative Theory ⧫→ Theory that deals with form rather than function or subject.

Forms, Open and Closed ➻ Closed forms suggest that the limits of the FRAME are the limits of artistic reality, while open forms suggest that reality continues outside the frame.

FORTRAN ➻ See COMPUTER LANGUAGES.

44/16 ➻ Shorthand for 44.1 kiloHertz 16-bit encoding, the standard for audio CDs. Compare 96/24, DSD.

Found Footage ➻ The use of previously filmed material, sometimes purposely "found" within another film. Less concern is paid to placing the footage in its historical context than in a COMPILATION FILM. Avant-garde filmmakers like Bruce Conner, Joseph Cornell, Kenneth Anger, and Ken Jacobs made liberal use of found footage.

4:4:4, 4:2:2, 4:2:0, 4:1:1 ➻ See COLOR-DIFFERENCE SAMPLING.

Fourier Series ➻ See Fast Fourier Transform.

Four-Walling ➻ The practice of renting a film theater outright at a fixed rate rather than sharing in the proceeds with the owner or operator of the theater.

FOX ➻ (1) Founded in 1986 by film distributor TWENTIETH CENTURY FOX, this attempt at a fourth American television network enjoyed remarkable success, thanks in large part to the fluidity of the television broadcast network business in the late 1980s and 1990s as CABLE TELEVISION grew in importance, but also because of canny programming strategies devised by Fox chief Barry Diller, who attacked one night at a time rather than spreading product thinly throughout the entire PRIMETIME schedule. In January 1994 the network marked its maturity by beating CBS in the bidding for a National Football League contract. See WB, UPN. (2) Short for TWENTIETH CENTURY FOX studio.

Fox Movietone ➻ The brand name for TWENTIETH CENTURY FOX'S successful newsreel series. See MOVIETONE.

FPS ➻ (1) Frames Per Second. (2) Feet Per Second.

FR-3 ➻ The third French television network, formed in the 1970s after the breakup of the state-owned system.

Fractal ➻ A geometry devised in 1977 by mathematician Benoit Mandelbrot that suggests that patterns in images (as well as in the natural world) can be described as progressively more detailed repetitions of themselves. The result is an algorithm that allows for powerful COMPRESSION techniques as well as attractive and interesting DIGITAL graphics.

Frame ➻ (1) Any single image on the film. (2) The size and shape of the image on the film, or on the screen when projected. (3) The compositional unit of film design. See FORMS, OPEN AND CLOSED. (4) In traditional television, two FIELDS, which produce a complete television image.

Frame Grabber ⇒ Software that can accomplish a realtime capture of a single video frame.

Frame Rates ⇒ In silent days, when cameras were often hand-cranked, the frame rate was an artistic variable. Although the standard was 16 frames per second—just fast enough to avoid FLICKER—the cameraman often OVERCRANKED or UNDERCRANKED intentionally for effect. Early projectionists also enjoyed this artistic freedom at the other end of the process, responding to their audiences in a way that has been impossible since. With the advent of sound, the frame rate needed to be standardized (so that the sound would be in sync with the image). The chosen rate—24 frames per second—must have seemed luxuriously hi-tech to filmmakers of the time: after all, it required 50 percent more filmstock than the silent standard. Although the inventors of television adopted Hollywood's ACADEMY APERTURE as the ASPECT RATIO of the new medium, they found it much simpler to tie the Frame Rate to the frequency of the alternating current that drove the electronics.

Thus, in the U.S. and Japan, where 60 Hertz current is the standard, the television frame rate is 30 frames per second. (Although in common parlance we say NTSC video's frame rate is 30 frames/sec, in fact it is 29.97 frames/sec). In Europe, AC runs at 50 Hertz and the frame rate is 25 frames per second. In PAL/SECAM countries, film destined for television is shot at 25 frames so that it matches frame for frame. In NTSC countries, however, film has to be run through a FILM CHAIN to be converted to the television frame rate. The SHOWSCAN projection system, which runs at 60 frames per second, has demonstrated how much value a higher frame rate can add to the cinematic experience. Now, as we enter the age of digital HDTV, we are about to regain some of the flexibility that was lost in 1929. The REFRESH RATE of a computer monitor (which is not quite the same thing as a Frame Rate) can range from 60 frames per second to 80 and higher. Moreover, it is often adjustable. See PAL/SECAM CHEAT.

Frame Relay ⇒ A more advanced form of X.25 PACKET-SWITCHED network technology.

Framing ⇒ The organization of the contents of a SHOT with respect to the limits of the screen. See ASPECT RATIO.

Franchise Film ⇒ A film that engenders a profitable series of sequels or SPINOFFS, or that otherwise begins a lucrative trend, such as *Nightmare on Elm Street*. The longest-running franchise is James Bond.

Free Cinema »+ The nonfiction, DOCUMENTARY movement in film in Britain in the fifties, whose theory was developed by Karel Reisz, Tony Richardson, and Lindsay Anderson.

Freeze Frame »+ A freeze shot, which is achieved by printing a single frame many times in succession to give the illusion, when projected, of a still photograph.

Frequency »+ See WAVE MECHANICS.

Frequency Doubling »+ The weakness of the NTSC television system is the relatively low vertical resolution (525 lines). LINE-DOUBLING techniques improve the quality of the picture. The weakness of the PAL and SECAM systems is the lower frequency of the signal (50 Hz). Frequency-doubling circuitry improves the quality of these pictures.

Fringe »+ In television, DAYPARTS that bracket PRIMETIME. Early Fringe is generally considered to be 5 pm to 7 or 7:30 pm; Late Fringe, 11 or 11:30 pm to midnight. See ACCESS TIME.

Fringing »+ An ARTIFACT, or inconsistency, in analog imaging. The edges of color areas are outlined or emphasized when they shouldn't be; usually caused by registration problems in the camera.

Front Projection »+ A more precise method of combining images than REAR PROJECTION. Live action is filmed against a highly reflective screen. An image from a slide or movie projector is projected on the screen by means of mirrors along the axis of the taking lens so that there are no visible shadows cast by the actors. Since the screen is exceptionally reflective, and since the live actors are well lit, no image from the projector is visible on the actors or props in front of the screen. The system was refined by Douglas Trumbull in the late 1960s for Kubrick's *2001: A Space Odyssey*. See CHROMA KEY.

FSS Band »+ See SATELLITE BANDS.

FTP »+ File Transfer Protocol, one of the basic components of the INTERNET along with HTTP and SMTP.

Full-Face Shot »+ Framing a person squarely facing the camera.

Full-Motion, Full-Screen Video »+ During the CD-ROM era, no computers had enough processing power to accommodate a DATA RATE sufficient to produce video that filled the screen and that also ran at 24- or 30-frames-per-second. You had to choose: speed or size. The advent of DVD with its much higher data rate and its MPEG-2 CODEC made full-motion, full-screen video possible for the first time.

Full Shot »+ A shot of a subject that includes the entire body and not much else. Also known as a medium long shot.

FX ➤ Hollywood lingo for SPECIAL EFFECTS, SOUND EFFECTS, OPTICALS, and DIGITAL EFFECTS.

G ➤ See GIG, GIGA.

Gaffer ➤ The chief electrician on the set; in charge of the lights. His assistant is the Best Boy.

Gaffer's Tape ➤ Two-inch wide silvery fabric-based adhesive tape used on the set to hold down wires, fix lights in the correct position, patch together broken props, tack up the lunch menu—or just about anything else. In your local hardware store they probably call it "Duct Tape," because heating and air-conditioning guys have adopted it as a quick (if sloppy) way to seal ducts. But now you know better.

Gag ➤ A joke, but more precisely a physical joke in silent films, or a "sight gag" in sound films (where it's what you see that's funny, not what you hear).

Gain ➤ Tech-speak for the volume of an audio signal.

Game Glove ➤ A mouselike cursor controller worn like a glove and operated by movements of the hand, for VIDEO GAMES.

Game Show ➤ A popular type of radio/television program based on the parlor game as spectator entertainment. In the 1950s large cash prizes gripped the attention of viewers. The discovery that contestants were fed answers resulted in a scandal that marked the end of a certain kind of marketing innocence in the U.S. Jeopardy has been running nearly 40 years, a record for any television show (except SOAP OPERAS).

Gamma ➤ The measurement of the contrast latitude or range of a FILMSTOCK or electronic image. If you plot the input against the output on a logarithmic scale, you have the CHARACTERISTIC CURVE. The word "gamma" is used to refer both to the curve itself and the slope of the curve (expressed as the tangent of the angle of its slope). A high gamma signifies high contrast. In film, the input is exposure and the output is the density of the emulsion. In electronics, the input is voltage and the output is LUMINANCE.

Gas Plasma ➤ A type of video display. The technology dates from the 1960s but such displays did not gain popularity until the late 1990s. Each SUBPIXEL in the display is filled with a mixture of neon and xenon gases. When the mixture is excited by an electrical potential, the gas becomes a plasma, emitting ultraviolet radiation in the process. The ultraviolet radiation, in turn, lights up phosphors on the surface of the subpixel. Gas Plasma displays share technological elements with both of their more popular cousins—the CRT and the LCD displays. Like the LCD, the subpixels in a Gas Plasma display are each individually addressed by a circuit grid, avoiding the scanning problems inherent in CRT technology and allowing a flat screen. Like a CRT, however, Plasma displays use phosphorescence to produce a stronger light than LCDs are capable of. In the plasma state the electrons are dissociated from their nuclei and energy is released. See ACTIVE-MATRIX LCD.

Gate ➤ The channel through which film passes in a camera or projector at the point at which it is exposed.

Gateway ➤ (1) A technology that allows a single HOST to transfer a connection from a user from itself to another host computer. (2) What INTERNET PORTALS were called, at first.

Gauge ➤ See FILM GAUGE.

General Release ➤ Widespread simultaneous exhibition of a film with as many as 2,000 prints in circulation, as opposed to limited FIRST-RUN, or PLATFORMING.

Generation ➤ The film in the camera when the shot is taken is "first generation." A print of this negative will be "second generation." An internegative made from this positive will be "third generation," and so on. Each generation marks a progressive deterioration in the quality of the image. While this deterioration applies equally to analog magnetic recording, such as VIDEOCASSETTES, it has no meaning in the digital world where every copy is indistinguishable from the "original"—a frightening thought in Hollywood and elsewhere. See COPY PROTECTION.

Genie ➤ Like COMPUSERVE, General Electric owned a major time-sharing system in the 1970s, called GE Information Services Company. It didn't take long for GEISCO to imitate Compuserve with Genie. Genie faded away in the early 1990s.

Genlock ➤ LOCKing clock GENerators in order to synchronize two video signals.

Genre ➤ A type of film following certain archetypal patterns, such as the Western, the Gangster film, the Science Fiction film, or the Detective Story. See FILM NOIR, MOUNTAIN FILM.

Geosynchronous Orbit ➤ See SATELLITE COMMUNICATIONS. Compare LEO.

German Expressionism ➤ Style of filmmaking common in Germany in the early twenties, characterized by dramatic lighting, distorted sets, and symbolic action and character. The artistic movement also involved painting and theater. The style aimed to portray the often tormented emotions of the characters in the visuals. Compare EXPRESSIONISM.

Gest ➤ (Pronounced "guest.") In Brecht's theory of acting the Gest was the basic meaningful unit of the language of gesture.

Ghost Image ➤ (1) A type of double exposure in which one or more preceding frames are printed together with the main frame to give a multiple exposure. (2) The same effect in television reception (unwanted) caused by the reflection of signals from mountains or large buildings.

Gibbs Effect ➤ The MPEG-2 compression algorithm converts parts of the image into BLOCKS. This can cause problems with the sharp edges of animated films at some data rates, producing a ringing aura or fuzziness called the Gibbs Effect. Also called MOSQUITOES.

Gibi ➤ Proposed prefix for the binary magnitude associated with the decimal GIGA. See BINARY MAGNITUDES.

GIF ➤ See IMAGE FILE FORMATS.

Gig, Giga ➤ (1) A Gig is a job or engagement in the entertainment industry, from musicians' slang. (2) Colloquially, a prefix for billion. In the computer world the prefix is often used to mean 2^{30}, which is 1,073,741,824. Thus an 8 Gig (or gigabyte) hard drive holds 8,589,934,592 BYTES, not 8,000,000,000 bytes. The IEEE has proposed a set of new prefixes for BINARY MAGNITUDES to clear up this confusion. See also MEG, K, TERA.

GIGO ➤ Venerable computer industry shorthand for "Garbage In, Garbage Out," based on the inventory nicknames LIFO and FIFO—last in, first out; first in, first out.

Glass Shot ➤ A type of SPECIAL EFFECT in which part of the scene is painted on a clear glass plate mounted in front of the camera.

Glitch ➤ A technical problem in computers and electronics. An error in the reproduction of sounds and images. See ARTIFACT.

Global Positioning System ➤ See GPS.

GNU ➤ A version of UNIX written by veteran hacker Richard Stallman. The moebian acronym stands for "GNU's Not UNIX." (Meditate on this for awhile.) Stallman was an early proponent of the OPEN SOFTWARE movement. Compare LINUX.

GO Network ➤ See SEARCH ENGINES.

Go Wide ➤ A distributor goes wide with a film when he releases it in a large number of theaters simultaneously, usually after a LIMITED RUN. See PLATFORMING, EXHIBITION.

Gobo ➤ A wooden, opaque screen placed in front of a light in order to shield part of the subject from that light or to cast a shadow. See SCRIM.

Gold, Platinum ➤ The RIAA awards for best-selling singles, albums, and music videos. Gold records are issued to singles or albums that sell 500,000 copies or more. Platinum records are issued to recordings that sell one million. The first gold award was issued to Perry Como for "Catch a Falling Star" in March 1958. The first gold album was *Oklahoma!*, a few months later. In recent years the awards have been subject to widespread counterfeiting. The official RIAA awards now bear an official hologram. The plaques have become collectibles.

Golden Time ➠ Super-overtime that pays a film or television crew at least double.

Goldwynism ➠ A malapropism of the sort attributed to Samuel Goldwyn, such as "Include me out," or "Anyone who goes to a psychiatrist ought to have his head examined," or "A verbal contract isn't worth the paper it's written on."

GOP ➠ In DVD-VIDEO production, a Group of Pictures, an organizational method used to make the disc work more efficiently. A GOP is the basic unit of MPEG: a KEY FRAME followed by one or more DELTA FRAMES. In DVD-Video the limits for a GOP are 18 frames in NTSC and 15 frames in PAL.

Gourand ➠ A technique of 3-D MODELING.

GPS ➠ Global Positioning System. First devised for the military, then commercialized for airlines and ships, by the mid-1990s GPS systems were available for your own car. The GPS receiver is always in sight of three GPS satellites and thus can determine its latitude and longitude with extreme accuracy by triangulation. The system wouldn't work for automobiles without equally accurate and detailed road maps: a ship or a plane doesn't need to know that the off-ramp is less than 50 yards away—a car does.

Grabbed Image ➠ A still image digitized from a frame of video.

Grain ➠ A quality of the EMULSION of a film. Grainy emulsions, which have poor powers of DEFINITION, are sometimes preferred for their "realistic" connotations. The visibility of the grain varies inversely with the size of the FILM GAUGE and directly with the amount of OVERDEVELOPMENT.

Grammys ➠ On the model of OSCARS, the awards presented each year by the National Academy of Recording Arts and Sciences for achievements in records, tapes, and CDs. From "gramophone."

Grand Alliance ➠ The consortium of American broadcasters, manufacturers, and engineers who decided on the standards for HDTV and ATV. These standards differ from DVB, those established by the EBU, the Grand Alliance's European counterpart. As the debate shifted in the mid-1990s from an analog system of HDTV like the one pioneered in Japan years earlier to a purely digital system, the idea of a single standard gave way to a confusing spectrum of digital possibilities ranging from something approaching the Japanese standard of analog quality on the high end to more commercial ways to exploit the flexibility of the digital bandwidth on the low end.

On November 1, 1998, the date the FCC had mandated digital television broadcasting was to begin in the U.S., hardly any of the manufacturers, broadcasters, cable distributors, or producers were ready. The Grand Alliance was united by its disarray. CBS, NBC, and Sony were supporting 1080I, while ABC, FOX, and Panasonic preferred 720P. (Off the record, industry executives were noting that for the foreseeable future, digital television was likely to be 480P.) And no one was listening to the cable companies. The FCC had granted each television station significant new radio spectrum bandwidth to broadcast the new digital signals over the air. But the vast majority of Americans had given up their antennas for cable boxes long ago. To provide the extra bandwidth, the cable companies would have to invest billions; all converters would have to be replaced; and—by the way—in the summer of 1998 the industry realized that no standard had been set for the cable connection between the converter and the new digital television set! (Was the Grand Alliance a subtle plan by the FCC to prove the value of government regulation? Certainly, left to its own devices the FCC couldn't have done more damage than did this industry consortium.)

Graphic Equalizer ➤+ A sound control on tape or disc machines that divides the audio spectrum into three or more bands. The gain, or volume, can then be adjusted individually for each band.

Graphic Match ➤+ A CUT that maintains a parallel between one or more of the compositional elements of a shot, such as the shape of objects, their color, or the contrast of the scene. Compare MATCH CUT.

Graphical User Interface ➤+ See GUI.

Gravure ➤+ A type of printing that uses a depressed, engraved, intaglio surface to carry the ink rather than the raised, relief surface of LETTERPRESS. See also OFFSET.

Grayscale ➤+ In computer graphics, a display in which each PIXEL may be assigned several values of gray as well as pure black and white. The brightness values greatly increase the readability of the image, despite the lack of color information. Usually there are 256 gray values in the scale.

Grazing Effect ➤+ The way sound is absorbed by an audience in a theater. STADIUM SEATING improves the sound of the room as well as the sight lines.

Green Book ➤+ See CD STANDARDS.

Grip ➤+ The person in charge of props on a set.

Gross ➤ The total amount of monies collected at the BOX OFFICE for film admissions. The Distributor's share of these monies is known as rentals.

Gross Shipment ➤ The total number of CDs or other recordings delivered to retailers before returns are account for. See NET SHIPMENT, SHIP GOLD.

Ground Station ➤ The transmitter for a SATELLITE COMMUNICATIONS, television, or DSB system.

Gruner + Jahr ➤ See BERTELSMANN.

GSM ➤ Groupe Spéciale Mobile. A standard for digital cell phones in Europe and Asia.

Guerrilla Theater ➤ A type of theater dating from the 1960s performed in the streets and other public places, usually with a political aim. Compare HAPPENING.

GUI ➤ (Pronounced "gooey.") Graphical User Interface. The command and control operating system for microcomputers, first developed at Xerox's Palo Alto Research Center in the mid-1970s and later commercialized with APPLE's Macintosh operating system in 1984, that uses a pictorial system of ICONS within windows, all controlled by a mouse or other pointing device. Because such a GUI system is graphic rather than character-based, the screen must be controlled at the PIXEL level, opening up applications to images and sounds (as well as fonts and other printer's graphics). Compare CLI (CUI).

Haas Effect ➤ According to the Haas principle, sounds that reach the ear 20 to 40 milliseconds after a primary sound are integrated with the primary sound and increase its volume. This is sort of the auditory equivalent of PERSISTENCE OF VISION—albeit less useful to artists and technologists. Also called *Precedence Effect*.

Hacker ➤ (1) Someone who is adept at breaking into computer systems via networks. (2) Any computer hobbyist. Through the 1970s and well into the 1980s, the word "hacker" had no pejorative connotation; hackers were simply hobbyists. People who invaded mainframes via the networks were known as "Freaks," on the model of the "PHONE PHREAKS" of the late 1960s and early 1970s who had learned to manipulate the then-new DTMF telephone signaling system to their own advantage. (Not all of the Phone Phreaks were electronic geniuses who had built *Blue Boxes*; some were blind people with acute perfect pitch who could actually whistle the "dual tones" and "multifrequencies"—the soul of the DTMF system—to route their calls wherever in the world they liked.) Then, in 1987, in an article about a notorious break-in, a *New York Times* reporter inverted the definitions of the two words, and the negative connotation stuck. The press is mightier than the modem!

Halation ➤ A halo-like effect usually caused by light reflecting off the film base and registering on the emulsion.

Halftone ➤ The process of photoengraving using a BEN DAY SCREEN, which permits photographs to be reproduced by means of a printing press. The image is broken down into black dots (and white areas) of varying sizes, which the eye reads together as gray values. See COLOR PRINTING, GRAYSCALE, DITHERING, ANTI-ALIASING.

Ham Radio ➤ The familiar nickname for amateur radio broadcasting. Hams are licensed to broadcast on certain limited frequency bands with a limited-power signal, but these signals can reach around the world. Since the first crystal sets in the 1920s, Hams have enjoyed communicating with their counterparts all over the globe. Part of the hobby involved collecting QSL cards from other amateur stations with which you've established contact. (Nowadays, QSLs are often digital, which takes away some of the glamour.) Radio Hams were the forerunners of both computer HACKERS and web surfers. While hacking may have some of the same thrill of discovery and present a similar technical challenge, web surfing has neither: all stations are "local," and the only technical feat is spelling the URL. (Is the term "Ham" Cockney rhyming slang for "amateur"?)

Hammocking ➤ The practice of situating a new or weak television program between two strong, established programs so that the audiences for the strong programs will lap over into the time period occupied by the weak program. See LEAD-IN, LEAD-OUT.

HAN ➤ Home Area Network. (You guessed right!) Compare LAN, WAN.

Hand-Held ➤ In the early days, film cameras were simply too heavy to permit such shots. Since the development of lightweight portable cameras (like the ARRIFLEX), hand-held shots have become much more common. The invention of the STEADICAM further popularized Hand-Held camerawork.

Happening ➤ An abstract theatrical event of the 1960s, often more an experience than a drama, that relied on spontaneity and borrowings from other media. Happenings were usually one-time events. See PERFORMANCE ART, GUERILLA THEATER.

Hard Light ➤ A light that casts sharp, precise shadows. "High-contrast lighting." See SOFT LIGHT.

Hardware, Software ➤ In computer and media terminology, hardware refers to relatively permanent equipment, such as cameras, television sets, and computers; software is the term for materials the hardware was built to play, such as films, tapes, and programming. See FORM FACTOR.

Harmonics ➤ The series of overtones that, when combined with the basic tone, give character and depth to sounds. Harmonics are multiples of the base tone.

Hays Office ➤ See PRODUCTION CODE.

HBO ➤ A wholly owned subsidiary of Time WARNER, HBO was the first American cable television PAY TV NETWORK, founded in 1972, beginning national distribution via SATELLITE in 1975. The rapid growth of HBO—for which cable subscribers were charged a premium—spurred the growth of cable itself, and decided the business structure of the medium for decades thereafter. By the mid-1980s, HBO had been joined by dozens of other cable networks, both basic and premium services.

HD ➤ High Definition. (1) A half-inch metal particle tape used in digital video recorders. The maximum resolution is 1980 x 1025 pixels. HDW700 can record widescreen images. (2) The DSD layer on an SACD disc. (3) High-definition DTV in general.

HD-40 ➤ See PLUGS.

HDC ➤ High Definition Camera. A digital camera that uses a two-million pixel CCD. See MEGAPIXEL.

HDCD ➤ (1) High Density Compact Disc or High Definition Compatible Disc. Dual-layer, double-sided technology agreed-upon by competing SONY/PHILIPS and TIME WARNER/Toshiba camps in 1995 for DVD, the next generation of CD technology. With a maximum capacity of 18.8 gigabytes, the HDCD standard maintains the backward compatibility required by the computer industry with the high capacity for DVDs important to the entertainment industry. (2) High Definition Compact Disc. A system developed in 1992 by the Pacific Microsonics company that increased both the SAMPLING rate and the WORD length of standard CD recording to provide a more accurate digital recording that was downwardly compatible with standard CDs.

HDLD ➤ High-Definition LaserDisc. Japanese Laserdisc format for HI-VISION HDTV recordings.

HDSL2 ➤ Although it was never called that, HDSL technology underlies the two-pair T-1 data lines offered for years by local U.S. telephone companies. HDSL2, introduced in 1999, uses just one pair of phone lines. Compare ADSL, SDSL.

HDTV ➻ High-Definition Television. In development in Japan for years before its first public demonstration in the U.S. in 1981 (by SONY and CBS), analog HDTV attempts to match the image quality of 35 mm film, and largely succeeds. By expanding the number of SCAN lines from the standard 525/625 to 1,125 per inch and widening the ASPECT RATIO from 1.33 to 1.78, analog HDTV provides a stunningly detailed image and an experience markedly different from standard broadcast television, although at a cost of enormous BAND-WIDTH. Although the technology was widely demonstrated and discussed through the 1980s, actual scheduled transmissions did not begin until November 25, 1991, in Tokyo. (The date was chosen to commemorate the number of scan lines.)

The rapid development of DIGITAL technology during the 1980s also slowed development of HDTV systems as manufacturers began to reconsider their original ANALOG systems. After much discussion, the FCC established a broad range of standards for HDTV in the U.S. in 1996. The commission decided on a digital format which obviated all the work done in Japan in the 1970s and 1980s. Digital HDTV comes in several flavors: the number of lines of horizontal resolution can be varied, and the scanning can be either progressive or interlaced. The first U.S. broadcast of HDTV occurred in November 1998. See DTV, GRAND ALLIANCE.

HDVD ➻ The handle for High-Definition DVD, the next generation of DVD-VIDEO, still in the planning stages as of 1999, but already acronymed.

HDW700 ➻ A widescreen digital tape format. See HD.

Head End ➻ The control center of a CABLE TELEVISION system; the distribution center.

Head ➻ (1) The beginning of a film. (2) The electromagnetic or optical device that reads or writes to a soundtrack or tape. Compare PICKUP.

Helical Scan ➻ The high speeds required for VIDEOTAPE systems are achieved by moving the recording or playback HEAD as well as the tape itself. Multiple heads are mounted on a drum that is fixed at an angle to the plane of the tape so that the heads trace a shape something like a compressed helix on the tape. (A helix is a spiral, like a corkscrew.)

Hertz ➻ The contemporary term for "cycles per second." Frequencies are now measured in Hertz, kiloHertz (one thousand Hertz), megaHertz (one million Hertz), and gigaHertz (one billion Hertz).

HF ➻ High Frequency band. See ELECTROMAGNETIC SPECTRUM.

HFC ➻ Hybrid Fiber Coaxial cable networks use FIBER OPTIC cable to provide digital voice and video signals to a node that serves from

500 to 2,000 homes; traditional coaxial cable takes the signals from there. Compare SDV.

Hiatus »→ This is what television people call the breaks between shooting seasons, usually late spring. While Los Angeles school children may get summers off like the rest of the country, the industry has asynchronous vacation periods: hiatus, which is often devoted to other work, and Christmas: everyone has left town by December 15th.

Hi-Def »→ Generic jargon for "High Definition."

HI 8 »→ SONY's 8 mm answer to SUPER VHS with a resolution of over 400 lines of horizontal resolution per image. Also High Band 8.

High-End Audio »→ Since the advent of HI-FI audio in the 1950s, AUDIOPHILES have been obsessed with achieving perfect sound reproduction. Of course, there is no such animal. But that doesn't stop the hobbyists. The industry that caters to them is now known as High-End Audio. Because the experience of music is such a personal perceptual domain, there appears to be no monetary limit to the hobby. Indeed, there is no technology—not even automobiles—that can command such economic multiples. Whereas a normal consumer might spend $500 on a music system, a High-End Audio freak could drop $50,000 without any trouble and ten times that amount with a little effort. The video equivalent is HOME THEATRE.

Hi-Fi »→ The introduction of the 33 1/3 rpm "long-playing" record in the 1950s offered the recording industry a frequency response range that was very close to the spectrum of human perception. HIgh-FIdelity disks gave rise to a new industry catering to AUDIOPHILES: HIGH-END AUDIO. See RECORD PLAYER.

High Density Compact Disc »→ See HDCD.

High Key »→ A type of lighting arrangement in which the KEY LIGHT is very bright, resulting in high contrast.

High Sierra »→ The machine-independent standard format for CD-ROMs, created in 1986 at a meeting held at a Nevada hotel by that name. See CD STANDARDS.

Highlighting »→ Pencil-thin beams of light used to illuminate certain parts of the subject (most often the actress's eyes).

Hip Hop »→ See RAP.

Hi-Res »→ A HIgh RESolution computer image.

Hispasat »→ Spanish satellite television system.

Hiss »→ See NOISE.

Histogram »→ A statistical chart composed of rectangles set on a baseline whose areas and dimensions represent the values of the underlying data. From the Greek histos, "mast." Histograms are a common tool of graphics programs, used to indicate (and adjust) the range of CONTRAST or SATURATION values.

Hi-Vision ⟩⟩ The Japanese HDTV analog broadcasting system. An analog 1,125-line widescreen system based on MUSE compression, Hi-Vision debuted in Japan on 11/25/91.

HNN ⟩⟩ Headline News Network. See CNN.

Hollywood ⟩⟩ (1) A political subdivision of Los Angeles County located on the northern rim of the Los Angeles basin, Hollywood became a center for film production around 1913. (2) By extension, the American film industry, although only one major STUDIO— Paramount—maintains premises there. Of the other studios, two are in Burbank (Disney and Warner), one is in Universal City next to Burbank (Universal), one is in Culver City (SONY), and one is in Century City (FOX), all political or geographic subdivisions of Los Angeles. (3) A state of mind composed of equal parts American Dream, California Dreamin', and *A Star Is Born*, as in "Goin' Hollywood."

Hollywood Pictures ⟩⟩ See DISNEY.

Hollywood Reporter ⟩⟩ Founded in 1930 by William R. Wilkerson, the *Hollywood Reporter* has always been the insider's daily trade journal in the Los Angeles film community. *Variety* had a much broader purview, but was based far away in New York. Even *Daily Variety*, published in Los Angeles to compete with the *Hollywood Reporter*, has always been considered a little "distant." *Hollywood Reporter* was published for many years by Wilkerson's widow, Tichie Wilkerson Kassel, before she sold it in 1988 to Billboard Publications, Inc.

Hollywood Ten ⟩⟩ In 1947 the notorious House Un-American Activities Committee of the U.S. Congress (HUAC) began a widely publicized investigation of alleged Communist influence in the American film business. Ten witnesses subpoenaed refused to testify, regarding the Committee as unconstitutional. They were charged with contempt of Congress, imprisoned, and BLACKLISTED until the 1960s. Dozens of other filmmakers who were never charged with any crime were also blacklisted simply for being the subjects of investigation for "Un-American activities." The Ten: Alvah Bessie, Herbert Biberman, Lester Cole, Edward Dmytryk, Ring Lardner Jr, John Howard Lawson, Albert Maltz, Samuel Ornitz, Adrian Scott, and Dalton Trumbo.

Hologram, Holography ⟩⟩ Holography is a system of photography using LASER light that attempts to duplicate realistically the three dimensions of space and the PARALLAX effect in the resulting Hologram. Although the technology dates from the 1960s it hasn't progressed much. At the turn of the century its main use continues to be in specialty printing applications such as security badges.

Holosonic »→ On the model of HOLOGRAPHIC, describes the sense of dimensional reality present in a SOUNDFIELD created by a multichannel sound system.

Home Box Office »→ See HBO.

Home Page »→ The HYPERTEXT equivalent of a cover page for a WORLD WIDE WEB service; the main page of a web site.

Home Shopping Network »→ See USA NETWORK.

Home Theatre »→ Marketing concept for high-end video equipment that became popular in the 1990s. Home Theatres usually include very large-screen monitors, COMPONENT audio systems, LASERDISC or DVD-VIDEO players, and SURROUND SOUND or 5.1 speaker systems. With traditional movie theaters shrinking rapidly in size, the phrase is less hyperbolic than it might appear. All that's missing at home now is STADIUM SEATING.

Homes Passed »→ The number of homes that have potential access to a CABLE system. See PENETRATION.

Homevideo »→ VARIETESE for the CABLE/VIDEOCASSETTE market, now accepted as common parlance.

Honeywagon »→ Old Hollywood jargon for the portable toilets on location. See TRAILER.

Hop »→ (1) Each node that an INTERNET transmission goes through is known as a Hop. The fewer Hops, the better. (2) Satellite transmissions also hop from satellite to satellite or GROUND STATION.

Horizontal Resolution »→ See LoHR.

Horse Opera »→ Nickname for a Western.

Host »→ The computer that hundreds or thousands of users dial into on an ONLINE system. Compare SERVER.

Hot Bird »→ Nickname for a high-power satellite.

Hot Type »→ Jargon for metal movable type and LINOTYPE. It's hot because it is usually set with a linotype machine that molds molten lead into character slugs. See COLD TYPE.

Howl Around »→ British equivalent of FEEDBACK (and a lot more evocative).

HSB »→ Hue, Saturation, Brightness. One of several systems for quantifying color values in print and electronic media. See COLOR MODELS.

HSL »→ Hue, Saturation, Luminance. One of several systems for quantifying color values in print and electronic media. See COLOR MODELS.

HSN »→ Home Shopping Network. Dating from the late 1980s, HSN is both an important cultural and media landmark. It was the first broadcast format to depend entirely on viewer interaction for its economics. Because of the nature of the goods that sold best, HSN also marked the trivialization of marketing. See USA NETWORK.

HTML ➻ HyperText Markup Language, a coding system based on SGML that provides a standard for integrating graphics, multimedia, and HYPERTEXT references to distant texts in WORLD WIDE WEB documents.

HTTP ➻ HyperText Transport Protocol, the communications protocol of the WORLD WIDE WEB. *SHTTP* is the secure version of HTTP. See FTP, SMTP, HTML.

Hue ➻ See COLOR.

Hue Modulation ➻ A system for high-fidelity optical SOUNDTRACKS in which the sound signal is carried by the modification of the color of the track.

Hum ➻ See NOISE.

HUT ➻ Homes Using Television. The percentage of homes in a ratings survey with a television set in use during a given time period. In effect, the sum of all program ratings. SHARE is based on HUT.

Hype ➻ Promotional activity, especially of the extreme sort; from "hyperbole."

HyperCard ➻ APPLE Computer's landmark software that combined elements of an operating system, database engine, graphics system, and high-level programming language in an easy-to-use reference system based on the model of index cards in a box. HyperCard proved useful for early CD-ROM MULTIMEDIA programming. Not to be confused with HYPERMEDIA.

Hyperlink ➻ See HYPERTEXT.

Hypermedia ➻ A synonym for HYPERTEXT, but of course including other media.

Hypertext ➻ A text-only or text-image-sound format for computerized information sources that allows the user to navigate through the information in a nonlinear fashion. Imagine an encyclopedia where pointing to any word or combination of words in an entry would take you immediately to a separate entry for that term or to an illustration or demonstration of it. A hypertext format is the ultimate system of cross-referencing. See MULTIMEDIA, INTERNET, WORLD WIDE WEB, HTML.

Hyphenate ➻ Jargon for a filmmaker who fulfills more than one function, such as writer–director, actor–producer, or writer–producer. (The proper punctuation here is actually an N-dash, but who outside the publishing industry knows the difference? "N-dashate" just doesn't make it.)

I Frame ⇒ See MPEG-2.

i.Link ⇒ Another name for FIREWIRE for those who don't want to recognize the Apple trademark on the IEEE 1394 standard.

IBA ⇒ Independent Broadcasting Authority, former name of the Independent Television Commission, the organization that operates CHANNEL 3, formerly ITV, in the U.K. Compare BBC.

IBM ⇒ Thomas J. Watson, star salesman of the National Cash Register Company, took over the failing Computing-Tabulating-Recording Company in 1914. Within five years he had built it into a thriving supplier of business machines by aggressively marketing—mainly to the U.S. government—C-T-R's Hollerith tabulator, a punched-card sorter. In 1924 Watson changed the name of the company to International Business Machines to reflect burgeoning activity in Europe, Asia, and Latin America. By 1940, with sales approaching $50 million annually, IBM was the leading office machinery supplier in the U.S., dominating the market for tabulating machinery, time clocks, and electric typewriters. Although the company had experimented with early electromechanical computing devices in the 1940s, it did not enter the nascent "computer" market until after Remington-Rand introduced the UNIVAC in 1951. In 1952 Tom Watson Jr took over from his father and introduced the 701, IBM's first computer. System/360, an all-electronic family, followed in 1964, and by the late sixties the company totally dominated the worldwide computer market with a market share approaching 80 percent.

The U.S. government sued the company on antitrust grounds, a court action that was to continue for many years. Although the company weathered the challenge from the developing minicomputer market in the 1970s (DEC, Data General, Prime) and moved quickly to establish its presence in the microcomputer market of the 1980s, by the late eighties it began to topple of its own weight as infinitely cheaper micros challenged, then conquered, the expensive mainframes on which the company had built its fortune. In 1990, its last great year, IBM realized a profit of nearly $6 billion on sales of nearly $69 billion. Throughout the early 1990s, in the face of substantial losses, a series of CEOs drastically downsized the company—but without success.

Then outsider Louis Gerstner Jr took over as CEO in 1993. In a couple of years he was able to restore the company to its former financial glory. (By 1997, the company was again earning $6 billion, but on only slightly higher sales of $78.5 billion.) IBM had always promoted from within. Gerstner, who wasn't even in the computer industry before his appointment, was the shock the old institution needed. Although IBM's sales remain enormous, and the company is once again profitable, it has ceded its position as the monopoly power of the computer industry to MICROSOFT.

IC ⟫⟶ See INTEGRATED CIRCUIT.

ICM ⟫⟶ International Creative Management. See AGENT.

Icon ⟫⟩ (1) In the SEMIOTIC categories first formulated by philosopher C. S. Peirce and adapted by film theorist Peter Wollen, a sign that represents its object mainly by its similarity to it. See INDEX, SYMBOL. (2) In the computer business, pictorial representations of files, programs, or processes of the sort made popular by the Macintosh in the mid-1980s. Strictly speaking, the GUI icon should have a limited range of meanings: otherwise, it would be better to use words. (In the Peirce definition, similarity is the key to the meaning.) But programmers were so taken with the icon concept that they quickly adopted the idea for control buttons within programs, confronting the user with rows of little cartoons, most of whose meanings were inscrutable. Windows 95 solved this problem ingeniously with the popup definition: the words are there if you need them.

Iconoscope ⟫⟶ The earliest type of television camera tube. See IMAGE ORTHICON, CCD.

IDTV ⟫⟶ Improved Definition TeleVision, a transitional technology that aimed to get a better picture out of old-fashioned NTSC through the technique of LINE-DOUBLING.

IEEE ⟫⟶ Institute of Electrical and Electronics Engineers. U.S. professional organization that is involved in determining standards for computer and video protocols.

If-Come ⟫⟶ A free OPTION on a screenplay or other literary property. (Well, it's better than no option at all!)

ILA ⟫⟶ Image Light Amplifier. This video projection device uses a single liquid crystal to amplify an image. The source of the image is usually a CRT. Compare DMD, OIL-FILM.

Illustrator ⟫⟶ See ADOBE.

ILM ⟫⟶ See INDUSTRIAL LIGHT AND MAGIC.

IMA ⟫⟶ 4:1 compression audio codec which works with 16-bit audio. Based on the standard created by the Interactive Multimedia Association.

Image ⟫⟶ An image is both an optical pattern and a mental experience. (1) A single specific picture. (2) Generally, the VISUALS of film or media as opposed to sound. (3) A visual TROPE. (4) By extension, often a nonvisual trope; hence, we speak of aural, poetic, or musical "images."

Image File Formats ➻ Just as there are dozens of different word-processing TEXT FILE FORMATS, so there are scores of image formats. With images, however, unlike texts, certain formats have become standard. Compuserve's *GIF* (Graphic Interchange Format) has become ubiquitous on the Web. JPEG is almost as common, and better suited for photographs. The basic Macintosh format is PIC; BMP (for Bit-Mapped Picture) is the Windows equivalent. PNG (Portable Network Graphics) adjusts for differences in GAMMA among platforms. Finally, TIFF (Tagged Image File Format) is the standard in publishing because of its versatility and power. These are all BIT-MAPPED GRAPHICS formats. No such standards have developed for VECTOR GRAPHICS. See MOVIE FILE FORMATS.

Image Orthicon ➻ The standard television camera tube for many years. See also CCD, CATHODE RAY TUBE.

ImageSetter ➻ A high quality output device for black and white or color REPRO in preparation for commercial printing. Although ImageSetters normally output to photographic paper and have resolutions ranging to 2800 dpi, the basic technology is similar to the office LASER PRINTER. See POSTSCRIPT, DIRECT-TO-PLATE.

Imaging ➻ The ability of a multichannel sound system to appear to place the sources of the sounds at various places in the SOUNDSTAGE.

IMAX ➻ High-quality film format of Canadian origin that depends on 65 mm filmstock run sideways at 30 frames/sec in a projection system capable of filling a square-shaped screen as high as 80 feet. The antecedent appears to have been TODD-AO. Introduced in 1970, IMAX has had a long career in stand-alone installations, often in theme parks and museums. Many variants have been introduced: IMAX DOME projects the image on a domed screen with a fish-eye lens. IMAX 3-D employs LCD spectacles and headsets for sound enhancement. IMAX Solido, introduced in 1992, employs a domed screen to further extend the 3-D experience. See 3-D, SHOWSCAN.

IMDB ➻ Internet Movie DataBase. Founded in London in 1990 by Col Needham and others as an email discussion group, the IMDB has become one of the great success stories of the INTERNET collaboration ethos. In 1993, personnel at the University of Cardiff put this movie list on the World Wide Web. Over the next few years thousands of film buffs around the world contributed to the knowledge base of the IMDB as its volunteer staff of editors vetted the information. In early 1998 Amazon.com purchased the IMDB.

I-MPEG ➻ Intraframe MPEG, a variant of the standard used in digital video equipment that permits only SPATIAL, not TEMPORAL COMPRESSION.

In the Can ➻ A film is in the can when shooting is complete but before it has been edited. See POSTPRODUCTION.

Indeo ➻ INTEL's proprietary compression technology introduced in 1993, based on DVI, originally required an i750 chip to compress but only a Pentium or fast 486 to decompress. Compare SORENSON, MPEG.

Index ➻ In the Peirce/Wollen system, a sign that represents its object by virtue of an existential bond. For example, a clock or a thermometer "point to" what they signify. See ICON, SYMBOL. Computer GUIs make effective use of Indexes for scroll bars, progress gauges, and the like.

Indie, Indy ➻ (1) An independent producer or distributor. See MIRAMAX. (2) An independent television station (not a network AFFILIATE). The FCC defines such a station as one that carries no more than ten hours of network programming per week during PRIMETIME.

Industrial Light and Magic ➻ George Lucas's SPECIAL EFFECTS company grew out of the sophisticated FX work for *Star Wars* (1977). More recently ILM has been a leader in the application of digital technology to film. See THX.

Information Theory ➻ Theory that deals with the transmission of messages, considering problems of distribution, transmission, and reception. In film, for example, Christian Metz identifies five separate channels of information: IMAGES, graphic representation (words read from the screen), recorded speech, recorded music, and recorded sound effects.

Infoseek ➻ See SEARCH ENGINES.

Ingenue ➻ A young adult actress, or the artless role she may play. Compare STARLET.

Ink Jet ➻ A cheap and effective printing technology that became ubiquitous for computer printers in the early 1990s. A piezoelectric crystal vibrates a nozzle which squirts ink at the paper. Resolutions of 300 dpi and more are possible, making the Ink Jet printer an effective competitor to the LASER PRINTER on the low end of the market.

Insert Program ➻ See DROP-IN.

Insert, Insert Shot ➻ A DETAIL SHOT that gives specific and relevant information necessary to a complete understanding of the meaning of the scene. Examples: a letter, a telltale physical detail.

INT ➻ INTerior, or indoors, in a script. Compare EXT.

Intaglio Printing ⇒ A system of printing in which the printing surface is depressed. See RELIEF PRINTING, PLANOGRAPHIC.

Integrated Circuit ⇒ A highly miniaturized electronic system incorporating a number of otherwise separate elements (transistors, capacitors, etc.) in its design. In modern microelectronics, the intermediate step between the PRINTED CIRCUIT and the MICROPROCESSOR.

Intel ⇒ Founded in 1968 by Gordon Moore, Robert Noyce, and Andrew Grove to produce microprocessors, Intel has grown into the dominant producer of logic chips thanks in large part to its symbiotic alliance with MICROSOFT. Originally, the aim of the company was to make semiconductor memory practical. A side contract with a Japanese company, Busicom, in the early years led to the development of the 4004 logic chip, which was introduced in 1971 and immediately found applications in devices from calculators to VIDEO GAMES.

The 4004 chip included 23,000 transistors, a huge number at the time. In 1981 INTEL won a contract with IBM to produce the CPU for IBM's new personal computer. IBM had never relied on an outside supplier for such a critical part before. At the time Motorola may have been further advanced in CPU design, and Zilog was neck-and-neck with INTEL. IBM's choice of INTEL to produce the CPU, like its choice of MICROSOFT to produce the OS was to determine the course of microcomputer history for the next twenty years. In 1995 Intel introduced the Pentium Pro processor. With 5.5 million transistors and capable of 300 million instructions per second, the chip continued an unbroken string of confirmations of co-founder Gordon MOORE'S LAW: processor power doubles every 18 months.

Intellectual Property ⇒ This rather oxymoronic term gained currency in the late 1980s to refer to films, music, photos, books—any creative, artistic, or entertainment product—even including such copyrightable or trademarkable material as computer software, algorithms, and design metaphors. As the rising tide of digitization made it increasingly easy to copy such products, manufacturers and their lawyers sought to find ways to protect their monetary value. The adjective is misleading; it simply means to convey that such properties are not physical entities; intellectual properties may or may not display intellect, or even intelligence. See COPYRIGHT, PIRACY.

INTELSAT ⇒ International Telecommunications Satellite Consortium, established in 1964. Also the name of satellites launched by that organization.

Intensity ⇒ See COLOR.

Intentional Fallacy ⇒ The error of judging a work of art by its author's intentions. See AFFECTIVE FALLACY.

Intentional Technology ➤ See Technological Determinism.

Intent-to-Rent ➤ In video marketing, a measure of the market's interest in a tape before it is released.

Interactive Cable ➤ Cable television system in which the cable tuner can transmit as well as receive, allowing viewers to "talk back" to a central computer. Using their tuners, subscribers can choose specific programs for which they will be charged separately. Warner Cable's QUBE system was the first commercial interactive cable service in 1977. Qube subscribers could also respond to simple multiple-choice questions with the results of the poll displayed immediately, or order products directly. The vision of interactive cable was far ahead of the technology at the time and Qube was discontinued.

Interactive Medium ➤ See Distribution Flow.

Interactive Services ➤ Catchphrase of the early 1990s describing online computer networks where users can query distant information sources or communicate with each other interactively. By extension, Interactive Cable as well. See Videotext, World Wide Web.

Interactive Voice Response ➤ See IVR.

Intercut ➤ See Cross-Cutting.

Interlace ➤ System used in standard television to decrease flicker by dividing the frame into two parts or Fields: first the odd-numbered lines are painted on the screen, then the even-numbered lines. Comparable in effect to the double-bladed Shutter in film projection. (See Field, Raster.) Because computer monitors were not dependent on the existing television standards, designers of the first graphical monitors could avoid the flicker problem by increasing the frequency of the scan: if you project 60, 70 or 80 frames per second, there is no need to interlace fields. This is Progressive Scanning, which provides a noticeably more stable image. The new HDTV standards allow for Progressive as well as Interlaced broadcasting, and a debate has ensued over how best to use the available bandwidth: 60P (60 frames per second, progressive) with lower Video Resolution or 30I (30 frames per second, interlaced) with higher resolution? Some mavens think Progressive scanning is more important than higher resolution. See Line-Doubling, Line-Quadrupling. Compare Showscan, Imax.

Intermittent Movement ➤ See Pull-Down Mechanism.

Internegative ➤ A negative prepared from a positive print especially for the purpose of producing other positive prints from it.

Internet ➤ The network of networks that grew out of the U.S. Defense Department of Defense's Arpanet in the 1970s linked government, university, military, and commercial sites for electronic mail and online databases. By 1994 the Internet had become the common carrier for commercial EMAIL as well, and the introduction of WORLD WIDE WEB technology quickly transformed what had been essentially a scholarly network into the global basic medium for online publishing, as popular with college students as with corporate advertisers. By 1995 nearly all government support of the Internet had ended.

Interpreter ≫ See COMPUTER LANGUAGES.

Intranet ≫ On the model of INTERNET, a large private network, usually using Internet technologies.

Intrinsic Interest ≫ A quality of an object or an area of the image that draws attention to it even though the design of the image does not. See DOMINANT.

Intro ≫ A LEAD-IN in radio, as, for example, an introduction to a commercial. Compare OUTRO.

Inverse Telecine ≫ Converting 30 frames/sec video to 24 frames/sec, the reverse of TELECINE. DVD-ROM producers often employ this technology, and MPEG-2 coders do it with the intention of upscaling the frame rate on playback.

IP Address, IP Number ≫ See DOMAIN.

IRDA ≫ The Infrared Data Association protocol for infrared connections between laptop computers and desktops or other peripherals, up to 4 megabits/sec.

Iris-In, Iris-Out ≫ An old technique of punctuation that utilizes a DIAPHRAGM in front of the lens, which is opened (Iris-In) or closed (Iris-Out) to begin or end a scene. The iris can also be used to focus attention on a detail of the scene. It's named after the iris of the eye, a biological diaphragm—not the flower. See FOCUS-IN, FADE-IN.

IS ≫ Information Systems, the "computer department" in nearly all businesses. Throughout the mainframe and minicomputer eras, the IS department members ruled as priests of the new technology. Computer rooms were off-limits to civilians; only the white-coated IS guys could enter. If you wanted a report, you made a formal request to the IS department, and a few months later, maybe, you got it. The entrenched IS personnel were seriously threatened by the introduction of the personal computer. The situation was not unlike the introduction of the Vulgate bible. IS managers battled the PC at first, downplaying its capabilities and often denying purchase orders for these "toys." Workers in other departments fought back. One common ploy in the early 1980s was to cut three purchase orders, each for less than $1,000, to cover the total cost of an Apple II and the irresistible VisiCalc SPREADSHEET software. This way, the boss didn't have to approve the purchase, and the IS department was none the wiser. By the mid-1980s, IS departments had made peace with the PC revolution.

It had become clear that these new machines were complicated enough so that the priestly caste would always be needed. Laypeople might be able to operate a word processor or spreadsheet, but the heart of the new MS-DOS operating system was dark enough that IS ministrations were necessary when it came to jobs like hooking up a printer or setting mysterious "interrupts." Instead of working in the temple, now, IS clergy had moved out among the people into the common offices where their holy knowledge was dispensed in digital indulgences to the innumerate masses (see NUMERACY).

The new enemy became the Macintosh, Steve Jobs's vision of an appliance that anyone could operate—clearly anathema. "The computer for the rest of us," as the Apple marketing slogan had it, was never able to make serious inroads in the corporate market. The powerful alliance of the IS clergy and Microsoft continued even after the introduction of Windows, which, although it presented a GRAPHICAL USER INTERFACE, was still based on MS-DOS and—indeed—raised the level of OS complexity by a magnitude, further entrenching the IS clergy.

Semiotician/novelist Umberto Eco once wrote about the religiosity of the Mac–PC Manichean dichotomy, but he had it backwards: he thought Macs were Catholic because of the elaborate and controlling operating system, while PCs were Protestant, because they allowed all standards. He confused the signifier with the signified. Socially, the Mac represented a Lutheran attack on the far-reaching dominance of Rome/Redmond and its one holy and universal OS. (And, yes, UNIX is Jewish.) See MICROSOFT, APPLE.

ISDN ➠ Integrated Services Digital Network. A digital phone link for business or personal use that combines two 64-kilobit data channels with two voice-grade channels. Developed in the early 1980s, ISDN has been successful in Europe but never took off in the U.S., mainly because the phone companies did a poor job of marketing. DSL is quickly replacing ISDN.

ISO ➠ (1) An "isolated camera" generally used in sports coverage and assigned to follow the tight end, for example, no matter what else happens on the field. (2) The International Standards Organization.

ISO 9660 ➠ A cross-platform standard for CD-ROMs established in 1988, based on the HIGH SIERRA standard. See CD STANDARDS.

Isochronous ➠ A constant rate of data transmission is necessary for digital video and audio streams. Such a rate is Isochronous (on the model of synchronous, asynchronous).

ISP ➠ Internet Service Provider. The term is often used indiscriminately to refer to any company that provides any sort of INTERNET service. It should be reserved for organizations that provide connections to the network, either dialup or dedicated.

ITC ➠ The Independent Television Commission—the renamed IBA— that assigns franchises for Channel 3 in the U.K. and oversees independent television broadcasting and cable. Compare BBC.

ITU, ITU-R ➠ International Telecommunications Union, the 130-year-old body that controls telecommunications of all sorts. ITU-R is the subcommittee dealing with Radiocommunications.

ITV ➠ The original independent, commercial television system in the U.K., established in 1956 and funded by advertising. The ITV system, operated by the Independent Broadcasting Authority (IBA), was composed of 15 regional franchises that were awarded based on bids by various business entities. The best-known of these franchises were London Weekend Television and Thames TV, which shared the Greater London area. ITV also operated Channel 4, founded in 1982 and dedicated to alternative programming. In a hotly disputed auction in 1991 franchises were reassigned. ITV was renamed CHANNEL 3; the IBA was renamed ITC.

IVR ➠ Interactive Voice Response. The accepted term for a computerized telephone system, the kind that make you punch 47 buttons only to find out that the lights are on, but nobody's home. Whatever time we gained from DTMF we've lost double to IVR.

Jack ➠ See PLUGS.

Jaggies ➠ Colloquial term for the jagged outlines on typefaces and graphics caused by the limited RESOLUTION of computer monitors (and televisions). Also known as *staircasing*. See ANTI-ALIASING.

Jamming ➠ The practice of broadcasting noise signals to interfere intentionally with the signal of a radio or television station.

Janus ➠ Founded in 1956 by Bryant Haliday and Cyrus Harvey, later owned and operated by their Harvard classmate William Becker and his associate, producer Saul Turell, to distribute films on 16 mm, the company quickly became a leader in the growing field of NONTHEATRICAL DISTRIBUTION as the heightened interest in foreign films and ART FILMS combined with the growth of film studies in universities in the 1960s to widen distribution channels for movies. (While at Harvard, Haliday and Harvey had converted the neighboring Brattle theater into one of the first ART HOUSES, famous at the time for its Humphrey Bogart series.) In 1985, just as 16 mm distribution was peaking, Becker and Turell made a deal with Films, Inc. selling the entire Janus library, and invested a small part of the proceeds in the struggling VOYAGER company, soon to be a leader in LASERDISC and MULTIMEDIA CD-ROM, the technologies that would eventually replace 16 mm film in the nontheatrical markets. Saul Turell died in 1986; his partnership position was assumed by his son Jonathan.

Java ⇒ The name SUN gave to a set of technologies that they intended to position as a cross-platform foundation for software. Java had more success as a metaphor in the mid-1990s than it did as a programming tool. (It may be the first technical brandname since "Macintosh" that is neither an acronym nor a functional derivative.) Microsoft immediately countered with their own superset of Java, purposely muddying the threatening cross-platform waters.

Jewel Box ⇒ The standardized plastic case in which most audio CDs and many CD-ROMs are packaged. Perhaps the worst packaging design since the bubble pack, the jewel box is fragile, too small to provide an effective display, environmentally unsound, and difficult for many people to open. (The trick is to squeeze—gently!—at the top and bottom of the right side with your left hand while grasping the left and right sides with your right hand in back of the box, then pull back with your right thumb.) The small size of the box not only inspires additional cardboard or plastic packaging to lessen shoplifting losses, it also has led to the decline of LINER notes and art. The Super Jewel Box is sometimes used for DVD packaging. Compare KEEP CASE.

Jiggly Show ⇒ Slang term of the 1970s that came into use with the rise of *Charlie's Angels* and *Three's Company*. A program featuring one or more young women without bras who find opportunities to run, hop, skip, and jump, thereby exploiting preadolescent fantasies. *Baywatch* provided an interesting slant on the genre: beaches offer more bare skin than any other locale.

Jitter ⇒ Timing inaccuracies in a digital/analog converter of as little as 10 picoseconds can cause the degradation of the sound known as Jitter. The effects are: metallic treble, lost SOUNDSTAGE, and a synthetic quality. See TIME SMEAR.

Jog and Shuttle ⇒ These are analog-influenced controls for VCRs, DVDs and the like. Replacing digital buttons with old-fashioned analog knobs, they provide better control, continuous acceleration (the further you turn the faster it goes), and welcome physical feedback.

JPEG ➤ The Compression standard algorithm for digital still images developed by the Joint Photographic Experts Group. Compare MPEG. See Image File Formats.

Jump Cut ➤ (1) A cut that occurs within a scene rather than between scenes, to condense the shot. It can effectively eliminate dead periods, such as that between the time a character enters a room and the time he reaches his destination on the other side of the room. When used according to certain rules, jump cuts are unobtrusive. (2) Obtrusive jump cuts produce an ellipsis between shots, either by maintaining a consistent background and abruptly changing the positions of the actors, or by holding the positions of the actors and abruptly changing the background. In *Breathless* (1959), Jean-Luc Godard deliberately inserted jump cuts in shots where they would be quite obvious. Obvious, obtrusive jump cuts are still uncommon, however. Not to be confused with Match Cut.

K ➤ (1) Abbreviation for the Kelvin temperature scale. See Color Temperature. (2) Abbreviation for the prefix kilo (thousand), as in "That DP will set us back $120 K." (3) In the computer world K is often used to mean 2^{10}, which is 1,024, not 10^3, which is 1,000. Thus, for example, 640 K (or kilobytes) of RAM equal 655,360 Bytes, not 640,000 bytes. Although the values may be close enough at the kilo level, the disparity between the binary and decimal values increases geometrically at higher levels. The IEEE has proposed a set of new prefixes for Binary Magnitudes to clear this up. Compare Meg, Gig, Tera.

Ka-Band ➤ See Satellite Bands.

Karaoke ➤ In the early 1990s, this Japanese traditional barroom sing-along became an international phenomenon when video technology was applied to provide easily readable lyrics superimposed on the video that accompanied the soundtrack. Laserdisc karaoke players became common attractions of bars.

KBPS, KPS ➤ These are standard abbreviations for kilobits per second (kbps, kps) and kilobytes per second (KBps, Kps), but it is so easy to misconstrue them that it is better to spell it out.

Keep Case ➤ The term for the standard lightweight packing of DVDs. A slight advance over the Jewel Case, at least the Keep Case doesn't break so easily and offers 45 percent more area for cover art.

KEM ➤ A brand of flatbed editing table. See Steenbeck.

Kenworthy ➻ A highly flexible, servo-controlled MOTION-CONTROL apparatus that can be computer-programmed to photograph miniature sets in such a way that the proper compensation is made for the reduction in size of the subject. See MOTION-CONTROL SYSTEM, LOUMA.

Key Frames ➻ In TEMPORAL COMPRESSION schemes like MPEG-2, certain frames are reproduced in detail. These are the key frames. All other frames include only the differences from the key frames. These are the *Delta Frames*. See MPEG-2.

Key Light ➻ The main light on a subject. Usually placed at a 45-degree angle to the camera–subject axis. See FILLER LIGHT, BACKLIGHT.

Key Lighting, High or Low ➻ In high-key lighting, the key light provides all or most of the light in the scene. In low-key lighting, the key light provides much less of the total illumination.

Keykode ➻ Eastman EXR stock includes printed characters and bar codes spaced a foot apart on 35 mm stock and 6 inches apart on 16 mm stock. This is the Keykode. It is used to match footage. See TIME-CODE, VIDEO MATCHBACK.

Keystoning ➻ When an image is projected onto a surface that is not perpendicular to the projection beam the rectangular frame is distorted into a trapezoid—the shape of a keystone in an arch. See SCHEIMPFLUG ADJUSTMENT.

Kibi ➻ Proposed prefix for the binary magnitude associated with the decimal KILO (K). See BINARY MAGNITUDES.

Kidvid ➻ *Variety's* apt coinage for children's television programming.

Kill Fee ➻ A minimum payment made to a writer when a publisher decides not to use the piece the writer has produced. Compare PAY OR PLAY.

Killer Ap ➻ One of the more curious characteristics of the microcomputer revolution is that the invention is abstract. When the automobile was invented, everyone knew immediately what to do with it. Machines like the telephone and radio were invented to serve a specific purpose. Indeed, all the devices that support our information age have obvious and specific purposes—with the single exception of the microcomputer. It can do everything and anything—but out of the box, it does nothing.

In the mid-1970s, the first sales of micros were to hobbyists who were thrilled just to be able to make the lights on the front panel blink. For the device to realize its commercial potential, however, something more was needed: application software—programs that would make these machines do something useful. Any software application that actually causes a consumer to spend money to buy a machine to run it on is a Killer Ap. Dan Bricklin's and Bob Frankston's VisiCalc is generally regarded as the first Killer Ap. In the early 1980s, tens of thousands of corporate managers snuck purchase orders for Apple II's past their computer departments just to run this pioneering spreadsheet program.

Kilo ➻ See K.

Kinematoscope ➻ Developed by Philadelphian Coleman Sellers in 1861, this antecedent of the cinema consisted of a series of stereoscopic pictures printed on glass plates that were strung together by chain mounted in a box. The spectator turned a crank and saw moving images. See KINETOSCOPE.

Kineme ➻ Pier Paolo Pasolini's term for the basic unit of cinematic language, on the model of PHONEME.

Kinepolis ➻ See MULTIPLEX.

Kinescope ➻ A film record of a television show shot directly from a television screen (and therefore of poor quality). This was the only way to preserve live television in the early years. Once videotape became available in the early 1960s there was no need for Kinescopes.

Kinetograph ➻ Edison's film projector. See BIOSKOP, CINÉMATOGRAPHE, KINETOSCOPE.

Kinetophone ➻ Edison's sound film apparatus.

Kinetoscope ➻ Edison's peephole viewer which used a continuous loop of role film to produce moving images. See KINETOGRAPH.

Kino-Eye ➻ One of the first CINÉMA VÉRITÉ approaches to film esthetics, developed by Dziga Vertov in the 1920s. His film *Man with a Movie Camera* is a famous example.

Kiosk, Kiosque ➻ (1) The French MINITEL system that makes available tens of thousands of services through a simple set of public dial-in access points. Once users have dialed an abbreviated phone number, such as 3615, they are confronted with a menu that allows them to choose any one of thousands of services. (2) "Kiosk" is used in the U.S. to refer to a public-access terminal of the sort one might find in airports.

Knockoff ➻ Garment industry term adopted by the television industry to describe a copy of another program. For example: in the 1970s, *Beacon Hill* compared to *Upstairs, Downstairs*; in the 1980s, *Dynasty* versus *Dallas*. Compare SPINOFF.

Ku-Band ➻ See SATELLITE BANDS.

Kuleshov Effect ➻ When a viewer infers meanings from a MONTAGE that aren't logically inherent in the shots themselves, that is the Kuleshov effect. From experiments by Lev Kuleshov in which he alternated the same shot of an actor's supposedly blank expression with various emotionally charged shots. Viewers believed the actor's expression changed.

Lab ➺ Historical Hollywood term for a company that does Special Effects, Optical effects, color correction, and the like. Compare Post House.

LAN ➺ Local Area Network. A computer network, usually of microcomputers, in an office building or campus. Compare WAN.

LANC ➺ Sony's protocol for the external control of video devices—especially Laserdiscs—by external computer programs. Also known as *Control-L*.

Lands and Pits ➺ See Optical Disc.

Language, Language System ➺ Unwieldy English equivalents of the French terms *langage* and *langue*, respectively. Cinema is a "language" because it is a means of communication, but it is not necessarily a "language system" because it doesn't follow the rules of written or spoken language.

Lap Dissolve ➺ See Dissolve.

Laser ➺ "Light Amplification by Stimulated Emission of Radiation," first developed in 1960. The laser produces a concentrated, narrowly focused beam of light whose wavelength is pure. As a result, laser light behaves in unusual ways. It has applications in Holography, which would be impossible without it, and in piped transmission of electromagnetic signals; see Fiber Optics. It is also the basis for CD and Videodisc technology.

Laser Printer ➺ The merger of photocopier, laser, and computer technology in the early 1980s produced the Laser Printer, introduced by Xerox (the LaserJet) and Apple (the LaserWriter). For the first time, sophisticated, high-resolution printing technology was available in the small-business office environment. Just as important, the Laser Printer collapsed the time-consuming and expensive Typesetting stage in the publishing process. For the first time, the writer controlled the printing. While the quality of the output remains less than can be accomplished with traditional Phototypesetting and ink printing, the 300-dots-per-inch resolution of the standard Laser Printer is good enough to compete. The result is Desktop Publishing and a revolution in the sociology of print nearly equal to Gutenberg's movable type. In the basic Laser Printer (as in the photocopier) an electrostatic charge is transferred to a drum which picks up toner powder and deposits it on the paper. The toner is then fused to the paper by a heat roller. See Printing Technologies.

Laser Rot ⇒ Because Laserdiscs are so large, they are subject to the physical stress of bending, which can cause the layers to separate allowing oxidation of the aluminum layer that holds the pits and lands that record the signal. The deterioration of the signal is called Laser Rot.

Laserdisc ⇒ (1) The Disc technology first developed by Philips (with MCA) for their Videodisc product called Discovision, introduced in 1978. (2) Now the generic term for this technology. The Laserdisc was the first exploitation of Laser technology for writing and reading large quantities of information on a plastic disc. Unlike its CD and DVD descendents, however, an LD is not digital. Instead, the pits and lands on a Laserdisc are used to record analog waveforms for the video and audio. It took Laserdiscs a long time to get started and an even longer time to realize their market potential. Philips and its partners announced the imminent debut of the technology beginning in 1975. By the time the first disc players reached the market three years later, Sony and Matsushita had captured the home video market with their tape machines, which had the added advantage of being able to record as well as playback.

The Laserdisc quickly disposed of its competitors (CED, TeD, VHD), but sales grew slowly. By 1984 it had become the medium of choice for Videophiles. The discs were still quite expensive, and couldn't be rented like videotapes, but the quality of the image was superb. The Laserdisc offers almost twice the horizontal resolution of VHS tape. In 1987 a digital soundtrack was added to the spec. Most LDs today include both an analog and digital soundtrack. DVD-Video has not yet killed the format, and it may survive quite awhile. There are still a number of videophiles who think the analog video of the LD is superior to the digital video of DVD, just as many of their audiophile cousins consider vinyl superior to CD.

Late Fringe ⇒ See Fringe.

Laterna Magica ⇒ See Magic Lantern.

Latitude ⇒ See Exposure Latitude.

Laughtrack ⇒ Laughter, applause, and other audience reactions, usually artificially composed, that are added to a television program soundtrack in postproduction. Also called canned laughter.

Lavalier ⇒ A small microphone either pinned to a lapel or worn around the neck. Often a Radio Microphone.

Law of the First Wavefront ⇒ This principle states that the first sound wave reaching the ear determines our perception of the direction of the sound.

L-Band ⇒ See Satellite Bands.

LCD ⇒ Liquid Crystal Display, a technology for flat video screens that found its first use in digital watches in the 1970s, then was refined for computer displays in the 1980s, and entered the world of consumer electronics with SONY'S VIDEO WALKMAN at the end of the decade. Also used in early VIDEO PROJECTORS. When an electrical charge is applied to a liquid crystal, it darkens. Modern computer and television LCD screens are backlit to provide a source of illumination.

LCLV ⇒ Liquid-Crystal Light Valve. A video projection technology. Compare DMD.

LD ⇒ LASERDISC.

Leader ⇒ (1) A piece of FILMSTOCK of uniform color, usually black, added to the HEAD or the TAIL of a reel. (2) A length of film showing countdown numbers, which is spliced to the beginning of a reel.

Lead-In, Lead-Out ⇒ (1) A transition, verbal or visual, into or out of a particular segment of a television or radio show. See SEGUE. (2) In programming, a show that precedes or follows another show. A popular lead-in will deliver a larger potential audience to the show that follows it. See also HAMMOCKING.

Leased Channel ⇒ CABLE systems are generally required by their contracts with the area they serve to offer certain channels on a COMMON CARRIER rental basis to independent producers.

LED ⇒ Light-Emitting Diode. A small, long-lived light most often used for signal lamps in electronic equipment.

Legitimate Theater ⇒ Stage theater, with live actors, as opposed to VAUDEVILLE, dinner theater, arena shows, and the like. The adjective dates from the seventeenth century, when by law some theaters were legal and others were not.

Legs ⇒ Commercial endurance. A film that continues to draw audiences week after week is said to have "legs."

Leitmotif ⇒ Also leitmotiv. From Wagnerian opera, a recurring piece of music in a film score used to signal a particular character or evoke a particular mood. A type of MOTIF.

Lens ⇒ An optical lens bends light rays in order to focus them; a magnetic lens bends electron beams so that they can be controlled for the purpose of SCANNING.

LEO ⇒ Low Earth Orbit satellite. A geosynchronous orbit (see SATELLITE COMMUNICATIONS) is not the only way to set up a communications network. LEO satellites are grouped in orbits between 300 and 600 miles. Each one is over its service area for only a brief time, then hands off communications to the next partner in the group.

Letterbox ⇒ The printing technique employed for certain videotapes, LASERDISCS, and DVD-VIDEOS that displays the entire frame of a

WIDESCREEN movie within the confines of the standard television ASPECT RATIO. The top and the bottom of the television frame are left blank. If you don't letterbox a widescreen transfer, you must PAN AND SCAN.

Letterpress Printing ⟫ The traditional method of printing using raised type. Each sheet is printed separately. See ROTARY PRESS, OFFSET, XEROGRAPHY.

LF ⟫ Low Frequency band. See ELECTROMAGNETIC SPECTRUM.

LFE ⟫ Low-Frequency Effects. The .1 in 5.1, utilizing the SUBWOOFER.

Library Shot ⟫ A STOCK SHOT.

Licensing ⟫ (1) A merchandising arrangement between a film producer and the manufacturer of a product that gives the manufacturer the right to use a character or other INTELLECTUAL PROPERTY from a film in exchange for a fee, usually royalty-based. Licensed products commonly include clothes, posters, toys, and games. Increasingly, licensing is part of the marketing strategy, as when a fast-food chain ties in the release of mugs or other tangible goods to the release of a film. (2) More specifically, the right to use intellectual property—footage, music, dialogue, or images—for a set period of time without gaining any ownership interest. See SYNC LICENSE, PERFORMANCE LICENSE.

Lighting Cameraman ⟫ British for CINEMATOGRAPHER.

Lighting ⟫ Early FILMSTOCKS were relatively insensitive. At first, only the sun could provide enough illumination. As a result, the earliest studios were built to rotate to catch the rays of the sun. Huge, unwieldy ARC LAMPS were the mainstays of cinematic lighting from the twenties until the 1960s when quartz xenon lamps, together with filmstocks with much faster EMULSIONS, greatly increased the flexibility of the medium. Now, films shot entirely with AVAILABLE LIGHT are not uncommon, and complicated, controlled lighting has become a luxury rather than a necessity. The more light available, the smaller may be the opening of the DIAPHRAGM, and consequently the greater the DEPTH OF FIELD. Central to the calculation of EXPOSURE and lighting is the GAMMA, or CONTRAST of the filmstock, although techniques of PREFLASHING and POSTFLASHING offer interesting ways of manipulating the contrast. Lighting remains one of the basic techniques of the film medium. See BACKLIGHTING, BARN DOORS, COLOR TEMPERATURE, DIFFUSER, FILLER LIGHT, GOBO, GAFFER, HIGHLIGHTING, KEY LIGHTING.

Lightshow ⟫ The projection of more or less abstract light patterns either moving or still, using numerous techniques, including film. Lightshows became popular in the sixties as accompaniments to rock concerts.

Limited Run ⇒ Releasing a film in a small number of theaters, or for a set number of weeks. See Go Wide, Platforming, Exhibition.

Line 21 Technologies ⇒ Television features that use the VBI, such as Closed-Caption, Teletext.

Line Producer ⇒ See Producer.

Linear Track ⇒ An audio signal recorded on a VHS tape as a stripe at the top edge. The slow speed of VHS tape makes for a poor recording. Much better is a Hi-Fi track, which is recorded with the video in a Helical Scan.

Line-Doubling ⇒ A technique useful in Home Theatre applications for improving the apparent resolution of the broadcast image. In conventional television, the image is divided into two Interlaced Fields. The CRT gun paints first one field, then the other. In a line-doubling IDTV set the two fields are stored in memory so that the CRT gun can paint all the horizontal lines progressively, without interlacing. Thus two complete images are painted in each thirtieth of a second (in the NTSC system) or each twenty-fifth of a second (in PAL and SECAM). This increases the brightest of the picture significantly. The picture also appears sharper—even though the information defining the image has not increased. See Scanning, Line-Quadrupling, Frequency Doubling.

Line-Quadrupling ⇒ Like Line-Doubling, a technique useful in Home Theatre applications for improving the apparent resolution of the image. In addition to painting all the lines progressively as in line-doubling, line-quadrupling systems interpolate an equal number of additional lines. In an NTSC system, then, the total number of lines is 1,050 (2 x 525). Understand that these additional lines, which double the apparent resolution, are mathematical inventions. They didn't exist in the original image—but then, such Virtual Information is a hallmark of DV and DTV, and nobody seems to mind.

Liner, Liner Art, Liner Notes ⇒ LP records were packaged in cardboard sleeves, called liners, which fortuitously provided a broad canvas on the front for Liner Art, and space on the back for text describing in detail the record enclosed. Both the art and the text contributed significantly to the total experience for Audiophiles, as well as providing powerful marketing tools. Liner Art—especially from jazz albums of the 1950s—has become a collectible. Liner Notes provided an effective point-of-sale introduction to the music inside, especially for new artists. Compare Jewel Box, Keep Case.

Lines of Horizontal Resolution ⇒ See LoHR.

Line-Scaling Device ⇒ A Line-Doubler, Line-Quadrupler, or similar device, often used in video projection equipment.

Linkage ⇒ Pudovkin's term for Montage. See Editor.

Linotype ⟫ A typewriterlike machine that permitted the casting of lines of type quickly and cheaply, it was replaced beginning in the 1970s by computer typesetting techniques. See PHOTOTYPOGRAPHY.

Linux ⟫ A version of UNIX written by Finnish student Linus Torvalds in 1991. Torvalds released the SOURCE CODE on the Internet. Over the years, hundreds of programmers around the world contributed to its development. By 1999 it had attracted the attention of major computer manufacturers like IBM and Hewlett-Packard who declared their support even though Linux competed with their own proprietary products. Torvalds continues to control Linux with the help of a group of programmer acolytes. This OS is at the heart of the OPEN SOFTWARE movement.

Lip Sync ⟫ Synchronization between the movement of the mouth and the words on the SOUNDTRACK.

Lithography ⟫ A printing system based on the fact that oil and water do not mix, so that printing surfaces and nonprinting surfaces can be PLANOGRAPHIC yet separate. See RELIEF PRINTING, INTAGLIO.

Live ⟫ In television and radio a live broadcast is a broadcast in REAL TIME, as it happens. Even live broadcasts can be edited. It is common for radio TALK SHOWS to introduce a seven-second delay before broadcast so that if a caller utters an obscenity it can be muted. See DISC, TAPE.

Live on Tape ⟫ Of course, it's not actually live if it's on tape, but this contradictory phrase is meant to convey the information that the tape hasn't been edited before broadcast. Also, on the same model, "Live-on-film." A recording of a live performance.

Live Recording ⟫ A seeming contradiction in terms, "live recording" signifies that a record or tape was recorded on location, usually in front of an audience, rather than in a studio. The suggestion is that the performance has undergone a minimum of technical manipulation. See MIXING.

LMDS ⟫ Local MultiPoint Distribution Service. A recent variant of MDS, LMDSs have expanded service beyond television to telephone and Internet connections. Antennas have been reduced to foot-square dimensions and can be attached to windows.

LNB ⟫ Low Noise Block. The microwave head in the center of a DSB antenna that amplifies the microwave signal and reduces its frequency for transmission to the set. See TRIPLE-BAND LNB.

Local Loop ⟫ Telephone industry term for the circuit between you and the Central Office where the switching is done for your neighborhood.

Location ⟫ Hollywood jargon for any place that is not in a STUDIO.

Logo ➤ From LOGOTYPE. An identifying design meant to symbolize graphically a company or organization either in print or audiovisually. Michael Snow's ↔ (1969) was the first film to use a logo as a title. (It is also known as *Back and Forth*.) In June 1993, ♀, the artist formerly known as Prince, was the first artist to change his name to a logo. Even though his label, Warner, distributed numerous diskettes to the news media with renditions of this unique glyph, reporters resisted and the typographically lackadaisical referred to him thereafter as "the Artist Formerly Known as Prince," which suggested that he no longer had a name. Fans called him TAFKAP, or O(+> —a kind of SMILEY meant to suggest the glyph (although it is lying on its side). By 1999, this person from Minneapolis had decided that the glyph was intellectual property of the first order. He let it be known that he preferred to be known from now on simply as "The Artist," and sued several websites for misappropriating the logo that used to be his legal name.

Logotype ➤ In TYPOGRAPHY, a single piece of type that represents a whole word.

LoHR ➤ *Lines of Horizontal Resolution*. Video monitors are limited in their vertical resolution by their scanning rates. But there is considerable variation in horizontal resolution, which is measured in LoHR. A standard VGA monitor measures 640 pixels wide by 480 pixels high. SVGA monitors can go up to 1280 x 1024. However, it is important to note that the number of horizontal pixels in a line is not the same as the LoHR: it sets an upper limit, but many systems are incapable of resolving all the pixels available to them. DVD-Video (MPEG-2), for example, has an upper horizontal limit of 720 pixels, but the horizontal resolution is approximately 540 lines for a 4:3 image (and 405 for a 16:9 image). The LoHR is measured by counting the number of discernible lines in an image of an industry-standard reference print. See VIDEO RESOLUTION.

Long Lens ➤ See TELEPHOTO LENS.

Long Shot ➤ A long shot includes at least the full figures of the subjects, usually more. See FULL SHOT, EXTREME LONG SHOT.

Long Take ➤ See SEQUENCE SHOT.

Longform ➤ Television programming term for shows more than sixty minutes in length.

Longitudinal Timecode ➤ *LTC*. TIMECODE that is recorded as an audio signal on the address track or on an audio track of a videotape. Compare VERTICAL INTERVAL TIMECODE.

Loop ➤ (1) The technique that permits the intermittent motion PULL-DOWN MECHANISM of the camera and projector to operate effectively. Loops of film before and after the mechanism allow continuous motion to be translated into intermittent motion. (2) A short piece of film joined end to end so as to repeat.

Looping ➻ A POSTDUBBING technique. The performer attempts to match dialogue to performance while watching a short piece of the scene formed into a loop. See ADR.

LOP ➻ Paul Klein's influential if sardonic theory of television programming, which he expressed in a *New York* magazine article in 1970. According to Klein, a respected television executive of the time, people watch television, not specific shows, and they decide which channel to turn to by comparing programs to find the one that offends them least: "Least Objectionable Program." The theory was only strengthened by the advent of CHANNEL-SURFING. Today Klein might rephrase it as "LOS"—Least Objectionable Shot. With the power of the REMOTE in your hands, there's no need to hang around for the whole program.

Lo-Res ➻ A LOw RESolution computer image.

Lossless ➻ Non-Lossy. See COMPRESSION.

Lossy ➻ See COMPRESSION.

Lot ➻ HOLLYWOOD jargon for STUDIO premises, as in "They gave him an office on the lot." All of the Hollywood lots are extensive compounds, with many office buildings, SOUND STAGES, workshops, standing SETS, and backlot LOCATIONS.

Louma ➻ A very flexible CRANE that is controlled by servomechanisms and that uses a television camera and MONITOR so the operator can control the camera from a distance.

Low-Power Television ➻ During the early 1980s the FCC establishing a classification of Low-Power television broadcasting that allowed the addition of numerous small stations. The aim was to expand access to the airwaves. Abbreviated as LPTV or LTV.

LP ➻ A "long-playing" vinyl record that rotates at 33 1/3 rpm; an ALBUM. See HI-FI, RECORD PLAYER.

LPTV ➻ See LOW-POWER TELEVISION.

LTC ➻ See LONGITUDINAL TIMECODE.

LTV ➻ See LOW-POWER TELEVISION.

Luminance ➻ See CHROMINANCE.

L-VIS ➻ Live-Video Insertion System. Technology developed by Princeton Video Image, Inc. in 1998 to matte in billboards or products after a show has been shot or while it is being broadcast. Virtual PRODUCT PLACEMENT. The technology has interesting ramifications: from now on, any Product Placement deal in a film has a time limit. Today they may be eating Reese's Pieces, tomorrow, Mars Bars.

LW ➻ Long Wave. See RADIO BANDS.

LWT ➤ London Weekend Television. One of the more important independent television franchises in the U.K. in the 1970s and 1980s. See ITV.

Lycos ➤ See SEARCH ENGINES.

M ➤ See MEG, MEGA.

MAC ➤ (1) Common nickname for a Macintosh computer. (2) Multiplexed Analog Component. A television broadcast protocol used in European DSB systems, mainly by the French and the Scandinavians, now moribund. Variants were DMAC and D2MAC.

Machine Language ➤ Digital computers understand only a binary language of 1s and 0s. This is machine language. Most humans can't write such strings. Assembly language (or "Assembler") is one step up: usually three-letter codes represent commands. (Assembler is sort of like a language composed entirely of acronyms.) Only a few programmers can write Assembler. Most depend on high-level languages like C, Basic, or COBOL, which use englishlike words. In order for the machine to understand these language they must be either interpreted or compiled. See COMPUTER LANGUAGES.

MacOS ➤ The MACintosh OPERATING SYSTEM didn't have a name of its own (it was known only as System) until the early 1990s when Apple started licensing it to other manufacturers and it was christened MacOS. The first successful GRAPHICAL USER INTERFACE, MacOS remains the most eloquent computer interface. In large part this is the result of the Macintosh *Human Interface Guidelines*—a remarkable document that serves as a grammar for the interface, and explains numerous semiotic concepts underlying and supporting that grammar.

Macro Lens ➤ A lens that can focus to very close distances, as little as 1 mm from the surface of the lens.

Macro Zoom Lens ➤ A lens first developed by the Canon corporation in the 1970s that can focus from 1 mm to infinity and can zoom as well. It permits unusual effects.

Macroblock ➤ See BLOCK.

Macrocinematography ➤ The photographing of objects intermediate in size between those requiring magnification by a microscope and those that can be photographed by a normal lens.

Macrovision ➤ A copy protection system for DVD-VIDEOS. Also the name of the company that sells it. The code added to the signal may also inhibit legal viewing. See CGMS, CSS.

Made-for-Cable Movie ⇒ The high prices paid for feature films by HBO and other cable networks beginning in the late seventies and early eighties soon made it economical for those networks to produce their own films; hence the rise of movies made expressly for showing on cable networks. While they often share the reality-based approach of MADE-FOR-TV MOVIES, they generally have higher budgets and therefore approach—and sometimes exceed—theatrical features in quality.

Made-for-TV Movie ⇒ An awkward phrase for a type of filmed television, intermediate in style and construction between a dramatic program and a THEATRICAL FILM. A successor to the B PICTURE that gained currency in the late 1960s. See TELEFILM, MADE-FOR-CABLE MOVIE.

Magic Lantern ⇒ *Optical Lantern*. A simple projection device dating from the seventeenth century, consisting of a light source, a translucent image source, and a magnifying lens. A popular entertainment throughout the eighteenth and nineteenth centuries, the Magic Lantern show was the most important antecedent of the movies. See SLIDE SHOW.

Magnascope ⇒ Paramount's short-lived widescreen "process" used for a few films in the late 1920s. The effect was achieved by placing a magnifying lens on the projector to double the width (and height) of the image. Of course the lens also magnified the GRAIN. You have to appreciate the chutzpah. "They want wide screens? We'll give 'em wide screens! Throw a wideangle lens on that projector!"

Magnetic Disk ⇒ As used for the storage of information in computer systems, the magnetic disk combines the technique of magnetic tape recording with the advantages and accessibility of the DISK configuration. See FLOPPY DISK.

Magtrack ⇒ Magnetic SOUNDTRACK on film, as opposed to OPTRACK—optical soundtrack.

Main Level ⇒ Basic parameters for the MPEG-2 protocol, specifying a maximum resolution equal to CCIR 601. In MPEG lingo, "levels" specify parameters.

Main Profile ⇒ The basic syntax of MPEG-2 that serve a wide range of output systems (cable, satellite, disc). In MPEG lingo, "profiles" specify syntaxes.

Make-Good ⇒ See BONUS SPOT.

Maltese Cross ⇒ The most common type of PULL-DOWN MECHANISM. An elegant intermittent cam.

Manga ⇒ The Japanese word for comics has been adopted in English to signify Japanese comic-book art. The genre has become a collectible. See ANIME.

Market ⇒ See ADI, DMA.

Married Print ➤ A positive print of a film including both sound and image. See ANSWER PRINT.

Martini ➤ The last shot. Compare WINDOW, ABBY SINGER, CHAMPAGNE SHOT.

Mask ➤ (1) A shield placed before the camera lens to block off part of the image. (2) A shield placed behind the projector lens to obtain the correct ASPECT RATIO. See TV MASK, MATTE SHOT.

Mass Media ➤ Newspapers, magazines, radio, film, and television that reach large audiences. The term became popular after World War II to suggest a dichotomy between POPULAR CULTURE and high ART.

Master ➤ The original disc or tape from which all discs or tape copies are ultimately produced. Also used as a verb.

Master Shot ➤ A long TAKE of an entire scene, generally a relatively LONG SHOT that facilitates the assembly of component closer shots and DETAILS. The EDITOR can always fall back on the master shot: consequently it is also called a *cover shot*.

Mastering ➤ In the Optical Disc world, the process of burning a master disc to be used in replication. Compare PREMASTERING.

Match Cut ➤ A cut in which the two shots joined are linked by visual, aural, or metaphorical parallelism. Famous example: at the end of *North by Northwest*, Cary Grant is pulling Eva Marie Saint up the cliff of Mount Rushmore; match cut to Grant pulling her up to a Pullman bunk. See also MONTAGE. Do not confuse with JUMP CUT.

Match on Action ➤ A cut that shifts the framing of an action within a SCENE by continuing the movement within the first shot seamlessly in the second shot. A MATCH CUT is a variation of the match on action.

Materialist Cinema ➤ (1) A twentieth-century movement that celebrated the physical facts of film, camera, light, and projector and in which the materials of the art were in fact its main subject matter. Michael Snow, Tony Conrad, Paul Sharits, and Hollis Frampton were important figures in the movement. See STRUCTURAL FILM. (2) The cinema of filmmakers such as Jean-Luc Godard and Roberto Rossellini that combined some of the qualities of definition (1) with a strong conception of political change as dialectically materialistic—that is, as rooted in the basic conflicts of concrete economic realities.

Matrix Encoding ➤ Adding SURROUND Sound signals to a basic two-channel stereo signal by encoding the necessary information in the basic signal.

Matsushita ➤ Japanese electronics firm noted not for innovation but for marketing, Matsushita has carved a dominant position in the media industry by allowing rival SONY to pioneer a technology that Matsushita (whose brand names include Panasonic and Technics) then exploits. Always the follower, never the leader, Matsushita bought MCA/Universal in 1990, a year after Sony had purchased Columbia Pictures. In 1995 Matsushita sold most of its interest in MCA to Edgar Bronfman's Seagram Company while Sony held on to Columbia.

Matte Shot ⇒ A matte is a piece of film that is opaque in part of the frame area. When printed together with a normal shot it masks part of the image of that shot and allows another scene, reversely matted, to be printed in the masked-off area. If the matte changes from frame to frame, the process is called Travelling Matte or Blue Screen. See also Chroma Key.

Mavica ⇒ Sony's first attempt at a digital electronic camera, introduced in 1989. An all-digital process, it was not a commercial success at the time. Sony reintroduced the Mavica eight years later, when the time was right. See DVC. Compare Photo CD.

M-A-W ⇒ A "Model-Actress-Whatever," the 1990s descendent of the Starlet. Compare D-Girl.

M-Bone ⇒ Broadband Internet technology that allows full multimedia programming—at least for those equipped with the necessary broad-bandwidth network connections.

MBPS, MPS ⇒ These are standard abbreviations for megabits per second (mbps, mps) and megabytes per second (MBps, Mps), but it is so easy to misconstrue them that it is better to spell it out.

MCA ⇒ See Agent, Universal.

McGuffin ⇒ Alfred Hitchcock's term for the device or plot element that catches the viewer's attention or drives the logic of the plot, especially in suspense films. According to Hitchcock, the McGuffin can be ignored as soon as it has served its purpose. Examples are the mistaken identity at the beginning of *North by Northwest* and the entire Janet Leigh subplot of *Psycho*.

MD ⇒ Sony's MiniDisc.

MDS ⇒ Multipoint Distribution Service. A Common Carrier distribution service operating in the super high frequency band (microwave) to distribute private television programming on contract. MDS is widely used to distribute hotel programming and other Closed Circuit transmissions. It can also be used to distribute Pay TV direct to homes not equipped with Cable. The consumer installs a small microwave Dish. Compare DSS.

Mebi ⇒ Proposed prefix for the binary magnitude associated with the decimal Mega. See Binary Magnitudes.

Mechanical ⇒ Copy and artwork prepared to be photographed for Photoengraving plates to be used in printing.

Media ➺ (Singular: MEDIUM.) (1) Agencies or channels for the exchange, transmission, or dissemination of information. Especially "mass media," such as newspapers and magazines (print media); radio and television (electronic media); CDs, tapes, and movies (recording media). (2) The physical forms of these expressions; for example, paper, AUDIOTAPE, FILMSTOCK, VIDEOTAPE, MAGNETIC DISK, OPTICAL DISC. The plural "Mediums" is often used for this connotation to distinguish it from the political and social meanings that attach to "the media." For example, the phrase "mediums of expression." (3) Since the late 1960s, when vice president Spiro Agnew began his campaign against the "nattering nabobs of negativism," the phrase "the media" most often summons up an amorphous image of the political establishment who supposedly control the news media. Although the right gets more attention for its critique of "the media," criticism has been just as prevalent from the left.

Media Event ➺ An event staged to draw the particular attention of the media. The simplest and oldest example of a media event is the press conference. The development of television as the main social medium for news has led to more sophisticated media events such as the staged dramatization (for example, politicians' visits to newsworthy sites) and the demonstration.

Media Image ➺ The aura created in electronic and print media for an idea, company, product, concept, person, or political theory. See VALIDATION, CULTURE INDUSTRY.

Mediaguard ➺ ENCRYPTION system for CANAL + Seca conditional access.

Mediasphere ➺ On the model of CYBERSPACE, this virtual world focuses our attention on the reality created by the increasingly pervasive news and entertainment MEDIA.

Mediate ➺ (1) To serve as a vehicle for the transmission of information. (2) To change or modify that information in such a way that it fits the peculiar requirements of the print or electronic MEDIA.

Medium, Mediums, Media ➺ "Medium" is the correct singular, "media" the correct plural, although the latter term often appears—incorrectly—as singular, perhaps because the writer or speaker has an image in mind of a massive and monolithic establishment. Some academics now use the coinage "mediums" as a sort of super-intensive plural. That word seems useful when one wants to draw attention to the multiplicity of channels of communication. For example: "There are numerous print mediums," but "The media are angry at the president."

Medium Shot ➺ A shot intermediate between a CLOSEUP and a FULL SHOT, generally including a figure from the waist up.

Meg, Mega ➻ (1) Colloquially, a prefix for million, as in "He went 12 megabucks over budget on his last film." (2) In the computer world the prefix is often pressed into service to mean 2^{20}, which is 1,048,576, not 1,000,000 (10^6). Thus an 80 Meg (or megabyte) hard drive holds 83,886,080 BYTES, not 80,000,000 bytes. Generally disc storage is measured on the binary model while data transmission rates are quoted on the decimal model—thus a 2 Megabit/sec connection transmits data at 2,000,000 bits/sec. There is even a third definition of megabyte as 1,024,000 bytes—that's a thousand kilobytes (1,000 x 2^{10}). The IEEE has proposed a set of new prefixes for BINARY MAGNITUDES to sort out this mess. See also GIG, K, TERA.

Megapixel ➻ The earliest digital still cameras were geared to producing images for computer displays and thus usually limited to the VGA dimensions of 640 x 480 PIXELS. This level of resolution is not enough to produce a good photographic print. Megapixel cameras, which reached consumer price levels in early 1998, record a million pixels or more: a level that can produce a satisfactory 4 x 6 print. The advent of the Megapixel cameras combined with cheap DYE SUBLIMATION and advanced INK JET printers marked a real shift in home photography. See HDC.

Megaplex ➻ See MULTIPLEX.

Melodrama ➻ Originally, simply a drama with music; more precisely, the type of nineteenth-century drama that centered on the simplistic conflict between heroes and villains. More recently the word has come to signify any emotional drama.

Memex ➻ Physicist Vannevar Bush wrote a prophetic article for the *Atlantic Monthly* in July 1945 as World War II was coming to a close. It forecast much of the digital revolution to come. His vision of the device he called a Memex accurately described the personal computer of the future. It included a keyboard, removable memory, storage of images and sounds as well as text, and multiple viewing screens. Compare DYNABOOK.

Merchandising ➻ For a long time studios have had licensing departments whose function it was to wring a little extra cash out of certain films by cutting deals with toy companies, clothing manufacturers, and others. (Of course, Disney, with its collection of perennially popular cartoon characters, led the way.) In the 1980s merchandising became more closely associated with marketing as giveaways were arranged with fast-food chains and others to promote a film. By the late 1980s it made sense to Warner and other studios to horn in on the retail share of the business by opening stores devoted to a wide range of studio merchandise. Now certain films may earn more from their merchandise sales than from ticket sales. See PRODUCT PLACEMENT.

Metal Particle Tape ➺ Videotape or audiotape using pure iron, not an oxide, for improved frequency response and wider dynamic range.

Metonymy ➺ In rhetoric, a common figure of speech that is characterized by the substitution of a word or concept closely associated with the object for the object itself (hence, "gun" for "gunman"). Generally, an associative device, common in cinematic language. See INDEX, ICON, SYMBOL, SYNECDOCHE.

Metro-Goldwyn-Mayer ➺ See MGM.

Metteur en Scène ➺ From the French, a modest—sometimes derogatory—term for "director." See AUTEUR, MISE EN SCÈNE.

MF ➺ Medium Frequency band. See ELECTROMAGNETIC SPECTRUM.

MFC ➺ See MADE-FOR-CABLE MOVIE.

MFP ➺ Multi-Function Product. A dull acronym for a Fax–Copier–Scanner–Printer. (They could have called it a "cosfap.")

MGM, MGM/UA ➺ Metro-Goldwyn-Mayer was formed in 1924 through the merger of Metro Picture Corporation, Goldwyn Pictures Corporation, and Louis B. Mayer Pictures (all established six to eight years earlier) under the control of the massive theater chain Loew's, Inc. Louis B. Mayer ran the studio until 1951, when he lost control to Dore Schary. For the first twelve years of its existence—under the influence of Mayer's associate, the revered Irving G. Thalberg—the studio quickly established a reputation for high quality, literate pictures. After Thalberg died in 1936 (at age 37), the quality remained, but the focus shifted to light entertainment. The studio emphasized its compelling roster of stars during the 1930s and 1940s, and reached its zenith in the late 1940s and 1950s with a long string of bright and colorful musicals produced by Arthur Freed and his team.

As the stars aged and the musical faded, MGM fell precipitously. From the 1960s through the 1980s it limped along, supported mainly by its library. Las Vegas real-estate magnate Kirk Kerkorian first took control of the company in 1970, installing former CBS programming chief Jim Aubrey as president. Aubrey proceeded to slash costs and liquidate assets with abandon, even auctioning off the studio's incredible prop and costume collection in 1970. Kerkorian always seemed more interested in the MGM logo and the tradition it represented than in actual film production. In 1973, MGM stopped distributing its own movies, licensing them to UNITED ARTISTS and CIC. In 1981, MGM acquired the remnants of United

Artists, beginning a long series of complicated financial transactions described with gusto and elan by Peter Bart in his book, *Fade Out*.

In 1986, Ted Turner purchased MGM/UA (as it was then named) only to sell back the film and television production business to Kerkorian, who resold the lot to Lorimar-Telepictures. (The historic MGM studio became the home of SONY Pictures—COLUMBIA and TRISTAR—in the 1990s.) Turner retained the MGM libraries, which fed his cable networks for many years thereafter. Giancarlo Paretti's Pathé Corporation took control in 1990, after numerous complex deals. Paretti quickly lost control to his creditors. In 1992 Crédit Lyonnais took control of what remained of the once-great studio. In 1996 the bank sold MGM at auction for $1.3 billion to a group led by Kirk Kerkorian and including Frank Mancuso and the Australian broadcasting company Group Seven. It was the third time Kerkorian had purchased the company.

A year later MGM purchased several assets from Metromedia, including the remnants of Orion and Goldwyn Entertainment (founded in 1979 by Samuel Goldwyn Jr), and—most important—their film library. Once again MGM controlled the world's largest collection of films. Kerkorian took the company public in 1997. In 1999 MGM bought the 1,300-film Polygram library from Seagram, further adding to its collection. It also won a suit preventing Sony Pictures Entertainment from producing James Bond films. Holding on to this successful FRANCHISE (derived from its UA subsidiary) should prove lucrative enough to edge MGM back into the list of major studios. Mancuso left the company in 1999.

Mickey ⟫⟶ In the computer business, a unit of measurement. 1/200th of an inch is common. What does it measure? The movement of the mouse, of course!

Micon ⟫⟶ A moving ICON. See SPRITE.

Micro ⟫⟶(1) Standard prefix for a millionth, as in "microsecond": 0.000001 (10^{-6}) of a second. See also NANO, PICO, FEMTO. (2) Short for "microcomputer," a word that has nothing to do with "millionth." The relatively cheap computers introduced by DEC, Data General, and others in the late 1960s were quickly dubbed "minicomputers" because they were smaller than the so-called mainframes they challenged. Still, they were the size of a closet. When the first desktop computing devices appeared a few years later they were called microcomputers simply because they were smaller than minis—on the model of miniskirt and microskirt. Machines that reduce the FORM FACTOR by another magnitude are known as "hand-helds"—not "nanocomputers."

Microchip ⟫⟶ See MICROPROCESSOR.

Microcinematography ➠ Film photography through a microscope. See MACROCINEMATOGRAPHY.

Microphone ➠ A device that picks up sound waves, "focuses" them, and translates them into an electrical signal which can then be amplified.

Microprocessor ➠ A small electronic device performing the work of millions of TRANSISTORS arranged in circuits that are microscopically etched into the chip material, usually silicon, often no more than 1/4 inch square. The microprocessor was the third step in the development of modern microelectronics, after the transistor/PRINTED CIRCUIT and the INTEGRATED CIRCUIT. The development of microprocessor technology from the 1970s through the 1990s made possible the microcomputer revolution as well as the ensuing DIGITAL revolution. See MOORE'S LAW.

Microsoft ➠ Founded in 1975 by Harvard dropout William Gates and Paul Allen, Microsoft has been a dominant force in the microcomputer industry since the early eighties. Microsoft's singular coup was to win the contract from IBM to provide the operating system for IBM's entry into the personal computer market in 1981. The MS-DOS operating system (and its successor, Windows) has dominated the PC industry ever since, providing Microsoft with opportunities to develop a wide range of applications programming. Since 1985 Microsoft has championed CD-ROM technology, founding an electronic publishing division in the late 1980s to prepare for the coming "information generation" in the PC industry. Microsoft started development of its Windows graphical interface at about the same time that APPLE introduced its highly regarded Macintosh operating system in 1984. It wasn't until the introduction of Windows 3.1 in 1992, however, that Microsoft's own GUI began to overtake MS-DOS, and not until the introduction of Windows 95 in August 1995 that the operating system began to approach the Mac OS in utility. The company settled one government antitrust suit in the mid-nineties only to find itself back in court in 1998 charged with anticompetitive monopoly practices.

MIDI ➠ Musical Instrument Digital Interface. The standard for digital communications between musical instruments and computers.

MIME ➠ Multipurpose Internet Mail Extensions. A set of developing standards to provide more graphic control over EMAIL messages and allow the inclusion of graphics, audio, and movies.

Mimesis ➠ The Greek word for "imitation," a term important to the definition of REALISM.

Mini-8 ➠ See PLUGS.

Mini Plug ➠ See PLUGS.

Miniature Card ➻ See DIGITAL FILM.

Minicam ➻ A small, lightweight television camera that can be hand-held. See ENG.

MiniDisc ➻ (1) SONY 2 1/2-inch portable, recordable audio CD format that uses the proprietary ATRAC COMPRESSION technique to accommodate enough music on the small disc and caching to avoid skipping problems. Introduced in 1992 as a personal audio device, the MD competed with Philips's DCC. Neither succeeded. While Philips abandoned the DCC format in 1996, Sony reintroduced the Mini-Disc in 1998 with more success. Not to be confused with a CD single. (2) Any small magnetic DISKETTE.

MiniDV ➻ Like DVCAM and DVCPRO, a format for digital videocassettes.

Minimalist Cinema ➻ A kind of extreme, stylized REALISM: Carl Dreyer, Robert Bresson, early Andy Warhol. Minimal dependence on the technical power of the medium.

Miniseries ➻ A CLOSED-END television SERIAL with a limited number of episodes, usually based on a popular novel.

Minitel ➻ (1) France Telecom's VIDEOTEXT system based on the Teletel protocol. By 1990 more than 20 percent of French telephone subscribers were Minitel users and more than 12,000 services were available. A precursor of the WORLD WIDE WEB, Minitel echoed all of its features on a smaller scale more than ten years before the success of the Web and maintained its position in French culture for years after the Web united the world. (2) The little terminal upon which the Teletel system relied for its success.

MIPS ➻ Millions of Instructions/Second. A common measure of CPU speed, not as precise as FLOPS.

Miramax ➻ Founded in 1979 by New Yorkers Bob and Harvey Weinstein, this INDIE distributor quickly developed into a key player in the film industry and has remained so for twenty years. The Weinstein brothers cannily acquired saleable art films and made them profitable through shrewd marketing. By the late 1980s Miramax owned the best foreign film Oscar, winning it four years running. In 1989 they began to venture into production while continuing their string of import successes with products like *The Crying Game* (1992), *The English Patient* (1997), and the films of Roberto Benigni.

In 1993 the Weinsteins cashed out, selling Miramax to Disney, but continuing to run it as an independent subsidiary in New York, maintaining their image as Hollywood renegades. Bob works behind the scenes, while Harvey plays the role of the cigar-chomping mogul of yore better than anyone left alive in Hollywood. In

1999 the company pulled down ten Oscars, including Best Picture for *Shakespeare in Love*, beating the establishment favorite, Dreamworks' *Saving Private Ryan*. The Weinsteins were accused of buying the award with an expensive promotional campaign, but it was more likely that their comedy beat the widescreen war drama because it worked better on VHS—and these days far too many of the Academy members see their movies that way rather than in proper theaters.

Mirror Shot ➻ (1) A shot in a mirror. (2) A kind of GLASS SHOT.

MIS ➻ Management Information Services. The 1980s term for the "computer department" of a company. Today, the abbreviation is usually shorted to IS.

Mise en Scène ➻ From the French, the term usually used to denote that part of the cinematic process that takes place on the set, as opposed to MONTAGE, which takes place afterward. Literally, the "putting-in-the-scene": the direction of actors, placement of cameras, choice of lenses, lighting, sets, costumes, and so forth. Mise en scène is more important to REALISTS, montage to EXPRESSIONISTS. Compare METTEUR EN SCÈNE.

Mise en Shot, Mise en Cadre ➻ The design of an entire shot, in time as well as space.

Mitchell ➻ The brand name of the most common type of Hollywood camera during the Golden Age: a large, complex machine requiring several operators. Compare ARRIFLEX.

Mix ➻ (1) Optical: a DISSOLVE. (2) Sound: the marriage of several separate recording tracks such as music, dialogue, and SOUND EFFECTS. See DME. (3) Music: any one of several different versions of a song prepared for various forms of distribution or various purposes: music video, FM radio, CD, for example.

Mixed Mode CD ➻ See CD+.

Mixing, Mixage ➻ The general term for the work of the sound editor or mixer, who combines and edits various separate soundtracks into one final version. The tracks might include dialogue, sound effects, music, and ROOM SOUND. See DME, MONTAGE, COMPOSITING.

MLP ➻ Meridian Lossless Packing, developed by Meridian Audio, a small British company, as a lossless compression technique for DVD-AUDIO, and adopted as part of the standard in August 1998, beating out DTS and others. MLP can achieve a saving of 40 percent.

MMCD ➻ Sony's proprietary format for a portable MultiMedia CD player based on MPEG-1 video. A transitional technology that led to DVD. Compare DATA DISCMAN, CD-I.

MMDS ➻ Multi-point Microwave Distribution System. A broadcasting system using microwaves. See MVDS.

MNP ➤ Microcom Networking Protocol. A system of correction and compression PROTOCOLS introduced by the Microcom company that became a standard for data transmission via MODEM.

MO ➤ Magneto-Optical, a combination of technologies used to produce rewritable CD-ROMs. See OPTICAL DISC.

Mobile Wireless ➤ See WIRELESS.

Model Shot ➤ A shot using miniatures instead of the real objects or locations. Especially useful for staging great disasters.

Modem ➤ From MOdulator–DEModulator. A device to convert DIGITAL computer information into an ANALOG signal so that it can be communicated over telephone lines. Modems are ranked primarily by their speed, measured in bits per second. Since each alphanumeric character takes up at least 8 bits—and usually 10—a 28,800 bits/sec modem is potentially capable of transmitting or receiving 2,880 characters per second, which is about 500 words per second. Compare CODEC.

Modernism ➤ The dominant art and literary culture of the first half of the twentieth century, modernism was characterized by a strong urge to abstraction (as in CUBISM); a critical self-consciousness, which made the work of art often more important than its subject (as in the THEATER OF THE ABSURD); and—most important—the deep-rooted rebellious spirit that characterized the AVANT-GARDE.

Modulated Dolby Digital ➤ In order to include a digital soundtrack on a LASERDISC (which is analog) that signal has to be modulated to an RF signal.

Modulation ➤ The principle that makes it possible for electromagnetic waves to transmit messages. Information is translated into waveforms, which can then be imposed on—or modulate—a carrier wave. See WAVE MECHANICS, AM, FM.

Mogul ➤ One of the descendants of Baber, who conquered India in 1526, or a rich and powerful, often autocratic, person. The word is most often used to refer to the heads and owners of the great Hollywood studios.

Moiré Pattern ➤ A disturbance pattern on television or computer screens caused by the interference of two similar line patterns. In print the same effect is caused by the interference of two (or more) BEN DAY SCREENS.

Monaural ➤ Single-source tape or disc sound reproduction, as compared with binaural STEREOPHONIC reproduction.

Moneme ➤ The basic unit of formal choice in European linguistics, on the model of PHONEME.

Monitor ➤ A CATHODE RAY TUBE or television set connected directly to a camera or computer.

Monopack ➻ See TECHNICOLOR.

Monophonic ➻ A single channel of audio, as opposed to STEREO-PHONIC.

Montage ➻ (1) Simply, EDITING. (2) Eisenstein's idea that adjacent shots should relate to each other so that A and B combine to produce another meaning, C, which is not actually recorded on the film. (3) "Dynamic Cutting": a stylized form of editing, often to provide a lot of information in a short time. See MIXING.

Montage of Attractions ➻ A concept associated with Eisenstein's theory of EDITING: the construction of a system of ATTRACTIONS.

Moore's Law ➻ Near the beginning of the digital revolution, Gordon Moore, one of the founders of INTEL, posited that the maximum number of circuits that could be printed on a CHIP would double every eighteen months. Throughout the 1980s and 1990s this "law" proved surprisingly accurate.

Morph ➻ The seamless change of a visual form from one state to another, usually accomplished by a computer program. The technique became popular in the early 1990s in commercials in which one model car would appear to change into another model. *Terminator II* made extensive use of morphs. They were also used to striking effect in Michael Jackson's "Black or White" video.

Morpheme ➻ The basic unit of formal meaning in linguistics. See PHONEME, MONEME.

Morse Code ➻ One of the earliest systems of MODULATION, Morse code translates the Western alphabet into combinations of only two symbols: dots and dashes (short and long bursts of energy).

MOS ➻ Film shot without sound: "Mit Out Sound," ostensibly from the days when German directors first arrived in Hollywood.

Mosaic ➻ (1) Developed in 1993 at the Supercomputing Center of the University of Illinois (see NCSA), the Mosaic program provided the first popular graphical interface to the INTERNET'S WORLD WIDE WEB. Mosaic, and programs like it, contributed greatly to the growth of Internet activity during the mid-1990s. (2) See DISTRIBUTION FLOW.

Mosquitoes ➻ Fuzziness on the edges of a compressed image. See GIBBS EFFECT.

Motif ➻ A recurrent thematic element used in the development of an artistic work. See LEITMOTIF.

Motion-Control System ➻ Growing out of the pioneering work of Douglas Trumbull and others for *2001: A Space Odyssey* (1968), these devices were special effects workhorses of the 1970s and 1980s. A Motion-Control System is a robot that operates the camera (and sometimes the lighting and the models) following a set script. The photography can be continuous or one frame at a time. This is quite valuable for photographing models and for travelling mattes. The KENWORTHY was an early example of this technology. John Dykstra's Dykstraflex, developed at INDUSTRIAL LIGHT AND MAGIC, was another. Most of this work is now done digitally.

Mountain Film ➻ Weimar Germany's rough equivalent of the American Western, a genre of the 1920s and 1930s that dealt with the pioneering struggles of mountain climbing and parallel emotional conflict. A semi-action genre that glorified physical prowess, it attracted such filmmakers as G. W. Pabst and Leni Riefenstahl, although it is most closely associated with Arnold Fanck.

Movie File Formats ➻ Because they deal with still and moving images these are more complicated than IMAGE FILE FORMATS or TEXT FILE FORMATS. Nearly all audio and video formats depend on compression techniques. The necessary CODECS exist within various architectures, the most common of which is QUICKTIME. Although MICROSOFT periodically announces grudging support for QuickTime they continue to challenge it with their own products, first VIDEO FOR WINDOWS, then DIRECTSHOW. The third major architecture is REALAUDIO/REALVIDEO, the first STREAMING MEDIA format. The combination of the elaborate MPEG codec and the DVD-VIDEO standard presents another potential video architecture, although its main use is in the dedicated environments of DVD and DSS.

Movie Made for Television ➻ See MADE-FOR-TV MOVIE.

Movie Movie ➻ A movie about the movies. See REFLEXIVITY.

Movietone ➻ Warner gets the credit in the popular imagination for introducing sound to the movies, but Twentieth Century Fox stole a march on their crosstown rivals. The sound-on-film system they had licensed from Case laboratory quickly became the standard. Case's system was derived from Lee De Forest's PHONOFILM. In May 1927 Fox released a sound newsreel of Lindbergh's takeoff on his historic flight that should outrank the October release of *The Jazz Singer* in the history books.

Moviola ➻ A traditional brand of EDITING machine; also used generically. See STEENBECK.

MOW ➻ Movie Of the Week; Hollywood jargon for MOVIE MADE-FOR-TELEVISION.

MP ➻ See METAL PARTICLE TAPE.

MPAA ➻ Motion Picture Association of America. The Hollywood studios' professional organization and lobbying office was founded in 1922 (as the Motion Pictures Producers and Distributors of America) with the express purpose of protecting the industry from a rising tide of public indignation at the loose morals of Hollywood, both on screen and off. (The Fatty Arbuckle scandal is generally cited as the key event.) With multi-mogul savvy, the Association hired Warren Harding's Postmaster, Will Hays, a public figure of impeccable morals, to front for it. The results were: the Hays Office, which ruled Hollywood morals for twenty years; and the PRODUCTION CODE, which had a profound effect on what was seen on screen.

Gradually, the mandate of the office changed. The Central Casting Bureau was set up early on, and as years passed the Association turned its attention from morals to business. The name of the group was changed in 1945 when Eric Johnston took over. At the same time the Motion Picture Export Association (MPEA) was formed to promote foreign sales. By this time the industry was under siege, from the government's anti-trust case on one side, and from television on the other.

In 1966 the MPAA cast Lyndon Johnson's aide Jack Valenti as its head. He presided over the replacement of the Code with the current RATINGS system, then immediately turned his attention to increasing industry sales. He has served as Hollywood's figurehead ever since. Only the majors belong to the MPAA (and MPEA), hence the need for AFMA.

MPAA CODE ➤ See PRODUCTION CODE.

MP@ML ➤ MAIN PROFILE at MAIN LEVEL. The main format of MPEG-2 video, including the basic parameters and the rules of syntax.

MPEA ➤ Motion Picture Export Association. An arm of the MPAA set up to promote exports.

MPEG, MPEG-2 ➤ COMPRESSION standard algorithms for DIGITAL motion-picture video developed by the Motion Picture Experts Group. MPEG-1 is a low-bandwidth algorithm aimed at the CD-ROM level. MPEG-2 is the high-quality algorithm adopted in 1994 for DVD-VIDEO and DSS, and later digital television. In MPEG-2, the I Frames are the KEY FRAMES. Each I (for Intra) Frame is complete; subsequent frames include only changes from the I Frame. P Frames are Predicted from the previous frame. B Frames are derived Bidirectionally from both preceding and following frames. (See TEMPORAL COMPRESSION.) In DVD-Video applications the MPEG-2 can be encoded either CONSTANT BIT RATE or VARIABLE BIT RATE. In broadcast applications, only CBR is possible, since compression is done in real time. Compare JPEG. See AC-3.

MP4 ➤ The successor to the MP3 protocol, under discussion as of mid-1999.

MPS ➤ Medium Powered Satellite. Lower power than DBS, but more channels.

MP3 ➤ MPEG-1, Layer 3. A version of the MPEG compression standard that became popular in late 1997 for posting and downloading music tracks on the INTERNET. The 10:1 compression ratio of MP3 made it feasible to move music files over low-bandwidth connections. Many artists began distributing versions of their music via MP3, while thousands of hackers pirated commercial music and redistributed it in MP3. In 1998, a small company began distributing a portable player for MP3 audio, the Rio. The RIAA protested, but lost their suit. Interestingly, MP3 is not supported in the MPEG-2 audio specification. See RIPPER.

MPX Filter ➻ A circuit that removes the 19 kHz pilot tone from an FM radio broadcast. The pilot tone can interfere with DOLBY noise reduction.

MS-DOS ➻ See MICROSOFT.

MSN ➻ MicroSoft Network. Microsoft's surprisingly belated entry in the online market debuted in August 1995 at the same time as Windows 95. A proprietary system for Windows machines only, it offered AOL-like graphics and a similar, although much more limited, menu of services. It was already clear at the time that the WORLD WIDE WEB was going to replace proprietary services like MSN, so the service was DOA. Unscathed by this failure, Microsoft soon reinvented MSN as one of the world's leading ISPs, selling access to the Internet and, in the process, creating one of the top-ranked PORTALS.

MSNBC ➻ The first combined cable channel/website, founded by MICROSOFT and NBC, opened July 15, 1996.

MSO ➻ Multiple System Operator. A CABLE TELEVISION company that operates more than one local cable system.

MTS ➻ Multi-channel Television Sound, a STEREO sound system for television.

MTV ➻ Music Television. CABLE NETWORK founded August 1, 1981, by Warner-Amex Cable to serve as a showcase for the newly developed MUSIC VIDEO promotions, MTV went on to revolutionize the music industry as well as marking a major shift in the way Americans use television. Now owned by VIACOM, MTV's list of top videos—which apparently has little statistical basis—has become at least as important as disc sales figures or radio ratings. For the current generation of young people, the video now often supersedes the song. See also RAP.

Multiangle ➻ The DVD-VIDEO standard allows for up to nine separate video tracks—usually devoted to multiple camera angles. The viewer can switch instantly from one to another. This feature has become known as Multiangle. The word can also be used as a verb.

Multicast ➻ Distribution to many, but not all (as in broadcast). Compare UNICAST.

Multi-channel Television Sound ➻ See MTS.

Multimedia ➻ The combination of text, sounds, stills, and moving pictures in a publishing enterprise, usually using the medium of CD-ROM or DVD-ROM. The word has become shorthand for any digital media production. See DVD, CD-ROM, QUICKTIME.

Multipath Distortion ➻ When television signals reflect off buildings or mountains they can reach the receiver via two or more paths causing GHOSTS.

Multi-PIP ➻ Multiple Picture-In-Picture. A feature of digital television sets: as many as nine channels can be displayed at once in small boxes on the screen. Imagine watching an event like the Olympics this way! See PIP.

Multiple Exposure ➻ A number of images printed over each other. Not to be confused with MULTIPLE IMAGE.

Multiple Image ➻ A number of images printed beside each other within the same frame, often showing different camera angles of the same action, or separate actions. Also called SPLIT SCREEN.

Multiplex ➻ (1) The technique of imposing one PROGRAM SIGNAL on another to increase the channels available on each radio frequency. Multiplex is used for FM STEREOPHONIC broadcasting as well as for the transmission of entirely separate programming, such as MUZAK. (2) A building that houses multiple movie theaters to increase the amount of product offered to audiences while maintaining constant staff and other expense levels. Since a large part of a cinema's profit comes from concession sales, a properly programmed multiplex can greatly increase yield from a single concession stand. A Multiplex with six auditoriums is known as a Sixplex, one with eight as an Eightplex, and so on. A theater with too many screens is known as a *Megaplex*. The largest so far is the modestly-named Kinepolis, opened in 1988 in Brussels. Kinepolis has 26 screens—including an IMAX—and a total seating capacity of 8,000.

Multiscan Monitor, Multisync Monitor ➻ A monitor than can adjust to inputs with various SCAN RATES and VIDEO RESOLUTIONS.

MUSE ➻ MUltiple Sub-nyquist sampling Encoding. A tape format developed by NHK for HDTV. See HI-VISION.

Music Track ➻ One of three basic tracks, together with dialogue and EFFECTS, that are MIXED together to form the final SOUNDTRACK.

Music Video ➻ A short video made to illustrate (and market) a popular song. The first music videocassette prepared especially for the home market was Michael Nesmith's *'Lectric Lady Disco*, reviewed by *Variety* in April 1978, but the genre did not establish itself until HBO's MTV cable channel debuted in 1981. The Music Video phenomenon grew rapidly over the next ten years so that by the 1990s

MTV, its imitators, and its competitors had become the major international marketing medium for popular music, and for certain genres (Rap, for example) the video was sometimes as important as the audio.

Musique Concrète ⇛ See Concrete Music.

Mutoscope ⇛ A sideshow or Nickelodeon device that produced moving images by flipping cards attached to a drum, not unlike a Rolodex.

MUX ⇛ (v) To Multiplex a signal. (n) A multiplexing device.

Muzak ⇛ Specially programmed and performed music designed to produce a useful mood or effect, then broadcast or reproduced by tape as an aural environment.

MUZE ⇛ A proprietary kiosk-based online information system for music stores, also maintains a web database.

MVDS ⇛ Microwave Video Distribution System. A broadcasting system that uses omnidirectional microwaves on the 40 gHz band. Sometimes called MMDS.

MW ⇛ Medium Wave. See Radio Bands.

NAB ⇛ National Association of Broadcasters. The major trade association serving television broadcasters.

Nagra ⇛ Brand name of a widely used portable sound tape recorder, important in the history of Cinéma Vérité and Direct Cinema. The Swiss manufacturer has kept its edge from the analog sixties through the digital nineties.

Nagravision ⇛ Encryption system for satellite television mainly used in France and in other countries on channels owned by Canal +. Also called *Syster*. See VideoCrypt, Eurocrypt.

Nano ⇛ Standard prefix for a billionth (U.S.), as in "nanosecond": 0.000000001 (10^{-9}) of a second. See also Micro, Pico, Femto.

NAPLPS ⇛ (Pronounced "nap-lips.") The acronym for North American Presentation Level Protocol Standard, the American and Canadian Videotext Protocol used in various versions by Bell Canada and Prodigy in the late 1980s and early 1990s. Compare Minitel, Prestel, Telidon.

NARAS ⇛ National Academy of Recording Arts and Sciences. Founded in 1957 on the model of AMPAS to grant awards for excellence in recording that became known as Grammys.

Narrative ⇛ Story; more precisely, the linear, chronological structure of a story. An important concept in theories of Formalism. Contrast with Plot. See Story.

Narrative Film ➳ A film that tells a story, as opposed to Poetic Film.

Narrowband ➳ A service that provides only one data type: voice or video, for example. See Bandwidth. Compare Broadband, Baseband.

Narrowcast ➳ The distribution of a transmission to a limited, controlled audience, such as the members of a certain profession. Compare Broadcast, Unicast.

NATAS ➳ National Academy of Television Arts and Sciences. Formed in 1957 to bestow annual awards for excellence in television production (Emmys) on the model of film's Oscars, NATAS quickly grew to more than 11,000 members with chapters in 13 cities. Unlike AMPAS, membership in NATAS was open to "locals" as well as to core production personnel in Hollywood. When the presidency shifted from the Hollywood chapter to the New York chapter in 1976, a split developed. The Hollywood chapter (with more than 40 percent of the total membership) felt the "hinterlands" had exerted more control than they deserved, and withdrew from NATAS in 1977, forming an independent organization known as ATAS (Academy of Television Arts and Sciences). After a court battle, a compromise was reached between the two organizations: ATAS (the Hollywood group) retained the right to bestow Emmys for nighttime programming while ceding Emmys for all other Dayparts, local, sports, and news programming to the national group.

NATPE ➳ (Pronounced "nat-pee.") National Association of Television Program Executives. The professional organization for television programmers, NATPE is best known for its annual convention, which serves as the major marketplace for U.S. television Syndication rights—especially first-run syndication. Because the exhibitors happen also to be film/television producers with a sense of production values and the wherewithal to realize them, the NATPE convention also is the sine qua non of trade shows, with palace-size "booths" and much hoopla.

Naturalism ➳ A theory of literature and film that supposes a scientific determinism such that the actions of a character are predetermined by biological, environmental, sociological, economic, or psychological laws. Often wrongly used as synonymous with Realism, it does not mean simply "natural" in style. Filmmakers from Erich von Stroheim to Michelangelo Antonioni and movements from Film Noir to Documentary show the influence of naturalism.

NBC ➳ National Broadcasting Company. Former RCA subsidiary sold to General Electric in 1986. America's greatest broadcasting visionary, General David Sarnoff, founded the NBC Network in 1926. By the late 1930s NBC was running two radio networks (the "Red" and the "Blue") and pioneering television. From the 1950s to the

1980s, NBC ran a perennial second to CBS in the ratings race, although the network was responsible for most of the memorable innovations in television technology and programming, from color television to late-night talk shows and sophisticated comedy. After Fred Silverman took ABC to the head of the ratings class in 1977, decimating third-place NBC's affiliate count, NBC hired him away to do the same for them. He failed. But his successor, Grant Tinker, succeeded. By 1986 NBC, having been acquired by GE in its purchase of RCA, was ranked number one, where it stayed until the early 1990s, thanks in large part to the talents of programming chief Brandon Tartikoff. Tinker accomplished this feat with innovative programming such as *Hill Street Blues* and *L.A. Law*. NBC regained its dominant position in the mid-1990s thanks to a collection of popular sitcoms led by *Seinfeld*. See ABC, CBS, RCA.

N-Connector ➠ See PLUGS.

NCSA ➠ National Center for Supercomputing Applications. Government-financed institution based at the University of Illinois at Champaign/Urbana. Working here in 1993, student Marc Andreesen (and others) develop the MOSAIC browser that legitimized the WORLD WIDE WEB and served as the basis for NETSCAPE.

NCTA ➠ National Cable Television Association. The industry group for the U.S. Cable business.

Negative ➠ A film that produces an inverse record of the light and dark areas of the photographed scene. See REVERSAL FILMSTOCK, POSITIVE, PRINT.

Negative Cost ➠ The cost of the finished film not including projection prints, publicity, distribution, and exhibition expenses. See COSTS, P & A.

Neorealism ➠ A style of filmmaking identified with Vittorio De Sica, Roberto Rossellini, and Luchino Visconti (among others) in Italy in the mid- and late 1940s. Characterized by leftist and populist political aims, the use of nonprofessional actors, location shooting, simple plots usually dealing with the working poor, and some HAND-HELD camerawork. See REALISM.

Net Shipment ➠ The total number of CDs sold after returns are accounted for. See SHIP GOLD, SELL-THROUGH.

Netizen ➠ A citizen of the INTERNET.

Netscape ➠ Founded in 1994 by Marc Andreesen and Jim Clark, Netscape was the company that more than any other could claim to have founded the WORLD WIDE WEB. Its Navigator browser, based on Andreesen's MOSAIC developed a year earlier at NCSA, became the tool of choice for millions of pioneer web surfers. Intending to make its money on the sale of SERVER software (and site licenses for

Navigator for large corporations), Netscape allowed most folks to download the browser for free. The company went public in August 1995, 14 months after its founding. The offering was the most successful in history, presaging the Internet boom of the late 1990s. At the end of the first day, the market valued the company at $2.9 billion—even though it had yet to make a profit.

Although Netscape moved quickly to develop quality products, it had raised the ire of MICROSOFT, who quickly acquired a competing browser, which they christened Internet Explorer. Microsoft saw the browser as the basis of the next operating system. To allow Netscape to dominate the nascent browser market could mean the death of Microsoft. Explorer was given away free; Microsoft used all its considerable clout to force computer manufacturers and online services to bundle Explorer with their products; and they conceived a plan to integrate the browser with the Windows OS. They were later to be sued by the Justice department for these tactics, but the plan was successful. Netscape realized too late that their real future was as a PORTAL.

In November 1998 AOL announced that it was purchasing Netscape for a mere $4 billion. It may have sounded like a high price for a company only four years old, but it meant that investors in the initial public offering in August 1995 were earning only about thirteen percent per annum on their investment. They might have done better in bonds. Not to worry: the purchase was phrased as a stock deal. When it was finally concluded less than four months later the breathless runup in AOL's share price over this brief period meant that Netscape's shareholders received $10 billion—a 245 percent return on investment, or about 70 percent per annum. Not what Internet investors are looking for, but not bad in the real world.

Network ➺ (1) A system of interconnected BROADCAST stations. See AFFILIATE. (2) Any system of interconnected communication that joins two or more "nodes."

Neue Kino ➺ German cinema in the late 1960s and 1970s. In English, *New German Cinema*. Unlike many other movements, Neue Kino comprised a wide variety of personal styles and concerns: Alexander Klüge, R. W. Fassbinder, Wim Wenders, Werner Herzog, Margarethe von Trotta, and Volker Schlöndorff.

New American Cinema ➺ The "personal" cinema of independent filmmakers in the U.S. from World War II to the 1980s. Characterized by a lyric, poetic, experimental approach.

New German Cinema ➺ See NEUE KINO.

New Wave, Nouvelle Vague ⇒ (1) Godard, Truffaut, Chabrol, Rohmer, Rivette, et al. Strictly, filmmakers who began as critics for CAHIERS DU CINÉMA in the 1950s and who were influenced by André Bazin. (2) The term is also used more loosely to refer to either (a) all the young French filmmakers of the 1960s, or (b) any new group of filmmakers, or (c) any movement that purports to be "new" for marketing purposes.

News Corp ⇒ It's the stuff that Hollywood movies are made of. Young Rupert Murdoch inherited a couple of local Australian newspapers from his father in 1952. Over the next ten years he learned on the job. By 1964 he was strong enough to found the country's first national paper, *The Australian*. Having conquered his native subcontinent he turned his attention to the motherland. In 1968 he bought the U.K. tabloid *News of The World*, and its competitor *The Sun* the next year. Within a few years he felt he was ready for the big show in the U.S. He approached from the south. He bought the San Antonio *Express-News* in 1973 and founded *The Star* tabloid the same year. He followed this up in 1976 by buying the New York *Post*. People began to talk about Rupert Murdoch as a mogul. In 1981 Murdoch moved up another quantum level, purchasing the venerable *Times* of London, and outraging the British establishment in the process.

Throughout the 1980s his various U.K. newspapers were staunch supporters of Prime Minister Margaret Thatcher. He was in the news for breaking a major strike against his papers. He went on another buying spree in the mid-1980s, his major acquisition being TWENTIETH CENTURY FOX—his first major non-newspaper property. (Marvin Davis had grown bored with his toy.) He had the incredible luck to find Barry Diller at loose ends. Diller did the impossible for Murdoch, founding the FOX television network (although Murdoch found it necessary to become a U.S. citizen in order to purchase the necessary local stations from Multimedia). While Diller was working his magic on the film and television side, Murdoch continued buying up print properties in the late 1980s: book publishers (Harper & Row; Collins; Scott, Foresman), newspapers (the New York *Post*, again—he'd sold it earlier), and magazines—most important, *TV Guide*, which he purchase for a record $3 billion. (He was only able to recover from this mistake ten years later, thanks to the good graces of his friend John Malone of TCI.)

All this while, he was expanding his satellite empire, first with Sky TV (later B-SKY-B) in the U.K., then with STAR in Asia. In 1991, his arch-nemesis in British publishing, Robert Maxwell (born Jan Ludwik Hoch in Czechoslovakia) jumped off the back of his yacht.

But Rupert had no cause to celebrate. News Corp was bankrupt. It was saved, not through his own devices, but because the lead lending bank, Citibank, worked financial miracles to keep the company afloat. By the mid-1990s Rupert's children were old enough to take roles in the company, and one by one all three (Lachlan, Elizabeth, and James) found employment. ("This is the boss's son; he's going to start at the bottom for a few days.")

In 1996 Murdoch found a replacement for arch-nemesis Maxwell in Ted Turner. When regulators ordered TIME WARNER, which owns CNN and controls the New York cable market, to add a competing news channel to its New York service, Time Warner chose MSNBC over the new Fox News channel. In the ensuing brouhaha, Turner compared Murdoch to Hitler. In 1998 Murdoch engineered the purchase of the "Los Angeles" Dodgers from the traitorous O'Malley family, who had hijacked the team from its native Brooklyn thirty years earlier, and tried to buy Manchester United, the world's most profitable soccer team. He had never shown interest in sports before; one wonders: was he responding to the image of his new arch-nemesis? Turner's success had been grounded in sports franchise ownership. By the turn of the century the Murdoch family's holding in News Corp had been reduced to 30 percent. It was still run like a $12 billion family candy store. But John Malone, who purchased eight percent of the company early in 1999, may have other ideas.

News Group ➺ One of the earlier Internet inventions (preceding the World Wide Web), News Groups provide bulletin boards organized around a wide range of topics. See THREADED DISCUSSION.

Newshole ➺ The space in a newspaper or magazine, or the time in a broadcast allotted to news as opposed to advertising or commercials. In a successful newspaper, the newshole may be as small as 20 percent.

Newsreel ➺ THEATRICAL FILM news report or, by extension, any filmed actuality.

NHK ➺ Japan's public television network.

Nibble ➺ Half a BYTE.

NICAM ➺ Near Instantaneous Companded Audio Multiplex. A method of transmitting television stereo sound in which a digital signal is imposed on a subcarrier. Used in the U.K., Scandinavia, Italy, and elsewhere.

Nickelodeon ➺ (1) The earliest film theaters; the admission price was originally five cents—hence the name. (2) CABLE NETWORK devoted to children's and young adults' programming, founded in 1979 by Warner Amex.

Nielsen ➤ In the U.S., the most widely used RATINGS system, consisting of monitor boxes attached to the receiving sets of a DEMOGRAPHIC sample of viewers or listeners. The monitors can provide continuous, real-time information. Ratings are usually expressed as both a percentage of the total television universe and a percentage of the sets actually tuned in at the time (*Share*). "It got a 19.1 and a 32 share," means that 19.1 percent of all television homes watched the show and that group comprised 32 percent of the total audience with sets turned on at the time. The *NSI* (Nielsen Station Index) is a periodic report of local ratings for all U.S. markets. The *NTI* (Nielsen Television Index) reports average national ratings.

96/24 ➤ Shorthand for 96 kiloHertz 24-bit encoding, the standard for DVD-Video. Compare 44/16, HDCD, DSD.

Nintendo ➤ See VIDEO GAMES.

Nipkow Disk ➤ Invented in 1884 by Paul Nipkow: a spinning disk on which are arranged spiral patterns of apertures that permit a light beam to SCAN a subject.

Nitrate Print ➤ A film print made on cellulose nitrate, which—although it provides a rich and eloquent image—is extremely flammable as well as perishable. Replaced by safer acetate prints after the 1940s.

NMT ➤ Nordic Mobile Telephone. The standard for analog CELLULAR TELEPHONY in Scandinavia. See TACS, AMPS, CDMA.

Noise ➤ In electronics, the concept of noise has been elevated to an art. In video, any high-frequency disturbance is considered noise. In audio, there is a spectrum of noise. *White Noise* has a random amplitude over a wide range of frequencies. It can be used to smooth out background sounds to produce a more restful aural environment, or to provide a level of privacy. *Pink Noise* is also distributed over a wide frequency range, but has a constant amplitude at all frequencies. It is useful as a test tone. *Brown Noise* also covers a wide range of frequencies but the amplitude varies inversely with the frequency. Music is a kind of Brown Noise that isn't random. *Hiss* is limited to high frequencies; *Hum* is a low-frequency problem. See DOLBY, CDMA.

Noninterlaced Monitor ➤ A monitor with progressive scanning. Although computer and television monitors both use essentially the same CRTs, computer monitors generally do not INTERLACE the display, providing a clearer, sharper image. See also COMPONENT VIDEO.

Nonlinear Editing ➤ See DIGITAL EDITING.

Nonlossy ➤ See COMPRESSION.

Nontheatrical Distribution ➤ Distribution of films to schools, universities, clubs, and other essentially nonprofit organizations. Nontheatrical distribution grew considerably between the early 1960s and 1980s, when it was challenged by videotape distribution; some independent films rely on this market. See JANUS.

NOS ➻ See VACUUM TUBE.

Notch Filter ➻ See COMB FILTER.

Nouvelle Vague ➻ See NEW WAVE.

Novel-for-Television ➻ A MINISERIES.

Novelization ➻ A novel made from a film or SCREENPLAY. See TIE-IN.

NSI ➻ See NIELSEN.

NTI ➻ See NIELSEN.

NTSC ➻ The standard television protocol for the U.S., Canada, and Japan. Some wags think it stands for "Never Twice the Same Color." See TELEVISION STANDARDS.

Numeracy ➻ On the model of literacy, knowledge of and familiarity with the world of numbers, especially as it reveals itself in computer technology.

Nut ➻ The basic operating expense of a theater—rent, salaries, utilities, etc. Often recoverable before margins are split with distributors.

Nyquist Limit ➻ When DIGITIZING an ANALOG signal it is necessary that the SAMPLING rate be at least twice the highest analog frequency, otherwise spurious information will be produced (see ALIASING). Therefore the Nyquist Limit of a 44 kiloHertz sampling rate will be 22 kiloHertz, or half the sampling rate. See OVERSAMPLING.

O & O ➻ Owned and Operated. A local television or radio station owned and operated by a NETWORK. Until 1996, when the industry was deregulated, FCC rules limited each network to 30 television, 30 AM, and 30 FM O & Os. The limit had been increased from 6 to 12 to 30 over the previous twenty years, as broadcasters had to compete with cable.

OCR ➻ Optical Character Recognition. Software that can identify the graphical patterns of individual letters in order to convert them to their ASCII codes. It's not as easy as you may think, proving that the digital machines still have a way to go to challenge human eyes and the brains that support them.

Odyssey ➻ The first popular home VIDEO GAME system, introduced by Magnavox in 1972 at a price of $99. See PONG.

Off-Broadway, Off-Off Broadway ➻ See BROADWAY.

Offline Editing ➻ See DIGITAL EDITING.

Off-Network Programs ⇒ Programs now in syndication that were previously aired on a NETWORK.

Offscreen Sound ⇒ Sound whose source is not visible within the frame but that is part of the DIEGESIS.

Offscreen Space ⇒ The areas not visible within the confines of the frame but nevertheless part of the space of a scene (the DIEGESIS), behind the set, behind the camera, above, below, left, and right of the frame.

Offset Printing ⇒ A PLANOGRAPHIC printing process in which ink is transferred from the printing plate to the paper by means of flat rubber "offset" rollers. When combined with PHOTOENGRAVING techniques, offset is a quick, inexpensive, and easily accessible means of printing. See LETTERPRESS, GRAVURE, XEROGRAPHY.

Oil-Film ⇒ An early technology for theatrical video projection that used a charged film of oil to project the image on a large screen. GE's *Talaria* was one such projector. See DMD, ILA.

100Base-T ⇒ See 10BASE-T.

180-Degree Rule ⇒ A major rule of CONTINUITY EDITING that states that the camera must remain on one side of the narrative action in order to ensure consistent spatial relationships and direction of movement from shot to shot.

One-Reeler ⇒ A film of ten to twelve minutes in length.

Online ⇒ In the narrowest definition, online refers to systems that people dial up using modems attached to their computers, which allow them to query centralized databases on a "HOST system." "Online" can also mean instantly available, even on a smaller network, as in ONLINE EDITING. See WORLD WIDE WEB, SERVER.

Online Editing ⇒ See DIGITAL EDITING.

Open-End Series ⇒ An unlimited SERIES, one that has a narrative scheme that leads to no particular conclusion. See CLOSED-END SERIES.

Open Software ⇒ The movement, gaining strength at the turn of the century, to make all software SOURCE CODE easily copied and reusable. In an Open Software universe, the theory goes, thousands of programmers around the world contribute to the development of an algorithm producing code that is not only more stable but also more elegant. This is similar to the INTERNET ethos, where any page can be hyperlinked to any other. The LINUX operating system is central to the Open Software movement.

Open Up ⇒ (1) To open up a lens means to increase the opening of the DIAPHRAGM to permit more light into the camera. (2) To open up a narrative means to provide scenes or sequences in other than the main location. It is often thought that plays, when filmed, need to be "opened up."

OPT, Operation Prime Time ➻ Syndicate of independent stations formed in 1976 by Al Masini to finance and produce miniseries, generally in conjunction with Universal–MCA, to compete directly with network programming. Active until the late 1980s, OPT was too far ahead of its time. FOX succeeded, followed by Warner (The WB) and Paramount (UPN).

Optical ➻ An operation accomplished in the laboratory rather than on the SET or in the cutting room. Examples: DISSOLVES, FREEZE FRAMES, WIPES, GHOST IMAGES, and MATTE SHOTS. See POST HOUSE.

Optical Disc ➻ The generic term for laser-driven storage media such as VIDEODISCS, CDs, CD-ROMs, and DVD. The technology was first developed by PHILIPS and MCA for their DISCOVISION product and by SONY for its CD product. An optical disc is a DIGITAL recording that takes advantage of the short, coherent wavelengths of LASER light to encode a vast amount of data in a small space. Contrary to popular assumption, the optical disc technology does not actually encode a signal in light. The digitized signal is recorded on the plastic disc physically as a series of microscopic pits separated by lands. The laser is used as a simplistic PICKUP. It reads transitions between the pits and lands as ones and zeros; the microscopic beam of light is reflected from the lands but scattered from the pits. Because this binary encoding scheme is both digital and simple, an optical disc is relatively impervious to wear or distortion, unlike analog systems such as MAGNETIC media and PHONOGRAPH records. See EIGHT-TO-FOURTEEN MODULATION.

Optical Lantern ➻ See MAGIC LANTERN.

Optical Printer ➻ The machine that duplicates prints of a film. Many operations of a technical nature are performed on the optical printer, including OPTICALS, the balancing of color values (see TIMING), and the correction of CONTRAST.

Option ➻ A producer who cannot afford or doesn't want to purchase a script outright may buy an "option" on the script. The option gives him the exclusive right for a certain limited time to purchase the script from the writer at a set price. Like options in the commodities market, film options provide great leverage. (Too bad there isn't a market in Hollywood puts and calls.) See IF COME.

Optrack ➻ Optical soundtrack on film, as opposed to MAGTRACK—magnetic soundtrack.

ORACLE ➻ ITV's TELETEXT system. An arduous acronym for Optical Reception of Announcements by Coded Line Electronics. See also CEEFAX.

Orange Book ➻ See CD STANDARDS.

Orion ⇒ Founded by former UNITED ARTISTS executives Arthur Krim, Robert Benjamin, Mike Medavoy, William Bernstein, and Eric Pleskow in 1978, Orion appeared to have a good chance to survive as a real Hollywood studio. The company enjoyed a number of hits in the 1980s, established a television production arm, and Orion Classics, an art film distribution company, and absorbed Filmways in 1982. But as death and defection reduced the ranks of the founders, the company fell on hard times. Orion filed for protection under the bankruptcy law in 1991.

Orthicon ⇒ See IMAGE ORTHICON.

Orthochromatic ⇒ A type of black-and-white FILMSTOCK that is sensitive to the blue and green areas of the spectrum. See PANCHROMATIC.

OS ⇒ (1) Operating System. The basic software that acts as the office manager of a computer, controlling how and where files are written, the protocols for input from and output to peripheral devices, and the rules that applications must obey. See UNIX, MS-DOS, MacOS, LINUX. (2) Stage direction for OffScreen.

Oscars ⇒ Nickname for the awards presented annually by the Academy of Motion Picture Arts and Sciences for outstanding work. Oscars have provided a model for scores of other awards, not only to honor participants in an industry, but also because awards shows make cheap, effective television programming. None, however, matches the Oscars for influence, drama, or ratings, an indication of the continued primacy of motion pictures.

OSS ⇒ An OVER-THE-SHOULDER SHOT.

OTP ⇒ Opposite Track Path. See PTP, RSDL.

Out of Sync ⇒ An expression used to indicate that sound and image are not locked in synchronization.

Outro ⇒ A closing comment in radio, as, for example, a conclusion to a recorded commercial. Compare INTRO.

Outtake ⇒ A TAKE that is not used in the FINAL CUT of the film. Until the late 1970s outtakes were useless. Then television producers discovered that audiences were fascinated to watch actors flub lines, commit bloopers, or send up their fellow actors. Thereafter, for certain films and series, outtakes became a valuable byproduct of the final cut, as they were recycled on numerous television shows. Indeed, you get the feeling some filmmakers now shoot out-takes on purpose, as indeed was the case for *A Bug's Life* (1998) which opened featuring one set of outtakes, then switched to a second set three weeks later. The film was animated.

Overcrank ⇒ To speed up a camera; to shoot at more than the normal 24 frames per second, so that the resulting image will appear in slow motion when projected. See UNDERCRANK.

Overdevelopment ⇒ FORCED PROCESSING.

Overexposure ⇒ See EXPOSURE.

Overhead Shot ⇒ A shot taken from a point immediately above the main action with the camera pointed down.

Overlap Sound ⇒ A cut in which the cut in the SOUNDTRACK is not synchronous with the cut in the image. Often used in REACTION SHOTS.

Overnights ⇒ The NIELSEN ratings for the previous night's programming.

Oversampling ⇒ A technique for smoothing the output of a DIGITAL CD signal by using an output SAMPLING rate that is a multiple of the input rate, usually 4x or 8x. In 4x oversampling, every fourth output sample is filled with an original value while the other three samples are set to zero. This intermediate signal is then passed through a digital filter, which distributes the single original value equally among all four samples, which makes it cheaper and easier to clean up the resulting final signal. The technique is not dissimilar to DOLBY in the analog world. The technique has been carried over to digital video recording, where the 4:2:2 mode is common. The numbers refer to the oversampling rates of the Y, U, and V signals, respectively. See YUV, SAMPLING.

Overscan ⇒ Because a television monitor is subject to voltage reductions which may reduce the width of the RASTER, manufacturers build in Overscan so you won't see the edges of the image. The result is that the screen of the monitor acts as a window cutting off the edges of the larger image "behind" it. To make sure you aren't subject to Overscan losses, find a source for an SMPTE Resolution Chart. See EDGE BLANKING.

Over-the-Shoulder Shot ⇒ A shot commonly used in dialogue scenes in which the speaker is seen from the perspective of a person standing just behind and a little to one side of the listener, so that parts of the head and shoulder of the listener are in the frame, as well as the head of the speaker.

P Frame ⇒ See MPEG-2.

Pace, Pacing ⇒ The rhythm of a film, or the speed and economy of its narration.

Package ⇒ Film properties are almost always packaged by their producers or agents before they are sold to studios. The package contains two or more of the following BANKABLE elements: script, director, stars.

Packet-Switched Network ⇒ The technology that allows a single telephone line to carry hundreds or thousands of simultaneous data conversations. The data is packaged into packets of a certain number of bytes, and the traffic from numerous communicators is carried along the same line. Each packet carries an address so that the system knows where to deliver it. An analogy would be a road that carried hundreds of trucks, each of them getting off at a separate exit. The result is that a single voice grade telephone line can carry 100 to 1,000 times as much information as it could if that single line were devoted to a single data conversation. The INTERNET is a packet-switched network. See also X.25, FRAME RELAY, ATM.

Packing ⇒ To facilitate recording it is a good idea to "pack" the tape first. This is accomplished by fast-forwarding or reversing so that the tension on each part of the tape is the same.

PAD ⇒ Packet Assembler–Disassembler. The device that assembles data into packets for transmission over a PACKET-SWITCHED network, and conversely disassembles the packets at the other end. Now better known as a SWITCH or a ROUTER.

Page Description Language ⇒ A computer language that is constructed so that it can accurately describe the appearance of a printed page, including fonts, styles, and images. To do this efficiently and precisely, a PDL must be VECTOR-, not RASTER-, oriented so that it can control any printer, no matter what its RESOLUTION may be. See POSTSCRIPT.

Paint Box ⇒ Computer software for generating television and video graphics. See CHYRON.

PAL ⇒ See TELEVISION STANDARDS.

PAL-M ⇒ The Brazilian version of the PAL TELEVISION STANDARD uses 525 lines and 60 fields per second.

PALplus ⇒ Introduced in 1994, this transitional technology provides a downward compatible widescreen television image. On a standard PAL television set, the image appears LETTERBOXED. Information carried in the vertical blanking interval allows widescreen PALplus sets to present enhanced vertical resolution.

PAL/SECAM Cheat ⇒ Ever since Talkies, the projection speed of film has been fixed at 24 frames/sec. American television runs at 30 frames/sec (precisely 29.97 frames/sec). To show films on television and make up for this discrepancy the 3:2 PULLDOWN FILM CHAIN was devised. The 24 film frames are sliced and duplicated to produce 30 television frames. In Europe and most of the rest of the world, however, television runs at 25 frames per second. (Both the European and American television frame rates are linked to the frequencies of Alternating Currents in their respective areas.)

When feature films are shown on European television no Film Chain is employed. The result is that they run four percent (1/25) faster, and the pitch of the soundtracks is four percent higher. This may seem like an insignificant difference. It is not. Generations of European televiewers have grown up with a distorted sense of film—not only American films, but their own as well. (Unlike feature films, European telefilms are shot at 25 frames/sec, so this doesn't apply to them.)

Palette ➻ See COLOR MAPPING. Sometimes used as a synonym for CLUT.

Pan ➻ Movement of the camera from left to right or right to left around the imaginary vertical axis that runs through the camera. See TILT, ROLL. A panning shot is sometimes confused with a TRACKING SHOT, which is quite different. See also CAMERA ANGLE.

Pan and Scan ➻ The technique of frequent reframing to keep the center of interest within the frame used to prepare WIDESCREEN or ANAMORPHIC films for television projection in the standard television ASPECT RATIO of 1.33:1. Compare LETTERBOX.

Panavision ➻ Now the most widely used ANAMORPHIC process, it has largely superseded other similar processes such as CINEMASCOPE. "Super Panavision" utilizes 70 mm filmstock, unsqueezed; "Ultra Panavision" uses 70 mm stock with a 1:1.25 squeeze ratio. The Panavision company also makes other highly regarded cameras.

Panchromatic ➻ A type of black-and-white film that is equally responsive to all the colors of the visible spectrum. See ORTHOCHROMATIC.

P & A ➻ Prints and Advertising. The marketing budget for a film; the expenditure that is still necessary after a film is IN THE CAN. The P & A budget can now sometimes rival the NEGATIVE COST.

Panda 1 ➻ Noise reduction system devised by Wegener Corporation and used for satellite audio.

Panthéon ➻ In the system of rating directors in hierarchical categories common to the AUTEUR POLICY, Panthéon directors are the highest rated.

Pantone Matching System ➻ Pantone is a manufacturer of inks whose elaborate color matching system has become a standard in the graphics world for defining hue, saturation, and brightness. The source is a book with swatches printed in SPOT COLOR for each shade. Each swatch is numbered. Pantone also provides software that attempts to match the printed swatches, but correlating colors on a computer screen is a process fraught with difficulty. See COLORSYNC.

Par ➻ Common abbreviation for PARAMOUNT Studios.

Paradigm ➻ In SEMIOTICS, a unit of potential, as opposed to actual, relationship. The paradigm describes "what elements or statements go with what"; the SYNTAGMA, "what follow what."

Paradigm Shift ➻ In the history of computers and media, a change in the basic model of interaction. Examples: the shift from the command-line interface to a graphical user interface, or from desktop machines to laptops and notebook computers.

Parallax ➻ The apparent change in position of a viewed object caused by differences in perspective or point of view. Parallax is useful in providing a sense of depth to otherwise two-dimensional representations, especially in cinema, when it is a function of the moving camera. Parallax is a problem for photographers who sight their images through a viewfinder rather than the taking lens. The solution is the REFLEX CAMERA.

Parallel ➻ In the computer world, a port through which data is transferred several bits at a time—in parallel, over several lines. The parallel port is usually used to drive a printer. See SERIAL.

Parallel Action ➻ A device of narrative in which two separate scenes, often occurring simultaneously, are observed in parallel by CROSS-CUTTING. Developed largely by D. W. Griffith in the 1910s. Also called parallel montage. See ACCELERATED MONTAGE.

Parallel Montage ➻ See PARALLEL ACTION.

Parallel Sound ➻ Sound that matches its accompanying image. Compare CONTRAPUNTAL SOUND, OVERLAP SOUND.

Paramount ➻ Adolph Zukor founded his Famous Players Film Company in 1912 with the profits he made from distributing the Sarah Bernhardt *Queen Elizabeth* in the U.S. In 1914 the newly formed Paramount Pictures Corporation took over distribution of Zukor's films as well as those of the Jesse L. Lasky Feature Play company. Two years later, Zukor and Lasky merged to form the Famous Players-Lasky Corporation, proceeding to acquire numerous other small producers as well as their distributor, Paramount. From 1919 on, the company engaged in an ambitious program of theater acquisition. B. P. Schulberg became head of production in 1925 and reinforced the studio's reputation as a purveyor of witty and sophisticated films, often with a European flavor. W. C. Fields, Mae West, Bing Crosby and Bob Hope, Preston Sturges, and Billy Wilder maintained Paramount's strong suite in comedy for many years.

In 1949 the studio was forced to divest itself of its movie theaters, but it survived the 1950s with help from Alfred Hitchcock, Billy Wilder, and others. Charles Bluhdorn's conglomerate Gulf + Western acquired control in 1966. The fortunes of the company rose steadily during the next twenty years under the leadership of production executives Robert Evans and Barry Diller. Martin S. Davis took control of the parent company in 1983 and replaced Diller with Frank Mancuso in 1984. Mancuso continued the generally solid progress until his ouster in 1991. In 1989 Gulf + Western, by this time restructured to focus on media industries, changed its name to Paramount Communications. After a protracted bidding war against Barry Diller's QVC, Sumner Redstone's VIACOM acquired Paramount in 1994.

PARC ⇒ See XEROX PARC.

Passive Matrix LCD ⇒ An LCD display screen where the PIXELS do not emit light and are usually backlit. Compare ACTIVE MATRIX LCD.

Pay or Play ⇒ A contract term that guarantees an actor or technician payment whether or not the film is made. (It really should be "Play or Pay.")

Pay Television ⇒ Any of several systems of television financed by charges to the viewer rather than by advertising. First developed by Sylvester L. Weaver in Los Angeles in the late 1950s as a broadcast system, which became a model for modern CABLE TELEVISION.

Payola ⇒ The practice of paying a radio disc jockey to play a certain record, it was a scandalous practice in the 1950s. See PLUGOLA.

Pay-per-View ⇒ A system for charging CABLE TELEVISION customers fees for individual programs, which became more widespread in the late 1980s as cable systems increased their channel capacity and developed more sophisticated SCRAMBLING technology.

PBS ⇒ Public Broadcasting Service. Created in November 1969 by the *Corporation for Public Broadcasting*, the PBS network differs in one important respect from commercial networks: it does not control production of the programs it distributes to more than 300 public television stations across the country. It simply serves as a conduit for productions controlled by local stations, the most powerful and prolific of which remain WGBH (Boston) and WNET (New York). The *Station Program Cooperative* (SPC), devised in 1974, allows the stations to vote on which programs will be produced for national distribution. They then share in the production costs proportionately. Since 1990 the SPC has turned over a portion of its budget to PBS to use as it sees fit to promote more innovative programming. Funded minimally by act of Congress, PBS remains reliant on local station constituents who engage in regular fund-raising by selling "subscriptions" to the public. In addition, some productions are funded by the Corporation for Public Broadcasting, which preceded PBS and still exists.

PC Card ⇒ Formerly known as the PCMCIA card, this credit-card sized ROM storage device has become established as a standard, especially for laptop computers and PDAs. The PC Card comes in three flavors: Type I and Type II cards occupy one slot; Type III cards occupy two slots. See DIGITAL FILM.

PCI ⇒ Presentation Control Information. Data on a DVD-VIDEO disc used for the menu and controls. See DSI. The two together constitute an overhead of about one megabit/sec.

PCL ⇒ Printer Control Language. Hewlett-Packard's driver for its pioneering LaserJet printer. PCL is not a page description language like POSTSCRIPT.

PCM ⇒ Pulse Code Modulation, a technique for digital encoding of an ANALOG signal using SAMPLING and QUANTIZATION. Compare PWM.

PCMCIA ⇒ Personal Computer Memory Card International Association. A ROM storage device shaped something like a credit card. This least mellifluous of acronyms soon gave way to PC CARD.

PCS ⇒ Personal Communications Service. A lower-cost system of CELLULAR TELEPHONY using higher frequencies, digital encoding, and more TRANSPONDERS to offer service with wider reception (inside buildings or tunnels, for example) and including simple data services using a small screen on the phone, as well as voice. The first PCS service, Mercury One-2-One, debuted in London in 1993.

PCTV ⇒ Television tuner cards for PCs have been around since the early 1990s. PCTV is an attempt to bring some elements of HDTV to your local computer screen. For most of us, the computer screen we own has a much higher resolution than our television set. The computer screen also accommodates PROGRESSIVE scanning—unlike most television screens. Hence, it is, on paper, a much better television monitor. It's only drawback is that it is usually smaller than a television screen. However, if HDTV sets don't drop in price precipitously, PCTV may prove very attractive.

PD ⇒ Abbreviation for PUBLIC DOMAIN, outside of copyright protection.

PDA ⇒ Personal Digital Assistant. A palm-sized, usually PEN-BASED, microcomputer dedicated to note-taking and communications. APPLE'S Newton was the first to gain attention in 1993. The simpler, cheaper Palm Pilot achieved commercial success a few years later. Compare PCS.

PDL ⇒ Abbreviation for PAGE DESCRIPTION LANGUAGE.

Pedestal ⇒ A neighborhood distribution node for CABLE television. Pedestals usually look a little like tombstones by the side of the road.

Pen-Based Computing ➻ Computing system such as the Newton or Palm Pilot that uses a stylus to input information rather than a keyboard.

Penetration ➻ The penetration of a CABLE system is the percentage ratio of homes subscribing to HOMES PASSED.

Pentode ➻ See VACUUM TUBE.

People Meter ➻ The more sophisticated box the NIELSEN company developed in the 1980s to measure television ratings. It replaced the AUDIMETER.

Perceptual Coding ➻ Recent systems of digital audio compression encoding take advantage of psychoacoustic limitations in the human ear—mainly AUDITORY MASKING. This is called Perceptual Coding. Dolby's AC-3 is such a system.

Performance Art ➻ A union of dramatic and pictorial arts that became common in the 1970s; derived from 1960s HAPPENINGS.

Performance License ➻ A contract that allows you to perform a piece of music in a film or video production. Compare SYNC LICENSE.

PERL ➻ A common scripting language for website development.

Persistence of Vision ➻ The physiological phenomenon that makes cinema and television possible. An image is retained on the retina of the eye for a short period after it is seen so that, if another, slightly different image takes its place soon enough, the illusion of motion can be created. See PHI EFFECT.

Persona ➻ From the Latin for "mask." A character in a literary, cinematic, or dramatic work. More precisely, the psychological image of the character that is created, especially in relation to other levels of reality. The word is also used to refer to the public character of a star or other celebrity.

Personal Communications Service ➻ See PCS.

Personality ➻ In the media sense, a performer who doesn't act, but "is," whose value lies in the PERSONA or image created and projected. See CELEBRITY.

PerspectaSound ➻ An ingenious, if short-lived, technology introduced in 1954 as an alternative to stereo magnetic soundtracks. The mono optical track included subsonic control tones that routed the signal to left, center, or right speakers producing a pseudo-stereo effect. Compare FANTASOUND, which produced real stereo.

Peta ➻ Colloquially, a prefix for quadrillion. In the computer world the prefix is used to mean 2^{50}. A petabyte of storage thus would equal 1,048,576 GIGABYTES, not one quadrillion bytes. As of this writing, no one has to worry much about terabytes, much less petabytes. (And, no, I don't know what the prefix for quintillion is, but I'll find out and let you know in plenty of time.) See MEG, K, GIG, TERA, BINARY MAGNITUDES.

PGC ⇶ ProGram Chain. A specific sequence of CHAPTERS on a DVD-Video. A PGC can be written so that only the G-rated sequences of an R-rated movie are shown, for example.

Phase-Shift Keying ⇶ *PSK*. An advanced coding system for data transmission. See BAUD.

Phasing ⇶ Setting up an interference pattern between the left and right stereo signals in an audio system to create the illusion of SURROUND SOUND and a SOUNDSTAGE. Compare SURROUND DECORRELATION.

Phenakistoscope ⇶ Early PERSISTENCE OF VISION device developed by Belgian optician Joseph Plateau in 1832. A series of separate pictures depicting stages of an activity such as juggling or dancing were arranged around the edges of a slotted disk. When the disk was placed before a mirror and spun a spectator looking through the slots perceived a moving picture. (Greek for "deceitful view.") See ZOETROPE.

Phi Effect, Phi Phenomenon ⇶ The psychological perception of motion that is caused by the displacement of two objects seen in quick succession in neighboring positions. Compare with PERSISTENCE OF VISION, which is physiologically rather than psychologically defined.

Philips ⇶ This Dutch-based international electrical and electronic products conglomerate, which can trace its corporate roots to the last century, has been responsible, with SONY, for many of the innovations in consumer electronics during the past fifty years. Philips can lay claim to inventing, developing, or popularizing the AUDIOCASSETTE in the 1960s, the LASERDISC in the 1970s, and DVD technology in the 1990s (not to mention the electric razor in the 1950s). Then again, CD-I and DCC were also Philips products.

Phone Phreak ⇶ A person who makes a hobby of manipulating and studying the complexities of the telephone system. Similarly, COMPUTER FREAK. The phenomenon was first described by Ron Rosenbaum in his seminal 1971 article in *Esquire* magazine. See HACKER.

Phoneme ⇶ In linguistics, the smallest unit of speech or sound that is identifiable (the unit of the "signifier"). See MONEME, MORPHEME.

Phonevision ⇶ PAY-PER-VIEW system developed by Zenith Radio Corp. in 1947 which lasted until 1969, although never getting past the experimental phase. The descrambler in the customer's home was activated by the insertion of a ticket. The major test took place in Hartford, Connecticut, during the 1960s.

Phong ⇶ A technique of 3-D MODELING.

Phono Cartridge ➺ See TURNTABLE.

Phono Plug ➺ See PLUGS.

Phonofilm ➺ Inventor Lee De Forest never did convince Hollywood to adopt his optical-track sound system. He first demonstrated it in 1922 and made many short films during the next few years. His competition was Western Electric, the manufacturing arm of AT&T. Under the guidance of a technician named Edward Craft they proposed a sound-on-disk system. And who was Sam Warner to argue with the telephone company? Craft demonstrated what was to become VITAPHONE first in 1922 at Yale University. Craft took a silent film describing a technology Western Electric had just licensed and added sound to it for the demonstration.

Ironically, the name of the film—and the invention it celebrated—was "Audion," Lee De Forest's own brilliant invention! Here's a quote from official Lucent (corporate descendent of Western Electric) history: "Western Electric made a huge breakthrough in long distance transmission by securing the patent rights to DeForest's Audion tube." Read that twice. (There's a story here.)

Phonograph ➺ A device, either wholly mechanical, mechanical-electrical, or mechanical-electronic, for recording and playing back sound signals etched on a wax or plastic DISK. A stylus vibrates physically as it is carried along by the groove in which the information is encoded. These vibrations are translated into sound. See RECORD PLAYER.

Photo CD ➺ Kodak's ingenious system of digital storage of photographic images, introduced in 1992. Unlike SONY'S MAVICA, which debuted years earlier (and failed at the time), Kodak's Photo CD system applied digital technology to only part of the photographic process. Customers take their film to a local processing center where the photochemical images are digitized and stored on a MULTISESSION CD-R disc in a variety of resolutions. Because the disc is writable, additional photos can be added later. The images can then be played back on a television set or microcomputer equipped with a suitable CD-ROM player. Both the customer and Kodak, therefore, maintain their considerable investment in cameras and chemical photography. See ADVANTIX.

Photoengraving ➺ A photographic process for making a printing plate. Any original material, such as typescript, previously printed page, or line drawing can be reproduced quickly. See OFFSET, HALFTONE.

Photogenic ➺ Attractive as a subject for photography. See PRESENCE, PERSONA.

Photogram ➺ From the French; a STILL.

Photography ⤳ Literally "light-writing." Any system of recording images, especially those that use chemical technology. Although CINEMATOGRAPHY is the more precise term for motion picture photography, the more general term, photography, is often used synonymously: one speaks of photographing a motion picture rather than "cinematographing" it, for example. Increasingly, the term is used also to include electronic image capturing.

Photolithography ⤳ An OFFSET printing process using PHOTOENGRAVED plates that are PLANOGRAPHIC. See TYPOGRAPHY.

Photonics ⤳ On the model of electronics, the science of using light waves (photons) to carry and modify signals. The earliest photonic applications were developed for FIBER OPTIC communications. As the CHIP industry begins to hit the physical limits of electronics, Photonics offers a faster, smaller, cheaper future for computing.

Photophone ⤳ RCA subsidiary formed in 1928 to promote sound-on-film.

Photoplay ⤳ The out-of-date term for a SCREENPLAY.

PhotoRet ⤳ A Hewlett-Packard color printing technology that mixes inks rather than simply printing color dots next to each other. Also called Color Layering.

Photoshop ⤳ See ADOBE.

Phototypesetting, Phototypography ⤳ The reproduction of TYPOGRAPHIC materials, such as printing plates, via photographic means. Rather than utilizing metal type, phototypography depends on stored film images of the letters and symbols to be reproduced. Now largely replaced by computer typesetting techniques. See PHOTOENGRAVING.

PIC ⤳ See IMAGE FILE FORMATS.

Pica ⤳ A unit of measure used in typography; equal to 12 POINTS or 1/12 of an inch.

Pickup ⤳ (1) As in "negative pickup," a film made by one company that has been acquired by another company. (2) The device in a LASERDISC or PHONOGRAPH record system that reads the information on the disc. (3) An INSERT or CUTAWAY that is shot at a later date.

Pico ⤳ Standard prefix for a trillionth (U.S.), as in "picosecond": 0.000000000001 (10^{-12}) of a second. See also MICRO, NANO, FEMTO.

Picture Element ⤳ See PIXEL.

Picturephone ⤳ See VIDEOPHONE.

Pilot ⤳ A sample television program prepared to test the concept of a planned SERIES. Today pilots are often recycled as MADE-FOR-TV MOVIES or THEATRICAL FILMS.

Pink Noise ⤳ See NOISE.

PIP ➤ Picture-In-Picture. Available on high-end analog television sets and common on digital sets, this feature allows an additional channel to be presented in a small box on the screen so that the viewer can watch two channels at once. See MULTI-PIP.

Piracy ➤ Since the 1970s, audiovisual technology has become increasingly simpler, cheaper, and more democratic. As this happens, it becomes much easier to make unauthorized copies of audio and video products. This practice is called piracy. But the ethics of copying are not so clear.

Authors of INTELLECTUAL PROPERTIES have always been interested in reaching an audience as well as making money. Few authors of books would deny public libraries the right to lend their books free—with no remuneration to the author. If the libraries were to buy electronic versions of the books from the publishers and print individual copies for their patrons, how would that differ? Most consumers think nothing of videotaping off the air. Does it make an ethical difference if you videotape a film off a public channel as opposed to a PREMIUM CHANNEL? If you make a copy of another VIDEO-CASSETTE is that different from taping off the air? If you have a legitimate subscription to a cable television service that chooses to SCRAMBLE some of its basic channels as well as its premium channels, must you legally use the cable company's tuner? What if you just bought an inexpensive CABLE-READY television set? Can you use a BLACK BOX to DESCRAMBLE the basic services? If you buy music on a CD, do you have the right to make an AUDIOCASSETTE copy to listen to in the car? And what about computer software?

Clearly, if you make numerous copies of an intellectual property to resell at a profit that is both illegal and unethical, but the line that separates right from wrong in private use is not so clear. As the technology continues to develop, as images, sounds, and text are increasingly delivered in DIGITAL form, new ways for compensating authors will have to be developed.

Pirandellian ➤ An adjective derived from the name of the twentieth-century playwright Luigi Pirandello, whose work investigated the subtle differences between fiction and reality and described a world system in which illusion and actuality combined in intricate ways to produce a continuum of VERISIMILITUDE. Understand that he wrote about this phenomenon in the early years of the twentieth century, eighty years before our virtual world began to take shape.

Pit Art ➤ Instead of printed labels, some CDs and DVDs use etched pits to provide a faint reflection of print. This is Pit Art.

Pitching ➤ Presenting the idea for a film (or a book or other INTELLECTUAL PROPERTY) to the people who have the money to make it real.

Filmmakers pitch ideas to studio executives; writers pitch them to publishers. See Shopping.

Pits and Lands ➺ See Optical Disc.

Pix ➺ Varietese for movies, as in "Hix Nix Stix Pix."

Pixel ➺ PIcture ELement. Any one of the hundreds of thousands of individually addressable coded areas of light and shade that make up a television or computer screen image. A standard monitor in use at the turn of the century has more than 750,000 addressable pixels.

Pixellation ➺ An Artifact, or inconsistency, in digital imaging. In pixellated images, the Pixels are clearly visible. See Jaggies. Not to be confused with Pixilation.

Pixilation ➺ A technique of Animation in which real objects, people, or events are photographed so that the illusion of continuous, real movement is created or modified, either by photographing one frame at a time or later printing only selected frames from the continuously exposed negative. Example: some films by Norman McLaren. Not to be confused with Pixellation.

Plaiding ➺ (Pronounced "pladding.") The Moiré patterns produced by the interference of two Halftone patterns in a printed photograph, or the similar interaction of patterns on a video or computer screen.

Planographic Printing ➺ Systems of printing in which the image is essentially the same height as the nonprinting area, neither depressed nor elevated. Lithography is planographic.

Platforming ➺ Releasing a film in an increasing number of theaters week after week in an attempt to build word-of-mouth. Wider than a Limited Run, narrower than Going Wide.

Platinum ➺ See Gold.

Platter ➺ See Turntable.

PlayStation ➺ See Video Games.

Plinth ➺ See Turntable.

Plot ➺ The order and sequence of a Story; the complete set of events to be told. Plot is the "how" and "which" of narration; story the "what."

Plug ➺ A mention of a commercial product or service within the context of a show, program, or film production. See Product Placement.

Plugola ➺ The practice of paying a film, television, or radio Personality, star, producer, or director to obtain a Plug. See Payola.

Plugs ➺ First, let's get one thing straight: the plug is the male connector on the end of the wire; the female connector is variously known as the jack, receptacle, or outlet (the latter two terms being generally reserved for electrical—not electronic—connectors). The jack is on the device.

Until the microcomputer revolution of the 1980s, electronics buffs had a relatively simple time of it. Most connections were made simply by twisting wires around BINDING POSTS with screw closures. If you were an audiophile you might solder spade lugs or O-lugs to the ends of the wires to make connections and disconnections easier. The number of plugs you had to know about was limited, and therefore so was the number of adapters you needed in your kit. The most basic plug was the venerable *Phono* plug. 1/4-inch in diameter and more than an inch long, the Phono plug was a hefty connector. The shaft and the tip provided the ground and the hot leg; the tip had an indentation and ridge at its base that engaged a spring clip in the receptacle. When you plugged in a Phono plug and that spring clicked solidly in place, you had a sense of accomplishment and assurance that the connection was made. When you see switchboard operators in old movies flipping those wires in and out you're probably watching the Phono plug in all its glory.

The *RCA* plug became common in the 1960s. Smaller overall than the Phono, the RCA provided greater separation between the two legs of the circuit: the sleeve was the ground; the hot leg was on the pin in the center of the sleeve. Split into four leaves, the sleeve provided the snugness that prevented the plug from falling out—but there was no click, no sense of closure. 16-mm projectors used a plug that looked almost exactly like a Phono plug—except that it was 7/32-inch in diameter, but few of us had to deal with 16-mm projectors. The *Banana* plug borrowed the spring-blade technology from the RCA, but this time the shaft was composed of blades. Since the Banana plug was a single-wire device (you needed two of them to complete a circuit), this was easy.

If you used professional audio equipment in the sixties, you also had to know about the *DIN*. A German invention (from the Deutsche Institut für Normung, the German standards body), the DIN connector provided a model for later multi-line plugs. (The most common had three lines.) Like the Phono, the DIN provided a positive spring lock—this time on the plug side. But what was truly innovative about the DIN was its sexual orientation: the female side was on the plug! The pins were on the jack. Rightly or wrongly, this trans-sexual architecture never caught on, and the DIN remains unique. One version of the DIN is also known as a *Cannon* or *XLR*. The XLR is used for BALANCED audio connections. (By the way, don't underestimate the sexual connotations of plugs and jacks. The

Phono plug is shaped like an abstract penis. We confuse jacks and plugs in common parlance because it sounds like a jack should be masculine. And it's interesting that the profession of telephone operator opened new doors to women in the work world: they could plug those jacks as well as the men!)

By the early seventies things in the plug world were getting more complicated. The advent of stereo meant that you needed two of everything. The Phono plug was able to accommodate the stereo world by adding a ring between the tip and the shaft, but RCAs had to double up. Smaller electronic devices invited smaller plugs, and the *Mini* plug was born. 1/8 inch in diameter and a little more than 1/2 inch long, the Mini is still ubiquitous today. Cable television, with its coaxial cables, brought us a whole new set: the Screw-in (also called *TNC*, for "Threaded N-Connector"), the *N-Connector*, the *F-Connector* (on the model of the RCA a simple push-in plug with two blades on the sleeve instead of four), and the ingenious *BNC* (BayoNet or British Naval Connector), which combined the two ideas offering the speed of the F-Connector with the positive lock of the threaded connector.

By this time we had to worry about telephone plugs and jacks, as well. The sturdy four-prong of the sixties was giving way to the flimsy, easily damaged *RJ-11C*. Later, we would have to learn the difference between the RJ-11C and the almost indistinguishable RJ-45X. (The RJ stands for Register Jack, and, yes, there are more than 60 configurations.) Then there's the smaller version that connects the handset to the console. It's enough to make you want to go all wireless. (The RJ-11 has six potential lines, although only four or two are usually used—be careful to differentiate between two-wire and four-wire cables. The RJ-45 has eight potential lines, so it is a little wider.)

In the 1980s, with the advent of the personal computer, the world of plugs went supernova. At first it was relatively easy; there was the *DB-25* serial connection on the one hand, and the 50-pin *Centronics* parallel connection on the other. (Europeans also had to be familiar with the *SCART*, an oddly-shaped 21-pin plug from the "Syndicat des Constucteurs d'Appareils de Radio et de Television.") Computers needed a lot more lines than either audio or video signals. Even more important, the standards had now doubled. On the one hand, there were the logical standards. The familiar RS-232C is a logical standard. These standards tell you which signals are on which pins (more or less) but they don't tell you anything about the physical arrangement of those pins. DB-25 is a common physical standard (there are 25 pins and the sleeve is D-shaped so it can only be plugged in one way). It is most often used for RS-232C connections—but there is no rule that says it must be used only for RS-232C connections. Similarly, a 50-pin Centronics (physical) plug is most often used for a parallel (logical) connection, but it is also used for a SCSI connection.

Since not all signals were necessary for many connections, soon there were DB-9s and DB-15s on the backs of PCs. Apple tried to make sense of the burgeoning plug world with the introduction of the Macintosh in 1984, which used (in addition to DB-25s and Minis) the new *Mini-8* plug. Unlike the earlier PC plugs, the Mini-8 was round. Because of this geometrical change the arrangement of the pins could be varied in such a way that it was impossible to stick the wrong plug into the wrong jack. A hole that received only an inactive plastic prong added to this security. Thus, Apple could use the physical Mini-8 configuration for a variety of logical applications without worrying that we users would mess things up. In a sense, the Mini-8 was a vindication of the DIN idea—although all Mini-8s are sexually "straight."

The nineties brought yet further variants: Apple introduced the dense, square *HD-40* plug with the first Powerbook. (It can provide 36 lines—enough for SCSI connections.) The fifty-pin SCSI-2 connector (the Micro DB-50) united both physical and logical standards effectively. It is a sturdy, locking connector. The USB plug, on the other hand, amplifies the flaws of the RJ connectors; it is even more flimsy and prone to failure. Moreover, it fits into PC-CARD jacks, which are not USB devices. Most recently, the FIREWIRE standard has given us yet another plug type, a little more sturdy than the USB.

Clearly, the proper grammar of plugging has yet to be written.

PM ➻ Slang for Production Manager. See PRODUCER.

PMS ➻ See PANTONE MATCHING SYSTEM.

PMT ➻ PhotoMultiplier Tube. See SCANNER.

PN ➻ PseudoNoise. See CDMA.

PNG ➻ Portable Network Graphic. See IMAGE FILE FORMATS.

Poetic Film ➻ Non-NARRATIVE FILM, often experimental. Jonas Mekas's 1960s phrase to distinguish NEW AMERICAN CINEMA from the general run of commercial, narrative fiction film.

Poetic Realism ➻ Term coined by critic Georges Sadoul to characterize certain films made in France in the 1930s and 1940s noted for their realistic yet lyrical evocation of day-to-day life, moody cinematography, and striking yet naturalistic mise-en-scène. Key figures include directors Marcel Carné, Jacques Feyder, Jean Renoir,

Julien Duvivier, and Jean Grémillon; writers Jacques Prévert and Charles Spaak; and art director Alexander Trauner.

Point ➛ A unit of measure used in typography; equal to 1/72 of an inch. Twelve points make a PICA. (In Europe a Point is defined as .0148 inch, not .0138 inch as in the U.S. and U.K. No, I don't know why, but it's got to be some kind of metric thing.)

Point-of-View Shot ➛ A shot that shows the scene from the point of view of a character. Often abbreviated POV.

Polarized Light ➛ Light waves that vibrate in one plane only, common in many reflections.

Polarizing Filter ➛ A lens filter that POLARIZES light. When the plane of the filter is at right angles to the plane of a polarized reflection in the scene, the reflection is eliminated. Two polarized filters can be used together to produce a fade as one is rotated until its plane is at right angles to the other.

Polaroid ➛ (1) Proprietary name of Edwin Land's instant photo technology. (2) By extension, any instant picture. See also 3-D.

Polavision ➛ An instant movie system introduced by Polaroid Corp. in 1977, it proved too little, too late as VIDEOCASSETTE technology was already established in the marketplace. See EVR.

Polyvision ➛ The name for Abel Gance's triptych widescreen system used in *Napoléon* (1927).

PoMo ➛ Nineties college slang for POSTMODERN that indicates either mild contempt for or insouciant acceptance of that intellectual paradigm.

Pong ➛ The first successful arcade VIDEO GAME, devised by Nolan Bushnell and introduced in 1972. In 1973 Bushnell founded Atari to market the product. 100,000 Pong machines were sold in 1974. See ODYSSEY.

POP ➛ (1) Point Of Presence. A node for an ISP or telephone company. (2) Post Office Protocol. The preferred protocol for the reception of email. See SMTP.

Popular Culture ➛ Until the 1970s this term carried with it a derogatory connotation meant to suggest a dichotomy between the culture of the MASS MEDIA and the culture of high ART. One of the successes of the cultural revolution of the 1960s was the destruction of this dichotomy so that now, for example, "pop" music can be viewed from the same critical perspective as "serious" music, and movies are treated with the same degree of respect as poetry. (Like most of the "successes" of the sixties, this one backfired, the result being that junk pop is treated equally with high-art kitsch, and what we used to call "taste" is not politically correct.)

Porn, Porno ⇒ Pornographic film exploiting sex, specifically for erotic gratification.

Portal ⇒ Internet jargon, circa 1998, for web sites that act as GATEWAYS (which is what they used to be called).

Portapak ⇒ Reel-to-reel half-inch portable videotape system first introduced by SONY in 1969, eventually superseded by VIDEOCASSETTE technology. See BETA, VHS.

Positive ⇒ A film record in which lights and darks conform to the reality of the scene photographed; a projection print. See NEGATIVE, REVERSAL.

Post House ⇒ Current Hollywood term for the digital effects companies that are rapidly replacing the LABS that used to produce special effects optically and mechanically. The computer-based Post Houses have quickly become integrated into the professional film work flow as the industry moves toward digitization. As the term indicates, their purview is broader than the Labs they have replaced.

Postdubbing ⇒ See DUB.

Postflashing ⇒ A technique in which color FILMSTOCK was exposed, after shooting, to a neutral gray light source of a predetermined level and uniform density in order to mute the INTENSITY of the colors for a more realistic effect, to decrease the CONTRAST range of the FILM-STOCK to aid in AVAILABLE-LIGHT photography, or to bring out detail in shadow areas. Of course, this is now done digitially. See PREFLASHING.

Postmodernism ⇒ If the intellectual Modernists of the first half of the twentieth century concentrated on abstracting their arts, the Postmodernists of the last half of the twentieth century eschewed the AVANT GARDE, preferring an eclectic approach that synthesized many historical movements, usually self-consciously, often superficially. Donald Barthelme put the style in lethal context in a note in *The New Yorker* in 1975: "Postmodernism is dead; didn't I tell you? I heard it from Donald. It was the last of those lovely—and lucrative!—'movements' of the twentieth century. I'll miss it. What will we talk about now?" As it turned out: not much. As the century stumbled to a close twenty-five years later, the zombie of postmodernism continued to dominate the intellectual scene.

Postproduction ⇒ The period after the shooting of a film or tape during which the production is edited, dubbed, and prepared for distribution. See POST HOUSE. Compare PREPRODUCTION.

PostScript ⇒ The page description language that was developed to drive the LASER PRINTER and has since become the standard for IMAGE-SETTERS in the publishing industry. The initial work was done by John Warnock at XEROX PARC in the early seventies. He founded ADOBE in 1982 to market this product.

Poststructuralism ⟫ Intellectual movement in literary theory and philosophy beginning in the late 1960s (and in film theory beginning in the 1970s) that has to some extent succeeded STRUCTURALISM—or debated with it. Rather than privileging the signified over the signifier (see SIGN), poststructuralist discourse privileges the signifier, questioning the absolute fixity of meaning, the certainty of origins, the power of the author, and the naturalness of any system that organizes society. Whatever.

Post-Synchronization ⟫ Recording the sound after the picture has been shot. See LOOPING.

POTS ⟫ Plain Old Telephone Service. See PSTN.

POV ⟫ A POINT-OF-VIEW SHOT.

PPI ⟫ PIXELS Per Inch. See DIGITAL RESOLUTION.

PPV ⟫ See PAY-PER-VIEW.

PQIX ⟫ See ADVANTIX.

PR ⟫ Public Relations, upmarket press agentry.

Practical Lighting ⟫ (1) Normal light fixtures on the set, such as common household incandescent bulbs. (2) The technique of using such fixtures for AVAILABLE-LIGHT photography.

Practical Set ⟫ A realistically built set in which doors, windows, and equipment actually work, or a real location. A practical set does not have WILD WALLS.

Praxinoscope ⟫ Developed by Émile Reynaud in the late 1870s, an elaboration of the ZOETROPE in which a cylinder of flat mirrors was placed in the center of the picture drum. The increased illumination and the steadiness of the image made it possible to connect the Praxinoscope to a MAGIC LANTERN, achieving the first projection of moving images. See ZOOPRAXISCOPE.

Precedence Effect ⟫ See HAAS EFFECT.

Preflashing ⟫ The same as POSTFLASHING except that the FILMSTOCK was exposed before shooting rather than after. Pioneered by Freddie Young in *The Deadly Affair* (1966).

Premastering ⟫ Preparing the data to create a disc image ready to master an optical disc such as a DVD-VIDEO. Compare MASTERING.

Premiere ⟫ See ADOBE.

Premium Channel, Premium Service ⟫ A cable channel for which an additional fee is charged, such as HBO, whose availability to cable system operators beginning in 1974 greatly increased the marketability of CABLE TELEVISION.

Prepress ⟫ The work of preparing a book or other document for traditional printing. While much of the Prepress process (layout, halftone screens, pasteup, color separations) has been obviated by the growth of DESKTOP PUBLISHING, the Prepress profession still exists.

Preproduction ➺ The period before shooting of a film or tape begins during which the script is prepared and cast and crew are hired and rehearsed. Compare POSTPRODUCTION.

Preroll ➺ Videotape decks need time to get up to speed. This time is called Preroll, and varies between machines from about 3 to 10 seconds. When two decks need to be synchronized for editing, Preroll has to be added to the equation.

Presence ➺ The quality of intelligence, character, or personality a performer projects via the media: screen presence, stage presence. See PHOTOGENIC, TELEGENIC.

Presence Track ➺ Audio track of location background sound mixed under dialogue to enhance the realism of a scene. See AMBIENT SOUND.

Press Agent ➺ A vaguely archaic term for the person whose job is to gain publicity for a film (or any other product) in newspapers, magazines, and the broadcast media. Compare PR.

Presstype ➺ During the brief period between the appearance of consumer-oriented offset printing in the 1960s and WYSIWIG page-layout programs in the 1980s, Presstype was popular for do-it-yourself publishing. The body copy of a newsletter would be set on a typewriter (an IBM Selectric with a special font ball, if you were lucky). The headlines would be set with Presstype after the body was pasted up. These plastic sheets included numerous instances of each letter in each font. You transferred a letter to the MECHANICAL by rubbing the top surface of the sheet gently with a burnisher or ballpoint pen.

Prestel ➺ British Telecom's VIDEOTEXT system, the first in the world, which debuted in 1976.

Preview ➺ (1) A prerelease SCREENING of a film, usually held to gauge audience reaction with an eye to making final adjustments in the editing. See SNEAK PREVIEW. (2) Marketing euphemism for a TRAILER.

PrimeStar ➺ See DSS.

Prime Time ➺ The hours when most television sets are in use and that therefore offer advertisers the greatest potential audience. In the eastern U.S., 7:30 pm to 11:00 pm.

Prime-Time Access Rule ➺ The FCC's 1971 ruling that forbade NETWORKS from providing more than an average of three hours of prime-time programming per evening. The ruling was designed to open up prime time to local programming. The effect, however, was that local broadcasters turned en masse to SYNDICATED programming. The ruling was overturned in 1993.

Principle Photography ➺ The main shooting schedule, not including SECOND UNIT photography and miscellaneous PICKUPS.

Print ➺ A POSITIVE copy of a film.

Printed Circuit ➺ A miniaturized electronic circuit whose interconnections are printed on a circuit board. Devices such as transistors, resistors, and capacitors can then be plugged into the circuit rather than painstakingly wired in. Together with the TRANSISTOR the printed circuit was the first stage in the development of modern microelectronics; a precursor of the INTEGRATED CIRCUIT and the MICROPROCESSOR.

Printing Technologies ➺ See RELIEF, INTAGLIO, PLANOGRAPHIC, GRAVURE, LETTERPRESS, OFFSET, LITHOGRAPHY, SCREEN, LASER PRINTER, XEROGRAPHY, PHOTOLITHOGRAPHY, DYE SUBLIMATION, THERMAL WAX, INK JET, SOLID INK, DOT MATRIX, BAND PRINTER, and DAISY WHEEL.

Print-Through ➺ The transfer of magnetically recorded sounds and images from one part of a magnetic tape to an adjacent part, caused usually by incorrect storage practices.

Process Color ➺ See COLOR PRINTING, SPOT COLOR.

Process Shot ➺ REAR PROJECTION, MATTE SHOTS, OPTICALS, and the like.

Processing ➺ The chemical procedure of development that brings out the latent image in the FILMSTOCK. If a film has been UNDEREXPOSED it can later be OVERDEVELOPED, or forced, to regain some of the balance between light and dark. In AVAILABLE-LIGHT color photography, it is often necessary to push the film a few "stops" in development (overdevelop it) in order to regain a balanced image. See EXPOSURE, SPEED.

Prodigy ➺ IBM's consumer online service, which debuted with great fanfare in 1988. Prodigy differed from predecessors like COMPUSERVE by offering a graphical interface based on NAPLPS, the VIDEOTEXT protocol. (It was the only major service ever to use NAPLPS.) Even this minimal level of graphics tended to slow down the system, a problem further enhanced by Prodigy's distributed network architecture. (The main host controlled a network of subsidiary hosts around the country.) By the early 1990s, Prodigy was on the ropes as the AOL juggernaut gained speed. The WORLD WIDE WEB obviated any need for NAPLPS. (Even AOL's proprietary graphics worked better.) IBM eventually sold the brand name and what was left of the network.

Producer ➺ In film and television the person with overall financial and business responsibilities who usually serves as general manager of the project and usually hires cast and crew—or the people who do. The producer may be simply a business manager, or the guiding artistic force of the film. The producer usually employs several associates: middle management, if you will. The title Executive Producer is often given to financiers. A Line Producer is someone who has day-to-day control of the project. (The term comes from the

Business School differentiation between "Staff" management and "Line" management.) On a large Hollywood production the Production Manager serves as the "project manager" and often wields considerable power.

Product Placement ➤ The practice of selling the right to appear in a film to the manufacturers of various automobiles, soft drinks, and other products. Product placement became a lucrative sideline for producers in the 1980s. The featured role for Reese's Pieces candy in *E.T.* in 1982 is regarded as a landmark. In a way, it's the opposite of LICENSING. See PLUGOLA, VIRTUAL PRODUCT PLACEMENT.

Production ➤ (1) Any film or television program. (2) The period during which a film or program is being shot. Compare PREPRODUCTION, POSTPRODUCTION.

Production Code ➤ In 1922 the Motion Picture Producers and Distributors of America organization was formed in response to supposed public moral outrage at Hollywood's sex scandals. Its aim was to impose modest self-censorship in order to ward off government regulation. The organization was known colloquially as the *Hays Office* after its first president. The Hays Office performed no formal censorship, preferring to counter bad publicity with good. The first formal "production code" listing do's and don'ts dated from 1930.

When Joseph Breen joined the MPPA in 1934, the Code began to be strictly enforced, with the Catholic Legion of Decency offering none too subtle support. The Code strictly limited filmmakers for years. Such words as "damn," "hell," "nuts," and even "nerts" were forbidden, as were explicit violence, alternative social behavior, unpunished criminal activity, and even the depiction of men and women in bed together. Although the Code began to fade in the late 1930s and after World War II, it was not seriously challenged until the 1950s and did not fall until the late 1960s, when it was replaced with the current RATINGS system.

Production Manager ➤ See PRODUCER.

Profilmic Space ➤ See MISE EN SCÈNE.

Profilmic Special Effects ➤ See SPECIAL EFFECTS.

Program Signal ➤ The signal that carries the actual program information and that is imposed on the carrier wave. See WAVE MECHANICS.

Programmer ➤ (1) The executive in charge of PROGRAMMING at a NETWORK or station. (2) A B PICTURE; a minor film made to fill a program in the 1930s, 1940s, or 1950s. (3) A modestly budgeted film, between an A and a B picture, capable of playing at the top of a double bill, common in Hollywood before the rise of the B picture. (4) Someone who writes computer code.

Programming ➤ (1) The art and science of designing a television or radio schedule to obtain maximum audiences Demographically determined to appeal to advertisers. (2) The art and science of writing computer instruction code.

Progressive Download ➤ This works like Streaming Media allowing an audiovideo file to start playing before the download is complete. The difference is that a Progressive Download doesn't adjust the data rate for available bandwidth and the file has a limited size rather than being continuous and open-ended.

Progressive Scanning ➤ See Interlace, Scanning.

PROM ➤ Programmable Read Only Memory. A rom that can be programmed to hold a nonvolatile set of data. Compare eprom.

Promo ➤ A television or radio "house ad" or announcement advertising upcoming programs.

Prop ➤ Any physical item used in a play or film: chairs, tables, eyeglasses, books, pens, et cetera. From "property."

Property ➤ (1) A Prop. (2) Any of a number of possible versions of either a fictional or nonfictional story—in manuscript, playscript, typescript, or book form—that has potential commercial value in the Media. Properties can be recycled many times. *Cabaret*, for example, began as a book of short stories (Christopher Isherwood's *Berlin Stories*); one of the stories became the play *I Am a Camera*, which became the film *I Am a Camera*, which became the musical play *Cabaret*, which was the source of the record album, film, and soundtrack album of the same title: one property, seven exploitations. See Package.

Prosumer ➤ Marketing term for Hi-End audio and video, a combination of PROfessional and ConSUMER.

Protocol ➤ A communications protocol—like its diplomatic grandfather—is a set of rules and codes of conduct that facilitates interaction between parties with different cultures. (In this case, the cultures are electronic operating systems.) The set of rules is usually divided into different levels that represent the various tasks that need to be done: physical, graphic, presentation, for example. See Internet, Television Protocols, HTTP, X.25.

PS ➤ A feature of rds that identifies the Program Service being received.

PSK ➤ See Phase-Shift Keying.

PSTN ➤ Public Switched Telephone Network, the traditional telephone system, also referred to as *POTS*, for Plain Old Telephone System.

PSX ➤ Familiar abbreviation for the Sony PlayStation game system.

Psychoacoustics ⇝ The psychology of the perception of sound. See PERCEPTUAL CODING.

Psychoanalytic Film Theory ⇝ Rooted in the work of Jacques Lacan, this strain of theory considers film in relation to such Freudian concepts as the dream, dream interpretation, projection, and the fetish. Generally useful in examining the relationship between the spectator and the image, the theory was also useful to FEMINIST FILM THEORY.

Psychographics ⇝ Statistical measurements of television viewers' lifestyles used by advertisers, together with DEMOGRAPHICS, to increase efficiency.

PTP ⇝ Parallel Track Path. In a dual-layer DVD-VIDEO the data in the second layer is organized in the same direction. (CDs and DVDs, by the way, play from the center out—the reverse of LPs.) This is good if the second layer contains additional comments but it doesn't work well if the second layer is a continuation of the movie. In that case, you would prefer *OTP* (Opposite Track Path) so that the pickup can continue with only the slightest hesitation. OTP is the same as RSDL.

Public Access Television ⇝ Channels set aside on CABLE systems for use by any member of the public. See ACCESS.

Public Broadcasting Service ⇝ See PBS.

Public Domain ⇝ Until the 1976 revision, U.S. COPYRIGHT law allowed a copyright owner to maintain all rights in his INTELLECTUAL PROPERTY (books, films, music) for a period of 28 years, renewable for an additional 28 years. At the end of the period, the work entered the public domain and the original author or producer had no rights in it. Some film producers from the 1930s and 1940s neglected to renew their copyrights under the old system. These films fell into the public domain rather quickly and provided a source of exploitation for VIDEOCASSETTE manufacturers during the first flush of business in the 1980s. DVD-VIDEO manufacturers followed their cue fifteen years later. (The 1976 COPYRIGHT law, now in effect, provides for one period: the life of the author plus fifty years.)

Public Relations, PR, Publicity ⇝ While advertising costs money, "PR" uses the "free" channels of news operations to promote ideas, people, images, products, and services.

Pull-Back Shot ⇝ A TRACKING SHOT or ZOOM that moves back from the subject to reveal the context of the scene.

Pull-Down Mechanism ⇝ The device that makes INTERMITTENT MOTION possible: usually a Maltese Cross gear or a cam-mounted claw that pulls each frame into position in the aperture of the projector and holds it steady while the SHUTTER opens, then closes. The invention of a practical pull-down mechanism, which made cinema possible, is usually credited to Thomas Armat. Since the 1970s the development of rotating prism apertures has obviated the need for pull-down mechanisms. In such systems (found notably in high-speed cameras and modern editing tables such as the STEENBECK), the film moves continuously rather than intermittently past the aperture while the prism continually redirects the light beam toward the lens.

Pull Focus ⇒ See FOCUS PULL.

Pulse Code Modulation ⇒ See PCM.

Pulse Width Modulation ⇒ See PWM.

Punch-down Block ⇒ See 66 BLOCK.

Push Development ⇒ To overdevelop, or FORCE PROCESSING.

Pushover ⇒ A type of WIPE in which the succeeding image appears to push the preceding image off the screen.

Puter ⇒ Cute Internet slang for microcomputer. It may be a sign of the dominance of the device that we have so few colloquial synonyms for it.

PWM ⇒ Pulse Width Modulation, the system for digital encoding used in the DSD system. Compare PCM.

QAM ⇒ Quadrature Amplitude Modulation. An encoding system used with Cable TV.

QDesign Music Codec ⇒ A popular low-bandwidth CODEC in the late 1990s for CD-ROMs, DVD-ROMs, and the Web, designed especially for the reproduction of music.

QPSK ⇒ Quadrature Phase-Shift Keying. An encoding system for satellite television and MMDS.

QSL ⇒ Confirmation of reception. See HAM RADIO.

Quadraphonic Sound ⇒ A development of STEREOPHONIC reproduction in the early 1970s that used four channels of information rather than two in either FM MULTIPLEX broadcasting or discs and tapes. Two channels fed front speakers with basic stereophonic signals while the two remaining channels fed back speakers with slightly different signals to provide an environmental ROOM SOUND. Introduced by the recording industry in 1972, quadraphonic sound did not have the anticipated impact on the stereo marketplace. It failed quickly, only to be revived twenty years later in digital formats. See SURROUND SOUND, 5.1.

Qualcomm Pure Voice Codec ➤ A popular low-bandwidth CODEC in the late 1990s for CD-ROMs, DVD-ROMs, and the Web, designed especially for the reproduction of voice.

Quantization ➤ The job of converting an ANALOG signal into a series of numbers that can be stored as DIGITAL data. The precision of a given method of quantization depends on two factors: the SAMPLING rate and the quantization level. The quantization level is a measure of the detail of each sample. For example, CD-quality audio is sampled at a rate of 44.1 kiloHertz with a quantization level of 16 bits; thus any one of 65,536 values (2^{16}) can be assigned to each sample. Compare DSD.

Quantum Link ➤ See AOL.

QUBE ➤ Warner Cable's name for its pioneering INTERACTIVE CABLE system introduced in Columbus, Ohio, in 1977.

QuickTime ➤ APPLE Computer's operating system extension for digitized moving pictures, audio, and other time-based data, introduced in 1991. A central technology for multimedia and CD-ROM production in the early 1990s, this architecture has been cross-platform since the mid-1990s, and serves as the core specification for MPEG-4.

QuickTime VR ➤ APPLE Computer's extension of its QUICKTIME technology that allows viewers to control their perspective of a space or an object while it permits producers to create such virtual realities easily and inexpensively. Introduced in 1995. See VIRTUAL REALITY.

Quintaphonic Sound ➤ A film SOUNDTRACK system that provided five channels of sound information: three in front, two behind. The term is now in disuse. See STEREOPHONIC, QUADRAPHONIC, 5.1, DOLBY SR, SDDS, DTS.

Race Film ➤ From silent film days through the 1940s the film industry didn't ignore the African-American audience. Filmmakers, Black and white, produced these films to meet the market.

Rack Focusing ➤ A technique that uses SHALLOW FOCUS (shallow DEPTH OF FIELD) to direct the attention of the viewer forcibly from one subject to another. Focus is pulled, or changed, to shift the FOCUS PLANE, often rapidly, sometimes several times within the shot.

Radio ➤ (1) From the Latin for "the emission of beams." The transmission of information such as a PROGRAM SIGNAL encoded on a carrier wave within the RADIO SPECTRUM of the ELECTROMAGNETIC SPECTRUM. (2) More colloquially, any broadcast of sound without picture. See WAVE MECHANICS.

Radio Bands ⇒ By international agreement radio and television broadcasting signals are limited to certain frequencies. The ranges for radio are: Long Wave, 150 kHz to 450 kHz; Medium Wave, 520 kHz to 1620 kHz; and Short Wave, 2,000 to 30,000 kHz. FM radio operates at 66 to 72 mHz in Eastern Europe; 76 to 90 mHz in Japan; and 87 to 108 mHz in the rest of the world. In the U.S. these bands are referred to by their frequencies, but elsewhere the wavelength equivalents are more common. For example, 600 kHz (frequency) is 500 meters (wavelength) while 1500 kHz is 200 meters. See HAM RADIO, ELECTROMAGNETIC SPECTRUM, SATELLITE BANDS.

Radio Data System ⇒ See RDS.

Radio Microphone ⇒ Increasingly popular form of the device that uses a small transmitter instead of a cable to connect to the amplifier. Singers of the TIN-PAN-ALLEY era such as Frank Sinatra and Mel Tormé used the mike cable as a prop to dramatic effect. They seem lost, now, without the wire to fondle. On the other hand, if the radio mike had not become ubiquitous in the seventies and eighties, a number of latter-day Rock stars—hyperactive yet untrained in the subtleties of the cord—would have strangled themselves. Curiously, a forlorn vestige of the sensuous, romantic wire of yesteryear remains in the truncated tail of today's coldly efficient radio device.

Radio Spectrum ⇒ See ELECTROMAGNETIC SPECTRUM.

Radiograph ⇒ An image produced on a radiosensitive surface, such as photographic film, by radiation other than visible light.

RAID ⇒ Redundant Array of Inexpensive Drives, an ingenious technique of computer data storage that provides protection against drive failure and increases the speed of storage. The name clearly describes the strategy. RAID systems use a variety of methods to write data to a set of disks, including striping (writing parts of a file to separate disks) and mirroring (writing a file to two disks).

RAM ⇒ Random Access Memory. Volatile computer memory that depends on the presence of an electrical current to maintain itself, as opposed to a ROM, a MAGNETIC DISK, or an OPTICAL DISC, which are nonvolatile means of storage that don't require the presence of an electrical current. The work of a computer is done in the RAM, into which both programs and the data upon which they operate must be loaded, usually from a nonvolatile storage medium. The definition of RAM has very little to do with "Random Access" or "Memory" since most systems of storage are "random access" as well and since "memory" suggests permanence, the singular quality no RAM has.

Rap ➤ Genre of Pop music that burgeoned in the late 1980s, based on old traditions of verbal performance in African-American culture—"rapping," "doing the dozens," and so forth. Like all popular music since the 1960s, Rap had its roots in that seminal decade (The Last Poets, James Brown) but unlike the tired imitations of Rock, Rap could lay claim to a degree of innovation. Focusing on the poetic rhythmic elements of the lyric, Rap eschewed melody and harmony while keeping to conservative Rock rhythms. As a result, Rap relied more than most music on recording technology; depended heavily on the visual impact of MUSIC VIDEOS; increasingly emphasized the dance performances (*Hip Hop*) that accompanied the verbal raps; and also exploiting SAMPLING.

Rapports de Production ➤ In Marxian thought, the relationships in the productive system among producer, distributor, and consumer.

Raster ➤ The predetermined pattern of SCANNING lines that produces the image on a CATHODE RAY TUBE. See also FIELD.

Raster Graphics ➤ See BITMAPPED GRAPHICS.

Rasterize ➤ To convert a VECTOR GRAPHIC image into a BITMAPPED GRAPHIC image for printing or display. See RIP.

Ratings ➤ (1) In cinema, systems of classification based on sexual or violence factors. The British Board of Film Censors bestows three types of certificates: U (Universal); A (Adult, prohibited to children under 16 unless accompanied by an adult); and X (unsuitable for children under 16). In the U.S., the Motion Picture Association of America (MPAA) rates films in six categories: G (General); PG (Parental Guidance suggested for children); PG-13 (some material may be inappropriate for children under 13); R (Restricted to persons under 18 unless accompanied by an adult); X (prohibited to persons under 18); and NC-17 (No Children under 17), a replacement term designed to avoid the negative connotations of the X rating. (2) In broadcasting, systems for estimating audience size for television and radio programs so that prices can be set for advertisers. See NIELSEN, ARBITRON.

Ratio ➤ See SHOOTING RATIO, ASPECT RATIO.

Raytracing ➤ A technique of 3-D MODELING.

RBDS ➤ Radio Broadcasting Data System. The U.K. version of RDS.

RCA ➤ Founded October 17, 1919, with the backing of the U.S. government in an attempt to control first radiotelegraphy, then radiotelephony, the Radio Corporation of America was a combination of General Electric, American Telephone & Telegraph, Western Electric, and American Marconi interests. Under the leadership of Owen D. Young, then David Sarnoff, RCA dominated innovation in consumer electronics for fifty years, from the founding of the National Broadcasting Company in 1926, through early American television broadcasts in the 1930s, to the introduction of NTSC color television technology in the 1950s and 1960s. RCA's last attempt at innovation was the CED VIDEODISC system introduced in 1980. By this time, SONY and PHILIPS were thoroughly in control of the technological avant garde. GE acquired RCA and its subsidiary NBC in 1986. The company was later sold to THOMSON, the French electronics giant.

RCA Plug ➺ See PLUGS.

RDS ➺ Radio Data System. A broadcast PROTOCOL for transmitting limited data on a subcarrier of radio FREQUENCY. The Radio Data System, introduced in Europe in the 1980s (successfully) and the U.S. in the 1990s (unsuccessfully) requires special receivers with LCD screens to display the data, which is generally limited to traffic reports, and information about the audio being broadcast. Features include Traffic Announcement (TA), Program Service name (PS), Clock Time (CT), Alternative Frequency (AF), and Enhanced Other Network (EON).

Reaction Shot ➺ A shot that cuts away from the main scene or speaker to show another character's reaction. See CUTAWAY.

Reactive Technology ➺ Unidirectional technology. See DISTRIBUTION FLOW.

Reader ➺ A staff employee who reads scripts and other properties, making preliminary judgments and writing summaries for executives. The film company's first line of defense against the deluge of material would-be writers, producers, and directors submit to it. As a matter of policy, the major studios cover most novels published. See COVERAGE.

Real Estate ➺ In the VIDEODISC and CD-ROM businesses, the amount of space available on the disc, as in "How much real estate does that movie eat up?"

Real Time ➺ A concept borrowed from computer technology. The actual time during which a process or event occurs. A LIVE broadcast occurs in real time, for example.

Real-Time Access ➺ See ACCESS.

RealAudio, RealVideo ➺ Pioneering STREAMING MEDIA formats for Web broadcasting from the RealNetworks company, founded by Rob Glaser, a former Microsoft honcho. The debut of this software in the mid-1990s permitted the first practical application of Internet broadcasting. See MOVIE FILE FORMATS.

Realism ➺ In film, the attitude opposed to EXPRESSIONISM that emphasizes the subject as opposed to the director's view of the subject.

Usually concerns contemporary topics of a socially conscious nature and uses a minimal amount of technique. See Neorealism, Minimal Cinema, Formalism.

Reality Programming ➤ An inexpensive television entertainment genre that grew out of news programming and became popular in the 1980s. Through a combination of documentary, interviews, and—at its best—investigative reporting, reality programming spins entertainment out of the stuff of news.

Rear Projection ➤ A process in which a background scene is projected onto a translucent screen behind the actors so it appears that the actors are in that location. Superseded by Front Projection and Matte techniques, both more effective systems, and then by digital effects.

Record Film ➤ A film that provides a duplicate representation of the subject photographed with no pretense to artistic content.

Record Player ➤ See Turntable.

Red Book ➤ See CD Standards.

Reel-to-Reel ➤ A tape recorder that uses open reels of tape rather than closed Cassettes or Cartridges.

Reflex Camera ➤ A camera that incorporates a mirrored shutter so that the cameraman can observe the scene through the Taking Lens rather than a separate Viewfinder, thereby eliminating problems of Parallax distortion and greatly enhancing the photographer's ability to judge the elements of the scene.

Reflexivity ➤ Traditional term in literature and philosophy to describe a medium that shows awareness of its potential and means of construction, displays them openly, and deliberately reflects upon itself. In Hollywood there's a simpler term: Movie Movies.

Refresh Rate ➤ The rate at which a computer screen is repainted. See Frame Rate, Interlace.

Regenerative Circuit ➤ First developed by Edwin Armstrong, an amplification circuit that uses the principle of Feedback to strengthen the incoming signal.

Region Code ➤ The major Hollywood studios insisted on this "feature" of DVD-Video: the standard allows discs to be protected by region codes. Players manufactured to be sold in one region will refuse to play discs designed to be sold in other regions. The studios wanted this feature so that they could more tightly control distribution windows. The regions are defined by marketing, not by geography or politics. They are:

(1) Canada, U.S., U.S. possessions, and some islands in the Pacific.

(2) Japan, western Europe, Poland, Romania, Bulgaria, the Balkans, South Africa, Turkey, the Middle East, Iran, and Egypt.

(3) Southeast Asia and South Korea.

(4) Australia, New Zealand, South America, most of Central America, the Caribbean, Papua New Guinea, and most of the South Pacific.

(5) Russia, the other former Soviet Republics, most of Africa, India, Pakistan, Bangladesh, Nepal, Bhutan, Mongolia, Afghanistan, and North Korea.

(6) China and Tibet. Note: producers are not required to region-code DVD discs.

Region coding is also a feature of SONY PLAYSTATION game discs.

It seems region 2 is easier to get into than NATO.

Relational Editing ⇒ Editing of shots to suggest a conceptual association between or among shots. See MONTAGE OF ATTRACTION.

Release Candidate ⇒ See BETA.

Release Print ⇒ A print ready for DISTRIBUTION and SCREENING. See also GENERATION.

Relief Printing ⇒ A system of printing in which the printing surface is raised. See INTAGLIO PRINTING, PLANOGRAPHIC.

Remake ⇒ A second production of a film (or sometimes a television show) using different personnel. The concept remains more or less intact, but the script is often completely rewritten to fit the talents of the new filmmakers. Compare SPINOFF, KNOCKOFF.

Remote ⇒ (1) Television (or audio or computer system) control device that is separate from the set itself, communicating with the set usually via infrared signal. Because the remote can be operated from anywhere in the room, this device (together with more advanced systems of tuning and the multiplicity of cable channels) has changed the television experience, and therefore the business. Rather than locking on to one channel, as they once did, viewers now roam the field, moving with equal ease from channel 2 to channel 124. (2) A broadcast transmission from a site outside the studio.

Remote Control ⇒ As REMOTE controls became ubiquitous in the 1980s some manufacturers yielded to the temptation to put sophisticated—but necessary—functions on the remote but not on the console. After all, the little buttons on the remote were cheaper than the big controls on the set. The result was that, if you lost the remote, you lost control. Replacement remotes were clueless when it came to these additional features.

Rendering ⇒ When an image, movie, or soundtrack is too complex to be rendered in REAL TIME, the artist works with an approximation, then applies the desired effects later. This is called Rendering. See 3-D MODELING.

Rep, Repertory ➤ (1) In legitimate theater, a company that produces a season of several productions with the same personnel. (2) A cinema that schedules a wide variety of films. Usually the same film or film program plays for only one day; often the programs are designed around a theme. See REVIVAL HOUSE.

Repro ➤ Copy prepared to be photographed for PHOTOENGRAVING plates to be used in printing.

Reprography ➤ Chemical or electrophotographic systems of image-transfer printing, such as XEROGRAPHY and similar systems. See OFFSET, LETTERPRESS.

Resampling ➤ Changing the DIGITAL RESOLUTION of an image. When you Downsample, groups of pixels are averaged and combined. When you Upsample, however, the program has to invent pixels to fill in the blanks. This is done by various mathematical Interpolation formulas. But, take note: you haven't increased the DEFINITION of the image.

Resolution ➤ (1) The ability of a lens to define visual detail, usually measured as the number of lines per millimeter that can be separately identified. See DEFINITION. (2) By extension, the precision of any other visual device or system, such as a television or computer screen. See VIDEO RESOLUTION. (3) In digital imaging, any one of a number of different parameters. See DIGITAL RESOLUTION.

Response Time ➤ In the technology of sound reproduction, the minimum amount of time necessary for a system of amplifier and speaker to reproduce sound and therefore a measure of the acuity of the system.

Reverb ➤ Reverberation, an echo automatically added to an audio output. See PHASING.

Reversal Filmstock ➤ A stock whose emulsion will print POSITIVE after exposure and development. Consumer slide film is a Reversal stock.

Reverse Angle ➤ (1) A SHOT from the opposite side of a subject. (2) In a dialogue scene, a SHOT of the second participant.

Reverse Field Cutting ➤ See SHOT/REVERSE SHOT.

Reverse Motion ➤ The film is run through the camera backward so that when it is later run through the projector in the normal manner the illusion will be created that time is running backward.

Reverse Spiral ➤ See DVD-VIDEO DISC FORMATS.

Revival House ➤ A cinema specializing in older films. See REPERTORY.

RF ➤ Radio Frequency. Shorthand for any analog radio signal.

RF Dolby Digital ➤ See MODULATED DOLBY DIGITAL.

RF Interference ⇒ Radio Frequency noise that causes Glitches in an image or noise in sound. An Artifact, or inconsistency, in analog imaging.

RGB ⇒ One of several systems for quantifying color values in print and electronic media. See Color Models, Television Standards.

RG-59, RG-6 ⇒ Types of Coaxial Cable.

RIAA ⇒ Recording Industry Association of America. The professional organization for the recording industry, founded in 1952. See Gold, Platinum.

RIP ⇒ Raster Image Processor. A processor dedicated to Rasterizing an image in preparation for printing on a high-resolution printer. Because of the large amount of data required for high-resolution printing it makes sense to off-load the computation to a dedicated machine.

Ripper ⇒ Software to allow the capture of audio for conversion to MP3 format. Although the source of the term may seem to be "ripping off, " in fact, a ripper is used for "tearing out" a track as a file from a CD Blob.

RISC ⇒ Reduced Instruction Set Chip. As Microprocessor machine code became more complex the idea that computers might operate better with a dumber—but faster—CPU gained some popularity. The only widely available RISC chips have been the Motorola PowerPC series, developed in collaboration with Apple and IBM and first appearing in 1994. By the turn of the century, as Intel and its cloners continued to develop CISC processors that kept pace with the RISC architecture, the debate had quieted down. See CPU.

RJ-11C, RJ-45X ⇒ See Plugs.

RKO ⇒ The studio that would not die, RKO has suffered longer than most from corporate intrigue and infighting. With a history that can be traced back to 1909, Radio-Keith-Orpheum emerged as a player in 1928 with interests in production, distribution, and exhibition. Throughout the 1930s and 1940s RKO held its own against the majors with such films as the Astaire–Rogers musicals and *Citizen Kane*. Howard Hughes acquired the company in 1948. It quickly declined into a shell. The studio facilities were sold to Desilu in 1953. Hughes then sold the company to General Tire, who abandoned film for television production. The company tried to get back into feature film production in the 1980s. In 1989 majority control was purchased by Pavilion Communications.

Roll ⇒ The movement of the camera around the axis that runs longitudinally from the lens to the subject. See also Tilt, Pan.

ROM ⇒ Read-Only Memory. A CHIP that stores data in a permanent form. It is less important that you can't write to a ROM than it is that the storage is permanent. See PROM, EPROM. Compare RAM.

Room Sound, Room Noise, Room Tone ⇒ (1) The particular quality of sound in a certain location, mainly a matter of reverberation and echoes. (2) The basic, underlying sound present in a location, such as clocks, traffic, activity. Room sound is often recorded WILD and later mixed with dialogue and effects. See AMBIENT SOUND, SOUNDSTAGE, PRESENCE TRACK.

Rotary Press Printing ⇒ Curved printing plates are attached to a rotating cylinder to permit continuous rather than intermittent operation of the press. Rolls of paper rather than individual sheets feed the press. Pages are cut later. Rotary presses can operate at very high speeds. See LETTERPRESS, OFFSET.

Rotoscope ⇒ A device to project individual frames, one at a time, onto a drawing board so that a TRAVELLING MATTE can be created or the live action can be redrawn for ANIMATION.

Rough Cut ⇒ The first assembly of a film, prepared by the editor from the selected TAKES, which are joined in the order planned in the script. Finer points of timing and montage are left to a later stage.

Router ⇒ Like a PAD, a device to route packets over a LAN or the INTERNET.

RTF ⇒ Rich-Text Format. A word-processing format meant to serve as a common interchange format between word-processing formats. It almost works. Sometimes. What is needed is an SGML interface.

RTFM ⇒ Customer-service shorthand response for "Read the friggin' manual," which is what you have to do after all else fails.

Rushes ⇒ Prints of TAKES that are made immediately after a day's shooting so that they can be examined before the next day's shooting begins. Also called dailies. See ANSWER PRINT.

S

Saccade ⇒ The flick movement of the eye from one position to another that occurs not only when reading words but also when reading images and real scenes.

SACD ⇒ (1) Super Audio Compact Disc. The Sony/Philips candidate to replace the audio CD standard in place since 1982. The SACD disc has two layers: the bottom layer is an old-fashioned audio CD, playable on any CD deck; the top layer has the *HD* recording at a higher density read by a different laser, and using an advanced lossless compression scheme. The HD layer uses Sony's Direct Stream Digital (DSD) process to provide both stereo and surround-sound signals. The advantages of this approach are backward compatibility with the huge installed base of CD players and *Single Inventory*—retailers do not need to stock two different versions of the same title. Compare DVD-AUDIO. (2) Société des Auteurs et Compositeurs Dramatiques, long-time independent French INTELLECTUAL PROPERTY rights agency. Compare ASCAP, BMI.

SAD ⇒ Super Audio Disc. See DAD, SACD.

Safe Action Area ⇒ See TV MASK.

SAG ⇒ Screen Actors Guild, the main union for American actors. SAG negotiates industry-wide contracts with the producers groups. AFTRA is more important in the television business.

Sampling ⇒ (1) The technique of monitoring an ANALOG waveform at certain time intervals and translating values into numbers for storage, transmission, and re-creation. See NYQUIST LIMIT, OVERSAMPLING, QUANTIZATION. (2) The practice that became prevalent during the early 1990s among some musicians, especially in RAP, of digitally reprocessing "quotations"—or "samples"—from other musicians' work and using them as if they were their own.

SAP ⇒ Second Audio Program. With the advent of STEREO TELEVISION broadcasts in the 1980s, the second audio channel offered opportunities to broadcast entirely separate audio tracks (instead of the stereo differentiator), as, for example, with translations, or audio descriptions of the visual action intended as an aid to sight-impaired viewers. Compare CLOSED CAPTION.

Sat Card ⇒ Satellite Card. A SMART CARD that serves as a decryption key for DSB satellite broadcasts.

SATCOM ⇒ Proprietary name for RCA's communications SATELLITES.

Satellite Bands ⇒ The frequencies assigned to satellite transmissions have been divided into bands, each of which is devoted to a certain function.

C-Band: from 3.7 to 4.2, 4.5 to 4.8, and 5.85 to 7.075 gHz ("4/6 gHz"), used for DSB and telecommunications, especially in the U.S.

Ka-Band: from 17.7 to 20.2 and 27.5 to 30.0 gHz ("20/30 gHz"), allocated to HDTV and other uses.

Ku-Band: from 10.7 to 13.25 and 14.0 to 14.5 gHz ("10/14 gHz"), used for most satellite television in Europe, generally spot or local beams compared to C-Band wide coverage.

L-Band: from 0.39 to 1.55 gHz ("1.5gHz"), used for Digital Audio Broadcasting (DAB).

S-Band: from 1.55 to 5.2 gHz ("2.5 gHz"), community reception band.

X-Band: from 7.25 to 7.75 and 7.9 to 8.4 gHz ("7/8 gHz"), mainly telecommunications.

DBS Band: Direct Broadcast Satellite (11.7 gHz to 12.5 gHz), a section of the Ku-Band used for satellite television, mainly in Scandinavia.

FSS Band: Fixed Satellite Services (10.7 to 11.7 gHz) of the Ku-Band frequencies intended for business use, but now the main satellite broadcast band.

Telecom Band: The 12.5 to 12.75 gHz slice of the Ku-Band, first used by French Telecom satellites, but now includes broadcast.

Satellite Communications ➤ A satellite placed in *geosynchronous* orbit 22,300 miles above the equator will remain stationary with respect to the Earth permitting sending and receiving antennas to be permanently aimed at it. TRANSPONDERS on the satellite receive Earth signals, amplify them, and retransmit them. Satellite technology for telephone, television, and information transmission grew rapidly from the 1970s through 1990s and has had a marked effect on the television industry. By the late 1980s DSB systems were broadcasting direct to viewers and challenging the CABLE industry. See DSS, LEO, B-SKY-B, ASTRA, DIRECTV.

Saturation ➤ See COLOR.

S-Band ➤ See SATELLITE BANDS.

Scale ➤ If you are an actor or technician "working for scale," you have agreed to accept the minimum payment established by your union or guild.

Scan Converter ➤ Another name for a LINE-DOUBLER.

Scan Rate ➤ See REFRESH RATE.

Scan, Scanning ➤ (1) In television, the movement of the electron beam in regular patterns to cover the mosaic of receptor cells in the camera or the coating of phosphor PICTURE ELEMENTS (PIXELS) on the screen of the CATHODE RAY TUBE. (Or the switching of electronic signals to activate the array of pixels on an LCD screen.) See FIELD, RASTER, INTERLACE. (2) The process of digitizing an ANALOG image, such as a photograph. Like laser printers operating in reverse, SCANNERS use a laser or LED light source to read the density of each color in the image, pixel by pixel. This information is then digitized by the software. The higher the resolution of the scanner, the more samples it takes See SCANNER.

Scanner ➤ (1) A device that digitizes an image. Scanners come in two basic FORM FACTORS (flatbed or drum) and use two basic technologies: CCD or PhotoMultiplier Tube (PMT). The CCD is usually associated with the flatbed scanner and the PMT with the drum. The PMT drum scanner is the more precise device, used for professional print applications (although CCD scanners are catching up). The Photomultiplier tube captures a greater range of contrasts. In the drum scanner, the scanning head is vertically stationary, while the source image moves on the drum. In the flatbed scanner, the source is stationary; the scanning head traces each line as it moves down the page.

(2) A radio receiver that automatically searches one or more radio bands (police, fire, cellular, etc.) searching for signals. HAM RADIO enthusiasts have done this manually for years. Cheap handheld scanners became popular in the late 1980s with the rise of cell phones. Previously, all you'd hear on a scanner were professional police and fire calls—sort of like watching a television set that only got cop shows. Cell phones opened up many new genres of scanner drama—most of them related to soap opera—as scanner owners listened in on their neighbors' intimate phone conversations. Cellphone manufacturers soon countered with security systems and digital PCS ENCRYPTION.

Scarlet Book ➤ The Sony/Philips specification for Super Audio CD (SACD) based on Direct Stream Digital (DSD) encoding. See CD STANDARDS.

SCART ➤ See PLUGS.

Scenario ➤ (1) An outline for a SCREENPLAY. (2) A complete screenplay. See TREATMENT.

Scenarist ➤ Out-of-date term for a SCREENWRITER.

Scene ➤ A complete unit of film narration. A series of SHOTS (or a single shot) that take place in a single location and that deal with a single action, usually in a single time period. A relatively vague term. See SHOT, SEQUENCE.

Scheimpflug Adjustment ➤ A mechanism on a projector that tilts the lens to adjust for KEYSTONING.

Schüfftan Process ➤ An obsolete process—but important in its time—that combined a MIRROR SHOT with a MODEL SHOT to produce a composite image.

Scope ➤ Abbreviation of CINEMASCOPE, and by extension all ANAMORPHIC processes.

Scopitone ➤ See SOUNDIE.

Score ➤ (1) (n) The music for a film. (2) (v) To write the music for a film. (3) Ratings.

SCPC ➤ Single Channel Per Carrier. Digital television standards allow signals to be multiplexed in a variety of ways. SCPC devotes an entire CARRIER signal to one channel.

Scrambling ➤ ENCRYPTION. The practice of encoding television (and other electronic) signals to prevent reception by anyone without a proper DESCRAMBLER. Satellite systems scramble television signals to prevent consumers from receiving signals directly; cable companies scramble those cable channels that are TIERED for PAY TV, CLOSED CIR-CUIT, or PAY-PER-VIEW.

Screen ➻ (1) The surface on which a film or television image is projected. (2) A method of printing in which ink is forced through a fabric screen to make the desired impression, the blank areas having been covered with an opaque material to prevent the ink from coming through. (3) A glass plate etched with crossed lines used to make HALFTONE patterns. See BEN DAY SCREEN. (4) As a verb, to project a film for a selected audience, such as critics.

Screen Actors Guild ➻ See SAG.

Screen Gain ➻ The index of a screen's reflexivity.

Screening ➻ Sometimes a public PREVIEW, more often a private showing of a film for critics or insiders.

Screenplay ➻ The script of a film or television show, usually but not necessarily including rough descriptions of camera movements as well as dialogue. Originally, *Photoplay*. See SCENARIO, TREATMENT, TELE-PLAY, DÉCOUPAGE.

Screwball Comedy ➻ A type of comedy prevalent in the 1930s and typified by frenetic action, wisecracks, and sexual relationships as an important plot element. Usually about middle- and upper-class characters and therefore often involving opulent sets and costumes as visual elements. *It Happened One Night* (1934), *Easy Living* (1937), and *Bringing Up Baby* (1938) are prime examples. Highly verbal, as opposed to its predecessor, the SLAPSTICK comedy. See also BLACK COM-EDY.

Scrim ➻ An opaque plate placed in front of a light to cast a particular shadow, usually to create the illusion of natural lighting. See GOBO, DIFFUSER.

Script Girl ➻ An obsolete term for the script supervisor. See CONTINU-ITY.

SCSI ➻ (Pronounced "scuzzy.") Small Computer Systems Interface. A device-independent physical and logical standard for peripheral interconnections introduced in the mid-1980s. Up to 8 devices can be chained together. Basic SCSI has a transfer rate of 5 megabits/second. "Ultra Fast Wide SCSI" pushes the transfer rate to 40 mega bits/second. Compare FIREWIRE, USB.

SCSI-2 ➻ See PLUGS.

SCTV ➻ Yes, it's an acronym. No, it's not technical. SCTV (from Second City TV) was a seminal Canadian television series of the late seventies which provided a launching pad for such influential comedians as John Candy, Andrea Martin, Rick Moranis, Catherine

O'Hara, Eugene Levy, and Joe Flaherty. The original Second City troupe in the 1950s was based in Chicago (Mike Nichols, Elaine May, Alan Arkin). The Canadians appropriated the moniker for Toronto. The premise of the show was a television station with the call letters SCTV.

SD ⇒ The Toshiba/Matsushita/Time-Warner proposal for a successor to CD-ROM that was merged into the DVD standard in 1995.

SDDS ⇒ Sony Dynamic Digital Sound. Sony's proprietary multi-channel theatrical soundtrack comes in two flavors: SDDS-6 (5.1) and SDDS-8, which adds two behind-the-screen channels. Introduced in 1993, SDDS uses Sony's ATRAC compression which had been developed for the ill-fated MiniDisc. See DOLBY DIGITAL, DTS.

SDI ⇒ Serial Digital Interface. Used with HD tape recorders. Compare FIREWIRE.

SDMI ⇒ Secure Digital Music Initiative. The effort of the RIAA in early 1999 to devise—quickly—a security scheme for Internet music distribution to counteract the perceived danger from MP3.

SDRAM ⇒ Synchronous Dynamic RAM.

SDSL ⇒ Synchronous Digital Subscriber Line. A technique for distributing high volumes of information through the standard telephone network. Data moves at 1.544 megabits/sec (T-1 speed). Compare ADSL, HDSL2.

SDTV ⇒ Standard Definition TeleVision, a new acronym for old-fashioned TV. More precisely, SDTV refers to a digital 4:3 television image with no more than 720 lines of horizontal resolution. Four channels of SDTV can be transmitted in the same bandwidth as one channel of digital HDTV.

SDV ⇒ Switched Digital Video cable networks use FIBER OPTIC cable to provide digital voice and video signals to a pedestal that serves from 8 to 32 homes; traditional coaxial cable takes the signals from there. Compare HFC.

Seagram ⇒ See UNIVERSAL.

Seamless Branching ⇒ One of the advantages of the DVD-VIDEO format is that—unlike any preceding digital video format—it permits seamless branching. There is no time gap when you switch between shots. This permits the MULTIANGLE function of the format.

Search Engines ⇒ Indexes of either the WORLD WIDE WEB or the whole INTERNET that usually intend to be comprehensive; also the software that does this work. In reality, *Yahoo!*, the leading Search Engine, is valuable precisely because it is edited by humans—not automatically comprehensive like *AltaVista*, developed by DEC to show the power of their hardware, which claims to index all pages. Because the web is so vast and growing so rapidly, the Search Engines quickly became magnets for surfers.

Yahoo! took the lead early and has maintained it. The site was founded in 1994 by two Stanford graduate students, David Filo and Jerry Yang. The company went public in 1996 and was immediately valued at $300 million.

Six other Stanford graduates (Joe Kraus, Ben Lutch, Ryan McIntyre, Martin Reinfried, Mark Van Haren, and Graham Spencer) founded Architext Software in 1994 to produce search software. In 1996 they changed the name of the company to *Excite!* and went public. They quickly gained the number two spot behind Yahoo. In 1999 Excite was acquired for $7.5 billion by @Home, an aggressive cable-based ISP.

Although it was also founded in Silicon Valley in 1994, *Infoseek*, the third early Search Engine, did not have the same academic provenance. From the beginning it was a straight business venture by veteran entrepreneur Steven Kirsch (Mouse Systems, Frame Technology). Deals with MSN in 1995 and WEBTV in 1998 secured Infoseek's position. In 1998 DISNEY bought a large chunk of the company and the two collaborated on the *GO Network*, which debuted in 1999 and immediately became a leader.

The fourth of the pioneer Search Engines, *Lycos*, came out of Carnegie-Mellon University in Pittsburgh, where chief scientist Michael Mauldin developed the technology, also in 1994. In early 1999 Barry Diller's USA Networks proposed a circuitous merger involving USA's Ticketmaster subsidiary, but the deal fell through.

Seca ⇒ Conditional Access System (CA) developed by CANAL +, used also by BDB.

SECAM ⇒ See TELEVISION STANDARDS.

Second Run ⇒ See FIRST-RUN.

Second Unit ⇒ An auxiliary film crew whose job is to shoot material such as foreign location backgrounds, action sequences not using primary actors, or special shots not handled by the first unit.

Secure Digital Music Initiative ⇒ See SDMI.

SEG ⇒ (1) Screen Extras Guild. (2) Special Effects Generator— a piece of electronic equipment that allows a television TECHNICAL DIRECTOR to create FADES, DISSOLVES, WIPES, SPLIT SCREENS, and the like in real time.

Sega ⇒ See VIDEO GAMES.

Segment ⇒ A basic unit of the television program, especially of the type of show unique to radio and television.

Segue ➻ (Pronounced "segway.") (1) A bridging element from one SEGMENT to another in television or radio. (2) A smooth, seamless musical change of key.

Selectavision ➻ RCA's proprietary name for its dead VIDEODISC format, a variable capacitance system using a stylus in a groove.

Sell-In ➻ See SELL-THROUGH.

Sell-Through, Sell-Thru ➻ Term which became common in the eighties to indicate the final retail sales of a VIDEOCASSETTE and then, by extension, any audio or video disc or tape. A tape may "SHIP PLATINUM" but the sell-through may be much less than that.

The VIDEOCASSETTE business developed in an unusual way. Although early manufacturers of prerecorded videocassettes may have planned to sell them through retail outlets to consumers, individual entrepreneurs quickly realized that renting the tapes at a far lower price made sense. Most consumers don't want to own movies; they just want to watch them. Those videotapes that are sold, new or used, to consumers, form the sell-through market. The sell-through and rental markets are still not well defined, although sell-through titles (mainly children's programming, how-to, erotica, and a few PUBLIC DOMAIN classics) are generally priced under $30, while tapes aimed at the rental market are sold to the retailers at a list price of $50 to $100. The sales of the manufacturer to the retailer—whether intended for rental or sell-through—are referred to as *Sell-in.*

Semioclasm ➻ Roland Barthes's term for the destruction of the connotations and denotations of the cultural language that is necessary before those languages can be rebuilt afresh.

Semiology, Semiotics ➻ Theory of criticism studying signs, symbols, and signification pioneered by Roland Barthes in literature and by Christian Metz, Umberto Eco, and Peter Wollen in film. It uses the theories of modern linguistics, especially Ferdinand de Saussure's concept of signification, as a model for the description of the operation of various cultural languages, such as film, television, kinesics (body language), and written and spoken languages. Semiotics became popular with academics in the 1970s and led to the founding of many university film departments. See CINEMA STUDIES, SYNTAGMA, PARADIGM, DIEGESIS. Compare STRUCTURALISM.

Sensurround ➻ Universal used this process on *Earthquake* and several other films in the 1970s. Low-frequency noise was fed to a set of woofers in the auditorium to create a sense of foreboding. (*Jaws* did it with music!)

Sequence ➻ A basic unit of film construction consisting of one or more SCENES that form a natural unit. An ambiguous term. See SHOT, SEQUENCE SHOT.

Sequence Shot ➻ A long, usually complex shot, often including complicated camera movements and action. Also called *Plan-séquence* (the French term), or Long Take.

Serial ➻ (1) In film, radio, television, and print, a continuing story told in episodes, each of which has a specific place in the narrative. A serial has a definite beginning, middle, and end, as opposed to a SERIES. (2) In the computer world, a port through which data is transmitted one bit at a time—serially. Compare PARALLEL.

Series ➻ A continuing string of television or radio programs or films, with each episode sharing basic situations and characters but divorced from the others in terms of plot. The series may be either OPEN-ENDED or CLOSE-ENDED. See SERIAL, SPECIAL.

Server ➻ The term for either the machine or a piece of software running on it that provides an INTERNET (or LAN) service. The Domain Name Server keeps the table of domain names; the Web Server offers HTTP services; the Mail Server runs the EMAIL system. See HOST, DNS.

SES ➻ Société Européenne des Satellites. This group operates the ASTRA satellites, and is the largest satellite broadcaster in Europe. See EUTELSAT, B-SKY-B.

Set ➻ The location of a scene, usually artificially constructed on a SOUND STAGE.

Set-Top Box ➻ Also, "Set-Top Device." Any one of an increasing number of television gadgets from cable tuners to DSB receivers to CABLE MODEMS that sit on top of your television set and increase the clutter already there.

Set-Tuning Meter ➻ A more recent version of the AUDIMETER.

Set-Up ➻ A camera and lighting position. When large, unwieldy cameras and lights are used, the number of different set-ups required can become an important economic factor.

7.1 ➻ The MPEG-2 audio specification allows for two additional channels beyond the 5.1 AC-3 spec. The two extra channels are left-center and right-center.

Sexploitation ➻ Jargon term for sex EXPLOITATION film or PORN.

SFX ➻ SOUND EFFECTS.

SGML ➻ Standard Generalized Markup Language. A superset and precursor of HTML, SGML was instituted by the U.S. (for government publications) beginning in the 1970s as a way of bringing order to numerous computerized typesetting languages. each of which had its own method for indicating fonts, styles, and formatting. Its development continues. While it has been adopted by some professional page-layout programs, it has not yet invaded the word-processing world where it is most needed. See RTF.

SGRAM ➻ Synchronous Graphics RAM.

Shallow Focus ➻ A technique that utilizes shallow DEPTH OF FIELD to create a shallow FOCUS PLANE, usually to direct the attention of the viewer to the subject or action in that plane. See also DEEP FOCUS, RACK FOCUS, FOLLOW FOCUS.

Share ➻ See NIELSEN.

SHF ➻ Super-High Frequency band. See ELECTROMAGNETIC SPECTRUM.

Ship Gold, Ship Platinum ➻ When a CD ships 500,000 or more copies it is said to "ship gold." If the shipment is more than a million, that's "shipping platinum." Note that shipments don't equal sales; the recording industry, like the book industry, is subject to heavy returns. It is not impossible to "ship platinum and return gold." See SELL-THROUGH, GROSS SHIPMENT, NET SHIPMENT, RIAA, GOLD.

Shiss ➻ The increasingly common scratchy background noise that emanates from someone else's WALKMAN in an elevator, car, or other enclosed space.

Shooting Ratio ➻ The ratio between film actually exposed in the camera during shooting to film used in the final cut. On a feature film a shooting ratio of 20:1 is typical, and 30:1 is not uncommon. On documentaries a ratio of 50:1 or 100:1 is not uncommon. Of course, if you're shooting on tape rather than film you could care less about the shooting ratio—you can always reuse the extra tape.

Shooting Script ➻ SCRIPT for a film or television show that includes thorough descriptions of the sets and rough outlines of proposed camera movements and edits as well as dialogue. Useful as a guide during production.

Shopping ➻ An idea for a film (or a book or other INTELLECTUAL PROPERTY) is said to be shopped when it has been presented to a large number of potential buyers or investors. The word carries the connotation of worn out. See PITCHING.

Short ➻ A film usually less than thirty minutes in length. Compare FEATURE.

Short-Circuit Sign ➻ According to Christian Metz, the condition of the cinematic SIGN in which the SIGNIFIER is the same as the SIGNIFIED.

Shortflight Series ➻ See MINISERIES.

Shot ➻ A single piece of film, however long or short, without cuts, exposed continuously. A film may be composed of more than a thousand shots, or it may seem to be a single shot. See SCENE, SEQUENCE, TAKE, CLOSEUP, CAMERA ANGLE, PAN, and ZOOM. Also DETAIL, FULL,

LONG, MEDIUM, EXTREME LONG, ESTABLISHING, TWO-SHOT, AERIAL, POINT-OF-VIEW, MASTER, FOLLOW, STOCK, DOLLY, TRACKING, and INSERT SHOTS.

Shot/Reverse Shot ➵ See ANGLE/REVERSE ANGLE.

Showcase ➵ Multiple exhibition of a film in a selected number of theaters. See FIRST-RUN, FOUR-WALLING, GENERAL RELEASE.

Showscan ➵ Douglas Trumbull's high-quality film format that uses 70 mm film projected at a rate of 60 frames per second to achieve unusually high levels of video fidelity. Trumbull began developing the technology as early as 1975. It has yet to develop broad commercial appeal, although it is a favorite of cutting-edge experimenters, especially since it fits so well with HDTV. Even at the high end, Gresham's law applies: 30 frames/sec IMAX thrives while 60 frames/sec Showscan is moribund.

Showtime ➵ Merger of two CABLE NETWORK competitors to HBO (Showtime and The Movie Channel), offering a diet of Hollywood movies. Showtime was founded in 1978 by Viacom, The Movie Channel in 1979 by Warner.

SHTTP ➵ See HTTP.

Shuffle ➵ To play CD or tape tracks in random order, without repetition.

Shutter ➵ The device that opens and closes an aperture on a camera or projector. Shutters on projectors are double-bladed so that each frame is actually projected twice. 24 frames/sec film thus has an effective frequency of 48 frames/sec, which is enough to prevent FLICKER.

Shuttle ➵ See JOG.

Side View ➵ A shot of a character viewed from the side. Compare FULL-FACE SHOT, THREE-QUARTER VIEW.

Sight Gag ➵ See GAG.

Sign ➵ In SEMIOTICS, the basic unit of signification composed of the *signifier* (which carries the meaning) and the *signified* (which is the concept or thing signified). In written language, for example, the word "tree" is the signifier, the idea of the tree the signified; the whole sign is composed of both elements, and the actual tree is called the referent. In cinema the signified, the idea of the tree, remains the same, but the signifier, the image (or even the sound) of the tree is much more complex. See MONEME, PHONEME, MORPHEME, SHORT-CIRCUIT SIGN.

Signal ➵ In the electronic media, the coded message of the program that is imposed on the carrier wave. See WAVE MECHANICS.

Signal-to-Noise Ratio ➵ The ratio in decibels between the audio or video signal and the noise inherent in the medium. The higher the

Signal-to-Noise ratio the better the quality of either audio or video on either tape or disk.

Signature Edition ➻ Marketing term for a LASERDISC or DVD-VIDEO on which a little extra care has been lavished, usually including a DIRECTOR'S CUT, additional footage, a "making of" documentary, or some other personal touches.

Signified, Signifier ➻ See SIGN.

Simple Profile ➻ A simpler subset of the MPEG-2 video standard: No B FRAMES. Compare MAIN PROFILE.

Simulcast ➻ A simultaneous broadcast—usually of a musical performance—on a television station and an allied radio station.

SimulCrypt ➻ A proposed DVB standard for untangling the welter of ENCRYPTION algorithms used in satellite broadcasting. It's really a simple idea: broadcasters would include the codes for all encryption methods in the data stream so that any receiver could find the one it understands. See VIDEOCRYPT.

Single ➻ (1) A short record, usually 45 rpm, seven inches in diameter, with one song on each side. See ALBUM, CASSINGLE. (2) A SHOT of one person.

Single Inventory ➻ See SACD.

Single-System Sound ➻ A system formerly used for news film in which both sound and image are recorded simultaneously, consisting of a camera that includes a recording HEAD, and FILMSTOCK, one edge of which is striped with magnetic recording material. See DOUBLE-SYSTEM SOUND.

Sitcom ➻ Situation comedy; a type of program, first in radio, then television, usually a half hour in length, that is centered on a limited number of characters—often a family—located in a particular situation. It's usually not the situation that is funny, but the group of people. See DOMESTIC COMEDY.

16/44 ➻ Shorthand for 44.1 kiloHertz 16-bit encoding, the standard for audio CDs. See SAMPLING. Compare 96/24, DSD.

16:9 ➻ The ASPECT RATIO chosen for WIDESCREEN HDTV. It doesn't match any of the commonly used cinema aspect ratios, but it is a neat multiple of 4:3.

Sixty, :60 ➻ See SPOT.

66 Block ➻ Also called a Punch-down Block. For anyone interested in the art of electronic connections (see PLUGS), the 66 Block, used in multiline telephone installations, is a thing of beauty. About a foot long and three inches wide, the 66 Block provided 50 pairs of connections on one side and fifty on the other. Many, but not all, 66 Blocks provide a 50-pin CENTRONICS jack on one side or both. A 25-pair telephone cable can be wired in on the left with two-pair, four-pair, or more lines coming out on the right. If the connections go straight through, a bridging clip links the output post on the left with the input post on the right. If you need to route, for example, the second pair on the left to the twentieth pair on the right, you use narrow-gauge wire. Each post is a small clamp. The connections can only be made with a special tool: the "Punch-down tool" pushes the wire into the clamp of the post, strips the insulation (because of the tightness of the clamp) and clips the wire just underneath the post: a neat and clean connection in no time. Before the 66 Block, telephone lineman had to wind each wire around a brass post and screw it in.

Skating ➤ See TURNTABLE.

Skew ➤ Each broadcast Satellite has a different angle above the horizon for your position. This is its Skew.

Sky TV ➤ Rupert Murdoch's pioneering DSB SATELLITE television system, founded in 1988, later merged with British Satellite Broadcasting to form B-SKY-B.

Skycam ➤ The invention of cameraman Garrett Brown in the early 1980s, the Skycam system suspends a camera from computer-controlled wires leading to four posts situated at the corners of a sports stadium or film set. The cameraman operates the device from a stationary control panel via a video monitor. The result is an image seemingly free to fly. See STEADICAM.

Slapstick ➤ A type of comedy, widely prevalent during the silent-film era, that depends on broad physical action and pantomime for its effect rather than verbal wit or character dialogue. See SCREWBALL COMEDY. The "slapstick" was a common prop in VAUDEVILLE that made a loud, funny noise when hit.

Slate ➤ See CLAPPER BOARD.

Slide, Slide Show ➤ A Slide is a frame of—usually—35 mm film that has been mounted in a cardboard or plastic holder. A group of Slides is held in a tray. The slide projector loads them one at a time. A continuation of the projected still-picture mode that began with the MAGIC LANTERN. Compare FILM STRIP. See REVERSAL FILMSTOCK.

SloMo ➤ SLOW MOTION replay in television sports coverage.

Slot ➤ (1) See TIME SLOT. (2) The allocated position of a satellite. If the satellite is geosynchronous, its slot is equivalent to a longitude. Compare SKEW.

Slow Motion ➤ The camera is OVERCRANKED so the film runs through faster than the normal 24 frames per second, so that when it is later projected at the normal rate the action will take more time than in reality. See FAST MOTION.

Smart Card ➻ A plastic card, like a credit card, but with an embedded microprocessor instead of a magnetic stripe, the Smart Card was invented by Roland Moréno in France in the early 1980s. The original aim for the device was to serve as electronic cash. The user would charge up the card at the bank and amounts would be deducted by merchants. The smart card found some success in France in the late 1980s as a phone card. The British immediately countered with a cheaper version: their phone cards simply expanded the magnetic stripe to cover the enter back of the card, and made the stripe recordable. The Smart Card (like other attempts at debit cards) never succeeded in the U.S. although a number of companies tried to find a use for this ingenious solution in search of a problem. The card has been used by some health maintenance organizations to record the owner's complete health records. This seems a brilliant use of the technology, and one hopes the practice spreads. Perhaps the most common use of the Smart Card has been as a decryption key for software and satellite broadcasts. Compare DONGLE.

SMART ➻ System Managed Audio Resource Technique, an ersatz acronym for a coding system—part of the proposed DVD-AUDIO standard—to allow producers to control the downmix from SURROUND SOUND to STEREO.

Smartmedia ➻ See DIGITAL FILM.

SMATV ➻ Satellite Master Antenna TeleVision, TV distribution system for multiple dwellings from a single antenna. Compare CATV.

Smearing ➻ An ARTIFACT, or inconsistency, in analog imaging. A phase shift in the signal causes the image to spread, usually to the right.

Smiley ➻ A combination of easily typed letters and punctuation meant to suggest a face: for example, :-)   :-(or :-p : a smile, a frown, a tongue sticking out. Smileys became popular in the 1980s as online chat systems grew. They offer a kind of emotional punctuation. When you think about it, the precursors of smileys—the question mark and the exclamation point—offer a very limited gamut.

SMPTE ➻ Society of Motion Picture and Television Engineers, the professional society for cinematic technicians in the industry.

SMPTE Timecode ➻ See TIMECODE.

SMTP ➻ Simple Mail Transfer Protocol, one of the basic components of the INTERNET along with HTTP and FTP.

S/N ➻ SIGNAL-TO-NOISE RATIO.

Sneak Preview ⟩⟩ An unannounced public screening of an unreleased film scheduled either for testing or for generating word-of-mouth publicity.

Snow ⟩⟩ An ARTIFACT, or inconsistency, in analog imaging. A grayish haze caused by signal noise covers the image.

Snuff Film ⟩⟩ A PORN film that supposedly shows a real murder. Named after a 1973 Argentine production imported into the U.S. several years later, accompanied by much outrage. This obscene genre was exploited years later by the Hollywood production *8 mm* (1998). See SPLATTER.

Soap Opera ⟩⟩ A type of continuing, never-ending serialized drama pioneered in radio, later a staple of daytime television, that deals with basically domestic situations, everyday problems, and common middle-class characters—usually housewives. Almost always daily in frequency, the soap opera soon evolves an extraordinarily involuted and tangled plot, since so much is made to happen to so few so often. Soap operas were often sponsored by soap and detergent products, hence the name. Often shortened to "Soap."

Socialist Realism ⟩⟩ The Stalinist dogma of art that had little to do with either socialism or realism but that insisted that Art serve the purposes of the State. Its aim was to tell simple stories with a clear style whose upbeat conclusions proved the wisdom of government policies.

Soft Focus ⟩⟩ Filters, Vaseline, or specialty lenses soften the delineation of lines and points, usually to create a romantic effect.

Soft Light ⟩⟩ Low-contrast lighting. Lighting that de-emphasizes the contrast between light and shadow. Compare HARD LIGHT.

Soft Matte ⟩⟩ Shooting a WIDESCREEN feature film without matting the top and bottom of the ACADEMY APERTURE ASPECT RATIO so that the film will be easy to show on television later, and not require PAN AND SCAN.

Software ⟩⟩ See HARDWARE.

Solarization ⟩⟩ A chemical or electronic process of reversal or shift of the color spectrum so that blues become yellow, reds cyan, and greens magenta, or some variation thereof. See COLOR.

Solid Ink ⟩⟩ A high quality color printing process in which CMYK solid ink sticks are run through rollers to deposit the ink on the page. The solid ink is not absorbed into the page, so DOT GAIN is less problematic. Compare DYE SUBLIMATION, THERMAL WAX.

Solid-State ⟩⟩ The adjective for electronics built with TRANSISTORS, ICs, and MICROCHIPS—and without VACUUM TUBES.

Sony ⟩⟩ With PHILIPS, this Japanese electronics firm founded by Akio Morita in 1946 has been responsible for many of the innovations in consumer electronics during the past fifty years. Sony can lay claim to inventing, developing, or popularizing the TRINITRON television picture tube, the WALKMAN AUDIOCASSETTE player, and the VIDEOCASSETTE recorder in the 1970s; the audio CD and CD-ROM in the 1980s; and DVD, DIGITAL PHOTOGRAPHY, and the PLAYSTATION game machine in the 1990s. In the late eighties and early nineties, Sony prepared for the next generation of consumer electronics by investing heavily in programming sources, purchasing CBS Records in January 1988 and COLUMBIA Pictures/TriStar in November 1989. In early 1999 Sony announced that it was shifting strategic emphasis from hardware to networking as it attempted to catch up with the INTERNET revolution.

Sony 3324 ➢ A 24-track professional audiotape format, REEL-TO-REEL, used for 5.1 productions.

Sony Pictures Entertainment ➢ The umbrella organization for COLUMBIA, TRISTAR, and Sony's other film properties.

Sorenson Codec ➢ Developed by a company whose specialty is medical imaging, the Sorenson video CODEC provides high compression and high quality. See MPEG.

Sound ➢ See ACTUAL, ASYNCHRONOUS, CONTRAPUNTAL, COMMENTATIVE, SYNCHRONOUS, OVERLAP, PARALLEL, CONCRETE, and DIRECT SOUND.

Sound Advance ➢ Because film images are projected one at a time and thus require an INTERMITTENT MOTION while sound must be played back continuously, projectors are designed with a loop between the gate and the sound head. The distance between these two is the Sound Advance: 21 frames ahead for 35 mm, 26 frames ahead for 16 mm, but 24 frames behind for 70 mm magnetic. When the sound is out of sync it's because the projectionist (if there is one) has set the loop at the wrong length.

Sound Bite ➢ A short clip used in radio or television news. The phrase became common in the 1980s to describe simplistic political slogans that fit in less than 30 seconds of airtime. Of course, media-savvy politicians had long ago learned to assure themselves of newscast exposure by reducing complex issues to easily quoted quips.

Sound Bridge ➢ Sound associated with one scene that briefly carries past the cut to the next scene (or begins during the previous scene) to enhance CONTINUITY. Compare SEGUE.

Sound Effects ➢ All those created sounds that are not dialogue or music. See SOUNDTRACK.

Soundfield ➢ The impression of dimensional sound produced by a multichannel sound system. A more precise term than SOUNDSTAGE.

Soundie ➤ Short films of musical groups made to be played in "soundie" movie jukeboxes, which had a brief vogue in the 1940s. The idea that musicians should be seen as well as heard was revived again in the 1960s with the similar *Scopitone* device, which failed even more quickly. Finally, the concept caught on when MTV was founded in 1981. By then, perhaps the music wasn't gripping enough to survive on its own without the images.

Sound-on-Film ➤ (1) One of two competing technologies in the early days of sound film, the other being Sound-on-Disk. (2) A film camera that records sound on a magnetic stripe on the filmstock at the same time as capturing the image. (Of course, all video cameras do this.) See SINGLE-SYSTEM SOUND.

Soundstage ➤ (1) A hangar-like sound-proofed building providing large open spaces for the construction of film and television sets. The large numbers of soundstages built in the 1920s and 1930s made possible Hollywood's notorious assembly-line work flow during the Golden Age. Compare BLACK MARIA. (2) In HIGH-END AUDIO and HOME THEATRE, the technical term for the perceived three-dimensional space provided by STEREOPHONIC or 5.1 sound systems. The equipment should project a Soundstage larger than the actual physical environment.

Soundtrack ➤ (1) Optical soundtracks operate by the modulation of a beam of light that creates a band on the film that widens and narrows to encode the information of the signal. Magnetic soundtracks, like tape recordings, encode the information electromagnetically on a magnetic coating. The final soundtrack, whether optical or magnetic, is usually a mixture of several primary tracks— effects, dialogue, and music. See also VARIABLE AREA SOUNDTRACK, SVA, STEREOPHONIC SOUND, 5.1, DOLBY SR, SDDS, DTS, THX, SURROUND SOUND. (2) Short for an audio record of the film's music released as a spinoff product.

Source, The ➤ An early proprietary online service, perhaps the first aimed at consumers rather than computer hackers. Founded by William von Meister in 1981. See COMPUSERVE, DELPHI.

Source Code ➤ The programmer's original composition before it has been compiled into MACHINE LANGUAGE. Machine code is not readable by other programmers; source code is. See COMPUTER LANGUAGES, OPEN SOFTWARE.

SP ➤ (1) See BETACAM. (2) See SIMPLE PROFILE.

SP@ML ➤ SIMPLE PROFILE at MAIN LEVEL. Compare MP@ML.

Spaghetti Western ➤ A European Western, usually filmed in Spain or Italy, and popularized in the 1960s by the films of Sergio Leone.

SPAM ⮞ The practice of transmitting junk-mail email (or posting indiscriminately to NEWS GROUPS). Traditional junk-mailers incur significant costs, which act as a barrier to entry, but Spammers pay nearly nothing to transmit thousands (or millions) of emails, which makes the practice especially pernicious. Opponents of Spam have suggested laws to control the practice (difficult to enforce) or putting a cost per message on all emails (contrary to the INTERNET ethos). At least Spam is a lot easier to dispose of than postal junk mail, and less ecologically problematic.

Spatial Compression ⮞ See COMPRESSION.

SPC ⮞ See PBS.

S/PDIF ⮞ Sony/Philips Digital Interface Format, a standard protocol for transmitting digital audio signals between components.

Spec ⮞ Speculation; without a contract, as in "I wrote the script on spec."

Special ⮞ A single television program that is not part of a series, serial, or other continuing structure.

Special Effects ⮞ A broad term for a wide range of devices and processes, including some kinds of work performed by stuntmen, MODEL SHOTS, OPTICALS, in-camera effects, MATTE SHOTS, REAR PROJECTION, SOLARIZATION, and much more. Christian Metz differentiated between what he called *Profilmic Special Effects*, which do not distort the image, and *"Cinematographic Special Effects,"* which do distort the image. See POST HOUSE.

Special Effects Generator ⮞ See SEG.

Speed ⮞ (1) Camera and projector speed: the standard for sound films is 24 frames per second; for silent films, between 16 and 18 frames/sec; for American and Japanese television, 30 frames/sec; for all other television, 25 frames/sec. (2) Lens speed: a measure of the ability of a lens to capture and admit light. The faster the lens, the more light admitted. See F-NUMBER. (3) Emulsion speed: the ability of an EMULSION to capture and fix light. The faster the speed of the emulsion, the less light is needed for a proper exposure.

SPFX ⮞ SOUND EFFECTS.

Spider ⮞ A program that automatically "crawls" the Web collecting information about websites, usually to report back to a SEARCH ENGINE. See BOT.

Spike ⮞ A peak in the DATA RATE for a digital audiovideo signal. When your DVD-VIDEO picture seems to break up momentarily, that's a Spike.

Spinoff ⮞ A television series created out of elements (usually characters, but sometimes situations) of an earlier series. The spinoff champion is *The Mary Tyler Moore Show* of the 1970s, which spun off *Phyllis*, *Rhoda*, and *Lou Grant*.

Splatter ⟫→ Exploitation genre concentrating on gore and violence.

Splice ⟫→ The physical joint between two pieces of film. There are two basic ways to do this: A cement splice can be made by scraping the emulsion off the area between the frames, coating the film with glue, and overlapping the other piece of film. A tape splice (or butt splice) is accomplished by butting up the two ends of film and taping them together, usually with a Mylar tape. This is less permanent but quicker. In either case, the two pieces of film are held by their sprockets in a splicer, a device that lines them up, cuts, scrapes, and trims tape.

Split Screen ⟫→ Two or more separate images within the frame, not overlapping. Accomplished on an OPTICAL PRINTER (for film) and a SEG (for television). See MULTIPLE IMAGE.

Spot ⟫→ A television commercial, usually 10, 20, 30, or 60 seconds. Colloquially, a spot is referred to by its length, as in, "They still have a few :20s left between 8 and 8:30."

Spot Beam ⟫→ A narrowly focused satellite signal.

Spot Color ⟫→ Most COLOR PRINTING processes create a spectrum by combining three or four primaries. Spot Color is the term for pre-mixed ink. From a graphic artist's point of view it is only a way to enhance the design. For a color professional, however, Spot Color affords a level of precision that isn't possible with process color.

Spotlighting ⟫→ Lighting a particular, often very small, area for effect.

Spread Spectrum ⟫→ One of the technologies that has made cellular phones successful, Spread Spectrum allows the broadcast of a relatively secure signal by changing the carrier from one frequency to another in a set pattern that only the receiver can understand. It was originally invented in 1941 by film actress Hedy Lamarr and composer George Antheil. They intended it as a security device to prevent the jamming of torpedo guidance signals, but it wasn't implemented until twenty years later. In 1997 Lamarr, then 84, was finally presented with an award for her accomplishment.

Spreadsheet ⟫→ Business analysis has always had a dimensional aspect: there are line items in a budget (the rows) and months and years over which they spread (the columns). For many years accountants and businesspeople used what they called "analysis pads" to do their sums and projections. The pads came in many flavors according to the number of columns and rows and the groupings thereof. Just after the Apple II was introduced, two business-school students in Cambridge MA—Dan Bricklin and Bob

Frankston—came up with the idea that a program could produce the rows and columns. What's more, it would instantly calculate the sums and differences. And even better, you could make a change in one number in the upper left and see it reflected immediately in the totals on the bottom and on the right.

It was this "what-if" capability that turned their program, *Visicalc*, into the first KILLER AP. Thousands of B-school graduates engineered purchases of Apple IIs for their companies just to run it. After the IBM PC was introduced in 1981, Visicalc declined quickly. It didn't run on the new MS-DOS machines and Lotus 1-2-3 did. Moreover, Lotus, the first program to use a menu bar, was more efficient. By the late 1980s even Lotus was in decline as Microsoft's Excel became the standard. Just because it's computerized doesn't mean it's better. Spreadsheet programs can produce "spreadshit": garbage in, garbage out, as the saying goes. And sometimes you learn something useful by working out the numbers by hand, with a pencil, on an old-fashioned analysis pad.

Sprite, Sprite Track ➤ Small graphic elements added to a movie or video game. Unlike the images of the movie, sprites are programmed with position and timing information. A good example would be a bouncing ball over lyrics. In order to make a movie interactive ("clickable") you need to add active areas to the image. Invisible sprites can be used for this purpose. Sprites are stored in their own track, separate from audio and video tracks.

Sprockets ➤ (1) The regularly spaced and shaped holes in FILMSTOCK that enable the film to be mechanically advanced. (2) The gears that engage the sprocket holes and drive the film.

Squarial ➤ A small, square satellite antenna, originally developed for B-SKY-B.

Squib ➤ A very small explosive charge in a capsule, used to simulate a gunshot or the like.

SR ➤ See SURROUND SOUND.

SR•D ➤ Another way to say DOLBY DIGITAL.

Stadium Seating ➤ Movie theater architecture that became popular in the late 1990s. Each row of seats is elevated above the one before it, as in a sports stadium, so that each spectator has a clear line of sight. IMAX theaters pioneered this design. See GRAZING EFFECT.

Staircasing ➤ See JAGGIES.

Stamped Multisession CD ➤ See ENHANCED CD.

Standard ➤ In the worlds of consumer electronics and microcomputers, a set of technical specifications that is usually one of several competing sets and therefore not really a "standard." When a national or international body sets a true standard (Group III fax, for example) the technology develops more rapidly. When companies compete with each other to establish true standards (color television, VHS vs BETA), the battles provide interesting technological history.

Standing O ≫ Theater slang for Standing Ovation.

Standup Comedy ≫ Comedy performance genre with its roots in VAUDEVILLE in which usually one, sometimes two, comedians deliver a running commentary or theatrical performance, hopefully humorous, on any subject. From the great vaudeville performers of the early years of the twentieth century to the current proliferation of clubs and comedy CABLE NETWORKS, standup has become the great American artform, surpassing even the musical as a native expression of our culture, a potent distillation of drama and performance values, enhanced by the lively intelligence of the comic spirit.

Star ≫ (1) A performer in film (and by extension other media) who is set apart from other actors by virtue of CELEBRITY. A star has a distinct PERSONA that reaches far beyond any particular role. Simply put, a star has enough box-office clout to sell tickets. From the earliest days of the film industry, stars were an integral part of both the business and the art. Mary Pickford, Douglas Fairbanks, and Charles Chaplin quickly gained fame that reached far beyond the movie houses. Such celebrity was not unknown in the nineteenth century: Charles Dickens drew crowds wherever he lectured. But the advent of movies, which could distribute thousands of mass-produced moving images within days, amplified the phenomenon by several magnitudes. Compare CHARACTER ACTOR. (2) Southeast Asian DSB system, part-owned by NEWS CORP.

Starlet ≫ A young actress who is being groomed for stardom or who is ambitious for it. She is valued more for looks or personality than for talent, and she tries to exploit them. Compare INGENUE.

Station Break ≫ The required interruption of radio and television programming to identify the station broadcasting.

Station Program Cooperative ≫ See PBS.

Steadicam ≫ The invention of cameraman Garrett Brown (developed in conjunction with Cinema Products, Inc.), this system permits hand-held filming with an image steadiness comparable to TRACKING SHOTS. A vest redistributes the weight of the camera to the hips of the cameraman; a spring-loaded arm damps the motion of the camera; a video monitor frees the cameraman from the eyepiece. Because it replaces expensive and time-consuming dolly tracks, the Steadicam results in lower production costs. First used by Haskell Wexler on *Bound for Glory* (1975). See SKYCAM.

S

Steenbeck ➸ A particular brand of editing table that is much more flexible than the old standard MOVIOLA.

Step Deal ➸ A staged production arrangement where certain criteria must be met before payments are made and the project continues.

Stereo, Stereophonic Sound ➸ In reality, sound is heard from many sources and the binaural ability of the two ears creates a sense of dimensionality. Stereophonic sound, which uses two or more speakers and tracks, approximates the binaural experience. Stereophonic headphones come closest to mimicking reality, since each ear then hears only one track. Stereophonic records were first marketed in 1958. See BINAURAL RECORDING, QUADRAPHONIC SOUND, 5.1.

Stereo Television ➸ An idea whose time should have come much earlier, television broadcast signals that include two stereo audio signals instead of one monaural signal together with sets equipped to receive them did not arrive in the U.S. until the mid-1980s. (The system was pioneered in Japan several years earlier.) See SAP.

Stereopticon ➸ A nineteenth-century device that produced a 3-D still image. The camera had two lenses separated by about 2 1/2 inches, the average distance between the pupils of the eyes. When the pairs of photographs were viewed in a Stereopticon each eye saw a different image. The slight differences produced the sensation of STEREOSCOPY.

Stereoscopy ➸ Photography utilizing two separate, paired images—one for each eye—to re-create a sense of depth in the image. There are, however, many psychological and technical problems that contemporary stereoscopy cannot overcome. "Orthostereoscopy" is normal stereoscopic vision. "Hyperstereoscopy" increases the distance between the cameras to more than the distance between human eyes, creating the illusion of depth where human eyes could not perceive it. "Pseudoscopic stereoscopy" reverses the left image with the right, creating complicated psychological reactions. "Pseudostereoscopy" consists of those techniques—overlapping, PARALLAX, and movement in the frame, for example—which two-dimensional photography uses to create the illusion of depth. See STEREOPTICON, HOLOGRAPHY.

Still ➸ A single photograph; more precisely, a frame enlargement or similar publicity photograph from a film. A PHOTOGRAM.

Stock Shot ➸ (1) A library shot, one that is literally borrowed from a collection, such as World War II shots or airliners in flight, or ESTABLISHING SHOTS of New York City. (2) Any unimaginative or common shot that looks as if it might as well have been a library shot.

Stock ➸ See FILMSTOCK.

Stop-Motion Photography ➤ A technique in which the camera operates one frame at a time, allowing objects to be adjusted between frames. Responsible for much trick photography. See FAST MOTION, PIXILATION.

Store and Forward ➤ Video or other media that are not broadcast live, but made available on the Web for downloading at a later time. See VIDEO ON DEMAND.

Story ➤ The events that are narrated, together with the ideas and emotions they engender. The story is the "what" of narration; PLOT is the "how" and "which."

Story Editor ➤ A middle-level studio executive charged with searching out and processing sources for films, both original scripts and published books. READERS work for Story Editors.

Storyboard ➤ A series of drawings and captions (sometimes resembling a comic strip) that shows the planned shot divisions and camera movements of the film—its DÉCOUPAGE. Storyboarding is now often done with software.

Straight-to-Video Movie ➤ See DIRECT-TO-VIDEO.

Streaking ➤ An ARTIFACT, or inconsistency, in ANALOG imaging. A bright area distorts the brightness level elsewhere in the image. Also a problem with some digital LCD screens.

Streaming Media ➤ Normally in Internet communications, the entire file of a movie or an audio must be received before your browser can begin to play it. Since audiovideo files are very large, this can be annoying. Streaming media technologies (QUICKTIME, REALVIDEO) allow the file to begin to play before it has completely downloaded, and adjust the DATA RATE to the available bandwidth. Streaming also allows Internet NARROWCASTING (or UNICASTING), where the "file" is in effect endless.

Street, To ➤ A tape or disc is said "to street" when it becomes available in the market—"on the street."

Strip ➤ A television series aired every weekday at the same time of day, usually SYNDICATED.

Stroboscope ➤ A light that flashes on and off rapidly in precisely timed cycles. The rate can be varied, which sometimes produces dangerous psychological effects, such as epileptic attacks. Some AVANT-GARDE films experimented with stroboscopic effects.

Structuralism ➤ The study of society, psychology, and related phenomena as arrangements of parts, usually called CODES. The extraction of meaning from a literary, film, or other text based on a close analysis of its construction. The anthropological studies of Claude Lévi-Strauss in the 1950s form the basis for Structuralism. Closely allied with Semiotics, Structuralism is more ethnographic than linguistic.

Structural Film ➤ A film in which the codes and structures of social arrangements are evident. Structural films of the late 1960s and 1970s took seeing via cinema as their subject matter, dispensed with both drama and narrative, and concentrated on camera movement and editing tricks such as Loop printing and the Flicker effect. See Cinestructuralism, Materialist Cinema.

Studio ➤ (1) A film or television production facility, including sound stages, offices, editing rooms, and the like. (2) By extension, the six major production/distribution companies that dominate American film distribution and own or rent physical production facilities in Los Angeles: Universal, Disney, Warner, Paramount, Fox, Sony. (Columbia Pictures was renamed Sony in 1991; Columbia moved onto MGM's famous lot in 1990; MGM had moved to an office building previously; United Artists, which never owned any real estate, was absorbed into MGM in 1981, then disappeared in 1991 when MGM was bought by Pathé.) Dreamworks is the most recent attempt to found a studio. See Hollywood.

Stunt ➤ A physical action that calls for unusual prowess, such as falling out of a window or crashing a car, and is therefore performed by a professional stunt man or woman standing in for the actor.

Stunting ➤ The television programming practice of scheduling a new show in a time slot that is more favorable than the one it will eventually occupy. See Double Pumping.

STV ➤ Subscription TeleVision. The broadcast equivalent of pay Cable television systems.

Stylus ➤ See Turntable.

Subcode ➤ See Code.

Subjective Camera ➤ A style that allows the viewer to observe events from the point of view of either a character or the Persona of the author. See Point-of-View Shot.

Subpictures ➤ These are used as overlays in the DVD-Video system to present subtitles, menus, and the like. There are 32 subpicture streams available in the DVD-Video specification. Each is limited to 4 colors from a palette of 16 colors and 4 contrast values from a palette of 16. Simple effects, such as scroll, fade, move, and color are permissible.

Subpixel ➤ The dots that together make a Pixel on a screen. Three are necessary in most instances, one for each of the three primary colors.

Subsidiary ➺ A minor interest of the image, often controlled by the DOMINANT.

Subtractive Primary Colors ➺ See COLOR MODELS.

Subwoofer ➺ A speaker dedicated to very-low-frequency special effects. See 5.1, SOUNDSTAGE.

Sundance Institute ➺ Founded in 1980 by Robert Redford, this Utah-based organization has proved a major force in independent film. It is well known for its annual film festival, and has lent its name to a CABLE CHANNEL that promotes independent film.

Sunday Ghetto ➺ Jargon for the time periods on Sunday when few television sets are in use and in which NETWORKS commonly schedule their public service programming.

Super Audio CD ➺ See SACD.

Super Technirama 70 ➺ See TECHNIRAMA.

Super VHS ➺ Enhancement of the VHS format developed by JVC Corp. that increases the bandwidth of the luminance subcarrier, resulting in greater picture detail, equivalent to approximately 100 lines of horizontal resolution greater than standard VHS. Introduced in 1987 in conjunction with the so-called S-VIDEO cabling system. Requiring suitably equipped VCRs and monitors, S-Video cable keeps the luminance and chrominance signals separate. SONY quickly answered the challenge of S-VHS with their own ED BETA and HI -8 formats.

Superheterodyne Circuit ➺ A radio circuit, invented by Edwin Armstrong, that mixes a signal generated within the receiver with an incoming PROGRAM SIGNAL in order to amplify the program signal.

Superimposition ➺ See MULTIPLE EXPOSURE.

Superstation ➺ After the success of HBO as a cable network made SATELLITE dishes common equipment for cable system operators, Ted Turner made his local station in Atlanta, *WTBS*, available on the satellite, thus becoming a "superstation," seen on hundreds of cable systems across the country. The rich diet of old movies and sports (Turner owned the Atlanta Hawks and Braves which WTBS carried) proved attractive to system operators and viewers alike. Other successful superstations are WGN (Chicago) and WOR (New York).

Surface Noise ➺ The basic random sound level inherent in any recording medium—film, tape, or disc. See also DOLBY.

Surrealism ➺ (1) A movement in painting and film during the 1920s that relied heavily on dreamlike, illogical narrative and imagery, Surrealism was best represented in film by the work of Salvador Dali and Luis Buñuel. (2) A film style reminiscent of that movement, either fantastic or psychologically distorting.

S

Surround Decorrelation, Surround Delay ➤ One channel of a STEREO sound system is slightly delayed to increase the sense of separation.

Surround Sound ➤ The strategic placement of speakers along the side and back walls of theaters designed to immerse the audience in ambience and sound effects. The technique has become an important feature of HOME THEATRES: usually a center speaker and two back speakers are added to the basic bipolar STEREO array. The surround-sound effect can also be simulated by altering the PHASING of the speakers in a two-speaker system. See 5.1, DOLBY SURROUND.

SVA ➤ Stereo Variable Area. The optical soundtrack printing technique used with the DOLBY STEREO technology.

SVGA ➤ Super VGA monitor standard: up to 1280 by 1024 pixels; up to 16.7 million colors. See VIDEO RESOLUTION.

S-VHS ➤ See SUPER VHS.

S-VHS-C ➤ Super VHS Compact. See VHS-C.

S-Video ➤ See SUPER VHS.

SW ➤ Short Wave. See RADIO BANDS.

Sweeps ➤ Those periods during the year—traditionally November, February, and May—during which all local television markets are rated simultaneously by a ratings service, such as NIELSEN. Because of this, networks concentrate their best programming during sweeps months.

Sweet Spot ➤ The best spot for experiencing a HOME THEATRE performance or listening to a HIGH-END AUDIO system.

Swish Pan ➤ Also called flick pan, zip pan, whip pan. A PAN in which the intervening scene moves past too quickly to be observed, appearing blurred. It approximates psychologically the action of the human eye as it moves rapidly from one subject to another. See SACCADE.

Switch ➤ In networking, a more advanced type of ROUTER.

SWL ➤ Short-Wave Listener. A hobbyist. See HAM RADIO.

Symbol ➤ (1) In the Peirce/Wollen system, a SIGN that demands neither resemblance to its object nor any existential bond with it, but operates by pure convention. See INDEX, ICON. It is interesting to note that the new language of computer GUIs avoids this type of sign in favor of ICONS and INDEXES. Perhaps Symbols develop as the last stage of semiotic evolution. Sometimes the symbolic meaning conflicts with the Iconic. For example, the Macintosh trash can (or more politically correct Windows recycling bin) works Iconically if you want to dispose of a file but Symbolically if you want to eject a disk: you have to learn that meaning. (2) More generally, something that represents something else by resemblance, association, or convention.

Symmetrical Compression ➺ See COMPRESSION.

Symptomatic Technology ➺ See TECHNOLOGICAL DETERMINISM.

Sync, Synch, Synchronization ➺ Mechanical, electrical, electronic, or crystal clock devices are used to keep sound and picture in proper relationship to each other. See LIP SYNC.

Sync License ➺ A contract for using prerecorded music in a film or video production. Compare PERFORMANCE LICENSE.

Synchronic ➺ In SEMIOTICS theory, a phenomenon is synchronic when all its elements belong to the same moment in time and do not depend on a change of state across time. See DIACHRONIC.

Synchronous Sound ➺ Sound matched with its source, which is visible in the frame of the image, or sound whose source is understandable from the context of the image. Compare ASYNCHRONOUS SOUND, COMMENTATIVE SOUND.

Syndication ➺ An alternative to NETWORKS distribution of television and radio programming. Programs are sold by the producer or distributor directly to the local stations rather than to the networks. Most network television series are profitable for producers only when they enter syndication after several years of a network run. Programs such as GAME SHOWS, TALK SHOWS, and REALITY PROGRAMMING are often sold only to local stations, bypassing the networks entirely. This system is known as first-run syndication. The FCC's so-called *Fin-Syn Rules* of 1970 prohibited the broadcast networks from owning or managing the rebroadcast of prime-time network programs. These rules helped to engender a thriving market in syndication. The networks were still arguing the case more than twenty years later when the FCC finally rescinded the rules in 1993. First-run syndication became an increasingly important market in the 1980s as the dominance of the networks waned. See ACCESS TIME, STRIP.

Syndie, Syndy ➺ Slang for SYNDICATION.

Synecdoche ➺ In rhetoric, a common figure of speech in which a part signifies the whole (or the whole a part); hence a "motor" is understood to be an "automobile." Generally, a metaphorical device basic to cinematographic language. Closely associated with the similar concept of METONYMY. See INDEX, ICON, SYMBOL.

Syntagma ➺ A SEMIOTIC term. A unit of actual rather than potential relationship. Syntagmatic relationships exist between or among the present elements of a shot or a statement in film. The syntagma describes what follows what, rather than what goes with what. Contrast with PARADIGM. Also "syntagm."

SYSOP ⇒ SYStem OPerator. The manager of a BBS or similar online system.

Syster ⇒ See NAGRAVISION.

TA ⇒ A feature of RDS that provides Traffic Announcements.

TACS ⇒ Total Access Communications System. The standard for analog CELLULAR TELEPHONY in the U.K., China, and elsewhere. See AMPS, CDMA.

Tail ⇒ The end of a reel of film, or a shot or sequence.

Take ⇒ A version of a SHOT. A filmmaker shoots one or more takes of each shot or SET-UP. Only one of each group of takes appears in the final film.

Taking Lens ⇒ The LENS that transmits the image to be photographed. On some cameras, a separate lens is used as the VIEWFINDER. Compare REFLEX CAMERA.

Talaria ⇒ See OIL-FILM.

Talk Radio ⇒ A radio format consisting of conversations between a host and performer or PERSONALITY. Telephone calls from members of the audience are a key attraction of the format.

Talk Show ⇒ (1) A common type of television program consisting of light interviews, conversation, and occasional performances or news items. (2) A TALK RADIO show.

Talking Heads ⇒ Jargon for a television news SEGMENT or documentary sequence in which subjects simply talk to the camera, or to an unseen interviewer.

TAP ⇒ Theater Alignment Program. A project of George Lucas's THX to establish standards for theatrical film projection.

Tape ⇒ A recording medium using a thin, flexible plastic base coated with electromagnetic particles. The good news is the bad news about tapes: they are linear. This geometry allows the physical form factor of the medium to closely parallel the logical form of the audio or video they record, so that—like film—they are easy to edit: you can cut and splice precisely. However, tapes cannot be stamped out like discs. They must be duplicated by rerecording, which is time-consuming and expensive. And they are difficult to navigate. There's no quick way to get from the end to the beginning. Compare DISC, LIVE.

TBC ⇒ See TIME-BASE CORRECTION.

TBS ⇒ Turner Broadcasting System. Also Turner Entertainment. The umbrella for Ted Turner's influential activities in cable television, sports, and film. Turner had been in the outdoor advertising business (billboards) before he got involved in television. When he put his local Atlanta UHF station WTBS on the satellite in 1979, he created the first SUPERSTATION and changed the course of CABLE TV. In 1980 he founded CNN, with HBO the Killer Aps of Cable. TNT followed in 1988, designed as an outlet for the MGM film library he then owned. By the early 1990s he was in bed with major cable owners like TCI. They prevented him from concluding his long-time dream of buying one of the original broadcast networks. Weeks after failing yet again to purchase CBS, Turner announced he was selling out to TIME WARNER. At the time he joked, "I'm tired of being small. I want to find out what it's like to be big for awhile." As the vice chairman of the world's largest media conglomerate Turner has shared the credit for improving the financial condition of the company in the late 1990s.

TCI ⇛ Started in 1956 as a local cable system by rancher Bob Magness, TCI, based in Denver, was built by CEO John Malone into the largest cable system operator in the U.S., with a hand in many cable channels and other entertainment interests. After the deregulation of the cable industry in 1984, TCI moved aggressively to acquire cable systems, buying more than 150 companies in the late 1980s alone. As the largest operator, owning more than 25 percent of the cable boxes in the nation, TCI gets the best prices from cable networks, and this powerful position has enabled Malone to buy into a number of program channels: TCI and its sister company, Liberty Media, own pieces of more than 30 percent of the cable networks. In 1993 and early 1994 TCI was engaged in merger talks with Bell Atlantic, which fell through due to antitrust worries. Undaunted, in 1998 Malone merged with AT&T. The company became the Broadband and Internet Services division of AT&T.

TCP/IP ⇛ Transmission Control Protocol/Internet Protocol, the set of communications standards on which the INTERNET is based.

TDM ⇛ Time Division Multiplexing. See CDMA.

Teaser ⇛ A short promotional SPOT. A teaser for a film is usually shown in theaters many months before the release date. Compare TRAILER.

Tebl ⇛ Proposed prefix for the binary magnitude associated with the decimal TERA. See BINARY MAGNITUDES.

Technical Director ⇛ The television crew member in charge of control-room decisions—such as which camera to use when—during the taping or broadcast of a show.

Technicolor ⇛ The first successful color film system. Although two-color Technicolor using the DYE-TRANSFER process applied to two separate pieces of film existed in the 1920s, *Becky Sharp* (1935) was the first full three-color Technicolor FEATURE to use the SOLARIZATION of the subtractive primaries (cyan, yellow, magenta) to achieve the full range of color we associate with the process. In 1942 Technicolor Corporation introduced the *Monopack* system, which required only one camera rather than three and therefore made color filming flexible, but it was not until the late sixties that color became the norm and black-and-white the exception.

By that time the Technicolor technology had been superseded by EASTMANCOLOR, yet Technicolor continued to survive as a process because it used dye-transfer technology and therefore gave better color values and a much longer-lasting print than did Eastman's straight chemical process. By the 1970s Eastmancolor had become the universal standard and the Technicolor process was moribund. For a long time the only plant that still processed Technicolor was in China—until that plant, too, was closed in 1992. The film preservation movement of the 1990s led to the revival of the dye transfer process and Technicolor resumed processing in 1996 with a new print of *Giant*. See COLOR.

Technirama ⇒ Perhaps the most complicated WIDESCREEN process invented in the 1950s, this creature of the Technicolor company used all of the tricks. The film was shot on 35 mm stock running horizontally. It was also anamorphically compressed. Then it was printed with further anamorphic compression so that the resulting 35 mm print could be projected with a normal CINEMASCOPE lens. (Sometimes a Technirama film was shown with a horizontal projector.) The key here is that the increased size of the horizontal image provided extra detail, even when printed vertically. SUPER TECHNIRAMA 70 was shot the same way, but printed on 70 mm stock so that no anamorphic lens was needed. The process lasted about ten years, from 1956 through the mid-1960s.

Techniscope ⇒ A WIDESCREEN process invented by the Italian subsidiary of Technicolor in 1963 using a two-hole pulldown to save on filmstock. *Once Upon a Time in the West* (1969, Sergio Leone) and *American Graffiti* (1973, George Lucas) were shot with this process.

Technological Determinism ⇒ A theory of the relationship between technology and society that sees the historical development of technology as separate from and independent of social, political, and economic forces. In this view, technologies arise independently, and then determine the shape of societies associated with them. Symptomatic technology also assumes that research and technology are self-generating, but sees their development in a slightly different way: historically, according to this theory, technologies become symptomatic of their societies. Intentional technology, on the other hand, views technological phenomena as the direct products of social, political, and economic forces.

TeD ⟫ A moribund Videodisc format developed by TElefunken and Decca, that used a plastic-foil disc and a stylus. The TeD system was marketed briefly in 1975.

Telecine ⟫ The link between TELEvision and CINEma. Originally Telecines, or Film Chains, were used simply to capture a movie in real time for broadcast. Today, more elaborate Telecines are also employed to digitize films either for Digital Editing or for the production of DVD-Videos. The term now has a broader connotation encompassing the entire burgeoning relationship of film and video. A 3:2 Pulldown Mechanism is used to convert the 24 frames/sec rate of theatrical motion pictures to the 30 frames/sec rate of NTSC television. Compare Film Scanner.

Telecine House ⟫ A Post House that specializes in Telecine conversions. Also, a *Transfer House*.

Telecom Band ⟫ See Satellite Bands.

Tele-Communications, Inc. ⟫ See TCI.

Teleconference ⟫ A telephone conversation among three or more people. A conference call can be a broadcast to hundreds of listeners, or it can be a conversation among a few. Not to be confused with Videoconferencing.

Telecopy ⟫ See Fax.

Telefilm ⟫ Originally, any filmed program prepared for television broadcast. The word has taken on the connotation of the awkward Made-for-TV Movie.

Telegenic ⟫ Attractive as a subject for television; on the model of Photogenic.

Telegraphy ⟫ Literally, "writing at a distance." A system of communication by wire or broadcast (radiotelegraphy) that translates messages into simple coded signals. See Morse Code, Telephony.

Télématique ⟫ French term to indicate the combination of computer and telecommunication technologies. See Minitel.

Telemetry ⟫ Literally, "measurement at a distance." The technology of monitoring scientific instruments and measuring devices at great distances by wire or radio.

Telephony ⟫ Literally, "sound at a distance." A two-way, interactive system of communication by voice rather than coded message using wires or broadcast (radiotelephony).

Telephoto Lens ⟫ A lens with a long Focal Length that acts like a telescope to magnify distant objects. It has a very narrow Angle of View and flattens depth perception. See Foreshortening, Wide-Angle Lens.

Teleplay ➽ (1) A play specially written for television. (2) Any script for a television program, on the model of SCREENPLAY.

Telepresence ➽ VIRTUAL REALITY technology that allows the viewer to control a camera (and sometimes also robotic tools) situated in another place, often a hostile or difficult environment, such as the interior of a reactor, or another planet. See WEBCAM.

TelePrompter ➽ A mechanical CUE CARD system. Early Teleprompters used paper rolls on which the dialogue was printed, then projected that roll on a screen or half-silvered mirror, often angled in front of a television camera lens so that a newscaster, speaker, or actor could read his lines and still appear to be looking directly into the camera. In the 1980s, the paper roll was replaced with a computer monitor.

Telestrator ➽ Formerly proprietary, now generic, term for software that allows a commentator to add pen marks to a television image. Sportscaster John Madden made it famous with his football play diagrams.

Teletel ➽ France Telecom's VIDEOTEXT technology. See MINITEL.

Teletex ➽ A moribund plan of the 1970s for advanced TELEX communications, based on ASCII code rather than BAUDOT, and operating at a blindingly fast 2400 BAUD. The technology was superseded by EMAIL and FAX before it had a chance. Not to be confused with TELETEXT.

Teletext ➽ A system for broadcasting information—with a limited degree of interactivity—via the VERTICAL BLANKING INTERVAL of the standard television channel signal. The technology was introduced by the BBC's CEEFAX service in 1976. During the early 1980s both CBS and NBC ran teletext experiments for awhile, but the technology never caught on in the U.S. since so few sets were equipped with teletext decoders. Teletext systems broadcast several hundred pages of textual information (weather, sports, ads, and the like) in the vertical blanking interval of the signal. The decoder "grabs" the individual pages the viewer requests as they come by, stores a few, and displays them on the television screen. Compare VIDEOTEXT with which it is often confused.

Teletype ➽ Antiquated technology for transmitting alphanumeric information from a local keyboard to a distant printer. The *TTY* (Teletype) protocol is still in use for communications devices for the deaf.

Television ➽ Literally, "sight at a distance." A system of unidirectional communication of images and sounds by either wires or broadcast. See CABLE TELEVISION.

Television Novel ➽ See NOVEL-FOR-TELEVISION.

Television Protocols ⇒ There are three main systems of electronic analog color signal transmission. *PAL* (Phase Alternate Line) is used by the U.K. and Western Europe, excluding France. *SECAM* (Séquential Couleur À Mémoire) is used by France and Eastern Europe. *NTSC* (National Television System Committee) is used by the U.S., Canada, and Japan. NTSC is a 525-line, 60 Hz system; PAL and SECAM are 625-line, 50 Hz systems. A fourth system, RGB (Red-Green-Blue) is used for most computer color monitors. See also PAL-M.

Telex ⇒ An early system of textual telecommunications that connected individual keyboard/printers via telephone lines and MODEMS. Still in use in some parts of the world, but now almost entirely replaced by FAX and ELECTRONIC MAIL. See BAUDOT.

Telidon ⇒ The Canadian PROTOCOL for VIDEOTEXT that gave birth to NAPLPS. The word is now in disuse. See also MINITEL, PRESTEL.

Temporal Compression ⇒ The enormous quantities of data that result from the raw digitization of a movie would overwhelm even the most advanced CPUs. SPATIAL COMPRESSION reduces each individual frame by a significant percentage, but more compression is needed. Temporal Compression schemes measure the changes between frames and register only the differences. In most compression algorithms the COMPRESSIONIST decides how often the KEY FRAMES will be recorded. The frames between the key frames are called delta frames. (This game can get complicated: see MPEG-2.)

One consequence of temporal compression is that most frames (the delta frames) simply aren't there. Only the key frames are fully recorded (well, fully recorded with spatial compression). This is why it is difficult to "rewind" a DVD-Video: if you're moving backwards, the delta frames don't have their frame of reference. Another interesting consequence is that the length of the film in minutes or hours has little to do with the eventual size of the digital file. Andy Warhol's eight-hour-long *Empire* might very well produce a smaller file size than almost any two-minute film by Chuck Workman. Empire is a static shot of the Empire State Building; only the lighting changes, and it changes very slowly. In Workman's kaleidoscopic films, the complete image changes every few frames.

Ten, :10 ⇒ See SPOT.

10Base-T, 100Base-T ⇒ See ETHERNET.

Tera ⇒ Colloquially, a prefix for trillion. In the computer world, the prefix is often used to mean 2^{40}—not 10^{12}. A terabyte of storage thus equals 1,024 GIGABYTES, not one trillion bytes. The IEEE has proposed a set of new prefixes for BINARY MAGNITUDES to clear this up. See also MEG, K, PETA.

Terminator ➥ A SCSI chain requires electronic signal damping at each end. The pluglike devices that do this are called terminators. Sometimes the termination is internal, which makes things confusing. SCSI is a very unstable standard. If your SCSI chain isn't working, try adding or subtracting a terminator—even though the book says not to.

Terrestrial Broadcasting ➥ Broadcasters who use antennas rather than satellites are known as terrestrial broadcasters.

Text File Formats ➥ Whereas graphics programs developed common interchange standards early on, word processors did not. ASCII text is, of course, a standard, but it includes no information about fonts or formatting. Each word processor or page layout program has its own file format. The only equivalent to GIF or JPG in the text world is RTF (Rich Text Format), but it often doesn't work very well. This may be one reason MICROSOFT's Word has come to monopolize word processing: despite its drawbacks, it serves as a standard. HTML attempts to provide a standard for Web-based text, but browsers interpret it differently and it still lacks sophisticated formatting. In the more complex arena of page layout, there is a veteran standard, SGML, but it is not widely supported yet. See POSTSCRIPT, ACROBAT.

TF-1 ➥ The first French television network, formed in the 1970s after the breakup of the state-owned system.

TFT ➥ Thin-Film Transistor. A technology for manufacturing ACTIVE MATRIX LCDs.

Thaumatrope ➥ Considered the earliest of the nineteenth-century optical illusion toys that, by exploiting the phenomenon of PERSISTENCE OF VISION, foreshadowed the development of cinema. The Thaumatrope ("magical turning") consisted of a round disk, mounted on a string, with a picture on each side. When the disk was twirled rapidly the images appeared superimposed: dogs in their doghouses and birds in their cages, for example. See PHENAKISTOSCOPE.

THD ➥ See TOTAL HARMONIC DISTORTION.

Theater of Cruelty ➥ Antonin Artaud's theory of theater that emphasizes the stage as a concrete physical space requiring its own physical language. By "cruelty" Artaud meant a theater that was "difficult"; that insisted on the involvement of the spectator in the theatrical process; that was free from "subjugation to the text"; and that returned to basic, mystical, cathartic values. See EPIC THEATER.

Theater of the Absurd ➥ Theatrical genre of the 1950s and after that emphasized the lack of reason, logic, and control in human existence through such techniques as fragmented narrative, satirical commentary, nonsensical dialogue, abrupt shifts in tone and character, and the pointlessness of plot. Samuel Beckett and Eugène Ionesco were the playwrights most closely associated with this genre, whose influence has been wide and deep since the 1950s, evident across a broad range of the arts, from experimental cinema to television Sɪᴛᴄᴏᴍs, from Monty Python (who did it at least as well as Beckett) to pop art and the novels of Donald Barthelme. As an attempt to deal with the unfathomable horrors of the post-war world, Theater of the Absurd succeeded very well, providing a new, transcendent logic and reason that is the foundation of the Pᴏsᴛᴍᴏᴅᴇʀɴ culture.

Theatrical Distribution ⇒ The standard distribution of films through commercial exhibitors, as opposed to Nᴏɴᴛʜᴇᴀᴛʀɪᴄᴀʟ Dɪsᴛʀɪʙᴜᴛɪᴏɴ.

Theatrical Film ⇒ A film made to be seen in theaters rather than on television, in classrooms, or elsewhere.

Thermal Wax ⇒ A high quality color printing process in which the CMYK inks are carried on a wax substrate that is melted on the paper. Compare Dʏᴇ Sᴜʙʟɪᴍᴀᴛɪᴏɴ, Sᴏʟɪᴅ Iɴᴋ.

Third-World Cinema ⇒ The cinema of the developing nations of Latin America, Africa, and Asia in the 1960s and after.

1394 ⇒ See Fɪʀᴇᴡɪʀᴇ.

Thirty, :30 ⇒ See Sᴘᴏᴛ.

Thirty-Degree Rule ⇒ A basic guideline for Cᴏɴᴛɪɴᴜɪᴛʏ Eᴅɪᴛɪɴɢ that requires that camera angles vary between shots by at least thirty degrees in order to suggest that the cut has narrative purpose. Conversely, shots whose camera angles vary less than this amount are noticed simply as breaks and call attention to themselves. James Whale's horror films of the 1930s break the thirty-degree rule with brilliant theatrical effect.

3224 ⇒ See Sᴏɴʏ 3224.

Thomson ⇒ Founded in 1893 in France to produce electrical equipment, Thomson now ranks fourth in the world in consumer electronics after Mᴀᴛsᴜsʜɪᴛᴀ, Sᴏɴʏ, and Pʜɪʟɪᴘs. (And that's only Thomson Multimedia, the consumer products company. Thomson-CSF—a separate company—is a major defense contractor.) After expanding too rapidly in the 1970s, a bankrupt Thomson was nationalized by the Mitterand government in 1983. In 1987 Thomson bought the GE and RCA television brands from General Electric. In 1996 the French government announced that it would sell Thomson Multimedia to Korea's Daewoo for one franc, but the plan was cancelled after public protest. Thomson is currently being privatized. In 1998 Microsoft, DirecTV, NEC, and Alcatel bought 30 percent of the company in equal shares.

Threaded Discussion ⇒ A new form of communication spawned by NEWS GROUPS on the World Wide Web. Think of an outline: the subject may initially be divided into three categories, A, B, and C. A may be divided into four subcategories: A.1, A.2, A.3, and A.4. Subcategory A.1 may be further divided into A.1.a, A.1.b, A.1.c, and so on. Threaded discussions allow large groups to hold a large number of narrow, specific discussions.

Three-Camera Technique ⇒ Shooting with three camera rolling all the time is an expensive way to make a movie, so it is rare in film. But it is a very effective way to shoot a television show in front of a live audience, and most TV shows are done this way. Lucille Ball is credited with inventing the technique for *I Love Lucy* in the early 1950s.

3-D ⇒ Filmmakers have experimented with systems that attempt to recreate a STEREOSCOPIC experience since at least the 1920s. From 1952 to 1954 3-D movies were a fad in competition with the new WIDESCREEN processes to get audiences out of their homes and away from the television screen. The problem is, somehow, to project two images at once: one for the right eye and one for the left. The first attempts at 3-D cinema used the *Anaglyph* process: one image was printed in red, the other in blue-green and the spectators wore spectacles that separated the two. (The eye behind the red lens saw only the blue-green image, and vice versa.)

This worked OK for black-and-white movies (although your eyes were still sensitive to the colors so you saw red and green fringes everywhere), but obviously was useless for color film. The Polaroid system was used during the heyday of 3-D in the 1950s. The left and right images were polarized: one was vertical, the other horizontal. But the spectacles were a bother—especially if you already wore eyeglasses. Moreover, there were psychovisual issues to deal with. (See STEREOSCOPY.)

The root of the problem is that a movie is projected for a group of people, each of whom is sitting in a different place. This may be acceptable when the film is limited to two dimensions but it makes good 3-D difficult if not impossible. (A STEREOPTICON, however, works well because there is one viewer, with a singular point of view.) More recently IMAX 3-D has come closer to fulfilling the dream. Viewers still wear spectacles, but now they are LCD lenses that are open and shut via an infrared signal as the left and right images alternate. See HOLOGRAPHY, VIRTUAL REALITY.

3-D Modeling ⇒ The most resource-intensive job that contemporary digital graphics software has to do is 3-D modeling. The aim is not to produce a three-dimensional image as in 3-D cinematography, but to render a 2-D image with some of the SEMIOTIC character-istics that fool us into thinking we're looking at a picture that has depth—even without binocular vision. These include perspective, relative placement, and variations in color, texture, and illumination for the objects in the scene.

Mathematical algorithms such as PHONG and GOURAND calculate differences in color, texture, and illumination. Because these calculations are so processor-intensive the artist works initially with WIRE-FRAME representations of the shapes—stick drawings, if you will—where grids of lines suggest the shapes. The process of applying the necessary calculations for the final image is called RENDERING. RAY-TRACING is one effective rendering technique.

Three-Point Lighting ⇒ The arrangement of KEY, FILL, and BACKLIGHT-ING that serves to model the subject while continuing to maintain balanced illumination in the shot.

3/4-Inch SP ⇒ See BETACAM.

Three-Quarter View ⇒ In this shot the subject faces to the side of the camera (although not necessarily at the 45-degree angle the term suggests). Compare FULL-FACE SHOT, SIDE VIEW.

3:2 Pull-Down ⇒ The standard movie frame rate of 24 frames per second is not easily converted to the NTSC television frame rate of 30 frames per second (precisely 29.97 frames/sec). The 3:2 Pull-down ratio is used in FILM CHAINS to translate film to video. The first film frame occupies three video FIELDS, the second film frame occupies two fields. Since each video frame is composed of two video fields, two of every five video frames will have field pairs with information from different film frames. This can cause flicker when video frames are frozen. PAL and SECAM frame rates are 25 frames per second; films shot for transmission in these systems are often shot at the 25 frames/sec rate to avoid similar problems. See PAL/SECAM CHEAT.

Throughput ⇒ The amount of data that a connection can transmit and, by extension, the quantity of work accomplished. On the model of input and output.

THX Sound System ⇒ Not a technology, but a set of standards for sound quality in movie theaters (and now in HOME THEATRE) developed by Lucasfilm and named after George Lucas's early science-fiction film *THX 1138*. See TAP.

Tie-In ⇒ Any commercial venture that is connected to a film or media program; for example, the simultaneous release of a NOVELIZA-TION or a soundtrack album, or a fast-food restaurant giveaway.

Tier ⇒ CABLE TELEVISION systems usually offer a basic level of service as included in the subscriber contract, while PAY TELEVISION channels are grouped together in tiers—levels—for which higher prices are charged.

TIFF ➵ See IMAGE FILE FORMATS.

Tilt Shot ➵ The camera tilts up or down, rotating around the axis that runs from left to right through the camera head. Compare PAN, ROLL.

Time Banking ➵ A variation of a BARTER deal in which the local station receives programming in exchange for credit toward commercial time that the syndicator sells.

Time-Base Correction ➵ Circuitry in a video recorder that corrects for horizontal misalignment. Time-Base errors appear as serrations, with wavering at the edges of the image.

Timecode ➵ Traditional filmstock has one great advantage for editors: you cut between physical frames—either a frame is included in the cut, or it is not. When images are recorded electronically, however, whether analog or digital, this advantage is lost. Timecode attempts to make up for this loss, providing references for the EDIT DECISION LIST in the form hh:mm:ss:ff. The code is on a separate channel so it doesn't interfere with the picture. Also called SMPTE Time Code, after its sponsor. See VERTICAL INTERVAL TIMECODE, LINEAR TIMECODE.

Time-Lapse Photography ➵ Extreme FAST MOTION. A typical speed might be 1 frame every 30 seconds so that 24 hours of REAL TIME would be compressed, when projected, into 2 minutes of film time. As a scientific tool, time-lapse photography makes it possible to study activities, such as the opening of a flower, that occur too slowly in nature to allow us to perceive them. The opposite of time-lapse photography is extreme SLOW MOTION, which has a similar use in studying phenomena that occur too quickly in nature to be observed.

Time Shifting ➵ The practice of videotaping broadcast television programs in order to watch them at a more convenient time.

Time Slot ➵ In radio and television, a structured time period into which a show must fit. In the U.S., time slots are generally measured in half hours.

Time Smear ➵ One of the more serious distortions of digital sound, Time Smear spreads the energy of a transient point both before and after the event. It is caused by the filters necessary to block spurious images in the signal. The higher the sampling rate, the more gentle the filter can be; the more gentle the filter, the less Time Smear. See JITTER.

Time-Sharing ➵ Mainframe computers, no matter how big or how fast they were, did one thing at a time. As minicomputers began to challenge them, the concept of Time-Sharing developed. In a Time-Sharing system numerous WORKSTATIONS are connected to one computer. Each user has access to all the facilities of the machine. The operating system allocates resources as necessary to each user.

Time Warner ⇒ See WARNER.

Timing ⇒ The process of correcting and matching color values in various shots and scenes shot at different times of the day, in different places, or under different lighting conditions so that the PRINT will be uniform. The job is now often done by the TELECINE specialist. See ANSWER PRINT.

Tin Pan Alley ⇒ The great age of American popular song, from the twenties through the forties, closely allied with the growth of American musical theater, and echoed since mainly by jazz vocalists. The style has experienced a minor revival in the 1990s as a new generation of singers has come of age. Tin Pan Alley songs usually adhered to a strict formula of 32 bars, with verse (seldom actually performed) and chorus. The lyrics, always important, form a body of remarkable poetry—as yet unnoticed by literary academics.

TNC ⇒ See PLUGS.

TNT ⇒ Turner Network Television. Having enjoyed some success as a cable SUPERSTATION with his local television station WTBS, Ted Turner founded the cable network TNT on October 3, 1988 to serve as a distribution conduit for the large number of movies to which he had recently obtained the rights through his erstwhile deal for MGM-UA. The Turner Classic Movies channel took over some of this responsibility in the 1990s.

T-Number ⇒ See F-STOP.

TOC ⇒ An acronym from the publishing industry for Table of Contents that has moved into general language thanks to the spread of DVD and similar technologies.

Todd-AO ⇒ A WIDESCREEN system of the 1950s and 1960s using 65 mm film (70 mm for projection) that ran horizontally, increasing the frame size. The film was shot and presented at 30 frames/sec—the first format to increase the frame rate. (If Todd-AO had succeeded, the marriage of film and television would have progressed much more rapidly and easily.) The format had a six-channel soundtrack at first recorded on 35 mm magnetic film that was interlocked with the picture film. Later, the soundtracks were striped on the picture filmstock. The first Todd-AO film was *Oklahoma!* (1955). The process got its name from Mike Todd, a famous producer of the time, and the American Optical company that developed it for him. Todd-AO provided a model for later superfilm formats, like SHOWSCAN and IMAX.

T-1, T-2, T-3, T-4 ⟫ A T-1 is a dedicated phone line with a BANDWIDTH of 1.544 megabits/second, using two pairs of phone lines. T-2 is rated at 6.312 megabits/sec, T-3 at 44.736 megabits/sec, and T-4 at 274.176 megabits/sec. Compare ADSL, SDSL, HDSL2.

Tone ⟫ (1) A general term for photographic CONTRAST. (2) The musical quality of a sound.

Tonearm ⟫ See TURNTABLE.

Tonys ⟫ On the model of OSCARS, the awards presented each year by the American Theater Wing in association with the League of American Theaters and Producers for achievements in BROADWAY legitimate theater. Named for Antoinette Perry, the first awards were given for the 1946–47 season.

Toontown ⟫ A locution for the closed world of cartoon characters popularized by *Who Framed Roger Rabbit* (1988).

Toplighting ⟫ Lighting from above the subject.

Tops and Tails ⟫ The beginnings and ends of audio or video tapes.

Toslink Cable ⟫ A FIBER OPTIC cable developed by TOShiba for digital audio signals. Common on LASERDISC players.

Total Harmonic Distortion ⟫ Spurious sound in an audio signal resulting from the harmonics of the basic frequency.

Touchstone Pictures ⟫ See DISNEY.

Touchtone ⟫ See DTMF.

Track ⟫ (1) The SOUNDTRACK. (2) Any one of a number of separate parallel recording channels on TAPE that can be played together or separately and later MIXED or modified in a number of ways. (3) The rails on which a camera moves for a TRACKING SHOT.

Track Record ⟫ Slang term used to refer to a filmmaker's experience. The quality of the track record is often not so important as the fact that it exists.

Tracking Shot ⟫ Generally, any shot in which the camera itself moves from one point to another, either sideways, in, or out. The camera can be mounted on a set of wheels that move on TRACKS or on a rubber-tired DOLLY, or it can be HAND-HELD. Also called "travelling shot."

Trades ⟫ Hollywood lingo for VARIETY and HOLLYWOOD REPORTER, the industry's daily trade newspapers, which wield surprising power in the industry. "I hope there was nothing in the trades this morning, was there?!" worries one assistant to another in the opening shot of Altman's *The Player*.

Trailer ⟫ (1) A short publicity film describing a soon-to-be-released "coming attraction." The studios now prefer to call them *Previews*, but the old word still survives. Compare TEASER. (2) One of the mobile homes used as offices and dressing rooms on location. Also *Winnebago*, from a common brand.

Transcoder ➤ Circuitry or software that translates between and among PAL, SECAM, and NTSC.

Transducer ➤ Any device, such as a microphone or video camera, that converts audio or video into electrical signals.

Transfer House ➤ See TELECINE HOUSE.

Transistor ➤ A semiconductor device that, like a VACUUM TUBE, can amplify or otherwise modify an electronic signal. Because the transistor was so much smaller and more durable than its predecessor the vacuum tube, it had a profound effect on electronic technology. See PRINTED CIRCUIT, INTEGRATED CIRCUIT, MICROPROCESSOR.

Transponder ➤ An electronic device that receives a signal, amplifies it, and retransmits it, as, for example, on communications satellites. A combination of a receiver and transmitter.

Travelling Matte ➤ A MATTE SHOT in which the matte changes from frame to frame to follow the action. See ROTOSCOPE, CHROMA KEY.

Travelling Shot ➤ See TRACKING SHOT.

Treatment ➤ A general description of a film, somewhat longer than a simple outline but shorter than a full SCREENPLAY. See SCENARIO.

Trim Bin ➤ See DIGITAL EDITING.

Trinitron ➤ Proprietary SONY technology for an advanced CATHODE RAY TUBE design: prisms allow all three electron guns to use the same lens, and the phosphor mask is vertically rectangular rather than circular, and thus compensates for the effect of gravity on the electron beams.

Triode ➤ See VACUUM TUBE.

Triple-Band LNB ➤ An LNB that can receive DSB signals from the FSS, DBS, and Telecom SATELLITE BANDS.

TriStar ➤ The new studio that almost made it, TriStar Pictures was formed in 1982 as a joint venture of COLUMBIA Pictures, CBS, and HBO. TriStar acquired Loew's theaters in 1986. As first CBS, then HBO lessened their involvement, TriStar became a kind of independent subsidiary of Columbia. SONY acquired TriStar in its deal for Columbia in 1989. For awhile in the early 1990s under the leadership of veteran production executive Mike Medavoy it looked as if TriStar would survive and thrive. But Medavoy left in early 1994, and within a year the adolescent studio had been merged into Columbia as Sony attempted to stem losses. It was the third studio, after UNITED ARTISTS and ORION, to fold shortly after a Medavoy departure.

Trope ➻ Any artistic device, such as a figure of speech or a symbol; a CONNOTATIVE twist or turn in meaning. As a comprehensive art, film can avail itself of the tropes of many other arts. In addition, it has tropes that are unique: the SWISH PAN, for example, or RACK FOCUSING.

Trucking Shot ➻ A TRACKING SHOT.

TrueType ➻ See ADOBE.

TTY ➻ See TELETYPE.

Turing Test ➻ Named for Alan Turing, who suggested it in a seminal paper in 1950, "Computing Machinery and Intelligence." The Turing test posits that if a machine can fool you into thinking it's a person, then the machine could be considered intelligent. In other words, "if it walks like a duck, and talks like a duck…." The fallacy here is profound: what kind of *person*? I know people who remind me of VCRs—you know, blinking all the time, stuck on 12, unprogrammable, can't do anything but play tapes, useless without a television set. Does that make a VCR intelligent?

Turnaround ➻ When a studio changes its mind about a project, that project is put in "turnaround," available to be sold to others.

Turner Entertainment ➻ See TBS.

Turnerize ➻ Slang for COLORIZE. Ted Turner championed colorization.

Turntable ➻ Of all the devices that define our times (most of which were invented in the late nineteenth century) only Edison's Record Player does not depend on modern technology. Electric light and power, the automobile, the airplane—even movies and still photography—all depend on prior technical developments. But the Phonograph could have been invented by Da Vinci. A little understanding of musical instruments and clocks was all that was needed. How ironic, then, that after more than a century the technology not only survives, but thrives—at least in the world of AUDIOPHILES. For all its powerful technology digital audio systems still can't match the analog record player for musical reproduction (yet).

    The modern Turntable has certainly benefited from technical innovation, much of it, paradoxically, since the debut of the CD which replaced it in most homes. It remains an art object (unlike any other player) where the physics of reproduction is apparent and visible, and industrial designers have more interesting elements to work with than just switches and dials. The *Platter* is, of course, the engine of the device. It rests on the *Plinth*, whose steady support is integral to the success of the system. A separate *Tonearm* carries the *Cartridge*—the heart—where the essential job of converting mechanical signals into electronic signals is done. The *Stylus* tracks the groove in which the audio signal has been preserved. It is attached to the Cartridge by the *Cantilever*.

Most Tonearms are pivotal, but records aren't cut this way; most cutting heads track tangentially: that is, the head moves on a rail over the disk always maintaining a 90° angle, or tangent, to the groove. Pivotal tonearms are offset—or bent—25° to approximate the tangent, but this introduces a force called *Skating*, pushing the stylus in to the center of the record. An *Anti-Skating Mechanism* attempts to correct for this, balancing the Skating force. The offset is the horizontal angle; the *Vertical Tracking Angle* is also a concern. This is adjusted by moving the pivot point of the Tonearm up or down. The *Vertical Tracking Force* is the pressure of the Stylus in the groove. Although this is measured in grams, the area of contact between the Stylus and the groove is so small that the pressure is actually several tons per square inch! (By the way, the geometry of disks presents many problems in the digital world, too—see CAV and CLV, for example—and the solutions are just as ingenious, but hidden inside our disc players where we can't admire them.)

Each of these naked elements of the modern Turntable presents opportunities for designers. Exotic ceramics are found in the most expensive platters, rare woods are used for some of the most admired Cartridges; rubics, sapphires, and diamonds are the materials for some Styli and Cantilevers. In short, Turntables are organic—almost alive—in a way that digital systems never can be.

TV Mask ➻ A mask used in the camera viewfinder to block off those areas that will not be reproduced on the rounded rectangle of a television screen. The area within the mask is the *Safe Action Area*. Compare SOFT MATTE.

TVRO ➻ TeleVision Receive Only, the name for DISHES sold to consumers in the 1980s and early 1990s to allow them to pirate network signals. Compare DSB, DSS.

Tweeter ➻ A high-frequency speaker. Compare WOOFER.

Twentieth Century Fox ➻ Lacking the personality of PARAMOUNT, the grit of WARNER, of the glitz of MGM, "20th Century-Fox" was the unsung major studio during Hollywood's Golden Years, seldom receiving the measure of respect it deserved. In fact, the studio has had one of the more consistent records through the years. The Fox Film Corporation was founded in 1915 by Hungarian immigrant William Fox, a Nickelodeon entrepreneur. In the 1920s Fox employed directors like John Ford, Raoul Walsh, and F. W. Murnau, and introduced the MOVIETONE sound system, which set the standard for more than fifty years. At the end of the decade the company nearly became the dominant force in Hollywood, but Fox's attempt to gain control of Loew's, Inc., owner of hundreds of theaters and MGM, failed during the stock market crash. The company was saved by its new star, Shirley Temple. In 1935 Fox merged with production company Twentieth Century, founded several years earlier by Darryl F. Zanuck and Joseph M. Schenk.

Continuing its technological lead, the studio introduced CINEMASCOPE in 1953, leading the way to widescreen. Darryl Zanuck and his son Richard controlled the studio through most of the 1960s; Dennis Stanfill was chairman through most of the 1970s, a period that saw a number of hits—*Star Wars* (1977) being the most significant. Oilman Marvin Davis bought the company in 1981, then sold it to Rupert Murdoch in 1985. Murdoch installed Barry Diller as chairman and CEO. Diller created the FOX television network—a major coup—before resigning in 1992 to find new worlds to conquer in the multimedia business.

Twenty, :20 ⇒ See SPOT.

24/96 ⇒ Shorthand for 96 kiloHertz 24-bit encoding. Compare HDCD, DSD.

Twinax ⇒ See COAXIAL CABLE.

Twisted Pair ⇒ Originally, telephone wires in a standard phone set were twisted around each other to dampen electromagnetic interference. Now, most "twisted pair" phone cables are flat. In either case, the twisted pair provides limited BANDWIDTH for the transmission of a signal. Compare COAXIAL CABLE.

Twofer ⇒ A discount ticket, especially in the legitimate theater, often at half price. From the expression "two for the price of one."

Two-Reeler ⇒ A film lasting approximately twenty minutes. During the silent period a two-reeler was, more often than not, a comedy. See ONE-REELER.

Two-Shot ⇒ A shot of two people. Likewise, Three-Shot.

2:2 Pulldown ⇒ Transferring 24 frames/sec film to video by repeating each film frame as two video fields. See DVD-VIDEO FRAME RATES, 3:2 PULLDOWN.

Two-Way Cable ⇒ See INTERACTIVE CABLE.

TWX ⇒ An advanced form of TELEX, now moribund.

Typage ⇒ Eisenstein's theory of casting, which eschews professional actors in favor of "types" or representative characters.

Typography ⇒ Literally, "writing by type." The composition of printed materials. The simplest and earliest form of typography used movable type as the direct printing agent, as in LETTERPRESS. Movable type can also be cast to produce a "stereotype" plate, which can then be used as the printing agent. The plate can be curved to fit a ROTARY PRESS. Movable type can furthermore be used to print a REPRO from which a PHOTOENGRAVING plate can be made, which is then used as a printing agent. In the 1970s PHOTOTYPOGRAPHY, in which film negatives of the letter forms replace metal movable type, came to prominence. During the 1980s, to a large extent, computer typesetting techniques replaced phototypography.

Four major processes are used in traditional printing: LETTERPRESS uses a relief image in which the letter forms are raised; GRAVURE uses intaglio, in which the letter forms are depressed; SCREEN and OFFSET (lithography) are planographic—that is, the letter forms are essentially the same height as the nonprinting areas. During the 1980s LASER PRINTING, an offshoot of XEROGRAPHY developed for computer printers, began to challenge traditional forms of printing. Office Laser Printers are generally capable of a resolution of 300–600 dots per inch, as compared with the 1,200 to 2,650 dots per inch of computerized phototypesetting.

UA ➤ See UNITED ARTISTS.

UDF ➤ Universal Disc Format. A file system proposed by the Optical Storage Technology Association for optical discs. DVD-ROM uses a hybrid version of UDF that is backward compatible with ISO 9660.

UFA ➤ Universum Film AG. An ambitious attempt by the German government in 1917 to form an organization that could compete in world markets, UFA enjoyed a brief period of success, distributing the films of directors like Ernst Lubitsch, Robert Wiene, Fritz Lang, F. W. Murnau, and G. W. Pabst, but fell on hard times in the 1920s as the American industry dominated world markets and sucked talent out of Germany. The death knell was sounded in 1927 when a Nazi supporter gained control of the company. See BABELSBERG.

UHF ➤ Ultra-High Frequency band. See ELECTROMAGNETIC SPECTRUM.

Ultimedia ➤ IBM's early 1990s proprietary technology for dedicated MULTIMEDIA, now moribund, used a large-format disc instead of the CD-ROMs common at the time.

Ultrawideband Radio ➤ A proposed new system for local area communications that broadcasts a very weak signal over almost the entire radio spectrum. Because the signal is so weak at any single frequency it is not supposed to interfere with traditional communications. The system broadcasts digital pulses rather than analog waves.

U-Matic ➤ SONY's 3/4-inch videotape system that introduced cassette technology to video for the first time in 1971. Still preferred to 1/2-inch cassettes by some professionals and used in business.

Undelivered Audience ➤ When a broadcaster promises a certain level of audience ratings to an advertiser and falls short of that goal, the difference between the guarantee and the actual rating is "undelivered audience." See Bonus Spot.

Undercrank ➟ To slow down a camera; to shoot at less than the normal 24 frames per second so that the image, when projected at 24 frames/sec, will appear in Fast Motion. See Overcrank.

Underexposure ➟ See Exposure.

Underground Film ➟ (1) Independent film made without connection to the usual sources of funding and distribution, usually on small budgets; noncommercial cinema. (2) Experimental cinema in the U.S. between World War II and the late 1960s. See Avant-Garde, New American Cinema.

Underscan ➟ Decreasing the raster size of a television image so that the edges of the picture are visible. Why would you want to do this? Perhaps to check a test pattern, or because you were worried that you were missing part of the movie. (Note that most computer monitors have controls that allow you to do this easily.) Compare Overscan.

Unicast ➟ In contrast to Broadcast or Narrowcast, an Internet unicast distributes a program to a single user. See also Video on Demand, Streaming Media.

Unicode ➟ The international standard 16-bit BCD system that assigns a numerical code to most characters in most script systems currently in use in the world. The successor to ASCII, which it incorporates, Unicode is an ambitious undertaking to bring order to written language. As an 8-bit system ASCII had only 256 possible values available. (In reality, only the first 128 of these—lower ASCII—were standardized. The eighth bit was originally intended as a parity check.) This made sense when ASCII was established: it was a time when computers were just beginning to realize that lowercase letters existed and the differentiation between a typesetter's curly quotes and a typewriter's straight compromise was interesting only to artists and publishers. At the time 128 characters seemed like more than enough.

The development of bit-mapped graphics displays, however, made it possible to display any character from any script—if the coding existed. As a 16-bit system Unicode raises the number of distinct codes to 65,536. Even with the heavy burden of Han (the Chinese ideographic script—Unicode's version is called Unihan) this seems like enough. (Unless too many other rock musicians follow the lead of the Artist Formerly Known as Prince. See Logo.) As of early 1999 Unicode supported all major script systems. The list of unsupported scripts had been reduced to Myanmar (Burmese), Cherokee, Ethiopic, Khmer (Cambodian), Thaana (Maldivian),

Mongolian, Moso (Naxi), Pahawh Hmong, Rong (Lepcha), Sinhala (Sri Lankan), Tai Lu, Tai Mau, Tifinagh, Yi (Lolo), and Canadian Syllabics. Most had already passed muster for future inclusion. See TEXT FILE FORMATS.

Unidirectional Medium ➻ See DISTRIBUTION FLOW.

Unifrance ➻ The quasi-governmental French film export agency. Compare EXPORT-UNION, MPEA, AFMA.

Unitalia ➻ The quasi-governmental Italian film export agency. Compare EXPORT-UNION, MPEA, AFMA.

United Artists ➻ As its name indicates, United Artists was intended to be a vehicle for filmmakers and served that purpose well for fifty years before its ignominious death in the 1980s. Founded by stars Mary Pickford, Douglas Fairbanks, and Charles Chaplin, and director D. W. Griffith in 1919 to produce and release their own pictures, UA thrived in the 1920s, also releasing films by Gloria Swanson, Buster Keaton, and Rudolph Valentino. In the 1930s it was best known for Sam Goldwyn's and Alexander Korda's productions. It nearly failed in the 1940s, but was saved by Arthur Krim and Robert Benjamin, who took control in 1950.

For the next thirty years United Artists' previous liability—its lack of a studio infrastructure—became its greatest asset, as location production grew in popularity, antitrust decisions freed theater owners from their ties to the other distributors, and changing business models in the industry freed filmmakers from long-term studio contracts. UA became a public company in 1957 and was taken over by insurance conglomerate Transamerica in 1967. Throughout the 1960s and 1970s UA thrived, releasing the James Bond series and Woody Allen's films, among many others, and receiving numerous Oscar nominations.

In 1978 top executives Krim, Benjamin, Mike Medavoy, William Bernstein, and Eric Pleskow left in a dispute over Transamerica's corporate employment policies, which clashed with the Hollywood culture. They immediately formed ORION Pictures. United Artists' days were numbered. The financial disaster of *Heaven's Gate* (1980) sealed the coffin. Transamerica sold the company to MGM in 1981. In 1983 the two companies were merged as MGM/UA Entertainment, and United Artists effectively was closed. After numerous changes of ownership and colorful financial shenanigans chronicled dramatically by Peter Bart in his book *Fade Out*, the company landed in the lap of the French bank Crédit Lyonnais in 1992. By this time it was little more than a shell.

United Paramount Network ➻ See UPN.

Universal ➡ The oldest surviving studio and the only one to own its own city, Universal was founded in 1912 by Carl Laemmle, and pioneered the move to the San Fernando Valley when it acquired the land for "Universal City" outside of Burbank in 1915. From the 1920s through the 1940s Universal was king of the B PICTURES, devoted almost entirely to those low-budget enterprises. In 1946 the company merged with International Films. Decca Records acquired a controlling interest in the mid-1950s, and the company began to concentrate on higher-quality productions. It was best known in this period for Douglas Sirk melodramas and Rock Hudson–Doris Day comedies. In 1962 the Music Corporation of America (*MCA*) acquired control of both Decca and Universal. Founded in 1924 by Jules Stein as a talent agency, MCA was quickly forced by an antitrust consent decree to sell its agency business.

From that time until 1995 the studio was run, at first, by Stein and Lew Wasserman, then by Wasserman and his long-time associate Sid Sheinberg. Through the 1960s and 1970s Universal City Studios, Inc., dominated television production. The company also entered the theme-park business early, offering tours of its studio lot, eventually building a "studio" in Florida to serve as a draw for tourists. For twenty years, MCA-Universal enjoyed a close relationship with Steven Spielberg, whose production company Amblin Entertainment had its headquarters on the lot. In 1990 MATSUSHITA purchased MCA, Inc., for $6.1 billion. Wasserman and Sheinberg remained in control. In 1994 Steven Spielberg left to form his own studio, DREAMWORKS, with associates Jeffrey Katzenberg and David Geffen. In 1995 Matsushita sold most of its stock in the company to Edgar Bronfman's *Seagram* Company and the long reign of Wasserman and Sheinberg came to an end.

UNIX ➡ Developed by Ken Thompson, Dennis Ritchie, and others at Bell Labs beginning in 1969, UNIX was intended from the start to be an open operating system that would lend itself to TIME-SHARING. Because AT&T, owner of Bell Labs, was prohibited from entering the computer market at the time, the company gave UNIX away to Universities and others for a small license fee, a decision which further enhanced its openness. Except for the kernel—some code at the core of UNIX—the OS was written in a high-level language, C (written especially for the development of UNIX), which made its functions easily available to programmers. Over time UNIX has grown into a family of operating systems, most proprietary (Hewlett-Packard's HP-UX, IBM's AIX, Sun's Solaris), others open (BSD from Berkeley, LINUX). Because of its prevalence in the universities and its strong networking component, UNIX became the dominant OS on the INTERNET. It remains the only operating system with a presence on just about every platform.

Uplink ➻ See DOWNLINK.

Upload ➻ See DOWNLOAD.

Upmix ➻ See DOWNMIX.

UPN ➻ United Paramount Network. Following the success of FOX and the debut of THE WB, VIACOM'S PARAMOUNT joined the party, creating the sixth commercial U.S. television network. The company is half-owned by Herb Siegel's Chris-Craft, which also has a major stake in WARNER.

Upsample ➻ See RESAMPLING.

Upscale ➻ In DEMOGRAPHICS, the group of young, upwardly mobile people with sophisticated tastes and relatively large amounts of disposable income whose presence in an audience is greatly valued by advertisers and whose tastes, therefore, increasingly affect television programming.

URL ➻ Uniform Resource Locator, the named address of any page on the INTERNET, especially HOME PAGES. In an address such as http://www.Readfilm.com/Dictionary, the part before the colon specifies the protocol to be used (in this case, HTTP); the words separated by periods after the colon constitute the address of the machine on the Internet; and the optional characters after the slash indicate a subdirectory on that machine. The "WWW" tag is not required for a World Wide Web site. It was useful when the Web was young to identify web sites to users, but is disappearing rapidly from URLs. You can name a web server anything you like. The last part before the slash is always the root-level domain and the preceding word the DOMAIN. A ~ in the string after the slash is used to transcend complicated directory paths.

Originally the machines linked together to make up the Internet were identified only by their IP ADDRESSES, numbers of the form 123.123.123.123 (each of the four groups is limited to numbers between 0 and 255). When the domain name system was instituted, Internet addressing took a quantum mnemonic leap past telephone addressing—and even geographical addressing. Words are always easier to remember than numbers.

USA Network ➻ Cable industry legend Kay Koplovitz developed the USA CABLE NETWORK in 1980. Unlike most of its competitors USA offered a broad spectrum of entertainment. In 1988 it began to develop some original programming. By that time the network was owned by PARAMOUNT and MCA. UNIVERSAL (the successor to MCA) bought out VIACOM (the successor to Paramount) in 1997 after a contentious court battle. In 1998 Barry Diller purchased USA, together with the television production and distribution operations of Universal in a deal that gave Seagram (majority owner of Universal) 45 percent of HSN. HSN—the would-be national network Diller was stitching together from the Home Shopping Network, Silver King (a group of local stations), Savoy Pictures, Ticketmaster, and web site CitySearch—was renamed USA Networks, Inc.

USAT ≫ Ultra Small Aperture Terminal. An antenna for satellite reception less than half a meter wide. See VSAT.

USB ≫ Universal Serial Bus. A medium-speed standard for computer–peripheral connections which allows data rates of either 1.5 or 12 megabits/second. The higher rate is sufficient to support telephony and MPEG-2, for example. USB became popular after the introduction of Windows 98, which supports the standard, in July 1998. Up to 128 devices can be chained together. Compare SCSI, FIREWIRE.

USSB ≫ See DSS.

Vacuum Tube ≫ A glass tube that is either evacuated or filled with an inert gas and that provides a proper atmosphere for the electronic manipulation of a signal imposed on a grid between a cathode and an anode. Many AUDIOPHILES still prefer these to SOLID-STATE devices, and search out what they call NOS (New Old Stock), tubes manufactured decades ago but never used. Some of these tubes are no longer manufactured, although Russian companies are still in the market. Most tubes are TRIODES (anode, grid, and cathode); PENTODES add two additional grids for greater efficiency. See AUDION, TRANSISTOR.

Validation ≫ The peculiar ability of the media to define an acceptable social reality and therefore, in part, to govern what we consider true or "real."

Valve ≫ British for VACUUM TUBE, descriptive of its function not its shape.

Variable-Area, Variable-Density Soundtrack ≫ The optical soundtrack technology that ruled from the 1930s to the 1980s, developed by RCA, encoded the audio signal by varying the area of the waveform. But other technologies had been tried, too. The Variable Density Soundtrack varied the grayness of the track. Another variant used a spectrum of colors. See SVA.

Variable Bit Rate ≫ *VBR*. A kind of COMPRESSION technique that allows more complex video on lower-bandwidth connections. The

COMPRESSIONIST decides which sections of the film will be compressed at which rates. Compare CBR.

Variable Frame-Length Movie ➻ A format supported by QUICKTIME that allows frames of different durations. Hey! Why not? It's all digital! (Imagine the MALTESE CROSS that would have been necessary to do this in the old days!)

Varietese ➻ The slangy jargon invented by *Variety* to chronicle goings on in the entertainment industry since 1905. Examples: to ankle (to quit one's job), BIOPIC, CHOPSOCKY, diskery (record company), helmer (director), HOMEVIDEO, to ink (to sign), KIDVID, NUT, ozoner (drive-in theater), oater (Western), SITCOM, sci-fi (science fiction), VENUE, web (network). *Variety* also never referred to "movies" (it was always "pictures" or "films") or "money" (always replaced by "coin"). As the new owners continued the modernization of the paper, reviewers' cryptic "sigs" (signatures) were eliminated in 1991, but some of the colorful jargon remains, and continues to brighten the paper.

Variety ➻ Founded by Sime Silverman in 1905 to cover the nascent VAUDEVILLE business, this entertainment industry trade newspaper quickly became as colorful—and nearly as entertaining—as the industry it covers. During its heyday it was regarded by most journalistic connoisseurs as the classic TRADE newspaper. The Silverman family, who controlled *Variety* for three generations, were quick to recognize new trends in the entertainment biz, from movies to radio, from television to "vidcassettes." The slang the paper's highly knowledgeable reporters invented to cover their beat not only added many colorful words to the language, it also described new phenomena precisely and meaningfully. (See VARIETESE.)

In 1933 a second publication, *Daily Variety*, began publishing locally in Los Angeles to compete with the *Hollywood Reporter*. During the great age of the entertainment business (1920–1990), *Variety* chronicled developments with savvy wit. In October 1987 the paper was sold to Cahner Magazines, operators of a string of trade papers, who proceeded to modernize it. *Variety* is now more readable, if less quirkily entertaining. Since the early 1990s the paper has been run by veteran writer-producer Peter Bart. Compare HOLLYWOOD REPORTER.

Vaudeville ➻ The theatrical performance tradition popular in the U.S. and Europe from the 1890s through the 1920s which, through its mixture of music, comic sketches, STANDUP COMEDY, and dance, greatly influenced the development of both film and television in the twentieth century and continues as the groundbase of our popular entertainment culture.

VBI ⇒ See VERTICAL BLANKING INTERVAL.

VBR ⇒ VARIABLE BIT RATE.

VCD ⇒ Video CD, a specification of the WHITE BOOK that allowed for the storage of up to 74 minutes of video on a standard CD-ROM using MPEG-1 compression. This was a transitional technology of the mid-1990s that was soon superseded by DVD. However, VCD products have been very popular in Asia. Not to be confused with CDV (or DVC, for that matter)!

V-Chip ⇒ The Clinton administration's ill-conceived idea to legislate a kind of parental control on broadcast television. Sets equipped with the V-chip would be programmable by parents not to display certain programs and channels.

VCR ⇒ A VIDEOCASSETTE recorder or player.

VDT ⇒ (1) Video Dial Tone, the concept that on-demand video should be as readily available as a dial tone. (2) Video Display Terminal. A CRT. Terminology of the 1970s, now in disuse.

Vector Graphics ⇒ See BITMAPPED GRAPHICS.

Venue ⇒ VARIETESE for a theater or auditorium.

Verisimilitude ⇒ The quality of appearing to be true or real; a more precise descriptive term than REALISM, since the latter word has special theoretical connotations in film and the arts. To a certain extent, verisimilitude is the aim of realism.

Verism ⇒ General realism in art, literature, and film.

Vertical Blanking Interval ⇒ The section of BANDWIDTH on a television channel that is visible as the black band at the top and bottom of the picture when the picture rolls. Although it is a very small part of the total channel bandwidth, it has enough room to carry a significant amount of data. It is used in CLOSED CAPTION and TELETEXT transmission systems. It is also used in VIDEODISC formatting to carry information about chapters and frame numbers. The VBI comprises lines 1 through 21 of FIELD one and 263 through 284 of field two.

Vertical Interval Timecode ⇒ *VITC* is recorded within the video signal, during the vertical blanking interval. See SMPTE TIMECODE, compare LONGITUDINAL TIMECODE.

Vertical Resolution ⇒ The number of lines in a video image that can be perceived from the top of the image to the bottom. This is not necessarily the same as the number of lines in the RASTER. See VIDEO RESOLUTION, LINE-DOUBLING.

Vertical Tracking Angle, Vertical Tracking Force ⇒ See TURNTABLE.

VGA ⇒ Video Graphics Array, a monitor standard: 640 by 480 pixels, 16 colors. See VIDEO RESOLUTION.

VHD ⇥ Video High Density. A capacitance VIDEODISC system without grooves, developed by MATSUSHITA and JVC; it died quickly. Compare CED.

VHDTV ⇥ Very High Definition TeleVision. Experiments to exceed a vertical definition in excess of 2,000 lines.

VHF ⇥ Very High Frequency band. See ELECTROMAGNETIC SPECTRUM.

VH-1 ⇥ MTV's second music CABLE NETWORK offers more widely varied music skewed to an older audience.

VHS ⇥ JVC's half-inch VIDEOCASSETTE format introduced in the U.S. in 1977 and popularized by MATSUSHITA to compete with SONY's earlier and technically superior BETA format. By aggressively marketing VHS and convincing other Japanese manufacturers to adopt the standard, Matsushita's VHS came to dominate the home market by 1980. Acronym for "Video Home System."

VHS-C ⇥ Compact VHS VIDEOCASSETTE with a playing time of about 20 minutes and standard VHS resolution of 250 lines horizontally developed by MATSUSHITA to compete with SONY's 8 mm CAMCORDER format. Although small enough to fit in a compact camera, the VHS-C cassette can be loaded into an adapter to be played on a standard VHS VCR. Also Super VHS-C (*S-VHS-C*), with a resolution of more than 400 lines horizontally, comparable to HI-8.

Viacom ⇥ Viacom was spun off from CBS in 1970 to comply with the FCC's FIN-SYN RULES, taking over the network's program syndication division. Throughout the 1970s and 1980s the company was active first in the cable industry, then in pay cable, acquiring systems, then stations, in numerous states, founding SHOWTIME in 1978, and acquiring Warner's share of MTV in 1986. In 1987 Sumner Redstone's National Amusements movie theater chain bought 83 percent of the company for $3.4 billion, winning a bidding war against Carl Icahn and a Viacom management group. In 1994 Redstone beat Barry Diller and QVC in an even more notorious bidding war for PARAMOUNT Communications. Shortly thereafter he also purchased Blockbuster Entertainment, the leading video store chain. The debt incurred for these pythonesque purchases weighed heavily. Redstone spent the next five years divesting bits and pieces of the empire and quarreling with various managers. One lucky break: Paramount's share of revenues from *Titanic*.

Vid ⇥ VARIETESE for VIDEO.

Video ⇥ (1) The picture portion of a television signal. See AUDIO. (2) Independent television art, usually on TAPE, often produced for VIDEOTAPE distribution rather than commercial BROADCAST. (3) Short for MUSIC VIDEO or Rock Video.

Video CD ⇥ See VCD.

Video Cut ➺ A version of a film edited especially for Videocassette release, including scenes and shots dropped from the theatrical release, usually more explicit sex.

Video Dial Tone ➺ The concept, which gained currency in the mid-1990s, of universal access through the telephone or cable network to a multiplicity of video products on demand.

Video for Windows ➺ Microsoft's challenger to Apple's QuickTime. Replaced by DirectShow in 1998.

Video 8 ➺ Sony's 8 mm Videocassette format introduced in the late 1980s for its Camcorder and Video Walkman products. Slightly larger than an Audiocassette, the Video 8 Cassette was soon challenged by the VHS-C format. Compare HI 8, Digital 8.

Video Games ➺ Whether they are played on dedicated boxes in arcades or at home on machines attached to the television set, Video Games for a long time constituted the most striking influence of the microcomputer revolution on popular culture. (Only the World Wide Web has challenged the game industry in this regard.) The first Video Games, utilizing the earliest 4-bit logic chips, appeared in 1972 (Pong, Odyssey). By 1982 Americans were spending $8 billion on arcade games and another $3 billion on home systems and cartridges—well in excess of consumer spending on either movies or music. After a shakeout in the mid-1980s, the introduction of *Nintendo*'s Famicon (1983 in Japan, 1985 in the U.S.) shifted the market from arcade to home and signaled the second generation of the game industry.

By 1989 Nintendo enjoyed monopoly control with 80 percent of the market. (Nintendo sales represented a full 20 percent of the entire U.S. toy market that year.) Nintendo's dominance began to crack with the introduction of 16-bit game machines in the early 1990s and governmental pressure on their anticompetitive practices (which included forbidding their developers from developing for any other game system). *Sega* started to move up in market share in the 1990s, only to be overtaken by Sony, a new entrant into the Video Game market. Sony's CD-based PlayStation, introduced in 1995, grew to dominate the market by the end of the 1990s. See Emotion Engine.

Video Matchback ➺ The process of cutting a film negative to match precisely the EDL produced in a nonlinear digital video editing system. Kodak's Keykode makes the job a little easier. In order for the matchback to be precise, the editing software must be able to work at 24 frames-per-second so that there is a direct match between the electronic frames and the physical frames.

Video on Demand ⟩⟩→ Proposed telephone-based or cable-based delivery system in which the viewer could request transmission of a movie or other program at any time she chose. See INTERACTIVE CABLE.

Video Output ⟩⟩→ As HOME THEATRE replaces old-fashioned television sets and as the medium becomes ever more digital, the once-simple connections between components of a High-End video system have become complex. As any computer manager knows, when there's a problem, "Cherchez la cable!" A new DVD-VIDEO deck or the latest video gizmo may provide you with the following cabling connections, in ascending order of effectiveness:

(1) RF Output (worst): the signal has been translated to Radio Frequencies; the audio will be mono only, even on stereo sets; the coaxial cable may require a 300-ohm:75-ohm adapter.

(2) COMPOSITE Video (satisfactory): all color and luminance information on one signal; uses an RCA plug.

(3) S-VIDEO (good): a COMPONENT signal on a 4-pin cable.

(4) COMPONENT Video (better): three separate cables, usually with RCA connectors. Be careful: these are probably YUV outputs. Don't plug them into RGB inputs. (In Europe the Component signal may be carried on a SCART cable.)

(5) Progressive Video (best): The Component YUV signals are provided with progressive scanning, usually with BNC connectors. Make sure you have a progressive-scan television. (Thanks to Jim Taylor for this succinct list.)

Video Projection ⟩⟩→ There is an array of sophisticated technology used to project video images. HOME THEATRE has been the proving ground for various Video Projection technologies that will eventually permit an all-digital movie distribution system. See DMD (Digital Micromirror Device), DLP (Digital Light Processor), LCLV (Liquid-Crystal Light Valve), ILA (Image Light Amplifier), OIL-FILM, LCD, LINE-SCALING DEVICE, EIDOPHOR.

Video Resolution ⟩⟩→ Whether employed as a television set or a computer monitor, a CATHODE RAY TUBE works by tracing a pattern of SCANNING lines. The vertical resolution of the resulting image is therefore limited by the number of lines in the RASTER. In NTSC video, the upper limit is 525 horizontal lines. Because some lines are used for other purposes (the VERTICAL BLANKING INTERVAL), the effective limit is reduced to 480 vertical lines. (This is why the first generation of graphical computer monitors—the VGA standard—offered 480 vertical lines of resolution.)

Horizontal resolution, however, is not limited by the raster pattern of the Cathode Ray Tube—nor is it constrained by it. If the horizontal resolution is equivalent to the vertical resolution there will be 640 lines on a standard monitor with a 4:3 Aspect Ratio. In television, the effective horizontal resolution is often far less. For example, the Notch Filter decoder used in cheaper sets reduces the horizontal resolution from 640 to around 300. This is similar to the resolution offered by VHS video. More expensive Comb Filters, introduced in the late 1970s, increase broadcast horizontal resolution significantly. Good Laserdisc players can provide horizontal resolution of 550 to 600 lines, and DVD comes close to 640 lines—more than twice the resolution of standard VHS tape.

As CRT manufacturers responded to the ballooning computer monitor market in the late 1980s and early 1990s they began to provide higher resolution devices. The SVGA (up to 1280 x 1024) monitor standard surpassed broadcast NTSC video and led the way to HDTV. Since HDTV is not limited to the 4:3 Aspect Ratio, it has become common to quote horizontal resolution in terms of lines "per picture height"—that is, the measure of the resolution of a horizontal area that is equal in length to the height of the image. For example, the total horizontal resolution of a 16:9 HDTV image equivalent to 640 x 480 on a 4:3 screen would be 853. To compare the two monitors effectively it is better to speak of 480 lines "per picture height." The Pixel array of the monitor determines the upper limit of video resolution, but just because a screen has 640 pixels horizontally doesn't mean the image that is displayed on it uses all that available detail. See Interlace, Digital Resolution, LoHR.

Video Walkman ⟫→ Sony's handheld portable Videocassette player introduced in the late 1980s, combining an 8 mm player with a color LCD screen. The small size was the result of Sony's expertise in miniaturization combined with the HI 8 cassette format and advances in color LCD technology.

Videoassist ⟫→ The use of video on the set to check shots immediately. The *videotap*, a small video camera that views the scene through the same lens as the film camera, allows other people besides the cinematographer to check the composition on a monitor elsewhere on the set. The tape that is recorded concurrently with the film being shot allows the director and others to check the shot immediately after it is completed so that fewer insurance takes are needed.

Videocassette ⟫→ The self-contained tape system that became a major means of distributing filmed entertainment product in the 1980s and that, as a by-product, turned most of the middle class into filmmakers—of a sort. By the mid-1980s JVC's VHS format, heavily marketed by Matsushita and RCA, had largely knocked Sony's

Beta format out of the market, although Sony had some success later with an 8 mm version. Videocassettes use 3/4-inch, 1/2-inch, or 8-mm magnetic tape enclosed in a plastic box with its own reels. The advantage is convenience: the tape itself need not be handled.

Videoconferencing ➺ Several technologies that allow the transmission of video signals over telephone Twisted Pair so that participants at a meeting at different sites can see as well as hear each other and use visual aids. Because of Bandwidth considerations, most videoconferencing systems transmit a succession of still pictures rather than Full-Motion Video. See Videophone, Compression.

VideoCrypt ➺ Smart-Card-based encryption system for DSB first used by B-Sky-B. VideoCrypt (I) is used in the U.K. while VideoCrypt (II) is used elsewhere in Europe. See Nagravision, Eurocrypt.

Videodisc ➺ In the 1970s, several means of recording video images on disc were developed and brought to market; only the Laserdisc survived. The RCA CED system inscribed the signal electromechanically. The TED system was entirely mechanical. The Philips/MCA Laserdisc system records the signal as microscopic "pits" and "lands" on a plastic disc, using lasers. See Optical Disc, CAV, CLV.

Videogram ➺ British for a Videocassette or Videodisc program.

Videography ➺ (1) On the model of Cinematography, the art and science of photography using a video camera. (2) On the model of Filmography, a list of videos.

Videophile ➺ A fan of video, mostly movies. The kind of person who invests in Home Theatre. Compare Cinephile, Audiophile.

Videophone ➺ AT&T demonstrated the first practical video telephone in 1964 at the New York World's Fair. This so-called *Picturephone* was introduced commercially in 1970 but never caught on as a consumer electronics product due to its high price and the lack of an installed base. By 1981 the system had found some utility in Videoconferencing. After adding Compression technology, AT&T reintroduced the renamed and redesigned Videophone in 1992. With a color image, it had a frame rate of 15 frames/sec, not quite good enough to impress potential buyers. In the 1980s Sony and other Japanese manufacturers had marketed black-and-white Picturephones, which sent series of still pictures. (Every time you pressed the button, another shot was taken and sent to your correspondent.) These failed.

Videotap ➺ See Videoassist.

Videotape ➺ A Tape system of television recording. Professional systems have historically used 2-inch- and then 1-inch-wide tape; amateur and semiprofessional systems use 3/4-inch, 1/2-inch, and 8-mm tape.

Videotex, Videotext ➨ There were online systems before the INTERNET: the ones that were distinguished by their ease of use and graphical interface were called Videotext. Subscribers usually used dedicated terminals or television screens, since few had their own computers (equipped with modems). The communications channel was usually the telephone line, occasionally a dedicated cable channel or broadcast frequency. The first videotext system, British Telecom's PRESTEL, was introduced in 1978, after a trial period that began in 1976. The concept was perfected by France Telecom with the MINITEL system, which debuted in 1981. Compare TELETEXT.

Videowall ➨ In museum installations or marketing presentations an array of television screens (usually rear-projection) driven by an equal number of LASERDISCS or DVDs and controlled by a computer program.

Viewdata ➨ The early British term for VIDEOTEXT, now in disuse.

Viewfinder ➨ Specifically, the eyepiece through which the camera operator observes the image. Non-REFLEX cameras have separate optical systems for viewfinder and TAKING LENS.

Viewing Ratio ➨ The ratio between the distance of a viewer from the screen and the height of the image on the screen. Our perception of RESOLUTION is greatly dependent on the viewing ratio, which is why large-screen televisions are successful only if you have a room large enough so you can sit far enough away from the screen to maintain the same viewing ratio you had with the cheap set.

ViewMaster ➨ A proprietary children's toy of the mid-twentieth century, a version of the STEREOPTICON. The 16 mm image pairs were ingeniously mounted on a disk that was notched so that an entire SLIDE SHOW could be presented: the viewer clicked a lever to change pictures.

Vignette ➨ A MASKING device, usually with soft edges. See also IRIS.

Vinyl ➨ The plastic out of which LP records are pressed, and by extension, LPs themselves.

Virtual Information ➨ In optics, a virtual image is one that is formed by extrapolating light waves back to a source that doesn't exist. We learn as children that there really is no one behind the mirror. In a sense the entire history of photography, film, recording, and their media descendants has been a series of exercises in virtuality: nothing exists behind the movie screen, either.

As the microcomputer revolution has overtaken us during the last twenty years, however, the rapid explosion of virtual information has matched or exceeded the exponential growth of computing power. We now deal with a world of perception a thousand times more virtual. Software algorithms produce information which looks like the real thing, but isn't: "virtual" information. We see this at one level in spreadsheet programs that produce—instantly and effortlessly—projections for businesses that could never survive in the real world. (MBA students learn to call these products "spreadshit.") We see it on another level in the galaxies of replicating facts and factoids available on the Internet.

But ethically, the increasing virtuality of information is of most concern in digital audio and video. In digital media we see colors, shapes, lines, and points, and hear tones, harmonies, and rhythms that really aren't there—or, more precisely—weren't there when the source was recorded. In the analog world the quality of an image was an index of its trustworthiness; not so in the digital world where the most precise images are often the most spurious. What we've gained in flexibility we've more than lost in trust. The story is told that Ingmar Bergman used to suffer sleepless nights worrying about the ethics of PERSISTENCE OF VISION: half the time people watching a movie are staring at a blank screen. (See SHUTTER.) Imagine how he might have felt about MPEG-2. See COMPRESSION.

Virtual Product Placement ➻ Insertion of billboards or products in a show after it has been shot and edited. See L-VIS, PRODUCT PLACEMENT.

Virtual Reality ➻ Term that first became popular in the early 1990s to describe game systems that strove for greater VERISIMILITUDE with 3-D techniques, headsets, and GAME GLOVES. The technology was aimed at arcade games first. The definition of the term was later broadened to include more general applications, such as TELEPRESENCE and QUICKTIME VR.

VIS ➻ Tandy's Video Information System, a multimedia format introduced in 1992 as a competitor to CD-I. It was even less successful than CD-I.

VistaVision ➻ Paramount's answer to Twentieth Century Fox's CINEMASCOPE in the 1950s. A nonANAMORPHIC process shot on 35 mm film running horizontally to increase detail, in which no action took place at the left or right of the screen so that exhibitors with different aperture masks could choose their own ASPECT RATIO from 1.33 to 2.0. Paramount couldn't convince theater owners to project the film horizontally. Although even vertical prints benefited from the increased detail, the process died after 1961. Hitchcock's *Vertigo* (1958) is perhaps the most famous VistaVision film. Compare TODD-AO.

Visuals ➻ (1) The IMAGES of a film as opposed to its SOUNDTRACK. (2) Any visual materials used in a lecture, meeting, or demonstration.

Vitagraph ➣ J. Stuart Blackton's early film company; a competitor to Edison's Vitascope and the Biograph company.

Vitaphone ➣ The sound system used in Warner Brothers' *The Jazz Singer* (1927), usually regarded as the first sound film. Ironically, the Vitaphone system recorded the sound on a disk that was coordinated with the picture. This technology had been tried often before and found wanting. It was nearly impossible to synchronize sound and image when the two were recorded on separate media. Vitaphone worked for *The Jazz Singer* because only certain parts of the film had sound, and thus were easier to synchronize. See Phonofilm.

Vitascope ➣ The projecting version of Edison's Kinetoscope exhibition machine.

VITC ➣ See Vertical Interval TimeCode.

VLF ➣ Very Low Frequency band. See Electromagnetic Spectrum.

V O ➣ Voice-Over.

VOB ➣ Video OBject. A blob (a large binary object) on a DVD-Video disc that includes all or part of the video of a movie.

Voice-Over ➣ The narrator's voice when the narrator is not seen, especially in television commercials. An off-screen narrative voice that comments on or counterpoints the images on the screen. See Commentative Sound.

VOR ➣ Voice Operated Recording. A feature of some tape recorders (often those intended for dictation) that runs the tape only when there is sound of a certain level to record. See Dictaphone.

Voyager ➣ Founded in 1984 by Bob Stein and Aleen Stein as Criterion to produce and distribute Laserdiscs, the company became known as Voyager when William Becker and Jonathan Turell joined the Steins as partners in 1985. By the mid-1980s Voyager had established a notable reputation as the leading producer of movies on Laserdisc, even as the medium itself seemed to be going nowhere. Voyager discs such as *Citizen Kane* and *King Kong* (both 1984) were landmarks in the history of the new audiovisual technology. In the late 1980s Stein became fascinated with the possibilities of Multimedia CD-ROM, digital cousin of the Laserdisc. Voyager's first multimedia CD, *Companion to Beethoven's Ninth*, by Robert Winter, was released in 1989 and became an immediate model for the new medium.

In 1991 Voyager introduced a line of Electronic Books on Diskette (later discontinued). *A Hard Day's Night* (1993) was the first digital CD-ROM to include a complete movie. In 1994 the German media moguls the von Holtzbrinck family bought a major interest in the company. Like all CD-ROM companies, Voyager was hit hard in the mid-1990s. The company was dismantled in 1998: the von Holtzbrincks took the brand name; Becker and Turell refocused on DVD-Video under the Criterion name; and Bob Stein and Aleen Stein went their separate ways.

VR ➤ See Virtual Reality.

VSAT ➤ Very Small Aperture Terminal. An antenna for satellite reception.

VSDA ➤ Video Software Dealers Association. The major U.S. trade association for the Homevideo market.

VTA ➤ Vertical Tracking Angle. See Turntable.

VTF ➤ Vertical Tracking Force. See Turntable.

VTR ➤ Video Tape Recorder. See VCR. Terminology of the 1970s, now in disuse.

Walkarounds ➤ Workers—often aspiring actors—who wear costumes of cartoon characters and animals and walk around theme parks. It's a sign of the tenuous line we now draw between reality and fantasy that patrons commonly beat on walkarounds, expecting them to bounce back like their animated originals. Well, it's better than waiting tables... maybe.

Walkie ➤ Short for "Walkie-Talkie," the ubiquitous tool of Assistant Directors and others on the set or on location.

Walkman ➤ Sony's miniaturized personal Audiocassette player, introduced in the late 1970s, that radically changed the social experience of music. What was once mainly a communal celebration became private and isolating as millions of music fans plugged up their ears as they walked, jogged, skated, or biked through the noise of the city. The word itself, originally proprietary to Sony, has become generic. Like the name of the corporation, it is an example of "Japanese English," an English neologism devised to work as well in Japan as internationally. See Shiss.

Walkthrough ➤ A rehearsal.

Wall Warts ➤ The ubiquitous and troublesome little transformers that power many electronic devices. There are few standards; they block neighboring outlets; and the cords are never long enough. Here's a workaround: Take a standard extension cord and cut it to a length of less than a foot, then wire in a thin plug that will fit your power strip or receptacle without blocking other outlets. The socket end of your little extension accord will accommodate two Wall Warts.

WAN ➤ Wide Area Network. A computer network, usually of microcomputers, that links several geographical locations. Compare LAN.

Want-to-See ➻ In film marketing, a measure of the audience's interest in a film before it is released.

Warm Colors ➻ The colors to the left on the visible spectrum: red, orange, yellow. Compare COOL COLORS.

Warner ➻ Brothers Harry, Jack, Albert, and Sam Warner formed the company that was to bear their name in 1923, two years later absorbing Vitagraph and First National. Even though their technology quickly lost out, it was the introduction of sound in *The Jazz Singer* (1927) that brought the company to prominence. Throughout the 1930s and 1940s, Warner Bros. films were known for their gutsy economy, social consciousness, and economically motivated realism. For more than 20 years, the brothers mined one genre after another—Gangsters, Musicals, Detective Stories, War, Film Noir—often producing the best examples of each as they left the artistic high road to MGM and PARAMOUNT. The studio reached its lowest point in 1956, when it was forced to sell its pre-1950 library. Seven Arts acquired Warner Bros. in 1967.

In 1969 an entrepreneur named Steven J. Ross gained control of the entity, and Warner's long rise to dominance began. Ross merged the company with his Kinney National Services, proprietors of parking garages and funeral parlors, changed its name to Warner Communications, and began refashioning his empire into one of the leading media companies of the 1980s and 1990s. He moved quickly into the music business, theme parks, publishing, sports, and cable television, and was well ahead of his competitors in recognizing the significance of the microcomputer revolution to the entertainment business.

As Ross wheeled and dealed in Manhattan, he left his managers in Burbank alone. In 30 years the studio has had only two management teams. Agent Ted Ashley reigned quietly but effectively from 1969 to 1980. The team of Robert A. Daly (CEO) and Terry Semel (COO) presided in the same manner until their surprising retirement in 1999 after one of the longest reigns in recent Hollywood history.

In 1989, three years before his death, Ross crowned his career by organizing the merger of Warner Communications with Time Inc. to form Time Warner, the largest media company in the world. Gerald Levin (from Time) took over the company after Ross's death. Burdened by the heavy debt incurred in the leveraged buyout, Time Warner sold significant shares to U S West and Toshiba. In 1995, only weeks after foiling Ted Turner's attempt to purchase CBS, Levin announced that Time Warner would purchase the Turner empire for $7.5 billion. See also WB, THE.

Wave Front, Law of the First ➺ See LAW OF THE FIRST WAVE FRONT.

Wave Mechanics ➺ Wave forms require a medium through which to be transmitted. Sound waves travel in air or water. Light and radio waves travel in the electromagnetic spectrum of particles. Any wave has two dimensions: the vertical—*amplitude*, or strength; and the horizontal—*wavelength*. The length of the wave is inversely proportional to its frequency, measured in cycles per second (also known as Hertz): the longer the wave, the lower the frequency. Receivers can be tuned to particular frequencies, thus making it possible for even narrow bands of the electromagnetic spectrum to carry numerous, separable signals. The PROGRAM SIGNAL is imposed on the carrier wave in either of two basic ways: either by the modulation of the amplitude (AM) or the modulation of the frequency (FM) of the wave. See also ELECTROMAGNETIC SPECTRUM.

Wavelength ➺ See WAVE MECHANICS.

WB, The ➺ Noticing the surprising success that FOX had developing the fourth commercial U.S. television network, Warner weighed in with The WB in 1995, stitching together a group of independent stations for limited network delivery. In 1998 a deal with cable giant TCI gave The WB access to 90 percent of American homes. See UPN.

Weather Channel ➺ CABLE NETWORK founded in May 1982, entirely devoted to—you guessed it! While it is surprising that a phenomenon so profoundly local as weather can command a national audience, The Weather Channel has managed to pull it off with a sophisticated database technology that localizes the forecasts for each market.

Webcam ➺ On the model of STEADICAM and SKYCAM, the Webcam has become one of the more intriguing Internet media. Soon after the WORLD WIDE WEB became a phenomenon in 1994, certain web sites began to broadcast still images from strategically placed still or video cameras. A savvy WEB SURFER thus has eyes all over the world. The factor that makes this trick so novel is that the images are captured in REAL TIME (or close to it).

   The first Webcams were used to show the weather in various cities. Later, certain web artists turned the camera on themselves. (This "reality-as-art" format had been foreshadowed by an Off-Broadway show in the 1960s called *The Family*. The actors simply lived on stage and you could pay a few dollars and watch them as long as you liked. Of course, you had to go to the theater.) Perhaps the most ambitious Webcam project was built by IBM for the July 1996 Olympics: cameras were stationed at more than twenty sports venues, giving fans unusual freedom. A year later the Pathfinder spacecraft broadcast live pictures from Mars—a major event in web history. See TELEPRESENCE.

Webring ⇒ A group of independent websites dealing with the same topic. Each site directs you to an index of the ring, or allows you to go to a random choice in the ring.

Webtop ⇒ Contrasting with desktop, Webtop services and programs store information on the Internet rather than your own disk. The advantage is that the data can then be shared. Imagine a personal calendar with a public face that let others know your schedule.

WebTV ⇒ Founded in June 1995 by Steve Perlman, Bruce Leak, and Phil Goldman—all ex-Apple technologists—WebTV targeted the large market of television viewers who don't own computers. An ingenious system that offers access to the World Wide Web and email over a television set, WebTV consists of a SET-TOP BOX that links to the company's own specially programmed servers to deliver web access. In what was a very rapid cash-out—even for the Internet— the founders agreed to sell the company to Microsoft in April 1997. The price was $400 million. The key technology involves adapting the INTERLACED SCANNING of the standard television set so that it can deal with print in a reasonable fashion. It should also be noted that the set-top box was the first widely distributed CABLE MODEM. The company makes its money through advertising and through licensing the technology to SONY, PHILIPS, and others, who sell the boxes.

Webzine ⇒ A ZINE.

West End ⇒ The LEGITIMATE THEATER industry in London. Compare BROADWAY.

White Book ⇒ See CD STANDARDS.

White Noise ⇒ See NOISE.

Wide-Angle Lens ⇒ A lens with a very broad ANGLE OF VIEW, it increases the illusion of depth and also exaggerates linear distortion. See FISH-EYE LENS, TELEPHOTO LENS, FORELENGTHENING.

Widescreen ⇒ Any one of a number of ASPECT RATIOS of 1.66:1 or greater. Almost all theatrical films today are widescreen. Widescreen processes are not necessarily ANAMORPHIC; some processes simply mask the top and bottom of the aperture during shooting or projection to increase the aspect ratio. TECHNISCOPE utilized a two-hole PULL-DOWN MECHANISM (rather than the 35 mm standard four-hole pull-down) in order not to waste filmstock while shooting. The resulting negative was then printed in a standard four-hole format for projection. The most common nonanamorphic widescreen ratios in use today are 1.66:1 (European) and 1.85:1 (American). See also CINEMASCOPE, PANAVISION, VISTAVISION, TODD-AO, TECHNIRAMA.

Widescreen Video ⇒ See ANAMORPHIC VIDEO.

Wild Shooting ➤ Shooting a sound film without recording the sound simultaneously. See Post-Synchronization, Direct Sound.

Wild Sound ➤ Sound recorded separately from images—and therefore not in sync with them—usually in order to obtain usable tapes of sound effects, such as Room Tone.

Wild Walls ➤ The walls of a set that have been constructed in such a way that they can easily be moved to facilitate the positioning of the camera. Camera angles are thus obtained that would not be possible on a Practical Set.

William Morris Agency ➤ See Agent.

Window ➤ (1) The period of release of a filmed product in a particular market. A theatrical film will follow theatrical release with Pay TV, airline, VCR, and network broadcast windows, for example. (2) A central concept of Graphical User Interfaces, it may have been misnamed. In the real world, windows don't come and go or lie on top of each other; pieces of paper do, though. (3) The last shot, as in "when do" we go home? Compare Martini, Abby Singer.

Windowbox ➤ An alternate to Letterboxing in which the left and right frame lines of the film frame are visible on the television screen as well as the top and bottom lines.

Window Dub ➤ A copy of a tape with Timecode showing.

Windows ➤ See Microsoft.

Winnebago ➤ See Trailer.

Wintel ➤ From WINdows and INTEL, the adjective to describe the dominant microcomputer environment of the 1990s—the remarkably lucrative symbiotic alliance between the leading chip manufacturer and Microsoft.

Wipe ➤ An Optical effect in which one image gradually replaces another image, usually moving horizontally, vertically, or diagonally across the frame. Very common in the thirties; less so today, although it has made a modest comeback (Spike Lee, for example). See Fade-In, Dissolve, Iris-In.

Wireframe ➤ A technique of 3-D Modeling.

Wireless ➤ (1) British for Radio. (2) More recently, a synonym for Cellular Telephony or regular telephone service that uses microwave antennas rather than Twisted Pair, Wireline, or Fiber Optic cable. Fixed Wireless is regular phone service, while Mobile Wireless refers to cell phones.

Wireline ➤ Wired. As Wireless transmission became more popular in the nineties, Wireline became the preferred antonym, since "wired" had so many hip connotations.

Woofer ➤ A low-frequency speaker. Compare Tweeter.

Word Processor ➤ The dedicated word processing machines of the 1970s provided the model for the Personal Computer. Descendants of the minicomputer revolution of the late 1960s, the Word Processors were the first computing devices designed to be used by just one person and dedicated to a single purpose. All were proprietary machines with software integrated with hardware from keyboard to processor to printer. As the PC revolution began with the introduction of the Apple II in 1977 it became clear that these new machines might be able to serve as Word Processors and thus find a useful niche quickly. Late in 1980, Archive, a small company in Davenport, IA, owned by an heir to the John Deere tractor fortune, introduced a CP/M based personal computer bundled with Wordstar software and a keyboard with a row of dedicated keys that transmitted Wordstar commands. This ingenious device also came with the first hard disk in a PC—a giant five-megabyte drive. The price was $8,000—but that was cheaper than a dedicated Word Processor at the time.

Work Print ➤ A quick print made from the NEGATIVE, often without having been color-corrected in any way, used for screening RUSHES, assembling a ROUGH CUT, and other editorial work.

Workstation ➤ Originally any one of a number of monitor/keyboard combinations attached to a TIME-SHARING computer, the term was appropriated in the 1980s for powerful individual microcomputers, usually running a variant of UNIX.

World Wide Web ➤ A system that provides relatively uniform standards for widely scattered information services on the INTERNET, including an addressing scheme that permits HYPERTEXT references to other sites.

Worm ➤ Write Once, Read Many. An OPTICAL DISC, CD-ROM, or DVD-R system of data storage that allows the user to write to the disc but not erase from the disc.

Wow and Flutter ➤ Distortion in the sound produced by tape, disk, or film soundtrack, caused by variations in motor speeds.

Woz Machine ➤ The CLV MAGNETIC DISK drive Stephen Wozniak developed for the Apple II.

Wrap ➤ To finish shooting a film, often followed by a "wrap party."

Wrap Beer ➤ A drink, sometimes provided by the producer, after the last shot of the day.

WTBS ➤ See TBS, SUPERSTATION.

WWW ➤ See WORLD WIDE WEB.

WYSIWIG ➤ (Pronounced "whizzy-wig.") One of the longest and least pronounceable acronyms (rivaled only by NAPLPS and PCMCIA, both now in disuse), WYSIWIG stands for What You See Is

What You Get. It came into currency in the mid-1980s with the advent of GUIs like the Macintosh to describe screens that could mimic real FONTS.

X-Band ⇒ See SATELLITE BANDS.

Xenon Lamp ⇒ An enclosed lamp filled with the inert gas xenon, which produces a very bright light of controlled COLOR TEMPERATURE and which has replaced the ARC LIGHT in most cinematic applications.

Xerography ⇒ An instant electrophotographic printing process. "Xerox" is a trade name for the first and most successful of a number of similar processes that are often grouped together under this generic title. Compare OFFSET, LETTERPRESS, ROTARY, GRAVURE.

Xerox PARC ⇒ The Palo Alto Research Center served as the Xerox company's think tank in the 1970s. Most of the necessary elements for the personal computer we know today were either invented or developed here, including the GRAPHICAL USER INTERFACE, the LASER PRINTER, and the POSTSCRIPT language. The prototype machine PARC demonstrated in the early 1970s was called the Alto. (Most of the elements of this machine had been demonstrated in 1968 by Douglas Engelbart at the Stanford Research Institute.) The Xerox company never realized any revenue from the seminal work that was done at PARC, despite the similarity of Laser Printer technology to their core product at the time, the photocopier. In 1981 Xerox did market a computer with a Graphical User Interface called STAR, but at $10,000 it didn't sell.

XGA ⇒ IBM's proprietary eXtended Graphics Array monitor format: 1024 by 768 pixels. See VIDEO RESOLUTION.

XLR ⇒ See PLUGS.

X.25 ⇒ An international standard PROTOCOL for PACKET-SWITCHED networks. X.25 was an important element of VIDEOTEXT systems of the 1980s, especially MINITEL. While it is still used commercially, it has largely been replaced by TCP/IP, the protocol of the INTERNET.

Yahoo! ⇒ See SEARCH ENGINES.

Y/C ⇒ A compromise approach to COMPONENT VIDEO that does not separate RGB information, but does separate luminance and CHROMINANCE signals. Used in HI 8, S-VHS, and SP formats.

YC$_b$C$_r$ ⇒ See COLOR-DIFFERENCE SAMPLING.

Yellow Book ⇒ See CD STANDARDS.

YIQ ⟫ One of several systems for quantifying color values in electronic media. Y stands for LUMINANCE, I and Q for the color difference signals. See COLOR MODELS.

YUV ⟫ One of several systems for quantifying color values in electronic media. Y stands for LUMINANCE, U and V for the color difference signals. See COLOR MODELS.

Zapping ⟫ The practice of editing or blanking commercials from a television program as a viewer records it, or using the REMOTE to mute sound or change channels during commercials.

ZDF ⟫ Zweites Deutsches Fernsehen, the second German television network.

Zine ⟫ An electronic magazine, usually on the INTERNET. Also *Webzine* or *E-zine*.

Zip Pan ⟫ See SWISH PAN.

Zoetrope ⟫ (1) From the Greek for "life" plus "turning"; an early antecedent of cinema, patented by George Horner in 1834, and consisting of a cylinder with a series of photographs or illustrations on the interior and regularly spaced slits through which a spectator observed the drawings, which appeared to move. See PRAXINOSCOPE. (2) Any one of a number of incarnations of Francis Ford Coppola's production company from the late 1960s to the 1990s (American Zoetrope, Omni Zoetrope, Zoetrope Studios, *Zoetrope* magazine), most of which failed financially. (3) New York Zoetrope, a book publisher specializing in film and media, and founded in 1975 by James Monaco during a period when Coppola wasn't using the word—now defunct. (It's a long story, but without a Chapter 7 or 11.)

Zoom ⟫ A shot using a lens whose variable FOCAL LENGTH is adjusted during the shot. The focal lengths of which the lens is capable range from WIDE-ANGLE to TELEPHOTO. Zooms are sometimes used in place of TRACKING SHOTS, but the differences between the two are significant.

Zoomed Video ⟫ Technology to allow analog or digital video to be displayed on a computer screen. Zoomed Video accepts direct input from a camera, VCR, or tuner.

Zoopraxiscope ⟫ Eadweard Muybridge's enlarged adaptation of the PRAXINOSCOPE, which included a projection system and which rivaled its predecessor for the first public screenings of moving images. See KINEMATOSCOPE.